BATTLE OF PLYMOUTH
NORTH CAROLINA
(APRIL 17-20, 1864)

THE LAST CONFEDERATE VICTORY

Juanita Patience Moss

HERITAGE BOOKS
2009

HERITAGE BOOKS
AN IMPRINT OF HERITAGE BOOKS, INC.

Books, CDs, and more—Worldwide

For our listing of thousands of titles see our website
at
www.HeritageBooks.com

Published 2009 by
HERITAGE BOOKS, INC.
Publishing Division
100 Railroad Ave. #104
Westminster, Maryland 21157

Copyright © 2003 Juanita Patience Moss

Other books by the author:
Anthracite Coal Art of Charles Edgar Patience
Battle of Plymouth, North Carolina (April 17-20, 1864): The Last Confederate Victory
Created to Be Free: A Historical Novel about One American Family
Forgotten Black Soldiers Who Served in White Regiments During the Civil War
The Forgotten Black Soldiers in White Regiments During the Civil War

All rights reserved. No part of this book may be reproduced or transmitted in any form or by any means, electronic or mechanical, including photocopying, recording or by any information storage and retrieval system without written permission from the author, except for the inclusion of brief quotations in a review.

International Standard Book Numbers
Paperbound: 978-1-58549-852-9
Clothbound: 978-0-7884-8074-4

THIS BOOK IS DEDICATED TO THE MEMORIES OF THE

"PLYMOUTH PILGRIMS"

15th Connecticut Volunteers
16th Connecticut Volunteer Infantry
2nd Massachusetts Heavy Artillery-Companies G & H
12th New York Cavalry-Companies A & F
24th Independent Battery B New York Veteran Light Artillery
85th New York Veterans Volunteer Infantry
2nd North Carolina Union Volunteers-Companies B & E
3rd Pennsylvania Heavy Artillery-Detachment Co. A
101st Pennsylvania Veteran Volunteer Infantry
103rd Pennsylvania Veteran Volunteer Infantry
10th U.S. Colored Infantry-Recruits
37th U. S. Colored Infantry Recruits
2nd U.S. Colored Cavalry-Recruits
U.S. Army Gunboats *Bombshell* and *Dolly*
USS Miami
USS Southfield
USS Massasoit
USS Whitehead
USS Ceres

Fig. 1. ***Seige of Plymouth historic marker***
From author's collection

"Now, comrades, I want someone to speak out loud and let the world know that we did something more than eat and drink and draw our pay for three and a half years that we served our country."

Jacob D. Brown, Co. D
101st Pennsylvania Volunteers
Marian, Pennsylvania
From a letter published by the "National Tribune
Veterans Newspaper"
Washington, D.C.
Thursday, October 3, 1889

THE BATTLE OF PLYMOUTH

TABLE OF CONTENTS

Illustrations	ix
Acknowledgements	xi
Prologue	1
Chapter 1 A Nation Divided	3
Chapter 2 A Small North Carolina Town	19
Chapter 3 Yankee Invasion of Plymouth	29
Chapter 4 The "Contraband" Problem	55
Chapter 5 Birth of the Ironclad Rams	65
Chapter 6 Ironclad Threat to Plymouth	77
Chapter 7 Lieut. Gilbert Elliott, CSA	85
Chapter 8 A Comedy of Errors	87
Chapter 9 General Henry Walton Wessells, USA	91
Chapter 10 Yankees Garrisoned at Plymouth	95
Chapter 11 A Union Soldier's Letter to His Mother	99
Chapter 12 Before the Battle	101
Chapter 13 A Surprise Sunday Attack	109
Chapter 14 The Rebel Goliath	121
Chapter 15 Captain James Wallace Cooke, CSN	127
Chapter 16 Lieut. Commander Charles Williamson Flusser, USN	.129
Chapter 17 Attacking the Forts	135
Chapter 18 General Robert Hoke, CSA	139
Chapter 19 Yankee Capitulation	141
Chapter 20 Sacred Flags	153
Chapter 21 Eyewitness Accounts	163
Chapter 22 Fate of the Defeated Yankees	169
Chapter 23 Escapees From Rebel Prisons	189
Chapter 24 Blacks During the Battle	199
Chapter 25 Properties Surviving the Battle	211
Chapter 26 Drowning of a Leviathan	229
Chapter 27 Final Reports on the Destruction of the CSS *Albemarle*	247
Chapter 28 Lieutenant William Barker Cushing, USN	251
Chapter 29 Demise of the Ships of War	255
Chapter 30 The War's Finale	259
Chapter 31 General Wessells Reports on the Battle of Plymouth	271
Chapter 32. Major James F. Mackey's Diary, April 16th to May 1, 1864	277
Chapter 33. A Northern Survivor's Story Twenty Years Later	281

Chapter 34. A Confederate Soldier's Personal Account	286
Epilogue	290
Bibliography	300
End Notes	310
Index	332
Thoughts From the "Plymouth Pilgrim" Historians	351

ILLUSTRATIONS

page

Fig. 1. Siege of Plymouth historic marker	v
Fig. 2. President Abraham Lincoln, Union	5
Fig. 3. President Jefferson Davis, Confederacy	5
Fig. 4. Gideon Welles, Secretary of Navy, USA	13
Fig. 5. Poster- "Men Wanted for the Navy"	14
Fig. 6. Integrated crew members of the USS Miami	17
Fig. 7. Arthur Rhodes' map of Plymouth	21
Fig. 8. Plymouth, N.C., 1863	24
Fig. 9. Sketch of Plymouth waterfront, 1864	24
Fig. 10. Three Confederate officers from Plymouth	27
Fig. 11. General Ambrose Burnside, USA	31
Fig. 12. Map of operations at Roanoke Island	32
Fig. 13. Map of early war operations in North Carolina	35
Fig. 14. Poster for Carteret County men to enlist in Union Army	39
Fig. 15. Fort Williams historic marker	45
Fig. 16. Spot where Fort Williams once stood	45
Fig. 17. USS Miami	48
Fig. 18. Ed Boots, re-enactor of 103rd Penna. Regiment	50
Fig. 19. Private Charles Mosher	53
Fig. 20. A slave becomes a soldier	57
Fig. 21. Stephen Mallory, Secretary of the Navy, CSA	65
Fig. 22. CSS Virginia	69
Fig. 23. John Ericsson	71
Fig. 24. USS Monitor	72
Fig. 25. CSS Albemarle being built at Edwards Ferry	75
Fig. 26. Captain James W. Cooke, CSA	82
Fig. 27. Lieutenant Gilbert Elliott	86
Fig. 28. General Henry W. Wessells, USA	93
Fig. 29. General George Pickett, CSA	104
Fig. 30. The Albemarle Ready For Action"	107
Fig. 31. CSS Albemarle engaging USS Miami and USS Southfield	125
Fig. 32. Lieut. Commander Charles W. Flusser, USN	133
Fig. 33. Map of Battle of Plymouth, April 17-20, 1864	137
Fig. 34. General Robert Hoke, CSA	139
Fig. 35. Confederate flags	153
Fig. 36. Flag of Co. B, 103rd Penna. Volunteers	155
Fig. 37. Port-O-Plymouth Museum	161

Fig. 38. A Plymouth Pilgrim in his Hardee hat	178
Fig. 39. Captain Henry Wirz, CSA	187
Fig. 40. Escapee John Lafler at age 54	194
Fig. 41. Officer escapees from Rebel Prison	198
Fig. 42. Private Crowder Pacien's enlistment record	203
Fig. 43. Ausbon House	214
Fig. 44. Latham House	215
Fig. 45. Grace Episcopal Church	218
Fig. 46. Ripley's "Believe It or Not"	218
Fig. 47. Methodist Episcopal Church	219
Fig. 48. Clark House	223
Fig. 49. Armistead-Pettiford House	225
Fig. 50. Harriet Toodle's property location	228
Fig. 51. Chart of engagement in Albemarle Sound, May 5, 1864	231
Fig. 52. *USS Saccacus* ramming *CSS Albemarle*	232
Fig. 53. Cushing's launch	236
Fig. 54. Cushing's torpedo	237
Fig. 55. *Picket Boat Number One*	239
Fig. 56. Cushing's daring and successful exploit	241
Fig. 57. Cushing's torpedo boat sinking the *CSS Albemarle*	242
Fig. 58. Sunken *CSS Albemarle*	246
Fig. 59. Lieutenant William B. Cushing, USN	254
Fig. 60. Robert Holmes' 100 year old oak tree, Avon, Conn.	266
Fig. 61. Tree marker of Robert Holmes' oak	266
Fig. 62. Crowder Patience (aka Pacien) at age 74	270
Fig. 63. Tombstone of Private Crowder Patience, Co. C, 103rd Penna. Volunteers	271
Fig. 64. General Robert E. Lee	274
Fig. 65. General Ulysses S. Grant	275

ACKNOWLEDGEMENTS

The Battle of Plymouth, April 17-20: The Last Confederate Victory was written at the suggestion of my publisher. After I had presented him with the manuscript of my historical novel he leafed through the pages. When he commented on the April 1864 battle at Plymouth, North Carolina, I was quite surprised. Few persons I know are aware of that battle, even those claiming to be avid Civil War buffs.

Craig Scott, publisher of Willow Bend Books, Westminister, Maryland, informed me that he had an interest in that particular battle with intentions of researching it, but instead other projects had intervened. He challenged me to write a nonfiction version of the battle I had described in *Created To Be Free*, promising that he would publish the new work.

He suggested that I research what already has been recorded regarding the individual regiments involved and then gather all of the information into one resource. Up for the challenge, for the past three years I have been pouring through letters, diaries, journals, books, and magazines, as well as traveling several times to Plymouth, North Carolina, even to attending the 2002 reenactment of the April 17-20, 1864 battle.

As I did after writing *Created To Be Free*, I have to thank my patient husband Edward, for driving "Miz Daisy" in my Chevrolet Venture van that has become my traveling library. Reba Burruss-Barnes, my efficient publicist, has cheerfully chauffeured me to Edenton and Plymouth, North Carolina, where my research began, two small towns across the Albemarle Sound from each other.

I thank every other person who helped me gather information for this book. When I began writing *Created To Be Free*, I discovered the names of the present day regimental historians on the Internet. The first person I contacted about my venture was Ruth Fulton, historian of the 103rd Pennsylvania Volunteers, the unit in which my great grandfather had served. Her grandfather, Private William Allison Fulton, had been a member of that regiment, also. She was the first to inform me of the well-attended re-enactment activities held at Plymouth, North Carolina each April.

Ms. Fulton suggested that I contact Harry Thompson, curator of the Port-O-Plymouth Museum. A Bertie County, North Carolina native, he possesses a wealth of information about Plymouth, as well as Washington and Bertie Counties before and during the Civil War. He also is very much involved with the annual re-enactment activities.

When I began researching for this book I contacted the other regimental historians who graciously shared pertinent information concerning their particular units include:

John Ball (85th New York Volunteers), great grandson of First Lieutenant John Lafler,

Ed Boots (101st Pennsylvania Volunteers), great nephew of Sergeant Edward Boots,

B. Conrad Bush, (24th N.Y Independent Battery Light Artillery), an avid Civil War buff,

Debra Miller Felice (101st Pennsylvania Regiment), descendant of Abraham Rice,

Scott Holmes (16th Connecticut Regiment), great great grandson of Robert Holmes,

Evan Slaughenhoupt, (103rd Pennsylvania Volunteer Regiment), great great great grandson of Silas Haggerty.

I have relayed the story of the Battle of Plymouth as objectively as possible from both the northern and southern perspectives. In order to do so, I quoted various sources in my attempt to put the events in chronological order. I also felt that some readers might be interested in knowing about the personalities and backgrounds of the major participants on both sides, as well as what happened to them after the war had ended.

My desire is that readers will find this book informative, interesting, and enlightening as I have searched for truth. Certain derogatory terms such as "nigger" and "darkey" are found in the writings from which I quoted because those were terms used during that period of history. In addition, "colored," "negro," and "mulatto" were being used as racial identifications on official documents. Therefore, those words must be included in this book of truth even though they will be offensive to some readers.

Unanswered questions still remain concerning certain events that took place at Plymouth during the four-day siege in April of 1864. Perhaps some answers can never be known since discrepancies are found even in the writings of eyewitnesses, especially those who wrote from memory years after the battle had ended. Others, while telling their stories, may have elaborated on their recollections or mistook names, dates, and times. Regardless, I, as well as present day historians of the "Plymouth Pilgrims," feel that the events at Plymouth, North Carolina on April 17-20, 1864, are worth the telling.

What I personally perceived last April at the reenactment activities was the genuine warmth and welcome being demonstrated by the residents of the town towards the descendants of the "Plymouth Pilgrims." They had come from many locales, some from as far away as Texas. They were intergenerational: gray-haired sages to babes being wheeled by their young parents. What they all shared was a genuine desire to honor the memories of the Federals who lost the Battle of Plymouth on April 20, 1864 with many surviving to later perish at Andersonville Prison.

I also observed the results of the great amount of time and energy the residents of Plymouth invested in the weekend activities. Many residents of the town enthusiastically participated in the annual activities. For instance, the Torchlight Walk through the streets of Plymouth, a very informative and enjoyable event, commenced at the United Methodist Church with a concert of music representative of the Civil War period.. Vendors set up tents in order to sell Civil War memorabilia. Filled with interesting artifacts concerning the battle, the Port-O-Plymouth Museum was open to the public.

An addition to 2002's activities was the presence of a new replica of the Confederate ironclad ram, *Albemarle*. Built on pontoons by New York native Guy Macken and his carpenters, the replica is three-fifths the size of the original. Once again the *Albemarle* is sitting at the wharf at Plymouth, North Carolina. [1]

A word of thanks goes to Joe and Sue Pate who invited me to join the descendants of the "Plymouth Pilgrims" in enjoying a sumptuous southern breakfast. The Pates presently are in the process of restoring the spacious antebellum Charles Latham House.

Readers just discovering Plymouth, North Carolina, may want to journey one April to the little town on the Roanoke River, eight miles from its mouth. *"While we are unable to walk in the shoes of our forefathers, participants (in the reenactments) at least walk on the same path... Living historians do not seek to glorify war, but attempt to gain a better understanding of life at that time by studying the arts and skills that would be lost to the future, as well as trying to understand the sacrifices made by soldiers, sailors and civilians on the battlefield or at sea."* [2]

Something, however, was missing at the re-enactment activities, so a descendant from Pennsylvania observed, then mentioning it to me. She was speaking about the lack of "colored" participation. Echoing the feelings of many African-Americans residing in Plymouth today, my response to her was, *"At that time in history the only presence we could have would be of slavery. For many of us to portray the conditions in which our ancestors had been forced to exist would be much too painful. We would not feel that we were adding anything positive."* My sincere hope is that this book will add something positive.

A number of people need to be thanked for helping me accomplish the task of writing this book. Because we have both settled in Alexandria, Virginia, I was able to call upon a former schoolmate from West Pittston, Pennsylvania, in order to gain pertinent naval information. He is Retired Admiral John Smith Jenkins, Senior Associate Dean Emeritus of Law, George Washington University Law School. Former colleagues Dr. June Bohannon Powell, retired Department Chairperson of Language Arts, Bloomfield High School, Bloomfield, New Jersey has edited the manuscript and Dr. Georgetta Campbell, retired West Orange Media Coordinator, has encouraged and prodded me to "reach beyond my grasp.".

My trips to Plymouth, North Carolina, put me in touch with retired New York City educator, Merion Baker Anderson, who introduced me to several members of the African-American community. By interviewing them, I heard more about the history of the town through the eyes of their ancestors, the majority having been slaves until the Civil War ended. Unfortunately, the persons who would have had the most information have died. However, I was able to glean some facts from several octogenarians, including Mary Pettiford Armistead, as well as from other residents, including Mrs. Princeton McDowell and her son, Reginald, owners of Toodle's Funeral Home. Their business is located on the Harriet Toodle property noted on the map drawn in 1864 of the Battle of Plymouth. Another Plymouth native, Helen Collins McNair, provided me with a written account of her ancestor, Annie Norman.

Rosalie V. Miller, librarian at the Shepard-Prouden Public Library, Edenton has aided me with my research for both books, *Created to Be Free* and *The Battle of Plymouth*. She is a collateral relative of Zebulon Vance, governor of North Carolina during the Civil War. Members of the staff in the Virginia Room, Fairfax Library, Fairfax, Virginia helped me to locate photographs of officers from both sides of the conflict. Pam Toms and Alex Meekins of the State Library in Raleigh, N.C. have also been helpful in my research. My most recent trip was to the Naval Historical Museum in Washington, D.C. where I was helped to find photographs of the ships associated with the Battle of Plymouth.

In November 2002 I attended the Heritage Festival on St. Helena Island, S.C. where I was fortunate to meet Janet Davidson Nash, the great granddaughter of Robert Smalls, mentioned in both of my books. He was a black Representative first and then a Senator from South Carolina during Reconstruction.

Many other persons have shared ideas with me; however, I do not remember all of their names, but I want them to know that I appreciate their help. So thanks to all of you who have been instrumental in helping me describe the little known battle that took place at Plymouth, North Carolina, April 17-20, 1864.

And with much gratitude to the Creator who orders my steps and directs my path.

Juanita Patience Moss
Alexandria, Virginia.
2003

PROLOGUE

Persons interested in the individual battles of the Civil War certainly are familiar with the notable ones like those fought at Antietam (Sharpsburg), Gettysburg, The Wilderness, The Crater at Petersburg, Bull Run (Manassas), Fredericksburg, and Vicksburg. Many persons, however, have never heard of the intriguing one that took place at Plymouth, North Carolina.

Even once they have heard of the battle, readers may then be forced to search the indices of a number of tomes before discovering any mention of what happened at Plymouth during four terrible days in April 1864. Many persons, even those quite knowledgeable about the Civil War, are totally unaware of the intense drama that unfolded there, drama filled with such critical elements as surprise, fate, intrigue, bravery, ingenuity, hope, daring, dedication, gallantry, victory, disappointment, and defeat. Therefore, many persons have no idea that the second largest Civil War battle in North Carolina took place at the small town of Plymouth, located on the south bank of the Roanoke River. There the Confederates were to taste their last victory.

Was the disgrace of losing the battle so great that the people back home in the North refused to talk about it? Was the disgrace associated with having one's son, brother, or husband become a prisoner of war and not returning home a hero as had other men just too hard to bear? Had the disgrace of their death and burial at Andersonville Prison clouded the minds of those left behind? If so, one hundred thirty eight years later the descendants of the "Plymouth Pilgrims" converging on Plymouth for the annual re-enactment activities have no such feelings of disgrace, only of pride.

Or might some historians have considered the battle at Plymouth too insignificant for discussion, since it had involved less than 3000 Union soldiers? Certainly that is a small number compared to the appalling totals of 51,112 men killed at Gettysburg, 34,624 at Chickawanga, 30,000 at Chancellorsville, 27,399 at Spotsylvania, and 26,134 at Antietam (Sharpsburg). However, it was not insignificant to the courageous men dubbed "Plymouth Pilgrims" who were fortunate enough to survive to tell their stories, or to descendants today honoring their ancestors who fought bravely in the Battle of Plymouth, April 17-20, 1864.

Chapter 1

A NATION DIVIDED

The scene unfolding at Plymouth, North Carolina, in April 1864 was only a small part of the much larger drama begun three years earlier on April 12, 1861, in the Charleston, South Carolina harbor where the Civil War was ignited. That terrible conflict has been called by many names: The War Between the States, The War Against Northern Aggression, The Second American Revolution, The Lost Cause, The War For Southern Independence, The War of the Rebellion, The Brothers' War, The Great War, and The Late Unpleasantness. Poet Walt Whitman called it "The War of Attempted Secession" while Confederate General Joseph Johnston named it "The War Against the States." Regardless by what name it was called, the war was *"the most horrible, necessary, intimate, acrimonious, mean-spirited, and heroic conflict the nation has known."* [1]

Ironically, many of the main actors choosing opposite sides of the conflict had graduated from either the Naval or Army Academy. For instance, West Pointers Generals Ulysses Simpson Grant and Robert Edward Lee both had fought for their country in the recent Mexican War, as had Confederate President Jefferson Davis. In 1861 his former political ally, Union General Benjamin Butler, enthusiastically had supported Davis as the Democratic nominee for President of the United States. Others choosing to serve on opposite sides included former shipmates Yankee Lieutenant Charles Williamson Flusser and Rebel Captain James Cooke, both later to play important roles at the Battle of Plymouth.

Even natives of the same state often found themselves on opposite sides, such as in the case of Union President Lincoln and Confederate President Davis, the two hailing from the border-state of Kentucky. Sometimes members of the same family chose opposite sides, resulting in Kentucky's being almost evenly divided in its loyalties. Two fifths of the eligible men from that state chose to clothe themselves in the cadet-gray uniform of the South.

The Flussers, a Louisville family, was such an example where the conflict truly became "a brothers' war;" for Unionist Charles Flusser disagreed politically with his mother, as well as with his brothers, Ottaker and Guy. Other split Kentuckian families included the prominent Clays, with four of Henry Clay's grandsons fighting for the South and three others for the North. One Breckinridge family member chose the North, while his brother chose the South. By a twist of fate the Rebel was captured by his Yankee brother at the Battle of Atlanta. [2]

*Fig. 2. **Abraham Lincoln***
Union President

*Fig. 3. **Jefferson Davis***
Confederate President

6

In another prominent Kentucky family, Senator John Crittenden had two sons serving on opposite sides: one a general in the Confederate Army and the other a general in the Union Army. Even Mary Todd Lincoln, wife of the President of the United States, had a total of seven brothers and brothers-in law wearing gray. [3]

All throughout the country many other families were being split apart as well, becoming bitter enemies over the issue of national versus state sovereignty. Examples included Confederate Jeb Stuart's father-in-law, the commander of a Union Cavalry unit. During the Battle of Port Royal, South Carolinia, Thomas F. Drayton, a brigadier general in the Confederate Army, was forced to fight against his brother Percival, a captain in the Union Navy. [4] Rear Admiral Samuel Phillips Lee, USN and General Robert E. Lee, CSA were Virginia cousins who chose opposite sides.

A man in the 17th North Carolina Troops of the Confederacy was captured at the Battle of Bentonville and to his great surprise, one of the guards at the prison where he was to be held was none other than his own brother serving under General Sherman of the Union. [5] In addition, at Plymouth, North Carolina, northern-born lawyer Charles Latham's three southern-born sons all served in the Confederate Army. [6]

To further illustrate the distressful situation, the following poignant poem was written by Jessie C. Moore of Kenawnee, Wisconsin. She was the 17 year-old daughter of Joseph Moore, Co. E, 14th Wisconsin Regiment. Her poem appeared in the *National Tribune* of Washington, D.C. on May 1, 1864.

The Blue and The Gray

I had two brothers once,
Warm-hearted, bold and gay.
They left my side—one wore the blue;
The other wore the gray.

One rode with Stonewall and his men,
And joined his fate to Lee.
The other followed Sherman's march
Triumphant to the sea.

Both fought for what they deemed the right,
And died with sword in hand.
One sleeps amid Virginia hills,
And one in Georgia's sand.

The same sun shines upon their graves,
My love for them must stay;
And upon my bosom lies,
This knot of blue and gray.

The North rallied against the South, Federals against Confederates, "Billy Yanks" against "Johnny Rebs." Each side at the outset denied that the issue of slavery was the catalyst igniting the acrimonious war. Rather, each side insisted that it was fighting for liberty just as their American forefathers had during the Revolutionary War. At first, though, neither view of liberty had anything to do with the status of slaves. However, northern abolitionists had other ideas, and so by the time President Abraham Lincoln delivered his eloquent Gettysburg address in 1863, the North was fighting for "a new birth of freedom." [7]

In addition, by fleeing behind Union lines the slaves themselves were opening the way towards making the war one against slavery. [8] Having become "contrabands of war," they forced the North to re-access its views on what liberty meant to all people living in America. This country, having been conceived on the ideals of freedom, was a paradox by keeping people enslaved. Therefore, from then on the North *"fought not just to restore the old union, not just to ensure that the nation born in 1776 'shall not perish from the earth,' but to give that nation 'a new birth of freedom.'"* [9]

Elected in 1860, "Black Republican" Abraham Lincoln, sixteenth president of the United States of America, had run on the platform advocating that slavery be kept out of the new western territories. [10] During the prior twenty years he had been speaking out against the institution of slavery, stating that *"slavery was 'an unqualified evil to the negro, to the white man...and to the State. The monstrous injustice of slavery...deprives our republic an example of its just influence in the world—enables the enemies of free institutions, with plausibility, to taunt us as hypocrites...'"* [11] Regardless of whether or not in agreement, a President of the United States of America was compelled to uphold the law of the land, and in 1860 the Constitution was protecting the institution of slavery in any state where the people wanted it.

Having denounced the Dred Scott decision of 1857, [12] Lincoln was of the opinion that the slaves should be freed, but at a gradual rate, and then colonized elsewhere with compensation given to their owners. However, later during meetings with black delegates where he had expected to advance his idea of colonization in Central America, Lincoln was opposed adamantly by black men influential in their respective communities, including the fiery abolitionist orator Frederick Douglass.

Even though he was vocal in his disapproval of the institution of slavery, Abraham Lincoln was not considered an abolitionist in the true sense of the word. For instance, in his first inaugural address, the new president had stated that he had *"no purpose, directly or indirectly, to interfere with slavery in the States where it exists,"* a pledge he reiterated in his first message to Congress on July 4, 1861. [13]

Therefore, abolitionist William Lloyd Garrison along with his northern cohorts was skeptical about the new president's seemingly paradoxical motives. The South, on the other hand, was quite certain that because of Lincoln's known anti-slavery views, states committed to slavery could no longer be part of the Union. They knew that in order for slavery to continue successfully as an institution, it must be allowed to expand into the new western territories. Therefore, on December 14, 1860, a call was issued in Georgia for deliberation on a possible Southern Confederacy, resulting in South Carolina's seceding from the Union on December 20th.

Ten other southern states quickly followed, totally upsetting the promising careers of many men who were the graduates of, or at the time students at the Army Academy at West Point, New York, or the Naval Academy at Annapolis, Maryland. They were men with bright military futures, pledged to serve their country, and willing even to die for it. However, the firing on Fort Sumter on April 12, 1861, abruptly changed the plans of countless numbers.

Consequently, many sons of the South were confronted with a heart wrenching decision: that of remaining loyal to the Union or remaining "loyal to their section." Robert Edward Lee, a Virginian, was one such man who, with heavy heart, chose the latter. He shed the blue uniform of which he had been so proud, then donning one of cadet gray. His very close friend, General Winfield Scott, advised him that he was making a very grave mistake, but Lee replied, "*I cannot raise my hand against my birthplace, my home, my children.*" (14)

American warriors, having been trained together with intentions of doing battle with foreign enemies, suddenly became adversaries among themselves. Ironically, the war tactics studied so diligently at the academies soon were to be used against one another. Federal and Confederate officers ultimately would lead the largest volunteer military forces in United States history with both sides equally certain that they were fighting for liberty. However, the two sides differed greatly as to what that liberty actually meant, and with neither side including a large population of men and women born in the United States—the slaves. (15)

By declaring its independence, the Confederacy intended to become a separate nation. However, it was devoid of any military forces. Quickly, though, two branches were formed, the Army first, encountering few problems. However, that was not the case of the Navy. Its major problem was that following the secession of Virginia, Arkansas, Tennessee, and North Carolina when resigned officers from the United States Navy reported to the newly created Confederate Navy Department, they were dismayed upon finding no ships available for their command.

Another problem was lack of manpower. Consequently, Secretary of the Navy Stephen Russell Mallory persuaded the Confederate Congress to pass a law stating that any man already serving in the Army would be allowed to volunteer for the Navy, if he so wished. Mallory found, however, even though hundreds of soldiers were willing to make the switch, many army commanders refused to release their men.

In such an emergency situation even some blacks were allowed to join the Confederate Navy in order to increase the numbers. For instance, Benjamin H. Gray at the age of twelve enlisted as a powder boy on the ironclad ram, *CSS Albemarle*. [16] Freed men were allowed to enlist, providing they had permission of the Navy Department or the local squadron commander. However, most of the slaves serving as officers' servants, coal heavers, and pilots, had been "volunteered" by their masters.

One young black pilot to make history was Robert Smalls who had been impressed into the Confederate Navy and forced to serve as a wheelman aboard the armed frigate *CSS Planter*. On May 13, 1862, when the captain and his mates decided to spend the night ashore, Smalls used the opportunity to seize control of the *Planter* anchored in the Charleston harbor, and then to turn her over to a Union squadron blockading the city. Following the end of the war and during the short-lived disastrous Reconstruction, Robert Smalls, by then a self-taught man, served five terms as a representative in Congress from the state of South Carolina. [17]

★★★★

After the assault on Fort Sumter, South Carolina, President Abraham Lincoln introduced an ambitious plan for blockading the entire eastern and southern coasts, thereby preventing the South from exporting and importing goods. However, at that particular time in history the United States Navy was weak, even though in the decade just prior to the war a number of sloops had been built and commissioned, as well as six steam-powered frigates including the *USS Merrimack*. So in order to carry out the President's ambitious plan, the Administration in Washington was forced to begin building a strong Union Navy.

Since Lincoln's blockade was intended to cover a distance of over 3,000 miles, extending from the Chesapeake Bay south around the peninsula of Florida, west into the Gulf Steam, and on to the Rio Grande River, the Union Navy was confronted with a serious problem. At the beginning of the war the majority of vessels were away in foreign waters, while others were being repaired in dry dock. Therefore, since only two functioning ships were on hand, Lincoln's ambitious proposal did not appear at all feasible. [18] So in order to resolve the situation quickly, James B. Eads of St. Louis was hired to build seven ironclad rams to be ready in just one hundred days, a contract he was able to honor to the surprise of many "nay-sayers." However, another major problem arose to face the government. There simply were not enough crewmen to man Ead's brand new rams. [19]

The Army, however, did not have the same problem as the Navy in recruiting men. In fact, some localities sponsored special hometown enlistment competitions, quickly filling Army regiments, each consisting of ten companies, A-K minus J, [20] 100 soldiers each. Some enlistees simply had the desire to be involved with something different while others were drafted. By those several methods the Yankee Army ranks began filling quickly, thereby, resulting in substantial manpower. However, that was not so in the case of the Navy.

Consequently, in order to increase Union naval manpower, trained seamen were offered incentive bonuses for volunteering. Another method used was that of diverting soldiers into the Navy. However, some of those men intensely disliked the confining environment onboard ships and thus becoming unruly and unmanageable.

Union Secretary of the Navy Gideon Welles entered into his diary his anxious thoughts concerning the dire shortage of seamen:

"*March 24, Thursday. We are running short of sailors and I have no immediate remedy. The army officers are not disposed to lose good men, and seem indifferent to the country and general welfare if their service can get along. Commodore Rowan writes that the times of the men are running out and no reinlistments; the army is paying enormous bounties. Between thirty and forty vessels are waiting crews.*

"*March 25, Friday. At Cabinet today, I brought up the subject of a scarcity of seamen. The President seemed concerned, and I have no doubt was. Stanton was more unconcerned than I wished, but did not object to my suggestions. I had commenced, but not completed, a letter to the President urging the importance and necessity of an immediate transfer of 12,000 men to the Navy. The army has by bounties got thousands of sailors and seamen who are experts. This letter I finished and had copied after my return....*

"*March 26, Saturday. I went early this A.M. to the President on the subject of procuring a transfer of seamen from the Army to the Navy. After reading the papers he said he would take the matter in hand, and before I left the room he rang for his man Edward and told him to go for the Secretary of War, but, stopping him before he got to the door, directed him to call the Secretary of State first. In this whole matter of procuring seamen for the Navy there has been a sorry display of the prejudice of some of the military authorities. Halleck appears to dislike the Navy more than he loves his country.*" [21]

*Fig. 4. **Gideon Welles, Union Secretary of the Navy***
From the National Archives

Fig. 5. **Poster used to induce men into the Union Navy**
Courtesy of John Ball

The United States Navy, even though integrated, had attempted prior to the war to restrict the number of blacks in the ranks to one twentieth of the total crew onboard a ship. During the Civil War, however, the chronic shortage of crewmen led Gideon Welles to suggest to the commander of the South Atlantic Blockading Squad that he open recruiting stations ashore for the enlistment of free blacks and "contrabands." As a result, the United States Navy had a high percentage of blacks serving in the lowest ranks, that of "boys" and "landsman." [22] For instance, on the *USS Miami*, dubbed *Miasma* by her crew, the number of blacks rose to be twenty-five of the total one hundred sailors.

The prejudice of many of the white officers and enlisted men, however, plagued the black sailors so much that they chose to remain together as much as possible. For instance, at Plymouth enlisting on the flagship *USS Miami* were a number of black sailors from the same families: Etheridge, Johnson, White, and Wilson. [23]

Besides being a mixture of blacks and whites, the crew of a typical Union warship consisted of older experienced seamen, as well as younger seventeen year-old boys away from home for the very first time. Consequently, Union ships had a much more heterogeneous group as compared with Confederate vessels.

Fig. 6. ***Integrated crew of the USS Miami***
Courtesy U.S. Naval Historic Center

Chapter 2

A SMALL NORTH CAROLINA TOWN

At one time the land on which the small town of Plymouth, North Carolina, sits was part of what was called the Long Patent granted on March 15, 1717, to Thomas Long. Almost half a century later on August 18, 1763, he sold it to Arthur Rhodes who named his newly acquired property "Brick House Plantation." Several years later, Rhodes sold 100 acres of his land to seven northern businessmen from Plymouth, Massachusetts. [1]

Arthur Rhodes' original layout of Plymouth was a parallelogram with four roads running parallel to the Roanoke River and five others at right angles to it. The town was later to become a very important port due to its being on a viable waterway. *"As early as 1820 Plymouth had more tonnage than any other town in Eastern Carolina. In those days it was not an uncommon sight to witness two hundred sailing vessels on the river, and as late as 1860 the importance of the town as a great trading and shipping point was maintained."* [2]

In order to approach the town of Plymouth from different directions the following roads were constructed

Washington Road entering at the southwest corner,
Lee's Mills Road (Acre Road), entering almost in the direct center as
    a continuation of Washington Road,
Columbia Road from the east, being almost perpendicular to Lee's
    Mills Road. [3]

The property on the south bank of the Roanoke River was divided into 172 lots with the new settlement being named "Plymouth" after the town in far distant Massachusetts. That bustling New England town was an important shipbuilding center with great need for the lumber and pitch provided in abundance by North Carolina long leaf pines, as well as for timber from the thick forests of cypress, oak, hickory, ash, gum, and white cedar.

Therefore, following the Revolutionary War, at Plymouth a flourishing trade existed in naval supplies, ship timber for masts and spars, shingles of cypress and juniper, cooperage material, as well as a variety of farm products. [4] Receiving tar, turpentine, and lumber transported from inland plantations, as well as large supplies of cotton and tobacco, Plymouth soon became a thriving town, the fifth largest port in North Carolina. A Customs House was built and products were shipped south to the West Indies, as well as north to the industrious cities of Norfolk, Baltimore, New York City, and Boston. [5]

Rapidly growing in both size and importance, Plymouth in the year 1799 became the Washington County seat, the county recently having been parceled from the territory of Tyrrell. By then the eighth largest settlement in the state, Plymouth on December 17, 1807, became the first incorporated town in Washington County.

★ ★ ★ ★

A mile or so above the town two creeks, one of which was called Welch's, emptied into the Roanoke River with the land between them being called Warren's Neck. A half-mile beyond the southeast border of the town and running in a southeasterly direction to the Roanoke was Coneby Creek, bordered on the west and north by a deep woody swamp. [6]

Due to the nearly impassable terrain in the area, viable waterways were extremely important for the transportation of cotton and other products grown inland to places where they could be sold. In that particular northeastern area of North Carolina, treacherous swamps, marshes, and morasses abounded. Therefore, being able to freely access the navigable rivers was a vital factor to the prosperity of the planters of the region.

Plymouth itself was surrounded by woody swamps lying to the south, as well as by a murky morass at the southwest corner within one hundred and fifty yards of where Washington Road (later to become Wilson Street) entered the town. Beginning 200 yards south of the town and about 100 yards north of the Columbia Road (later to become Main Street) was a miry impassable swamp. It was from one hundred and fifty to two hundred yards in width, extending north to the Roanoke River, a tributary of the Albemarle Sound. [7] Besides the water and mud hindering overland travel, there were also the thick impenetrable woods overrun with trees, thickets, shrubs, and tangling vines.

21

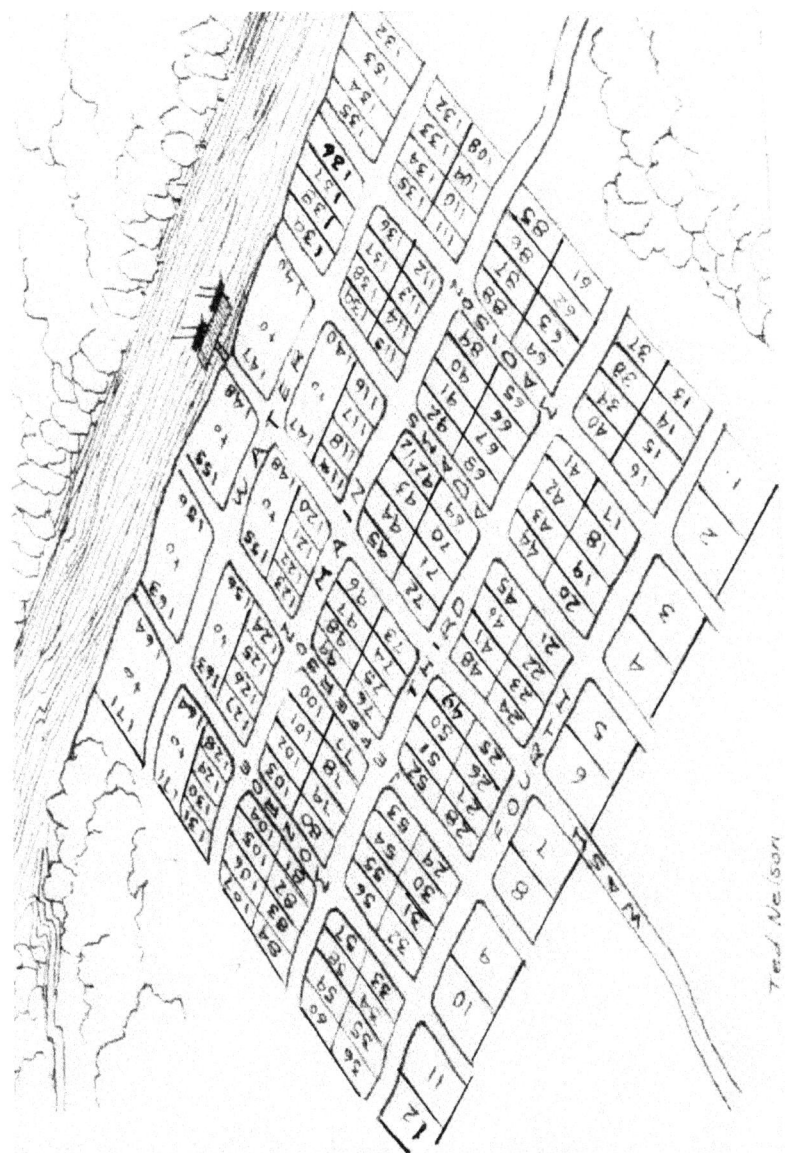

Fig. 7. Map of Plymouth by Arthur Rhodes
Courtesy of Washington County Historical Society

Because of those thick forests and the treacherous swamps abounding with poisonous copperheads and cottonmouths, for nearly 100 years the new settlers in the area had no idea of the existence of a large 16,000 acre body of water just a mere ten miles south of Plymouth. The lake was approximately six feet higher than the surrounding swampland and approximately eighteen feet above the Scuppernong River located six miles away. After discovering the lake and, according to folklore, naming it Phelps after the first man reaching it during an exploratory excursion, [8] ambitious and enterprising colonists initially thought of draining the lake. Plans were formulated also for the removal of the Scuppernong Swamp.

Ultimately, the men had a change of mind after realizing that the lake could be used as an excellent source for irrigation. Therefore, the lake never was drained. Instead, in 1784 three prominent men, Josiah Collins, a prosperous ship owner; Nathaniel Allen, a wealthy businessman, and Samuel Dickinson, a well-known physician, acquired all of the surrounding land to form the Lake Company. Afterwards, 10,000 acres of bogs were drained, canals dug, and crops planted. The opening and closing of canal gates provided the necessary water for growing abundant crops of rice, thus providing a great source of wealth for the three men. [9]

Even though located nearly 100 miles from the Atlantic Ocean, the town of Plymouth, North Carolina, was only 10.5 feet above mean sea level, resulting in a very flat surrounding countryside. Consequently, drainage ditches were a necessity on surrounding farms where the rich, dark, loamy soil was soaked by 55 inches of annual rainfall. [10]

Antebellum Plymouth was an important "Port of Entry," boasting in 1806 of twenty-four ocean-going sailing ships regularly anchoring there. Large quantities of produce grown in the agrarian South were being shipped in exchange for goods manufactured in the industrial North. For instance, timber from the North Carolina woods was needed greatly in the northern shipbuilding centers like Plymouth, Massachusetts. In addition, a large amount of Plymouth revenue was banked in Baltimore, Maryland. [11] Consequently, ties with the North had always been very strong.

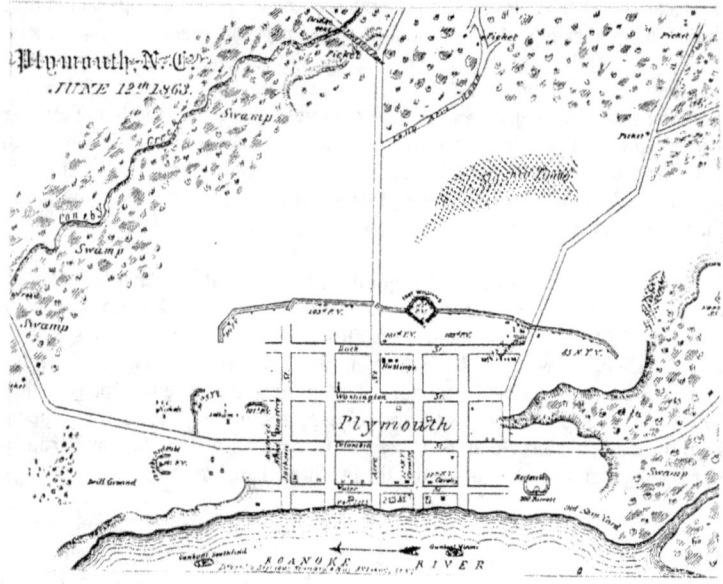

*Fig. 8. **Plymouth, N.C., 1863***

*Fig. 9. **Sketch of Plymouth waterfront, 1864**
"Pictorial History of the Civil War"*

Initially, when the ten deep-South states withdrew from the Union, North Carolina had refused to join them. A special convention called by Governor John Ellis had been held in the state capitol of Raleigh where two delegates from each county voted on whether or not North Carolina should secede. By only a small majority the vote determined that North Carolina would remain in the Union.

However, after the people of Virginia voted to join the Confederacy, North Carolina was alone, squeezed precariously between two Confederate states. Consequently, worried North Carolina politicians lobbied for another convention and once again by just a narrow margin, the electors voted to remain in the Union.

Then on April 12, 1861, South Carolina fired on Fort Sumter in the Charleston harbor, igniting the War Between the States. Secretary of War Simon Cameron telegraphed Governor John Ellis requesting that troops be raised in North Carolina for the purpose of invading South Carolina. [12] A highly incensed Governor Ellis sent an immediate response to the President of the United States stating that North Carolina would provide no such troops for punishing their neighbors. Ellis then called for a third convention at which time the voters declared secession. *"The last to secede, North Carolina sent more men to the war than any other state, had more men killed than any other state, and had less officers."* [13] Even so, all throughout the war residents of North Carolina would remain about 50% in favor of the Union.

At the beginning of the War Between the States many citizens of Plymouth were pro-secessionists, enthusiastically supporting the Confederacy. In fact, the First Regiment of North Carolina State troops was organized in the spring of 1861 at the racetrack near Warrenton where under the leadership of Major Louis Charles Latham a company of 152 enthusiastic Plymouth men proudly donned their brand new cadet-gray uniforms. [14]

However, Plymouth was a southern port tightly tied to the North by trade, and so in 1862, when the Yankees occupied Plymouth the first time, strong Unionist feelings were soon to surface. Local soldiers and sailors were recruited, including blacks escaping from bondage. Consequently, by the end of the war, a total of 2000 eastern North Carolina whites and 3000 eastern North Carolina blacks would have served the Union. [15]

Fig. 10. Three Confederate officers from Plymouth
Latham brothers and Whitehurst
From files at Washington County Library, Plymouth, N.C.

Chapter 3

YANKEE INVASION OF PLYMOUTH

The 1864 drama enacted at Plymouth really began in early 1862 after the Federals successfully had penetrated deep into southern states. A little more than a year later, General Orders, No. 62, dated April 22, 1863, commanded that the 18th Army Corps divide North Carolina into three districts.

Plymouth was included in the Sub-District of the Albemarle, the second of three districts of the Department of North Carolina. By April 1864, most of the land forces garrisoned in the small town on the Roanoke River were under the command of Union General Henry Walton Wessells. He only recently had been appointed as the replacement for Brig. General William H. Keim who died. Keim had been the first to command what originally was the District of the Albemarle, later renamed the Sub-District of the Albermarle. [1]

At that particular time Plymouth became the keystone of naval activities on the Chowan, Cashie, and Roanoke Rivers where approximately 2000 sailors on 30 Union ships patroled the waters under the command of Lieut. Charles Williamson Flusser. Confident of the protection being provided by gunboats on the Roanoke, General Ambrose E. Burnside garrisoned his land forces at Plymouth, an outpost to the main Federal base at New Bern (New Berne, Newberne).

In February of 1862, only months after the Union forces of Flag Officer Silas H. Stringham and General Benjamin F. Butler had captured Forts Hatteras and Clark on the Outer Banks of North Carolina, Major General Burnside arrived on Roanoke Island with 10,000 troops. He was accompanied by a motley flotilla of many varieties of boats, including sailboats, passenger steamboats, coal scows, ferryboats, tugboats, converted barges, as well as makeshift gunboats. Dubbed "Burnside's Expedition," with considerable ease it was able to overtake Roanoke Island being defended by less than 3000 Confederates and a "mosquito fleet" of seven gunboats. [2]

A most strategic spot for either side to hold, Roanoke Island was located just at the mouth of the Albemarle Sound. The swampy island of Sir Walter Raleigh, Virginia Dare, and "The Lost Colony" fame was only ten miles long and two miles wide, small in size, but large in importance. In an amphibious operation launched on February 7, 1862, from Fort Monroe, Virginia, General Burnside was able to successfully land his men on the southwestern side of the island. Then, while being supported by intense fire from the gunboats, 10,000 Union soldiers successfully attacked the Confederate forts located on the narrow waist of the island.

Fig. 11. **General Ambrose Burnside, USA**
*whose muttonchop whiskers led to a new word,
"sideburns" an anagram of his name*

Fig. 12. **Map of operations at Roanoke Island, N.C.**
Official Records of the War of the Rebellion

Outnumbered and outmaneuvered, Confederate Brigadier General Henry Alexander Wise was forced to surrender his stronghold of approximately 2500 men and 32 guns. Inexperienced in military tactics, prior to the war he had been a lawyer and a Democratic politician who had served four years as governor of Virginia, thereby making him the official executioner of the abolitionist John Brown. [3] Not only was General Wise to lose the Battle of Roanoke Island, he was to lose his son as well; for O. Jennings Wise was mortally wounded during the fray. [4]

Following the Federal victory, the three Rebel forts, Barlow, Blanchard, and Huger were renamed Foster, Parke, and Reno (also called Fort Point for Weir's Point) respectively, in honor of the Union commanders of the three brigades participating in the capture of Roanoke Island. [5] With the labor of freed blacks escaping up the Chowan River, the Yankees then proceeded to build an additional fort named after General Ambrose Burnside.

General Burnside had been successful in tightening the blockade. The main reason for the Federals' being there in the first place was to choke off Rebel maritime supplies. Afterwards, the Yankees garrisoned on Roanoke Island were under the impression that they always had to be ready for a surprise Rebel attack. However, at the beginning of the rebellion just the opposite was true; for at that particular time the defense of Richmond, Virginia, the seat of President Jefferson Davis, was far more important to the Confederates.

After his defeat, General Henry A. Wise reported to the Confederate House of Representatives Committee investigating the loss of Roanoke Island:

"Such is the importance and value of Roanoke Island, that it ought to have been defended by all means in the power of the Government. It was the key to all the rear defenses of Norfolk. It unlocked two sounds, Albemarle and Currituck; eight rivers, the North, West, Pasquotank, the Perquimans, the Little, the Chowan, the Roanoke and the Alligator; four canals, the Albemarle and Chesapeake, the Dismal Swamp, the Northwest Canal and the Suffolk; two railroads, the Petersburg and Norfolk and the Sea-Board and Roanoke.

It guarded more than four fifths of all Norfolk's supplies of corn, pork and forage and it cut the command of General Huger off from all its most efficient transportation. It endangers the subsistence of his whole army, threatening the navy yard at Gosport and to cut off Norfolk from Richmond, and both from railroad communications with the South. It lodges the enemy in a safe harbor from the storms of Hatteras, gives them a rendezvous, and large rich range of supplies and the command of the sea-board from Oregon Inlet to Cape Henry. It should have been defended at the expense of 20,000 men and of many millions of dollars." [6]

Another important objective of the Yankee presence in North Carolina was to destroy the bridge to Weldon where the railroad crossed the Roanoke River. However, since their supplies were coming from Wilmington and the railroad was the lifeline to their capitol, Richmond, Virginia, the Rebels were determined to prevent the enemy from destroying the bridge. Therefore, they built Fort Branch three miles southeast of Hamilton at Rainbow Banks in Martin County. The specific purpose of that fortification was to guard the bridge.

Throughout the war, Fort Branch was successful in preventing the Yankees from ever reaching the vital railroad bridge. Even after having been thwarted on the water, the men from the North unsuccessfully tried several times to storm the bridge by way of the land. [7] Possibly, if they had been able to accomplish that feat in 1863 or 1864, the war may have ceased at an earlier date.

Several regiments of Yankee soldiers, including the 103rd Pennsylvania Volunteers, arrived at Plymouth on May 3, 1863. On the previous day they had left New Bern aboard the steamer transport *Robert Collyer*. [8] Unknowingly, the men of the 103rd were entering into a situation to prove far more disastrous to their unit than had all of their previous service; thereby earning them the moniker of the "Hard Luck Regiment." [9]

Later, on August 31, 1863, the 101st and 103rd Pennsylvania Volunteers with the 85th, 92nd, and 96th New York Volunteers together were organized into the First Brigade under the leadership of Colonel Theodore F. Lehmann. Also included were one company of the 12th New York Cavalry and one battery of artillery, the 24th New York, neither unit actually being brigaded, taking their orders directly from the commander of the district, Brig. General Henry Walton Wessells. [10]

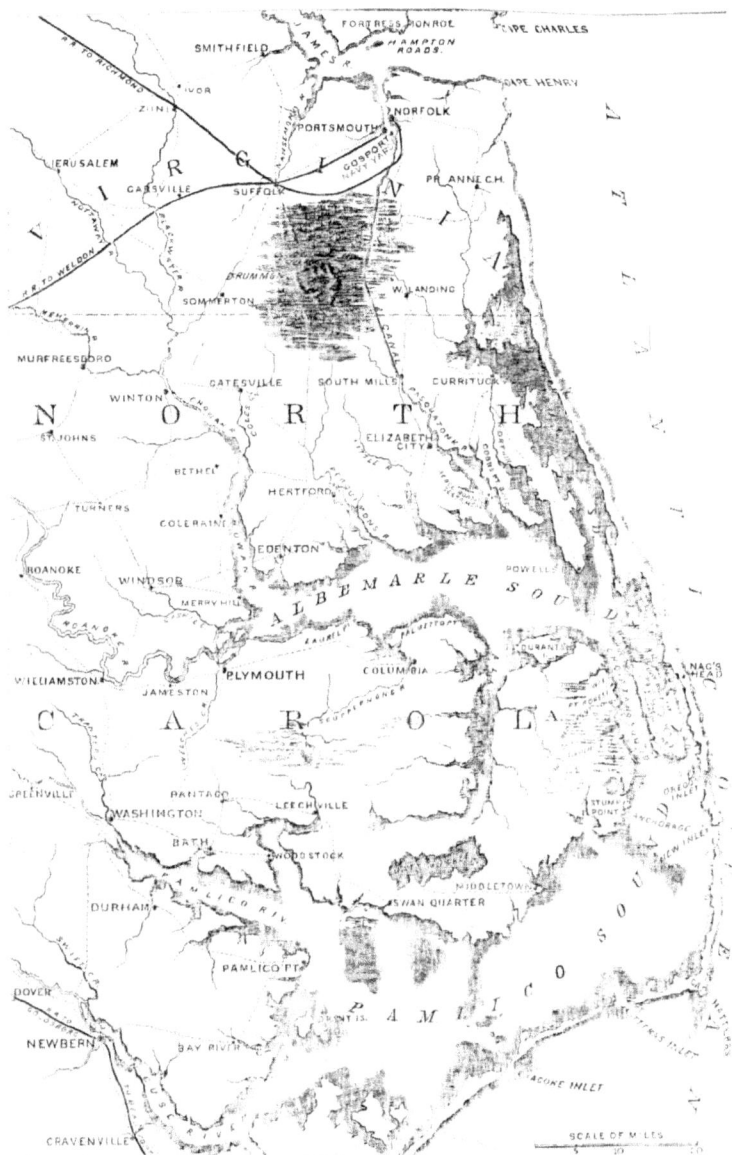

*Fig. 13. **Map of early war operations in northeastern N.C.**
History of the 103rd Regiment*

Sometime later after General Clark had withdrawn his troops to Williamston, the Federals peacefully moved in to occupy Plymouth. At that time approximately 200 troops were garrisoned there: members of Co. I of the 3rd Massachusetts Infantry (nine months' men), Co. C of the 1st North Carolina Infantry, and a company of the 1st North Carolina Cavalry, all under the command of Captain Barnabas Ewer, Jr. of the 3rd Massachusetts Regiment. [11]

Since the people of Plymouth owned few slaves and had a long history of lucrative trading ties with the North, they were generally supportive of the Federal cause. Therefore, town leaders remaining loyal to the Union had no difficulty facilitating the peaceful occupation of the Yankee troops. Commander Stephen C. Rowan when corresponding with his superior observed: *"The hearts of the people of North Carolina are not with the rebels; the woods and swamps are full of refugees fleeing from the terror of conscription."* [12] In general then, residents of the Albemarle Sound region were nominally pro-Confederate or pro-Union, adapting to whatever was necessary for their survival and peace *"when confronted by authority or threatened with conscription, violence, or the destruction of their property."* [13]

From neighboring Bertie County, for instance, out of the 1428 men serving during the Civil War, fifty-six percent were Confederates and forty-four percent Federals. Washington County, where Plymouth is located, was split fifty-fifty. [14] Due to the political divisiveness at that time, the state of North Carolina had not just one governor, but two. The Confederate governor at the state capitol in Raleigh was Zebulon Baird Vance, while the appointed Union military governor at New Bern was Edward Stanley.

Peace, however, was short-lived at Plymouth, for on December 10, 1862, began the first of three battles for the occupation of the important port on the south bank of the Roanoke River. The Confederates had been planning an attack on the town for some time. Their intended goal was to remove the "safety net" being provided at Plymouth for runaway slaves, conscription dodgers, Unionists, and white refugees disillusioned with the South's cause. Composed of the latter, two Union regiments of North Carolinians already had been formed, as well as in other areas of the state.

In addition, the Yankees were conducting raids from Plymouth on nearby towns and farms in search of decent food to supplement their unpalatable army rations. Dried meat, beans, and apples as well as hardtack were staples in the soldiers' diet. Hardtack was a hard three-inch square and one half-inch thick cracker used in the absence of fresh bread. Nearly unbreakable, it was labeled by the men "sheet iron," or better yet, "worm castle" since invariably the cracker hosted maggots and/or weevils. The only way to make the cracker edible was by crushing it into smaller pieces with a rifle butt and then soaking it in hot water or coffee or by frying it in grease. [15]

To the Union Men
OF
CARTERET COUNTY.

It is proposed to raise in Carteret County, one or more companies of volunteers, to be attached to the 1st Regiment N. C. U. Volunteers, under my command.

The men who are enlisted under this call, are intended to act as a Home Guard. Their head-quarters will be at Beaufort, where they will be equipped and drilled. They will not be moved from the county, except at intervals for battalion drill, nor will they be called upon to march to any other part of the State, unless upon an occasion of emergency. Their pay, clothing, rations, equipments and allowances, will be in all respects similar to those of the United States Volunteers.

The term of enlistment will be for the war.

EDWARD E. POTTER,
Col. Com'g 1st N. C. U. Vols.

Sept. 5, 1862.

Fig. 14. Poster for Carteret County men to enlist in Union Army
Courtesy of John Ball

The government fare being so unappetizing, the soldiers confiscated fresh fruits and vegetables, as well as chickens, hickory-smoked hams, and bacon. Even though North Carolinians who had taken the oath of allegiance to the United States had been promised not to have their property foraged, few officers were enforcing the rule. [16] So when the enlisted men returned to Plymouth from the countryside, they usually were carrying bountiful supplies of produce, certainly reason enough for the unhappy residents of northeastern North Carolina to want the detested "blue-bellies" gone.

Corporal Luther Dickey of the 103rd Pennsylvania Volunteers described two such foraging raids in 1864 when food and other items were destroyed deliberately:

"On Jan. 20, an expedition started from Plymouth under command of Lieut. Col. Maxwell for the purpose of capturing or destroying Confederate property which had been concentrated at Harrellsville, Hertford County, N.C. The expedition was highly successful; a large amount of property was brought away, and for want of transportation many wagons, large-quantities of salt and sugar, and 150,000 pounds of pork were destroyed....

Again on Jan. 26, another force commanded by Lieut. Col. Maxwell was dispatched into Bertie County to destroy and capture Confederate property. On this excursion 200,000 pounds of pork were destroyed, also a large amount of Confederate property; tobacco, cotton, horses, mules, and wagons were brought away. Lieut. Col. Maxwell's success in these enterprises call forth a complimentary order from Maj. Gen. Peck, commanding the Army and District of North Carolina, in which he said: 'The success of this enterprise is shown in the list of property taken or destroyed...This example of Col. Maxwell will be appreciated and emulated by the whole command." [17]

Sergeant Julian Wheaton Merrill of the 24th New York Independent Battery, the "Rocket Battalion," [18] recalled one of his foraging experiences:

"...A good share of our time has been spent in scouting, foraging and chasing guerrillas, this fall--both as cavalry and again as artillery, on "Gov." steamers which are sent with infantry inland, on the many rivers emptying into Roanoke Sound and navigable many miles from their mouth.

To give you an account of one of these expeditions would be to describe all, except in numbers of troops and results. Last evening a party returned, consisting of forty of the 12th Cavalry and thirty-five of the 24th Artillery (mounted). They brought in with them about half-a-mile of cattle, sheep, hogs, carts, negroes, furniture, &c, &c, and nine guerilla prisoners. They had been out four days.

Most of the household property was taken from the Pettigrew and Collins plantations--both of the Southern aristocracy, extensive landholders and strong secessionists. ...

> One of the guerrillas who was captured is one of two who a few days ago called one of two negro men, living with their families in the same hut, and then telling him to raise his hands, shot him dead. The other guerilla called out the other negro and ordering him to place himself in the same position, shot him. Provocation- "being negroes." Our forces were unable to catch hold of this second monster. It will be too much of a blessing for this one taken to receive his just deserts, (which he certainly will receive from Butler) for 'hanging is too good for him.'
>
> The property taken has been turned over to the quartermaster and he will make good use of it distributing it among the poor citizens who have come within our lines, or give U.S. credit for proceeds of sale. ...The citizens throughout these eastern counties of North Carolina are constantly coming within our lines and enlisting. Two companies of North Carolinians have been recruited here within a few months.
>
> A company of negroes of about one hundred (enlisted here) were sent to Norfolk day before yesterday. Contrabands arrive here from 'up country' by steamers, well loaded, on an average of once a fortnight. They are then sent to the colored colony on Roanoke." [19]

B. F. Blakeslee of the 16th Connecticut Regiment described raids conducted by Companies A, C, and H under Captain Hintz. He told about breaking up rebel cavalry camps and burning large quantities of cotton and tobacco, as well as capturing some prisoners. [20]

Corporal Luther Dickey of the 103rd Pennsylvania Volunteers wrote about an early Yankee expedition to Elizabeth City.

> "A 'wild cat' bank there was raided by the sailors. A large quantity of bank-notes, both signed and unsigned, were confiscated by the sailors and lavishly distributed to the soldiers. These notes were finely executed both in design and engraving. It was an easy matter to palm them off on the illiterate, white and black, in districts first invaded by the Federal troops. The garrison at Plymouth, for a time, found foraging made easier by using this spurious money. The parties robbed would catch their chickens for the 'Yanks,' while the latter stood quietly by. It is needless to say that the second visit to a place found no one willing to accept these new crisp bills in payment, and then downright foraging was resorted to..." [21]

The military governor Edward Stanley had complaints about the activities of the Yankee invaders when he wrote to Maj. Gen. J. G. Foster:

> "I deeply regret to be compelled, in the last hours of my stay here, to distress you by complaints of the outrages of our forces in the last expedition to Hyde

County. *In numerous instances, well authenticated, they entered and robbed the houses of loyal men, destroyed furniture, insulted women, and treated with scorn the protections which by your advice I had given them....*" [22]

So the determined Rebels, having been lying in wait for just the right time, launched an early morning surprise attack on Plymouth. The opportune time came the day after Lieut. Commander Charles Williamson Flusser had left the town unprotected when he sailed the *USS Commodore Perry* into the Chowan River.

In Flusser's absence the town was rampaged, beginning at dawn on December 10, 1862, when Confederate Colonel John C. Lamb totally surprised the Plymouth garrison. Companies of the 17th North Carolina Regiment were successful in capturing all of the pickets and in confiscating a substantial supply of munitions. Preparing to defend the garrison, Union Captain Barnabas Ewer lined his men across Main Street, but the Confederate cavalry quickly scattered them. The Yankees then reformed inside the Customs House.

"*Lamb directed his artillery fire on the Customs House, placing nine holes in it and blowing down one side of the upper story. Then he fired on the Union gunboat Southfield, placing one hole in her smoke stack and the other through the boiler.*" [23]

Unfortunately, during the ensuing battle the Union gunboats from the river unintentionally set fire to many buildings, resulting in the total destruction of what once had been a very pretty town. "*Ewer, observing his naval support withdrawing under fire, managed to get aboard a departing vessel, much to the disgust of witnesses.*"[24]

Many businesses were burned deliberately, as well as private residences from which frantic inhabitants garbed solely in their bed clothing were forced to flee into the frigid early morning air. While running in the street to escape her burning home, forty-three-year old Amanda Phelps was shot and killed. Her daughter Lucretia was Lieut. Commander Charles Flusser's special "lady friend."

Later in the month, in a letter written to his mother, Flusser shared the grief and anguish he felt:

Plymouth, North Carolina
28th Dec. 1862

My dear Mamma-

"*...The greater part of the town was burned on the 10th instant by the enemy during my absence. I heard the firing and returned to find the enemy fled, the town in ashes, and one of my lady friends murdered. I am very fond of her daughter. I found her kneeling at the feet of her dying mother, her dress disordered, her hair dishevelled,* *and her countenance the picture of woe. I vowed then, in my anger, to go higher up the river within the enemy's lines, and burn a town in their possession. This I could do without loss to our side. But, when I viewed the distress of the poor women and children turned out of doors in a cold winter morning, but half clad, and no time allowed them to save anything from their houses, I determined that I should never be a willing party to the infliction of such sufferings on the families of even our worst enemies..."* [25] Two months later, however, angry Unionists went up the river to Hamilton and torched a hotel that was owned by Lamb. [26]

When the attack on Plymouth was over, less than a dozen fire-scarred buildings remained standing. Describing what he remembered, Edward L. Conn sent the following account in 1909 to the *Raleigh News and Observer*:

"Col. Lamb with his little army not being able to drive off the gunboats to the river, withdrew from the town, and the Federal authorities immediately undertook fortification. They made fruitful use of their time for a year or more, building forts, erecting breastworks and cutting away the forest growth near the town." [27]

Regardless of differences in the analysis of the outcome, the Confederates became aware from their first attack on Plymouth just how well protected the Yankee troops were by the gunboats on the river. On the other hand, the Federals learned just how vulnerable they were on the land.

Consequently, forts were constructed immediately, connected by walls of dirt called earthworks erected protectively around the perimeter of the town, except on the east where swamps would curtail them. The largest of the fortifications was Fort Williams built on an elevated area in the center of Plymouth. A thirty-foot deep, 30-foot wide deep moat, and an impenetrable stockade enclosed the large pentagonal shaped fortification. [28] Mounting four thirty-two pounder cannons and six-pound brass pieces, the formidable Fort Williams commanded Acre Road as it entered the town from the south. [29]

At first, Fort Williams was surrounded by numerous "A" tents (one for each four men) used during the warmer weather, placed on wooden floors elevated two feet off the ground. Later, however, wooden huts were built for winter shelter. A kitchen and a dining area were constructed, streets paved with bricks, and arbors built to provide shade against the intense heat of the summer months. [30]

While some members of the 103rd Pennsylvania Volunteers remained outside the fort, Co.'s A and G garrisoned inside the bastion that had been named in memory of Brig. General Thomas Williams. Having died in action at Baton Rouge, Louisiana, on August 5, 1862, he was the first general killed commanding the Department of North Carolina. [31] Today at the intersection of Jefferson and Fort Williams Streets, a historical sign marks the spot where Fort Williams had stood.

*Fig. 15. **Fort Williams historic marker***
From author's collection

*Fig. 16. **Spot where Fort Williams once stood***
From author's collection

The smaller Fort Gray (Fort Warren to the Confederates) was built two miles up the Roanoke River for the purpose of cutting off Confederate land communications and to halt the enemy from coming down the river. Located at the southern terminus of Warren's Neck and facing Tabor Island, Fort Gray was isolated from the rest of the fortifications at Plymouth, being approachable only by water. The fort had been named for Colonel Charles Gray of the 96th New York Infantry Volunteers. He was killed on December 14, 1862, by a musket shot through his heart while he was leading a charge across the Neuse River at Kinston. [32]

Built on Sanderson's farm was a third fortification, Fort Wessells, also in an isolated spot. Some Federals called it the 85th Redoubt after the regiment erecting it, the 85th New York Infantry. [33] Called Fort Sanderson by the Confederates, it was protecting approaches from the southwest via Washington Road. The site of the fort was where presently Campbell and Wilson Streets intersect.

Placed on the western side of town at the waterfront was a fourth fortification. Battery Worth enclosed a 200-pound rifled gun and was built specifically to sink the rumored ram. The Confederates called that entrenched earthwork facing the Roanoke River Fort Hal. [34]

Close to the town's eastern limits, Latham's farm was located between Third and Fourth Streets. On that property an earthwork was built, Redoubt Latham to some and Coneby Redoubt to others. Four hundred yards from that redoubt another earthwork was erected on Bateman's farm bordering on Columbia Road. [35]

Another redoubt was named for Captain Alexander Compher, [36] Co. D of the 101st Pennsylvania. Also called Fort Comfort (most likely as a mispronunciation of the correct name), it was built on a hill in the backyard of a large white home owned by Jackie Dotson. The fort was equipped with two 32-pounders and two twelve pounders. Facing east, octagonal in shape, [37] the fort was located north and midway between Columbia Road and the miry swamp bordering the river. After the Confederate victory on April 20, 1864, the fort was renamed Fort Jones in honor of Colonel J. G. Jones of the 35th North Carolina Infantry who was killed in the siege. [38] At the present time in 2003, a water tower stands on the spot.

The ultimate goal of the Federal gunboats in the North Carolina waters was to form a successful blockade. In addition to preventing the South's vital exports of cotton and tobacco from reaching the Atlantic Ocean to be exchanged for English imports of efficient Enfield rifles and ammunition, the Yankees also intended to prevent the Rebels from being able to access supplies of essential salt for manufacturing gunpowder. Therefore, one company from each of General Wessells' regiments was required to be on Roanoke Island, blocking the Confederates, as well as keeping the Federals' supply channels viable.

So when Co. F of the 103rd Pennsylvania Volunteers arrived on the island on June 23, 1863, the men were not expecting to be replaced until six months has passed. Therefore, not until January 2, 1864, when Captain Cochran's Co. C fortuitously arrived on Roanoke Island would Captain Donaghy's Co. F return to Plymouth, disastrously rejoining the other eight companies of the 103rd garrisoned there.[39]

Just as General Burnside had been, General Wessells was quite confident that his small garrison at Plymouth could adequately defend the town due to the protection being afforded by the four gunboats on the Roanoke. Built in the Philadelphia Navy Yard, the flagship *USS Miami* was carrying six 9" guns, one 100-Parrott rifle, and one 24-pounder smooth bore howitzer. The *USS Southfield*, originally a Staten Island ferryboat, carried five 9" Dahlgren guns, one 100-pounder Parrott, and one 12-pounder howitzer. Both the *USS Ceres* and *USS Whitehead* carried several 20-pounder Parrott guns and howitzers.[40]

Therefore, the Federal gunboats were in full command of the Roanoke River.

Fig. 17. *USS Miami*
Courtesy of the U.S. Naval Historical Center

In 1871, J. W. Merrill of the 24th New York Independent Battery described the environment at Plymouth just prior to the disastrous battle on April 17-20, 1864:

> "In addition to our churches and schools, the gayer portion of the garrison interested themselves in concerts, balls and parties. 'Ferguson's Band' [41] was in as great demand as it is in the present winter seasons.
>
> The few whites who were left, and able to entertain did so. The officers of the different departments entertained and the soldiers did the same. Christmas was kept as a holiday and on New Years, the day was made jolly by a show of climbing greased poles for a purse, running sack races, chasing a greased pig, running races with wheelbarrows while blindfolded; the whole concluding with a grand scrub race of all sorts and sizes of horses."[42]

Following all of those festive holiday activities and with a promise of a thirty-day furlough within sixty days of re-enlistment, men already having served their three months stint were induced to re-enlist on January 1, 1864, for three more years. [43] At the same time, they were being issued brand new uniforms because General Wessells wanted all of the members of his brigade attired similarly. Heretofore, each regiment had been wearing a distinctive uniform of its own.

General Wessells ordered his men to wear the regulation army uniform with the long woolen dark blue frock (uniform) coat that had been the standard look at the beginning of the war. However, the men felt that the shorter length sack (fatigue) coat was much more comfortable to wear during battles. The general, however, was insistent that his men (18th Corps, Army of the James, 4th Division) look unique. For example, on the arms of each uniform were sewn veteran chevrons called a "hash." Wessell's Brigade wore veteran chevrons representing the color of the particular branch of the army (blue for infantry, yellow for cavalry, and red for artillery). In addition, each chevron was outlined with red to signify the soldier's re-enlistment during war times.

On an enlisted man's frock coat a badge (a green variegated cross) was sewn over the soldier's heart, whereas an officer's badge was a metal pin. Resembling a shamrock, it represented the 4th Division of the 18th Army Corps. When the patterns for the uniforms were distributed to seamstresses, all of the light blue trousers were constructed unsized. Because of that, a number of small metal disks the size of pennies were sewn along the openings. Each soldier, therefore, was to determine his trouser size by the number of disks required to keep his trousers up and in place, announcing, for instance, that he wore a "four penny size." Down the side of the trouser legs of the non-commissioned officers was sewn a stripe in the color of the military branch. The red stripe of the artillery inspired the nickname "red legs."[44]

Each officer and non-commissioned officer was issued a sword, even though not very sharp. Swords were used mainly for dress appearances, not expected for use in battle, except when all else had failed. They varied in length according to whether infantry, cavalry, or artillery.

In addition to their new dark blue frock coat and light blue trousers, the soldiers were issued elaborate black "Hardee" hats. The men detested being forced to wear them during the dress parades. That particular kind of hat was named for General William Hardee who in 1857 had designed the original Union dress uniform. It was also called the "Jeff Davis" hat because Jefferson Davis had been Secretary of War at the time he and Hardee collaborated on styling a standard dress uniform for the United States Army, first designing one for the cavalry and then one for the infantry. Hardee later was to become a general in the Confederate Army.[45]

On June 15, 1893, Charlie Mosher recorded in his diary:

"We have drawn regulation hats, much to our disgust. They are of black felt, stiff rims, one side cocked up with a brass spread eagle to keep it in place."[46]

Fig. 18. **Ed Boots, re-enactor,** *101st Penna. Volunteers From author's collection*

For an enlisted man the eagle was a metal pin; however, for an officer the soaring eagle was intricately embroidered on one side of his hat. Although on its front the Hardee bore a number such as 101 to identify the regiment, the state was never indicated. Also adorning each hat was another identification: a bugle for infantry, crossed sabers for cavalry, and crossed cannons for artillery.

The men much preferred wearing their dark blue caps called "kepis." A narrow black leather visor and a flat top flopping forward at a sharp angle were the chief characteristics of forage caps. A "kepi" was a French-style forage cap, differing in several details from the other types. How much the soldiers really detested the dress hats can be discerned in Captain John Donaghy's memoirs in which he writes the following concerning the soldiers' being dressed in proper attire:

"Keeping the clothing and equipment of the men up to the required state of completeness was a duty that took considerable attention on the part of the company commanders. The regulations allowed each enlisted man $42 per year for clothing, and each article had a fixed price. What he drew in excess of that amount was charged against his pay, and if he drew less than the allowance he was paid the amount so saved.

"On the marches at the beginning of our service when the men were fatigued, many of them threw away their great coats, or such articles as they thought they could spare. Afterwards experience, or their company commanders, forced them to replace the articles discarded. When it was the latter that exercised the compulsion, the man usually considered himself a victim of military tyranny.

While at Plymouth it was ordered that dress hats be added to the equipment of the men. The hats arrived, and the men assembled at their respective company headquarters to be fitted and supplied. Private M____of my company remained in his tent unwilling to receive a hat. I sent him a special invitation to come and be crowned, but he replied that he did not want to buy a hat, and that he did not believe that a free born American citizen could be compelled to buy what he did not want.

Barring his stubbornness M____was a good soldier, so I went to him and explained the necessity of his obedience, but it was of no avail. He flatly refused to take the hat. I ordered his arrest, and had him sent to jail in town. Next day he sent me word that he was sorry for his conduct and would take the hat. He was released." [47]

Because their furloughs had been granted, all of the men of the 24th New York Battery, spiffily attired in their new uniforms, were able to visit their respective homes, there to make a great impression with their smart appearance. *"On their return, Captain Cady* [48] *again made a change in the roster of the Battery; many vacancies having occurred by resignations, promotions, deaths and sickness."* [49]

Private Charles Mosher, among the fortunate number surviving the horrific conditions at Andersonville Prison, believed he was the only one in the 85th New York Infantry to receive his veteran furlough. It was granted because Mosher's father had become seriously ill and was desirous of seeing his son once again. So in February of 1864, Mosher traveled home to his family's farm near Chapinville just north of Canandaigua, New York. Sadly, however, upon his arrival he learned that his father had died two weeks before.

While he was home on furlough, twenty-one year old Charles Condit Mosher used $200 of his Ontario County re-enlistment bounty as a down payment for a residence for his recently widowed mother, his sister Sarah, and himself when he would return after the war had ended. He purchased a $600 house on Troy Street in Seneca Falls, New York, so as to be near his brother's home. [50] When Private Mosher returned to duty on March 24, 1864, he was two days past his thirty-five day limit. Fortunately, he was not reported AWOL (absent without leave).

When the Battle of Plymouth erupted on April 17, 1864, the veterans of the 101st and 103rd Pennsylvania Volunteers, as well as the other men in Mosher's regiment, the 85th New York, were waiting still for their promised furloughs. However, the men of 16th Connecticut were not, having been mustered in later than the others and "for the duration of the war." [51] Therefore, they would not be eligible for a furlough until August of 1865. Fortunately, by that time war would have ceased.

*Fig. 19. **Private Charles Mosher, 85th N.Y. Volunteers***
Courtesy of Wayne Mahood

Chapter 4

THE "CONTRABAND" PROBLEM

The story of what occurred at Plymouth, North Carolina on April 17-20, 1864 cannot be told fully without including information concerning the black presence as well. Due to the lack of solid information, however, the role of blacks has been underplayed in the drama that unfolded there.

Just prior to the War Between the States, the small community had been a pleasant peaceful prestigious place: population of 409 whites, 401 slaves, and 62 freed persons. [1] Few persons in Washington County were in possession of more than ten slaves, even if that many, with the exception of Josiah Collins of Cool Springs District. According to the 1860 census, his possession of 328 individuals made him the largest slave owner in the county. The fourth largest slaveholder was Alfred G. Garrett of Plymouth District, owning only 59.

The 1860 census also names fifty-eight "free persons of color" residing in Plymouth, the majority categorized as M (mulatto), products of decades of miscegenation, a characteristic of the South's "peculiar institution." Surnames of "free persons of color" living in Plymouth just prior to the Civil War included Archer, Ash, Banks, Bateman, Brooks, Bryant, Dempsey, Gaylord, Jones, Johnson, Lee, Newberry, Overton, Pearce, Sanderlin, Sparrow, Toodle, and Wilder. [2]

For instance, one "free woman of color" was Mary A. Lee, a forty two-year old baker listed in the 1860 census as "head of household." Her combined property value of $2,750 made her the wealthiest "free person of color" in Washington County prior to the Civil War. Interestingly, Mary A. Lee was the owner of a three-year old girl judged by the 1860 census taker as being a mulatto. Sometimes "free persons of color" would purchase a relative. Most often, however, it would be an aged one who could not fare alone. [3] The circumstances surrounding Mary A. Lee and the child owned by her are not known. What is known, however, is that the girl could not have been Mary's biological child because colored children always took the legal status of the mother.

In his diary Charlies Mosher makes mention of a black woman living in Plymouth:

> *"April 17,1864...About half past four o'clock, on my return from Black Biddy's with warm biscuits for supper (She is the colored woman who bakes for us sometimes.)..."* [4]

Whether Mary Lee and Black Biddy are one and the same cannot be determined, but the presumption would be that the woman Mosher is writing about was either a runaway living in the refugee shantytown, or she was a "free woman of color" living in town. Certainly she could not have been a slave if she were openly baking for Yankee soldiers.

★ ★ ★ ★

When Wessell's Brigade arrived at Plymouth in 1863, less than five hundred inhabitants in residence were not connected with the Union military forces. Many of that number were blacks, the majority of which still were living in bondage. Following the Emancipation Proclamation being delivered on January 1, 1863, and the Bureau of Colored Troops being established later on May 22nd, black men from Plymouth, North Carolina, enthusiastically enlisted in both the Union Army and Navy, having been promised their freedom if they did.

Three regiments of black soldiers formed at Plymouth: the First N.C. Volunteers of African Descent (later the 35th U.S. Colored Infantry), the Second N.C. Volunteers of African Descent (later the 36th U.S. Colored Infantry), and the Third N.C. Colored Infantry (later the 37th U. S. Colored Troops). [5] The names of several Plymouth men known to have enlisted in the 36th USCT were as follows: Edmund Beasley, Gaston Beckton, Abram Bell, Jacob Biner, Allen Brown, Joseph Bunch, Henry Gayer, Peter Herbert, David McRae, Gilbert Mizzell, Washington Nuby, and Frank Swift. All were later mustered into service in Portsmouth, Virginia. [6]

*Fig. 20. **A slave becomes a Union soldier***
Courtesy of the Fairfax Public Library, Fairfax, Va.

Black sailors from Plymouth included: Alonzo Holt, Alfred James, Fayette Norcom, Jim Norcom, Willis Norcom, Aaron Sanderson, Isham Shark, Henry Smellen, Washington Sparrow, Henry White, and York Yarrett (perhaps Garrett). [7]

The names of those particular blacks are not found on any census prior to 1870 because if they were living in Plymouth at the time, they would have been someone's property. Therefore, the 1870 census is the first to record all persons of color living in Plymouth, identified as either "B" or "M." Since oftentimes slaves were given or chose the surname of their owners, many surnames of Plymouth African-American citizens today reflect past ownership. Examples of such are: Armistead, Chesson, Collins, Davenport, Etheridge, Fagan, Garrett, Jones, Missell (Mizzell), Norman, Newberry, Phelps, Spruill, Walker, and Windley. Identical surnames can be seen on tombstones in the cemeteries of the Plymouth Methodist and Grace Episcopal churches. [8]

Oftentimes, the surname of a slave was changed when he or she was sold. For instance, a certain Windley slave automatically became a Garrett after having been sold to the owner of Garrett's Island, Alfred Garrett. [9] Therefore, identical surnames of African Americans today do not necessarily reflect a biological bond. They may just be suggesting a common point of origin.

Descendants of a slave born on March 19, 1830, at Somerset Place, Creswell, tell the story of a young slave girl named Annie sold to Robert Davis. However, after he developed financial problems, she became the property of Major Charles Louis Latham and his first wife, prominent citizens of Plymouth. Seemingly, years later when his second wife had disliked Annie, Latham sold the girl to a man whose surname was Murphy. However, just before the Civil War began, Annie was in the possession of Guifford Jones. After the war ended and she was free, she returned to Washington County where she married David Norman and gave birth to seven children. [10]

Another mention of her can be found in a brochure describing historic Plymouth:

"Annie Norman, a devoted house slave for the Charles Latham family, moved to Mackeys after the war and regularly walked ten miles from her house to town to visit the Lathams. As she got older, she was known to refuse a ride home in the Lathams' newly acquired automobile as she was afraid of it." [11]

A woman highly respected by both blacks and whites, Annie Norman, amazingly, lived to be 112 years of age. She died on June 9, 1942. [12]

Another black woman of special interest was young Amanda Speller. In June of 1863 she married George Washington, a "Col'd" cook in the 24th New York Battery.

Both hailed from Windsor in Bertie County. Unfortunately, Amanda was to become a civilian casualty of the Battle of Plymouth, for during the siege she was killed. [13]

The next year George Washington married Ellen Bond at Plymouth. Performing the wedding ceremony was Rev. Alford Pettiford, the father of Reuben Pettiford who in the future would become a well-off black citizen of Plymouth. The wedding license was given to the Provost Marshall.

The Washingtons produced four children: Lucy, Reuben, Cora, and Allen. George died in Windsor on April 9, 1888, from cerebro-spinal meningitis. Interestingly, depositions to obtain a widow's pension were given by sisters of George's first wife Amanda. In addition, one of Amanda's sisters was midwife to the births of Ellen's children. [14] Seemingly, the Speller and Washington families were relatives, or perhaps just very close friends.

★ ★ ★ ★

In 1863, hundreds of runaways were escaping not only to Roanoke Island, but also to Plymouth in order to be under the protection of President Abraham Lincoln's troops, albeit totally ignorant of the Yankees' reasons for being there. The slaves had no idea that the primary objective was to "preserve the Union." The slaves, moreover, were under the mistaken impression that the white soldiers from the North were their "saviors, come down South just to free them."

On the contrary, the majority of Yankee soldiers garrisoned at Plymouth never had seen a black person before the war. Perhaps many of the white men were as curious about colored people as was Samuel Boots of North Sewickley, Pennsylvania. On October 24, 1863, he wrote the following letter to his nephew, Sergeant Edward Boots of the 101st Pennsylvania Regiment. [15]

> "Dear Nephew...I suppose you have by this time, become pretty well acquaint with the characterists of the collourd man. I would like to have your opinion of him whether he can be brought on in equality with the white man wether the intelect is there if it was brought out. We hear a great deal about them here."

Although there is no record of his reply to his uncle, Sergeant Ed Boots wrote the following to his sister on February 10, 1864.

> "The school for the negroes still goes on. There are three teachers now. One old lady & two young ones. All from Massachusetts. I think. I am glad to see the negroes taught. They will learn how much we are doing for them & the more they learn, the more thoroughly they will be for the North. They will yet become good citizens, fit to take a share in the responsibilities that every man should feel." [16]

At Plymouth the number of refugees rapidly swelled as more and more slaves continued to arrive. They were fleeing from surrounding plantations such as Somerset, Sahara, and Pea Ridge owned by the wealthy slave owners, Josiah Collins, Ebenezer Pettigrew, and John Newberry, respectively. Many of the runaways, while attempting escape by water, were picked up by Union gunboats and then deposited either at Plymouth or Roanoke Island.

Therefore, during Federal occupation, Plymouth became a Mecca for runaway slaves, the number approximating 1,000 in two years. [17] The news had spread rapidly over the slave "grapevine" that "Old Pap" (as the 53-year old General Henry W. Wessells was affectionately called) would provide security for black refugees and their families. Since he would not turn them away, a huge problem was being created for the soldiers from the North, expected then to look after colored runaway slaves following them in droves just as the children of Hamlin followed the Pied Piper.

In his description of Plymouth, Private Warren Lee Goss of the Second Regiment Massachusetts Heavy Artillery recorded:

"...The place was a general rendezvous for fugitive negroes, who came into our lines by families, while escaping from conscription (impressment) or persecution, and for rebel deserters, who had become lean, hungry, ragged, and dissatisfied with fighting against the Union. Schools had been established for the young and middle-aged colored population...The whole place had a Rip Van Winkle look, as though it had composed itself into a long sleep to awake after the era of revolution and rebellion had passed...." [18]

The black refugees were being classified by the Federals as "contraband," a term first coined by General Benjamin F. Butler who considered the runaway slaves "spoils of war" like any of the Confederates' other possessions. [19] To their owners slaves were property or chattel just like their cattle and horses, harnesses, saddles, and saddlebags, as well as their caches of gold and silver. By escaping their bondage the slaves were causing many southern fortunes based totally on "black gold" to fade quickly, considering that in 1860 a strong male was worth $1,800. [20]

Therefore, the Yankees felt justified in allowing the runaways to remain at Plymouth, finally beginning to realize that the slave was the key to the wealth of the South. The first time in their lives paid to work, many of the black refugees were elated to contract with the Army as cooks, teamsters, personal servants, laborers, and laundresses for a salary of $10 a month. [21]

Not wanting to be thought of as mere "things," many blacks, however, objected to the term "contraband" being applied to them. Because they were no longer slaves, they wanted to be called citizens. However, even though they were not "things," they were not allowed at that time to be citizens of the United States. The ex-slaves had no idea that they were not even considered "whole" human beings. They did not know that according to the Constitution of the United States, each slave was counted as three-fifths of a person for taxation purposes and for congressional representation. [22] Therefore, each owner was very careful to account for each slave in his possession, albeit not by name, only by gender and age (for example, female, 65; male, 12).

So until that controversial problem could be solved, the escaped slaves were referred to as "colored refugees." Not until 1868 when Congress ratified the 14th Amendment to the Constitution of the United States, would the word "citizen" ever be used in reference to persons of African descent.

Written by J. B. Kirk of the 101st Pennsylvania, one description of how Yankees helped slaves become free was sent to the *National Tribune Veterans Newspaper* in Washington, D.C. and published on January 9, 1902:

"...Perhaps some account of the way we managed in the matter of taking the slaves away from the plantations may be interesting.

On Judge Donald's (or perhaps his name was Donnoly) plantation, which lies on the north side of Albemarle Sound, 150 slaves, ranging in age from, we'll say, a few days to 100 years, and I am satisfied that one of them had reached the latter age.

Their complexions varied about as much as their ages, ranging in color all the way from New Orleans molasses to a few saddle. The owner had 'seen de smoke way up de riber, whar de Lincoln gunboats lay,' and had taken his departure for more congenial latitudes, leaving the slaves in the charge of the overseer. One of their number turned up at Plymouth one day and requested 'Old Pap' to send to the plantation for them.

A pretty strong detail was ordered in charge of Lieut. Col. Maxwell of the 103rd Pa. for the purpose; but as the Colonel was going to look after some provisions gathered under the tithe law, he entrusted me to look after the slaves. Having everything ready, we took 'Joe,' our guide, and started. In due time we landed and proceeded up to the judge's plantation. Our road lay along a ditch or canal that Joe told me ran up into the 'Great Dismal Swamp.' It appeared as we got near the slave quarters that we were on the other side of the canal from them, but there was a temporary bridge there and across this bridge 20 or 30 came to meet us...."

That night as they boarded the gunboat heading for Plymouth, one hundred and fifty slaves passed from bondage to liberty.

Subsequently, due to the arrival of even more refugees, a shantytown emerged on the edge of the Great Dismal Swamp. With its source in southern Virginia the Swamp was a very dangerous place, characterized by deep tannin-tinted black water where a forest of cypress trees stood with upward protruding knobbed "knees." Propagating in that dark place were female *Anopheles* mosquitoes that caused malarial deaths, including those of the soldiers from the North.

Possessing few amenities of civilization, a medley of dilapidated shacks constructed of staves split from pitch pine logs housed the black refugees at Plymouth. By digging makeshift latrines, cleanliness and sanitation were attempted. Three zealous white missionary ladies, Sarah P. Freeman and her daughter Kate from Maine, along with Mrs. Coombs from Ohio, organized a school for blacks, many of whom, regardless of their age, were desirous of learning how to read, write, and cipher. [23]

When the battle at Plymouth erupted, the missionaries, along with other noncombatants, were put aboard the mail-boat, the *Massasoit*, a side-wheeler carrying ten guns, to steam east to the safety of Roanoke Island. Under the auspices of the New York Branch of the National Freedman's Relief Association (NFRA), they continued their work at the Freedmen's Colony, recently organized on the island. [24]

Having close ties to the American Missionary Association (AMA), an evangelical Congregational minister from Worcester, Massachusetts, Rev. Horace James, a former army chaplain, was appointed Superintendent of Negro Affairs for the District of North Carolina. [25] He was given the directive from the Federal Government to provide the refugees with the necessary tools and other essential implements conducive for survival on the island. Rev. James fervently believed that the only way the ex-slaves could raise themselves out of the degradation in which they had been forced to exist for generations was to own their own land. Therefore, his policy was that each family was to be allotted a plot of land on which to build a house and to cultivate a garden. [26] Another northern missionary, Rev. James' cousin Elizabeth Havard James from Medford, Massachusetts, arrived soon afterwards and set up a successful school for enthusiastic "contrabands" of all ages. [27]

Unfortunately, the Utopian colony Rev. James was expecting in 1863 to serve as a template for future settlements of former slaves was not successful. For one thing, it became much too overcrowded due to the large number of escapees from nearby plantations, especially after the boatload of refugees arrived in April of 1864 during the second battle for Plymouth.

Concerning the burgeoning number of refugees on Roanoke Island, Sarah Freeman wrote to Sergeant Julian Wheaton Merrill on December 12, 1864:

"*My dear adopted son,*
...I have been sick, but now am very well and able to labor and find plenty. I do, as you may well suppose when I tell you that instead of 800 of the colored people here to cloth and look after here, as we had in Plymouth we have 4,000 and a much more helpless destitute class than we had there." [28]

From Sara Freeman's letter, as well as one believed to be from Kate Freeman, readers will realize that the women had known Julian Merrill very well when all three were in Plymouth.

> "My little brother Whete,
> ...I never before so fully realized the horrors of this war. It has never been brought close to home to me as since Plymouth fell. It seems much more like a reality now than it did before as many noble brace spirits whom I knew so well were numbered among the prisoners. I did not know how much I was attached to my Plymouth home and the friends I made there until I was hurried away from them. You can better imagine than I describe the suspense with which we waited for intelligence from you all, listening meanwhile to the roar of the cannon, not knowing which shot was the death blow to some of my friends..." [29]

Also, after the battle of Plymouth was lost and the Yankee prisoners went off to Andersonville Prison, Sarah Freeman wrote to Mr. and Mrs. Merrill, attempting to reassure Julian Merrill's parents that he had been prepared spiritually to go to battle.

> "...He looked at me with much sincerity and said do you know that I have been living in anticipation of this for two or three weeks and believe that I have been in a measure prepared for it. I next went to the door and as I took his hand I said, May God bless you. I could not stop wishing his own Mother could see him as he then stood before his adopted Mother as he exited me."

One statement was certainly incorrect in the letter Sarah Freeman penned to the Merrills:

> "...The most we have been able to learn is that they are at Andersonville near Americus, and that it is a healthy place and that they are well cared for...." [30]

After the surrender of the Confederacy in 1865, the victors no longer would have any use for the black men returning to their families on Roanoke Island. The United States Government had returned all property to former owners. Government rations ceased. Teachers no longer were provided for the ex-slaves so eager to learn the necessary skills for survival. Everything tangible was taken away from the refugees who had found asylum at the Freedmen's Colony, thereby, forcing most to evacuate the island in search of livelihoods elsewhere. [31]

Many friends and families separated forever after they went to the mainland. A number, however, refused to leave the island, remaining in occupations not requiring ownership of a plot of land, such as fishermen and oystermen. In later years some freedmen were able to purchase land in order to become farmers. Still others became surfmen who made their livelihood by saving the lives of shipwreck victims. [32]

Chapter 5

BIRTH OF IRONCLADS

Due to the Union's plan to blockade Confederate traffic to the Atlantic Ocean, President Jefferson Davis' new government was forced very quickly to establish a navy. Therefore, by an act of Congress on February 20, 1861, the Navy Department was established with the appointment of Stephen Russell Mallory as Secretary of the Confederate States Navy Department. A lawyer from Key West, Florida, Mallory once had been his state's United States congressman. Ironically, in 1813 he had been born to Yankee parents when they were living in British Trinidad. However, soon after the death of his father, Mallory moved with his widowed mother to Florida.[1]

Fig. 21. ***Stephen Mallory, Confederate Secretary of the Navy***
Library of Congress

The idea of the Confederates' use of ironclads began with Mallory's declaration to the Congressional Committee on Naval Affairs.

"...I regard the possession of an iron-armored ship as a matter of the first necessity...."

With plans to build a formidable Navy, Secretary Mallory strongly felt that "wooden frigates, as they are now built and armed, will prove to be the forlorn hope of the sea, simply contests in which the question, not of victory, but of who shall go to the bottom first." [2]

He was emphasizing the necessity of building gunboats protectively covered with iron plates. Such ironclads were being used already by France and England, but only experimented with in the United States, never having been implemented by the Government. For instance, back in 1843 after obtaining $1,000 from the government to design an ironclad in Hoboken, New Jersey, Robert Livingston Stevens set about fulfilling the dreams of his deceased father, John Stevens, who had begun experimentation on ironclads during the War of 1812. The son, a wealthy mechanical engineer, naval architect, and inventor, attempted the building of an enormous ironclad to measure at least 400 feet in length and 45 feet in width.

Unfortunately, before the vessel reached completion, Robert L. Stevens died in 1856. Even though his brother, Edwin Augustus Stevens, contributed a vast amount of revenue towards the fruition of the ambitious project, the United States government at that time had no interest in ironclads. There was no demand or excuse for such unnecessary experimentation, and so until the Civil War erupted there were no iron-covered vessels sailing American waters. [3]

★★★★

The *CSS Virginia* was to be among the first of the Confederate ironclads. Commissioned on February 17, 1862, she originally had been the Federal frigate *USS Merrimack*, not to be confused with the *USS Merrimac*, a later vessel built by the Federals. The former was a 4,636-ton frigate, while the latter was a 684-ton iron hulled gunboat.

Unfortunately for the Union, its premier shipbuilding facility, Gosport Navy Yard, was located in the South at Portsmouth, Virginia, directly across the Elizabeth River from Norfolk. Even though by today's reckoning the Navy Yard was worth $400 million dollars, the Federals determined that it was far better to destroy it than to leave it to the enemy when Virginia decided to secede. Therefore, the Gosport Navy Yard was put to the torch, fulfilling Major General Benjamin Butler's prediction. *"The war is to be illuminated by burning cities and villages."* [4]

Throughout the war, wherever the enemy would be in occupation, quite often burning was the order of the day. Anything that could not be confiscated and used was torched, not only cities and villages, as General Butler had predicted, but also houses and barns, ships, railroads and bridges, horses and cattle, cotton bales, and fields of crops. All commenced when the Federals deliberately burned Gosport Navy Yard at Portsmouth, Virginia on April 20, 1861. [5]

At that same time a futile attempt was made to scuttle the *USS Merrimack* in order to prevent her from falling into the waiting hands of the Confederacy. So unsuccessful, however, was the Federals' attempt that the Rebels were able to completely restore the vessel, converting her then into the formidable ironclad *CSS Virginia*. [6]

On March 8, 1862, at 11:00 a.m., revolutionary naval history was made. At that time the first ironclad, the *CSS Virginia* (aka *CSS Merrimac*) created by the Confederates, tended by the smaller vessels *Roanoke, Beaufort* and accompanied by the *Jamestown, Patrick*, and *Teaser*, steamed down the Elizabeth River from Norfolk into the Hampton Roads. Their purpose was to attack the blockading Federal fleet.

Upon entering the Hampton Roads, they were to encounter first the 24 gun steam-sailing sloop, the *USS Cumberland* whose Union sailors were astonished when their cannonballs simply ricocheted off the tough hide of the *CSS Virginia (Merrimac)*. Therefore, being unchallenged, the well-protected Confederate ironclad had no difficulty in ramming her armored prow into the wooden hulled Federal gunboat, the *Cumberland*, thereby successfully sinking her. At a later time her commander, Lieut. Morris, would boast, *"We sank with the American flag flying at her peak."* Even so, one hundred and twenty one men were lost: one third of the entire crew. [7]

After having destroyed the *USS Cumberland*, the 10-gun *CSS Virginia (Merrimac)* then attacked the 50-gun frigate *USS Congress* successfully. Following their surrender, the Union sailors were released, but the officers were taken as prisoners. Then after having been set on fire by the enemy, the *USS Congress* continued burning until near midnight, at which time her magazine exploded, totally obliterating the Federal vessel. Thus on the first day of Battle of Hampton Roads, the superiority of ironclad ships over wooden ones clearly had been proven.

The Confederate ironclad did not remain unscathed, however, even though she proved to be far superior to the wooden boats, just as Mallory had predicted. Her smokestack was riddled, some armor loosened, part of her formidable ram broken off, and two large guns put out of commission. In addition, Flag-Officer Franklin Buchanan was shot and was moved ashore to a hospital. Even with all of those obstacles, the *CSS Virginia (Merrimac)* still had the upper hand, leaving the Confederates confident that victory certainly would be theirs in the morning.

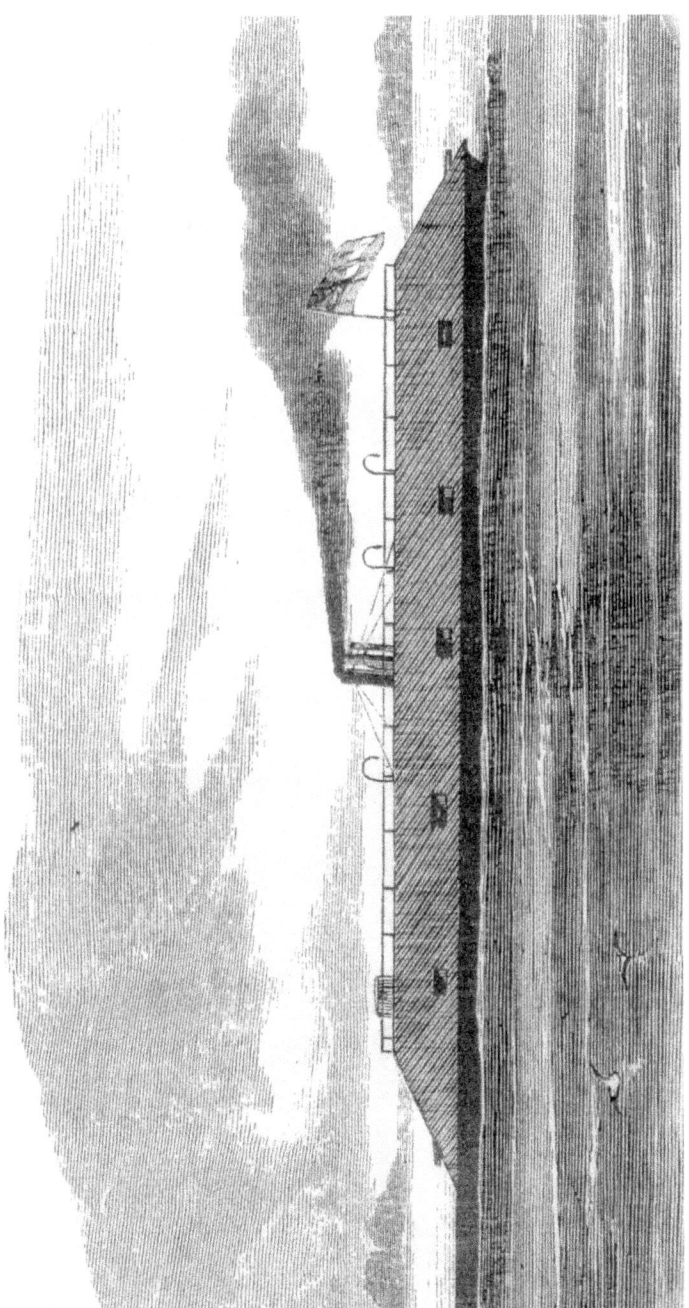

Fig. 22. **CSS *Virginia* (*Merrimac*)**
Courtesy of the U.S. Naval Historical Center

However, something was about to occur to change the expected outcome at the Battle of Hampton Roads; for at midnight, under the command of Captain John L. Worden, the *USS Monitor* arrived on the scene. She was the creation of an innovative European inventor, John Ericsson, who hastily had built the new Federal ironclad. Considered a genius, at the age of eleven he had been given a cadetship in the corps of Swedish engineers; and even before he had immigrated to America in 1839, he already was credited with several notable inventions.[8]

Fig. 23. John Ericsson

Described as looking like "a cheese box on a raft," smaller in size than the *CSS Virginia (Merrimac)*, the *USS Monitor*, was, however, the faster and more maneuverable of the two. John Ericsson had contracted with the United States Navy to have the ironclad completed within 100 days, a task, however, not accomplished until the passing of forty additional days. Upon her completion at the Brooklyn Naval Yard, the boat was without the masts and sails that Ericsson had been contracted to include. He adamantly refused to put them on his steam-powered creation.[9]

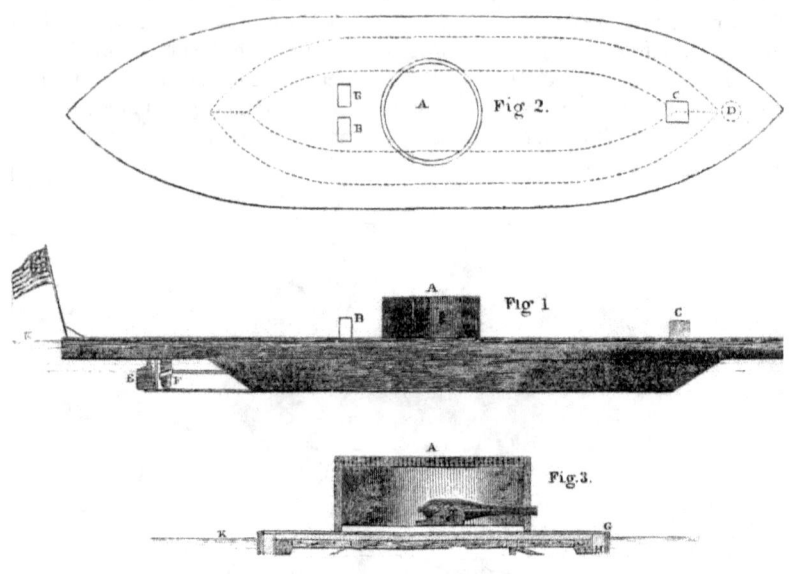

Fig. 24. **USS Monitor**
Courtesy of U.S. Naval Historical Center

Upon receiving a telegram from Secretary of the Navy Gideon Welles ordering the *USS Monitor* to proceed to Hampton Roads, Virginia, Captain Worden, who was to be her commander, was quite surprised; for the brand new ironclad was without crew, ammunition, or provisions. So very new she was that her guns had not been tested yet.[10]

Then due to Captain Worden's concern over her ability to navigate that high seas, the *USS Monitor* was towed south from New York's East River to Virginia by the tugboat Seth Low.[11] Fortunately encountering no mishaps, Ericsson's *Monitor* arrived in Hampton Roads where a different kind of naval warfare was about to be fought; for instead of being a one-sided confrontation of iron against wood, it would for the very first time in history be iron against iron.[12]

The *USS Monitor* arrived just in time to challenge the *CSS Virginia* (*Merrimac*), which with utmost confidence had returned at dawn to finish off the remaining United States boats: the *Roanoke*, the *St. Lawrence*, and the *Minnesota*. The latter two had grounded in the channel's shallow waters, and so easily became the object of attack by vessels much smaller in size than the *CSS Virginia* (*Merrimac*). Therefore, the *CSS Yorktown* and the *CSS Jamestown* had been able to maneuver much closer to the grounded Federal boats. Consequently, since the *CSS Jamestown* already had damaged the *USS Minnesota* seriously, the Rebels had not been at all wary of leaving her to sit overnight, crippled as she was.

However, when the *CSS Virginia* (*Merrimac*) returned intending to complete the job she had begun the day before, her crew while peering through the early morning fog was greatly surprised to discover the formidable ironclad *USS Monitor* protecting the floundering smaller *USS Minnesota*. At that point the tables turned; for the *CSS Virginia* (*Merrimac*) was drawn into an equally balanced contest with the *USS Monitor*. After a time of intense battle, the damaged Rebel ironclad was forced to retreat toward Norfolk. On that day the face of naval warfare was changed forever. Wooden battle ships had become obsolete. [13]

In a letter to General Cooper who was Adjutant and Inspection General, Benjamin J. Huger, commanding the Department of Norfolk penned his conclusions:

> *"This action shows the power and endurance of iron-clad vessels; cannon-shot do not harm them, and they can pass batteries or destroy larger ships. A vessel like the* Virginia *or the* Monitor, *with her two guns, can pass any of our batteries with impunity. The only means of stopping them is by vessels of the same kind."* [14]

On April 7, 1862, Secretary of the Navy Mallory wrote to Confederate President Jefferson Davis:

> *"It will be remembered that the* Virginia *was a novelty in naval architecture, wholly unlike any ship that ever floated; that her motive power and her obedience to her helm were untried and her officers and crew strangers comparatively to the ship and to each other, and yet, under all their disadvantages, the dashing courage and consummate professional ability of Flag-officer Buchanon and his associates achieved the most remarkable victory which naval annuals record."* [15]

Following the Battle of Hampton Roads, both sides of the conflict developed a sense of urgency for building fleets of ironclad boats. By utilizing Mallory's innovative ideas, standard specifications for building Confederate gunboats were implemented. For one, all exposed surfaces were to be protectively covered with iron plates and bows solidly reinforced with armor.

In addition, all vessels were to be fitted with rifled cannon and screw propellers. Mallory's hypothesis was that rifled cannon would give ironclads the capability of firing salvoes with much more accuracy from a farther range than could any of the guns in use at that time. He also believed that explosive shells, rather than solid shot, would cause considerable more damage to enemy ships. Finally, he knew that his use of a screw propeller replacing a paddle wheel would allow the engines and boilers to be placed safely below the water line.

The new modifications were enforced by Chief Navy Engineer John L. Porter; Commander John Mercer Brooke, Office of Ordnance and Hydrography; and Chief Naval Engineer William P. Williamson. [16] A Virginian, John Luke Porter had learned the craft of shipbuilding in his father's shipyard in Norfolk. A Naval Constructor at Pensacola, Florida, when the war erupted, John Porter had resigned his United States Navy commission, eventually becoming Chief Naval Constructor for the Confederacy.

William P. Williamson, another Virginian, had studied mechanical engineering in New York City after which time he was employed at the Gosport Navy Yard. In 1861 he was imprisoned after refusing to take the oath of allegiance to the United States, subsequently being dismissed from service. After joining the Confederate Navy, he became Engineer-in-Chief on duty in North Carolina waters.

The third member of the trio was the creator of the Brooke rifle, a cast gun reinforced by wrought iron, capable of firing a 100-pound shell at high velocity. [17] A Floridian, John Mercer Brooke was a graduate of the United States Naval Academy. After resigning his commission on April 20, 1861, he became a lieutenant of the Confederate Navy and then was appointed by Secretary Mallory to be in charge of armor and guns on ironclads. His many hours of research resulted in the critical discovery that when placed from 35 to 38 degrees from the vertical, an ironclad's casemate armor could deflect even the best enemy projectiles, the casemate's function being to house men and guns.

Initially, the three Confederates had been in collaboration on plans for building a formidable ironclad intended to serve as a floating fort. Ultimately, however, Porter's plan was the one implemented. From his drawing board the design for the ironclad ram, *CSS Albemarle*, emerged. [18]

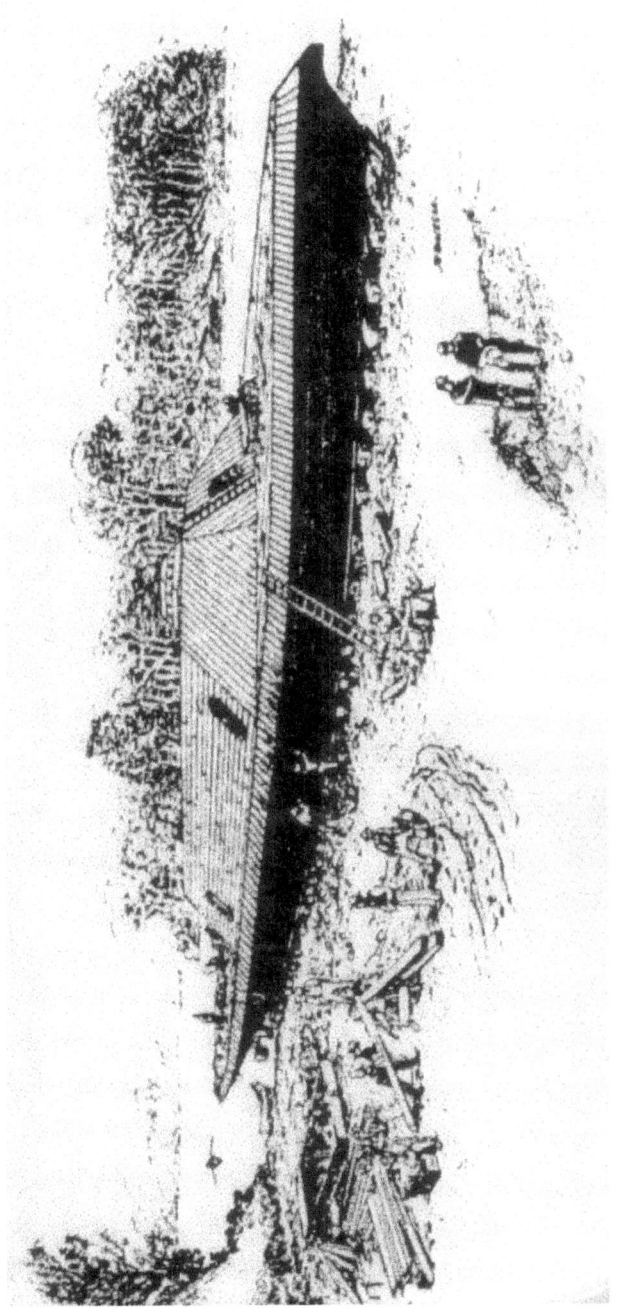

Fig. 25. ***CSS Albemarle being built at Edwards Ferry***
From engraving by J. D. Davidson, "Battles and Leaders," Vol. IV

Chapter 6

IRONCLAD THREAT TO PLYMOUTH

During late 1863 and early 1864, a steady flow of reports from spies and scouts had convinced the Yankees that the Rebels were only a short distance from Plymouth. The men from the North were cognizant of the fact that not too far up the Roanoke River, Confederate General George E. Pickett with his division were securely positioned at Williamstown, Rainbow Bluff, and Tarboro. However, the Rebels had not made any serious attempts from those or any other nearby places to dislodge Yankees occupying New Bern, Washington, Elizabeth City, Beaufort, Edenton, Winton, or even Plymouth. Every now and then, though, the Rebels would conduct a harassing raid.

The Federals at Plymouth were quite confident of not being seriously attacked due to the protection afforded by the four gunboats patrolling the Roanoke, as well as by the four forts and four redoubts in the town. On the south bank two miles up the river where two creeks emptied, there on a patch of land called "Warren's Neck" the Yankees had built the isolated earthwork, Fort Gray. A footbridge of single logs called a corduroy road was laid across the swamp, providing the only means of reaching the fort other than by the tugboat, *Dolly*. Today a lumberyard occupies that same area.

Isolated also, was a second earthwork, Fort Wessells, a half-mile south of the town, built there to protect approaches from the southwest via Washington Road. Presently, the area is a golf course. The largest of the fortifications, the "citadel" Fort Williams, commanded Acre Road (Lee's Mill's Road) as it entered the town in its direct center from the south.

On the right of Plymouth, just at the beginning of the swamp, the two-mile line of rifle pits connected Fort Williams, the Coneby and Compher redoubts with Battery Worth. Running parallel to the river, the earthworks continued eastward from Fort Williams in the center of Plymouth, ending at the eastern edge of the town. However, for two reasons no fortifications were built there, excepting the two redoubts on either side of Fort Compher (also called Comfort). First, there were not enough troops for manning any fortifications in that area. Only Co.'s D and E of the 101st Pennsylvania Volunteers had been positioned there. Second, the terrain was much too swampy. [1] Even so, with the four gunboats patrolling the Roanoke River the Federals were confident that the eastern end of Plymouth was sufficiently secure.

The Navy's protective presence bolstered the confidence of the Federal troops to the point that they believed they could maintain their hold on all of eastern North Carolina indefinitely. Not only were the four formidable gunboats present, in addition there was a motley assortment of shallow-draft vessels like those having participated in

"Burnside's Expedition" in February of 1862. They were double-enders, [2] ferryboats, and tugboats, all capable of easily navigating the rivers of northeastern North Carolina.

As early as 1863, rumors had reached the ears of Lieut. Charles W. Flusser, intimating the construction of a Confederate ironclad upriver from Plymouth. By the beginning of March of 1864, those rumors had escalated. Finally the rumors were supplanted by truth when a carpenter, formerly a worker on the ram, defected to the Union. He assured the Federals that, indeed, an ironclad was being built upriver, a boat to be just the right size for navigating the tortuous and dangerously narrow Roanoke River, which was a mere 130 yards across in some spots.

The carpenter was the first to furnish the Yankees with any concrete evidence concerning the mysterious Rebel ironclad, even though for some time informants had been relaying messages to and from both sides. Concerning such, on July 23, 1863, Charlotte Edmondston, an interested observer of the Rebels' shipbuilding activities, entered into her diary the fact that two Yankees, *"originally deserters from them to us, have redeserted and returned to their former friends.... My mind misgives me that they will yet work us mischief as they are remarkable intelligent and are possessed of full information as to the forces available for the protection of the boat...."* [3]

What was so unusual about the boat was that she was not being built in a shipyard. Instead, her keel had been laid in an unplanted cornfield located 30 miles south of Weldon on land belonging to William Ruffin Smith, Jr. who was the father of Peter Evans Smith. The younger Smith was a close friend of the talented shipbuilder Gilbert Elliott who had been commissioned to build an ironclad.

The property was named the Edwards Ferry Shipyard due to its proximity to a river crossing by that name. The location was about five miles from what today is called Scotland Neck. There on that unlikely spot, the famed ironclad ram *CSS Albemarle*, nick-named the "Cornfield Ironclad," was constructed.

The wealthy slave-owning Smith family, vigorous supporters of the Confederacy's cause, in addition to offering use of their land, also extended warm hospitality to Gilbert Elliott, as well as to the overseer of the project, Captain James Wallace Cooke. Prior to the war, young Elliott had been a partner in the shipbuilding firm of Martin & Elliott located in Elizabeth City. However, after General Burnside's capture of that place in February of 1862, the firm had been forced to close its doors. Very soon afterwards, eighteen-year old Gilbert Elliott joined the Confederate Army, later to resign in order to devote all of his time and energy to building the ironclad.

Gilbert Elliott's own words to the "Century Magazine" in 1888 were: *"No vessel was ever constructed under more adverse circumstances."* [4] In fact, all throughout the summer months of 1863, oppressive heat and humidity were intolerable for the crew of slaves and the white carpenters who had been hired by the master shipbuilder. Even so, the green pine timber had to be cut at the three portable sawmills that had been assembled by Cooke and Elliott. By the use of teams of horses, the unseasoned lumber was hauled to the forges erected at the makeshift "shipyard" where willing mechanics, all strong believers in the Confederate cause, had volunteered their services.

The most important part of the boat, the hull, had to be built first. The sixty-foot shield, an octagonal superstructure with a slope of thirty-five degrees, was to be solidly plated with iron. The hull finally was completed on October 6, 1863, and the *CSS Albemarle* was launched to float upriver to the Halifax Navy Yard. [5] There she received the final outfitting of the engines needed to drive her twin screws. However, the problem delaying her completion expeditiously was the serious shortage of necessary supplies, especially iron.

After having been assigned the responsibility of overseeing the building of not just one ironclad, but a total of three, James W. Cooke aggressively scoured North Carolina for necessary supplies. While doing so he earned the sobriquet "Ironmonger Captain." [6] His responsibility was to locate available sources of iron for rolling into plates to metamorphose vulnerable wooden gunboats into impregnable ironclads. He found that procuring sufficient iron was a daunting task because of its scarcity in the South. In time, however, Cooke was to determine that railroad iron would be the best available source. However, he was not able to get the needed cooperation from railroad owners, even among Tarheels who would have been helped considerably by the success of the ironclads.

The "Ironmonger Captain" finally was able find a suitable source for his needs from the unused railroad tracks belonging to the Atlantic and North Carolina Railroad Company, running between the towns of New Bern and Kinston. Those particular rails at the time were of no value to the Confederates because New Bern was occupied by the Federals. In addition to the railroad iron, Cooke had another source. Patriotic southern school children were collecting old iron pots, pans, and kettles to be donated to the Confederate cause.

The new governor Zebulon Vance, elected in September 1862, agreed to the out-of-state shipping of the railroad iron to Richmond, Virginia, but only if it were to be used for the defense of North Carolina, particularly for the building of ironclads. Eventually, a large amount of railroad iron was shipped from the Tarheels' state to the Tredegar Mills located in Richmond, Virginia. With the Mills rolling thirty tons per day, [7] the metal was hot-rolled readily into useable iron plates seven inches wide, two inches thick, and six inches long.

Transporting the railroad iron first to Virginia and the finished plates then back to North Carolina greatly taxed the Confederates' railway system, being used basically for transporting food and other essentials to the military. Thus the completion of the ironclads constantly was being delayed, causing James Cooke to become quite frustrated. His daunting responsibility was to supervise the building of three ironclads: the *CSS Neuse* at Whitehall (Seven Springs) on the Neuse River, an unnamed boat at Tarboro on the Tar River, and the *CSS Albemarle* at Edwards Ferry on the Roanoke River. Each one was behind schedule.

Catherine Ann Devereux Edmondston was the owner of the plantation called "Looking Glass" located near Edward's Ferry. From June of 1860, to the end of the war in 1865, she was penning in her journal much of what she was seeing and hearing. Over a year's time she faithfully recorded her astute observations concerning the construction of the *CSS Albemarle*. On February 16, 1864, when she had business at the County Court House in Halifax, she set aside enough time for inspecting the strange looking vessel. Mrs. Edmondston recorded that on that particular day she had seen the installed engines, as well as shafts and propellers on the ironclad, even though no official records supporting her claim ever have been found. She also mentioned that only the armor plates were yet in need of being bolted in place. [8]

The *Albemarle* was at last in the final stages of completion. The time had arrived for the most tedious job of all: that of affixing the iron plating to the exterior. For the job Peter Evans Smith invented the first "twist drill," "necessity being the mother of invention." Consequently, instead of taking twenty minutes to drill an inch and a quarter hole through the plates, the operation could be done in just four minutes. [9] In addition, as the holes were being drilled, instead of producing the iron powder so dangerous for men to inhale, safer iron shavings were formed.

During that frenzied time, Gilbert Elliott came to the realization that he needed to devote much more time to the building of the ironclad than he originally had anticipated. Therefore, with the intention of giving all of his attention to the task, he requested a release from his military duties so that he could work full time on the *Albemarle*. After finally securing the necessary four endorsements, he was released on January 20, 1864. [10] Gilbert Elliott's resignation from the Confederate Army was noted on the 17th N. C. Regiment's muster for Monday, February 29, 1864.

The unusual sight at Edward's Shipyard drew many curious persons who enjoyed making comical or disparaging remarks about such a strange phenomenon as a boat being built in a cornfield. A number of the more inquisitive observers, afraid they might miss something, would visit the site on a daily basis. During the first two weeks of April 1864, the visitors were detecting increased activity around and on the odd looking boat, viewed by many as a "chimerical absurdity". [11] Indeed the work was being stepped up because Captain James Cooke intended to keep the commitment he had made to General Robert Hoke: that of having the *Albemarle* ready for assisting his troops with the surprise attack on Plymouth planned for the 17th of April.

General Hoke's reason for appealing to the Confederate government to allow the *Albemarle* to participate in the impending battle was that he was certain he would need naval assistance to counteract the protection being provided by the Federal gunboats on the Roanoke River. At first, Captain James Cooke thought it an impossible feat to have the ironclad completed by April 17th. However, when he learned that her destination was to be Plymouth, Cooke vowed that the *Albemarle* would be there, completely finished or not.

A new quandary arose as the iron plates were being applied to the boat's exterior. It had to do with the relationship between the elephantine *Albemarle's* increased weight and the water level, as well as the presence of hidden shoals in that particular section of the Roanoke River. So in order to pass safely over the dangerous shoals, the *Albemarle* first steamed a short distance down river to Hamilton. All the while the protective iron plates were being attached to her body. However, on the 16th of April she still was not protected well enough for proceeding downstream to her destination of Plymouth as Captain Cooke had promised General Hoke.

Even with the job still incomplete on Sunday the 17th, the *CSS Albemarle* was placed in commission at 2:00 p.m. Then an hour later Captain Cooke ordered, "*Cast off all lines!*" With ten portable forges on board for emergencies and with numerous sledge hammers simultaneously echoing, the unfinished Confederate ironclad ram slipped her mooring at Hamilton to begin her tenuous journey down the Roanoke River, heading for the Port of Plymouth.

Luck certainly was with the Confederate ram. For one thing, the river's water level had risen much higher than had been seen in many years. Luck, therefore, allowed the *Albemarle* to avoid the hidden mines called torpedoes strategically planted to explode when the ironclad should pass over them. Luck also provided a scout, Frank P. O'Brien, an Alabama artillerist, who reported to the chagrined Captain Cooke that the Yankees had been made aware of the imminent approach of the ironclad. Consequently, in preparation the Federals had chained two gunboats together in a "vee." So in order not to be caught by the set trap, the forewarned Rebel ironclad hugged the shore, thereby thwarting the Yankee strategy. Luck was even piloting the ironclad: a man by the name of John Luck. [12]

Commander John Newland Maffitt who briefly commanded the *Albemarle* after Captain Cooke became ill in 1864 recorded his assessment of the ironclad:

> "The entire construction was one of shreds and patches; the engine was adapted from incongruous material, ingeniously dovetailed and put together with a determined will that mastered doubt, but not without some natural anxiety as to derangements that might occur from so heterogeneous a combination. The

Albermarle was built in an open cornfield, of unseasoned timber. A simple blacksmith shop aided the mechanical part of her construction."[13]

In his tribute to James W. Cooke, Maffitt commended the captain by writing *"Naval history affords no such remarkable evidence of patriotic zeal and individual perseverance."*[14]

Fig. 26. ***Captain James W. Cooke, CSN***
"Battles and Leaders of the Civil War"

CSS Albemarle [15]

Description:
Shallow-draft vessel.
Flat bottomed with straight sides.
Octagonal casement on a flat hull.
Constructed out of yellow pine and oak.

Plates:
From 2' below knuckle to deck covered with 2 layers of 1"iron.
Forward and aft decks covered with 1" iron.

Casemate:
2 layers of 2" iron plating on outside surfaces.
Grating top 46"long and 15' 6" wide.
Gun deck headroom within 7" from floor to grating top.

Casement
Sides angled 35 degrees from vertical.
Wall covering 2 layers of 2" iron.

Displacement	376 tons
Extreme length	158'
Extreme bean	35' x 3"
Deck width	32'
Hull depth from tip of floor (over bilge)	8' x 2"
Loaded draft	9"

Machinery:
2 screws
2 horizontal non-condensing engines (18' x 1' 7"),
    200 horsepower each

Gunports:

Port and starboard	2 each
Forward and aft	1 each
Holes	22" wide, 2' 6" inches high
Shutters	2' 8" wide, 5' 6" high
Shutter covering	2 layers of 2" iron

Prow: Solid oak
18' in length
Covered with iron plating 2" thick tapering off to a 4" edge

Speed: 4 knots

Chapter 7

LIEUTENANT GILBERT ELLIOTT, CSA

The talented builder of the *CSS Albemarle* was only eighteen years old when he was asked to work on the ironclad. The Confederates were in hopes that such a vessel would give them back control over the North Carolina waters, then in the hands of the Yankees.

The third child of Gilbert Elliott I and his wife Sarah Ann, Gilbert II was born on December 10, 1843, in Elizabeth City, North Carolina. Unfortunately, when the boy was but seven years of age his father died, leaving Mrs. Elliott with the responsibility of rearing five children.

Prior to the Civil War, the Elliott family already had been in the Elizabeth City area for three generations, having owned lots on the riverfront of the Pasquotank River. Gilbert Elliott's maternal great grandfather, Francis Grice, had been a Philadelphia shipbuilder during the Revolutionary War. His son, Charles Grice, migrating south sometime around 1795 to the warmer climes of North Carolina, purchased acreage including Lot # 4 on the riverbank in Elizabeth City. Charles Grice then converted that plot of land into the Grice Shipyard. [1]

Even though young Gilbert Elliott's career aspirations had been leaning toward the profession of law, during the fall of 1861 he found himself being drawn into the shipbuilding business. On May 20th of that year, North Carolina, the last state to secede from the Union, had joined the Confederacy greatly in need of gunboats. Because young Elliott had been preparing to follow in his lawyer father's footsteps, he was at that time employed by the Honorable William E. Martin, an Elizabeth City attorney. However, when Elizabeth City became occupied by the Federals in February 1862, Gilbert Elliott's career plans changed dramatically.

The important role he was to play in the unfolding tableau of Confederate defense of North Carolina waters began evolving slowly during the summer of 1861. During that period he was managing his absent employer's shipyard. The lawyer had gone to war with the 17th North Carolina Regiment. In addition, Elliott was serving as agent for William Martin's brother, Adjutant General James G. Martin.

On August 29, 1861, a majority of the 17th Regiment, including William Martin, was captured at Fort Hatteras when it was overtaken by the Federals. The Rebel captives were shipped to the North as prisoners of war. Eventually, Martin was exchanged, and upon his return to Elizabeth City, he reorganized the 7th Volunteers to becoming the 17th N.C. Regiment (second organization). During May 1862, Gilbert Elliott joined that particular unit and was appointed First Lieutenant with duties as Regimental Adjutant, receiving his training at Camp Johnson near Kinston.[2]

The direction of the drama sharply changed when the Secretary of the Navy, Stephen Mallory, had a special assignment for Gilbert Elliott, who at the time was serving in the Confederate Army. His expertise in shipbuilding was much needed for the construction of a formidable ironclad. Subsequently, Lieutenant Gilbert Elliott was granted a furlough of two years in order to build an ironclad on the Tar River.

Months later, on December 15, 1863 he was compelled to write to Colonel William F. Martin, the 17th Commander at Wilmington, North Carolina, citing his work on an additional ironclad, the *Albemarle*, as his reason for resigning his position as Regimental Adjutant, as well as from the Army.[3] On January 20, 1864 Lieutenant Elliott finally received the necessary permission to leave the Confederate Army in order to become Gilbert Elliott—civilian builder of the Confederate ironclad, the *CSS Albemarle*.

Fig. 27. Lieut. Gilbert Elliott, builder of the CSS Albemarle
"N.C. Regiments, 1861-1865," Vol. II

Chapter 8

A COMEDY OF ERRORS

Upon first hearing the disturbing report about an ironclad being built upriver near Tarboro, General Henry W. Wessells on February 4, 1864, wrote to the Department Headquarters at New Bern. He reported that "*a formidable expedition was in preparation by the enemy with the object of recovering possession of the Roanoke River.*" [1] At that time he requested that reinforcements be sent to Plymouth.

Three days later on February 7th, General Wessells wrote directly to the commander, General John J. Peck, whose headquarters were at New Bern:

"I believe it is perfectly reliable to state that a naval brigade has been organized in Richmond for the purpose of operating in these sounds and tributary rivers, and that they may be heard from any moment. But as it is better to prevent than to invite an attack on a small force, I request reinforcements, 3,000 effective men, until the emergency has passed, or till the designs of the enemy are fully developed." [2]

Again he wrote on February 10th to repeat the request:

"The State of North Carolina is of infinite importance to both hostile parties, and as the points occupied are so weak as to be harassed at any moment with impunity, I feel justified in repeating my request for re-enforcement, as I desire to have it on record." [3]

He reported frequently to his superiors that if Plymouth were to be attacked, he feared his forces would not be adequate to defend it successfully. However, General Benjamin Butler, commanding the Department of Virginia and North Carolina from Fort Monroe and his subordinate Major General John J. Peck, commanding the Department of North Carolina from New Bern, were not as concerned as General Wessells. For on February 20th the skeptical General Butler wrote to General Peck:

"I don't believe in the iron-clad. I believe Plymouth is as safe as Fortress Monroe provided you keep from being surprised." [4]

Again on March 9th, General Butler facetiously wrote to General Peck:

"With the force you have, we shall expect you to hold North Carolina against all comers. Don't let the army get frightened at the ram. She must have at least 2 feet of water to float in." [5]

Then on March 20th, General Peck wrote with much confidence to General Wessells at Plymouth:

> "*Without a naval force they might as well attack Fort Monroe. Demonstrations may be made, but no serious operations.*" (6)

On the same day General Wessells wrote to General Peck also:

> "*At all events I do not feel disposed to neglect their warnings, and in view of their importance I request a temporary reinforcement of 5,000 men. The presence of the gunboat, Com. Perry, now I believe in the James River, would, I think, put a stop to any further threats from the iron-clad above us on the river. I should regret making any report not justified by future events, but must depend upon the best information within my reach, and there is too much at stake to neglect any reasonable warning.*" (7)

General Peck relayed that information to General Butler who responded to General Wessells:

> "*You will have to defend the district with your present force, and you will make such dispositions of them as will in your judgement best subserve this end.*" (8)

On March 9, 1864, the newly appointed Federal General-in-chief Ulysses Simpson Grant was assigned the command of the United States armies. By the beginning of April he was consolidating forces with plans of abandoning Plymouth and Little Washington. His strategy was that the men so unnecessarily (in his opinion) garrisoned at those two small North Carolina towns should be sent to General Butler to fight at Bermuda Hundred, Virginia, in order to cut the Confederate's railroad communications with Richmond.

To Grant's way of thinking, Plymouth and Little Washington automatically would be safe from the Rebels following such a victory and no longer would there be a need for a force at either place. However, on that issue General Grant was moving much too slowly; for already the aggressive young General Robert Hoke, anxious to prove himself, was preparing for his surprise attack on Plymouth. Only recently had he been chosen by Confederate President Jefferson Davis to replace General George Pickett who in January of 1864, had failed miserably at ousting the Yankees from New Bern.

Dated April 12, 1864, General Hoke's orders read:

"GENERAL:
You are assigned to the special command of the land forces for an expedition against Plymouth, &c in Eastern North Carolina. Your force will be...immediately assembled at Tarborough.....As soon as you are prepared to move from Tarborough you will notify the commander of the gunboat Albemarle, and inform him at what time you propose to make your attack, so that he may co-operate as nearly as possible....In your movement on Plymouth, success will depend in great measure on celerity and secrecy, but great confidence is reposed on your well-known activity and energy....Should you succeed in the first step, in capturing Plymouth and opening the river, then your attention should be immediately directed to Washington and New Bern."[9]

Even as late as April 19th, General Grant would endorse General Butler's opinion by optimistically stating: *"General Peck should be able to hold Plymouth with the force he has."* [10]

To General Wessell's final desperate request just prior to the beginning of the battle, General Peck had responded:

"This is the time in April for rebel demonstrations in North Carolina, just in advance of the opening campaign in Virginia. Have they as many available troops in North Carolina as in April of 1863, when Longstreet made feints in order to deceive me and take my forces at Suffolk? Would not heavy detachments now endanger the operation of Lee? Under all the circumstance I think their demonstrations will be light." [11]

Actually, General Peck did not have the 5,000 men at his disposal to send to Plymouth as General Wessells was requesting. At that time there were only 10,150 men "present for duty" in all of the District of North Carolina, including the nearly 3,000 already garrisoned at Plymouth. [12] Help, instead, was requested from the Navy.

So on Saturday, April 16th, the gunboat *USS Tacony* commanded by Lieut. Commander Truxton arrived at Plymouth. However, by that time General Wessells mistakenly had been led to believe that the Confederates were not planning an attack on Plymouth at all. Unfortunately then, on the 17th just a few hours before Hoke's surprise attack, Wessells sent the *Tacony* back to New Bern where he felt she might be needed more. Indeed, it was a grave error on General Wessell's part.

He sent a message to General Peck to state his feelings on the matter, *"I cannot learn that there is any considerable force of the enemy on the river now, though such is the report from various source. I very much doubt if there is any design of bringing the thing (ironclad) down."* [13]

In his diary, Private Charles Mosher of the 85th N.Y. Infantry assessed the *Tacony* situation as follows:

> *"April 16 No drill to day. The gunboat* Tacoma *came in. She mounts 12 guns. Her commander had a dispute as to seniority with Lieut. Com. C. W. Flusser of the Miami. Flusser won out. The* Tacoma *put back for Newbern."* (15)

To make matters even worse, at New Bern General Peck received a false report from two Confederate deserters who stated that General Pickett (who was not even in North Carolina at the time) was planning an attack on Little Washington. So on April 17th, accompanied by two steamers of troops, the *USS Tacony* with her twelve guns was unnecessarily positioned at Little Washington on the Tar River instead of being at Plymouth on the Roanoke River where she was needed.

On April 21, 1864, "the comedy of errors" concluded when General Benjamin Butler, unaware that Plymouth already was in the hands of the enemy, telegraphed Major General Henry W. Halleck, the Federal Chief of Staff: *"'They* (the Plymouth garrison) *ought to hold out, and I have very confidence they will.'"*(16)

Chapter 9

GENERAL HENRY WALTON WESSELLS, USA

Henry Walton Wessells was born on February 20, 1809, in Litchfield, Connecticut, eight days following Abraham Lincoln's birth in Hodgenville, Kentucky. Having graduated from West Point in 1833, Wessells fought in the Seminole War of 1837-1840, first as 2nd Lieutenant of Infantry and after promotion on July 7, 1838, to First Lieutenant.

During the Mexican War, he was made captain, later winning the title of brevet-major for gallantry at Cherulusco and Contreras. In spite of being wounded, he demonstrated his bravery during the battle at Conteras when, after the color bearer was killed, Wessells quickly seized the regimental standard. Later his home state of Connecticut rewarded his gallantry by presenting him with a jeweled sword.

Having been assigned from 1849-1854 to duty on the Pacific Coast, Wessells, in 1855, participated in the Sioux Expedition. On June 6, 1861, he was promoted to major, and on August 22, 1861, appointed to colonel of the 8th Kansas Infantry, serving on the Missouri border.

Commissioned brigadier-general of volunteers on April 25, 1862, Wessells was assigned command of the Second Brigade, First Division, Fourth Corps. After the death of General William H. Keim and just days before the Battle of Seven Pines/Fair Oaks, Virginia, Wessells was assigned by General George B. McClellan to command the Second Brigade of Casey's Division. Following the Battle of Seven Pines/Fair Oaks he was brevetted lieutenant-colonel in the regular Army just as the Third Brigade of Casey's division was merged into Wessell's brigade. Subsequently, General Henry Walton Wessells became commander of eight regiments. While covering the retreat of the Army of the Potomac from Malvern Hill to Harrison's Landing, two regiments of the First Brigade (104th Pennsylvania and 56th New York) also were assigned, temporarily, to General Wessells' command. [1]

General Wessells was always neat in his appearance, although attiring in full military dress only when necessity dictated. Sometimes his identity was mistaken, therefore, such as when he was attired in the simple government brogans and trousers of an enlisted man. Often he might be found wearing the blue great coat of a private soldier, and on many occasions he could be seen tramping on foot among his men.

An early riser, the general had a habit of pacing leisurely in front of his headquarters as if in deep meditation. Corporal Luther Dickey wrote of the following incident:

"An enlisted man, Corporal Smith (assumed name), of the 85th New York, was on duty at the provost marshal's office, and, passing headquarters early one morning when the general was taking his accustomed exercise, he accosted him with a freedom and abandon common in army life only among those of equal rank. The following colloquy occurred, as afterward related by the corporal:

'Good morning, General!'

'Good morning!' quietly responded the general.

The corporal, halting as if to engage the general in conversation, continued, 'It's a fine morning, General!'

'Where do you belong?' asked the general.

'To the 85th New York, but I am on duty as a clerk at the provost marshal's office,' responded the corporal.'

'Ah,' said the general, and then hesitating for a moment, continued, 'When you return to the provost marshal's office, notify the provost marshal that you have orders to report to your company for duty, and I will see that the order is issued.'

Corporal Smith obeyed orders and his service at the provost marshal's office ended that morning."[2]

Even though always dignified and reserved, General Wessells was approachable and affable when his officers or men needed to discuss serious matters with him. Possessing the greatest respect for their commander and with almost a filial reverence, they affectionately referred to him as "The Old Man," "Old Billy," and "Dad Wessells." [3]

The Federal defense of Plymouth was depending on the joint effort of the army and navy. Therefore, with the troops being transported by gunboats, an easy camaraderie oftentimes developed between soldiers and sailors. The fact that Captain Charles W. Flusser of the United States Navy held General Henry Wessells of the United States Army in the highest regard is indicated in the following correspondence:

"I have the information about the roads, depots, etc, from Gen. Wessells. Where he obtained it I do not know, but he deems it reliable, and he, I think, is always correct. He certainly possesses the art, in a greater degree than any one else I know of, of sifting evidence, reconciling or rejecting conflicting stories, and seizing, the truth and the importance from out of a wordy mass of seeming irrelevant talk." [4]

Respectfully referred to as "Old Pap" by "contrabands" escaping from plantations to the safety of the Union lines, General Wessells allowed them to remain at Plymouth without fear of being returned to their owners as was allowed by the Fugitive Slave Act of 1850. Consequently, a number of black men enthusiastically enlisted in the Union Army, being assigned to regiments of the United States Colored Troops that were garrisoned in other areas, including the 37th USCT (originally the 3rd Regiment North Carolina Colored Infantry) at Norfolk, Virginia. Some other black recruits at Plymouth belonging to the 2nd United States Colored Cavalry had been awaiting orders when the battle erupted. Still other black soldiers remained at Plymouth after enlisting, being assigned as cooks in the white regiments garrisoned there, such as the 24th New York Battery, 85th New York Volunteers, and 103rd Pennsylvania Volunteers.[5]

*Fig. 28. **General Henry W. Wessells, USA***
History of the 103rd Regiment

Chapter 10

YANKEES GARRISONED AT PLYMOUTH

The "shakes" from ague were quite common among people living near swamps, the white soldiers from the North not being exempt. For instance, during a single week alone two hundred and forty men of the 85th New York Regiment reported sick. Although some were fortunate enough to survive their bouts of alternating chills and fever, others less fortunate died and were buried in the graveyard next to the unfinished edifice of the Grace Episcopal Church. [1]

Once the weather turned chilly, however, no new cases of the "shakes" appeared. What the reason was, no one knew. Not the Army doctors even, for during that period of history, no one was aware that the cause of the "shakes" was propagating in the swamps surrounding the town. *Anopheles gambiae* abounded there, the mosquito species hosting a minuscule protist parasite, *Plasmodium falciparum* that caused malaria. The female mosquito only transmits the dreaded disease known as ague, or malaria, or more commonly the "shakes." [2]

For some unknown reason, the "contrabands" did not have as high an incidence of the "shakes" as did the whites. No one could understand why for no one was aware at that time of history of such a thing as a parasitic relationship between a one celled organism and an insect, and certainly no one knew about a human blood condition called "sickle-celled anemia." Most people did not know even that blood was composed of microscopic cells, let alone that they could be crescent or sickle-shaped rather than round. Therefore, no one had any idea that a human carrier with a single gene for sickle-cell anemia was protected against developing the "shakes."

In Africa 40% of some black populations are carriers of the sickle-cell gene, providing them with an adaptive advantage because the malaria-causing parasite *Plasmodium* cannot live in cells that are sickle-shaped. [3] So unbeknown to any one, many of the displaced sub-Saharan Africans, "contrabands" in the North America's South, carried the protective sickle-cell gene. All that was known at the time was what could be observed. At Plymouth the percentage of blacks contracting malaria was far less than that of whites.

Spring once again had arrived in North Carolina. Sunday, April 17th was a beautiful sunny warm day. Following breakfast, regimental inspections were held. For instance, Colonel E. H. Fardella, an Italian from Sardinia, conducted the 85th New York's. There was no drill that day, and so immediately after inspection the men gathered for the compulsory Protestant service conducted by Colonel A. W. Taylor of the 101st Pennsylvania Volunteers, [4] the "Keystone Regiment."

April 17th was just an ordinary Sabbath in the lives of the Federals garrisoned at Plymouth, North Carolina, where they were still waiting, although no longer patiently, for their promised thirty-day furlough. Just a week prior, the disappointed troops had been read the General Order, No. 23:

> "In accordance with directions from the commanding general of the army and District of North Carolina, the following from Maj. Gen. Butler, commanding Department of Virginia and North Carolina, is published for the information of the Veteran Volunteers of this command:
>
> 'The paymaster has been ordered down to pay these troops. The continued threatening of the enemy has rendered it impossible to give them the furloughs which it is the desire of the commanding general they should have; but the time they have been delayed he will endeavor to make up to them by extra time at home.'"
>
> By command of Brig. Gen. H. W. Wessells [5]

As a result, by April 17th the veterans in the 103rd Pennsylvania Volunteers had received from the paymaster the $100 bounty due them from their first enlistment. [6] They also were given one or two installments of the new bounty, each installment being $50. In addition, they had received several months' pay that was due them, as well as one month's advanced pay.

Concerning the 85th New York Infantry's pay, Private Charles Mosher wrote in his diary:

> "On the first of last January the three regiments of our old brigade re-enlisted for three years or during the war. We are field veterans. Our first three years would have expired this coming fall. The terms of our re-enlistment were that we should have a thirty days' furlough as soon as troops could be sent to relieve us.
>
> On the first of this month the paymaster was here and paid us. All enlisted men received from two to three hundred dollars each, which exhausted the paymaster's money-drawer to such an extent that he could not pay the officers. The paymaster then made us this proposition. As our furloughs were expected daily would we keep enough money for our needs until we reached home, and take a paymaster check for the balance payable in Elmira, N.Y., then he could pay the officers and all would have money. To this we agreed." [7]

Many of the men garrisoned at Plymouth already had sent their pay home to their dependents, some of the money being deposited directly into banks for security purposes. However, other men had not done anything yet with their greenbacks and so with new uniforms on their backs and money "burning a hole in their pockets," they were more than anxious to go home after almost three years away. The orders were expected momentarily, perhaps on the very next boat from headquarters at New Bern.

Just the day before on Saturday the 16th of April, a company of the 16th Connecticut had experienced a great disappointment. Even though they were not due a furlough because they had organized later than the other regiments, those troops were not expecting to be reassigned to another location. Directly after Sunday's breakfast, they dishearteningly boarded the *Massasoit* to be transported east from Plymouth to Roanoke Island. There they were to join Co. C of the 103rd Pennsylvania Volunteers, Co. A of the 101st Pennsylvania Volunteers, and Co. A of the 85th New York Infantry already garrisoned there.

★★★★

On Sunday afternoon, April 17, 1864, the following 2,834 effective Federals remained garrisoned at Plymouth, North Carolina: [8]

ARMY

85th New York Vols., Colonel E. H. Fardella, with Co.'s C and H at
Fort Gray and Co. K at Fort Wessells, 544.
Nine companies of 16th Connecticut Vols., Colonel Francis Beach,
Lieut. Colonel John H. Burnham, 463.
Nine companies 101st Pennsylvania Vols., Lieut. Colonel A. W. Taylor,
409.
Nine companies 103rd Pennsylvania Vols., Colonel Theodore F.
Lehmann, 485.
Companies G and H, 2nd Massachusetts Heavy Artillery, Captain Ira
B. Sampson, 269.
Companies B and E., 2nd North Carolina Union Vols., Captains
Johnson and Hoggard, 150.
24th New York Independent Battery, Captain Cady, 122.
Detachments from Companies A and F- 12th New York Cavalry,
Captain Charles H. Roche, 121.
Unattached recruits, including Negroes who had been enlisted at Plymouth for the
37th U.S. Colored Infantry and 2nd U.S. Colored Cavalry, 245.

U.S. GUNBOATS
Bombshell, commanded by Acting Ensign Thomas B. Stokes, 20.
Steam launch *Dolly*, 16.

UNION NAVAL FORCES:
Southfield, commanded by Acting Volunteer Lieut. Charles A. French, 139.
Miami, commanded by Lieut. Commander Charles W. Flusser   137
Whitehead, commanded by Acting Ensign George W. Barrett   53
Ceres, commanded by Acting Master Henry H. Foster   45
Massasoit
Robert Collyer
DeWitt Clinton

Chapter 11

A UNION SOLDIER'S LETTER TO HIS MOTHER

Edward Nicholas Boots was born in the year 1834 in Marion Township, Beaver County, in Pennsylvania. In 1861 when the Civil War erupted he enlisted in the Union Army, becoming a member of the 101st Pennsylvania Volunteers. His frequent letters to his mother were to become important history because they revealed many personal details of what happened during the Civil War.

Plymouth, N.C.
October 11th 1863

Dear Mother,

Yours of September 30th arrived & found me in the enjoyment of that great blessing good health, for which I desire to feel thankful to the giver of all good. Your letter was a great pleasure to me. I should be glad to get one from you every day, but as that is impossible I will try to be satisfied with one from you every week. I am glad to hear that you still get to attend preaching. It is a great privilege; I know that I should be happy to enjoy it with you. We are altogether destitute of any preacher at this post & I know not when we shall have one. Prayer meetings are still carried on to some extent. I believe that the sabbath school has entirely ceased.

I had a very pleasant visit to Roanoke Island last week, but I have wrote about it to Horace & Dan. I came back to Plymouth on last Saturday evening. It was all the recreation that I have had this summer except a few rides with Lt. Col. Taylor. The sickness in the Regt. seems to be on the decrease for which we ought to all feel thankful. We have been among diseases constantly for many months. That so many of our lives have been spared is a great mercy. In the 85th N.Y. Regt. the sickness is still very bad-they had two hundred & forty sick one day this week. The deaths, comparatively speaking have been few, yet many fresh graves have been dug since we came to Plymouth. The greater part have been buried at the graveyard attached to a new Episcopal Church. The Post Quartermaster is now having the grave-yard fenced, which is a good thing as it was open to horses, mules, cattle, & every other thing that could abuse it. A church has existed before on the spot where the new one now stands. The inscription on the tombs date many years back. One especially I often look at erected to the memory of Louis Picot a native of sunny France, sleeping his last sleep on the marshy banks of the Roanoke. Like the soldier, he sleeps far from the land of his birth.

A body of rebel troops are within a few miles of us putting in force the rebel conscription act. The result of it is, that we are crowded with refugees coming within our line to escape it. Black as well as white are flying. The steamer Massasoit took a boat load of black refugees from Edenton to Roanoke Island last week. They are safe there.

I have seen numbers of white refugees & I can hardly say that I have seen a good looking man among them. The majority have dark hair, sallow complexions, high cheek bones, long visages, a treacherous looking eye, a shuffling sort of walk & almost any other ugly look that you can think of, but I am glad that we are able to afford them protection from the rebel despotism.

It appears to be generally supposed that we are to stay here for the winter. Winter quarters are being built here very fast. We shall soon have a small town of log huts. I think that you are doing right in buying that farm, but before you buy, be sure to find out all the claims that can come against it. You will no-doubt have to be very economical for a while to enable you to pay for it, but I think that you will be able to get through with it. You can use my money.

Your son,

E. N. Boots
Q.M. Dept 101st Reg. P.V.

P.S. I will answer Sylvia's letter soon. It is thundering & raining hard today. [1]

Having been captured on April 20, 1864, Sergeant Edward Nicholas Boots was never to return to his home again. Just five months after the Battle of Plymouth he died at Andersonville Prison, Georgia, succumbing on September 12, 1864, from the ravages of scurvy. He lies in grave #8606. [2]

Chapter 12

JUST BEFORE THE BATTLE

During the first week of July, 1863 the devastating news about the Confederate defeat at Gettysburg, Pennsylvania, had been most disheartening to many residents of North Carolina. People already had become weary of the war. Especially, they were bemoaning the fact that they had sent their brave boys off in a blaze of glory and, sadly, many were returning home in pine boxes. Then from Vicksburg, Mississippi, came the distressing report of yet another lost battle within the same time frame. Ironically, it had occurred on July 4th, Independence Day, further adding to the Confederates' humiliation at having lost two major battles. [1] Consequently, as a result of that last Federal victory the Mississippi River from Cairo, Illinois and south all the way to the Gulf of Mexico was under the total control of the Yankees.

Also quite perturbing to the Confederates was the fact that on the eastern coastline the Federals had successfully blockaded the Albemarle and Pamlico Sounds, resulting in stocks of unsold bales of raw cotton piling up in barns and sheds. In addition, hundreds of slaves were fleeing the large plantations, smaller farms, riverboats, job sites, as well as city and town residences. Deserters from the Confederate army were raiding, looting, and even murdering. Dissidents like newspaper editor William Woods Holden were supporting the "peace movement." [2] "Buffaloes" (white North Carolinian Union soldiers) and blacks were plundering while Yankee soldiers were pillaging. Most unsettling of all to the southerners, however, was the sight of former friends fraternizing with the insufferable Federal invaders. For North Carolinians loyal to the Confederacy all of that was just too much to bear, causing them to feel forgotten and deserted.

An example of just why the Confederates were so concerned about such socializing was recorded in Union Major James Mackey's diary on February 23, 1864: *"There was a ball at Hooker's. Officers and N. C. girls in attendance."* [3] Among those in attendance may possibly have been the Plymouth belle Lucretia Phelps escorted by the Yankee officer Lieut. Commander Charles Flusser.

Sergeant Major Robert H. Kellogg of the 16th Connecticut Regiment recorded an interesting happening:

"There's one thing, at least, to be said in favor of Plymouth. It was the home of a few 'true blue,' loyal Southerners—a very few, however. They were hard to find, and I fear they are yet. The loyal men before spoken of, and some who were not loyal, were blessed with numerous daughters, fair to behold, but apt to have a few little weaknesses, such as 'dipping snuff' and smoking corn cob pipes.

One of these men lived in a small house half way between the camp of the 16th and the eastern or left-end of the town, and was blessed (or cursed, I doubt if he knew which at times) with three daughters, and pretty ones they were. 'The prettiest I've seen yet!' was the emphatic declaration of each succeeding man who was lucky enough by dint of long watching or shrewd stratagem to get a peep at them.

For, be it known, the father was as watchful over these fair scions of his house, as any orge, read of in fairy tales, could possibly have been over his captives. Perhaps he had read some sensation tale of 'excesses of a brutal and licentious soldiery,' and thereupon resolved to keep his household uncontaminated from the least approach of such an insidious foe. I can not think he had taken a good square look into the honest faces of the 16th men, nor heard Chaplain Dixon preach to his crowded audience of boys in blue, every Sunday. At all events he seemed determined that no officer or soldier should form the acquaintance of his girls. On the other hand, our boys were quite as determined that they would become acquainted with them.

But how was it to be done? That was the question which was presented to the mind of many a one who had cast 'sheep's eyes' at that humble dwelling in the hope of getting a glimpse at its fair inmates. Many and various were the plans which were made, but alas!

The best laid schemes o'mice an'men.
Gang aft a-gley,
And lea'e us naught but grief and pain,
Or promised joy.

None had been successful until at last one day two members of Co. 'A' walked coolly and boldly into the forbidden cottage. First let me give the names of the ones who did it, then I'll tell how they did it. The persistent and successful schemers were Corporal Sam Belden, (remembered by every one of his surviving comrades to-day and by many friends in this vicinity), and Private John Quinn.

And this is the way the fort was taken. After much polishing of buttons and brushing of uniforms, they obtained possession of the Company Clothing Book and another volume of similar size, which they found in the Orderly Sergeant's tent; and on a pleasant afternoon quietly left the camp, unnoticed, and proceeded to the scene of interest.

A modest knock at the door brought out 'pater familias' or 'old tar heels' as the unsuccessful besiegers spitefully termed him. Corporal Sam coolly informed him, with that imperturbable gravity of countenance and manner for which he was celebrated, that they were deputed by General Wessells, who was in command of the post, to take the census of the town. There was no getting around that, for an *order emanating from such a source was not to be lightly disobeyed; so they were rather ungraciously admitted to the heretofore unvisited house—couldn't call it a mansion by any stretch of the imagination.*

Once seated inside, Corporal Sam as spokesman, commenced a series of questions which the U. S. Census Commissioners would have hard work to equal, Private Q. jotting down the replies of the blushing and confused girls, and of the astonished father.

Of course, by this cool and ingenious method they obtained the names of all, their ages, and other interesting information, and moreover they did it all with such suavity, and conducted themselves with such gentlemanly deportment, that from that day they were invited, happy, envied, and regular visitors at the forbidden house." [4]

Certainly General Robert E. Lee had not forgotten the Confederate sympathizers of northeastern North Carolina. Well aware of their plight, he was determining to do something about it by formulating a plan to retake both New Bern and Plymouth in order to get some river traffic opened. Also, he was well aware that the Yankees had in their possession large amounts of munitions, foodstuffs, blankets, shoes, and other necessities so desperately needed by the Rebels whose supplies were diminishing rapidly and not replaceable due to the Yankee blockade. Besides, General Lee was speculating, such a successful mission surely would make quite an impression on the Union sympathizers of North Carolina.

More than anything else, the Confederate sympathizers of northeastern North Carolina desperately wanted the insufferable Yankees gone from New Bern on the Neuse River, headquarters of the Union's Sub-District of the Albemarle, as well as from Plymouth on the Roanoke River. General Robert Hoke had an idea just how that could be done and he enthusiastically shared his ideas with General Lee who then conferred with the president of the Confederacy.

After having discussed the situation with General Hoke and concurring with him, President Jefferson Davis, however, offered the task to General Lee who promptly turned it down, but suggested General Hoke instead. However, President Davis chose to assign the job to a more experienced officer and one of higher rank than Hoke. [5] Major General George E. Pickett with his 13,000 troops was given the job of retaking New Bern, with General Hoke as a major participant. In addition to the large number of soldiers involved three hundred sailors and marines were led by Commander John Taylor Wood. [6]

However, the poorly coordinated assault quickly turned into a disaster for the Confederates. One disappointing outcome was that from the river Commander Wood was able to destroy only one docked Federal gunboat. Second, on the land General Pickett was unsuccessful in his endeavors at retaking New Bern. As a result of his failure in North Carolina, he was recalled to the Virginia theatre.

Fig. 29. **General George Pickett, CSA**
"Battles and Leaders of the Civil War"

Initially, Robert Hoke had been the one to suggest to General Lee that a plan should be formulated for retaking New Bern. Finally, after Pickett's disappointing failure at New Bern, President Jefferson Davis was willing to turn the task over to the audacious young General Robert Hoke.[7]

Hoke's campaign strategy was quite bold; for instead of attacking New Bern, as was expected, he would take his troops even farther east to Plymouth, the major Federal supply depot located only eight miles from the mouth of the Roanoke River. A surprise attack was bound to be successful, he was certain, once the protection of the Federal gunboats on the river was removed. He was confident that such a feat could be accomplished easily by the ironclad ram *Albemarle*, still being built upriver. So after securing the enthusiastic cooperation of Captain James W. Cooke, commander of the *Albemarle*, General Hoke confidently set his plans into motion.

Spies and scouts for each side were kept very busy reporting what was happening to the respective enemy. During early spring, throughout the Union garrison at Plymouth the disheartening news had spread like wild fire concerning the building of an ironclad upriver, thereby creating great concern among the Yankees. Then, after the Confederate carpenter had defected to the Union, the concern changed to alarm; for he verified the rumor that a special ironclad indeed was being built to be just the right proportions for navigating the winding, narrow Roanoke River right down to Plymouth.

Prior to that time, the setting was so very tranquil that several officers had felt secure enough to send for their wives and children. In his diary Major Mackey of the 103rd Pennsylvania Volunteers wrote about his wife's presence, as well as the "ladies" of Dr. Frick, Dr. Palmer, and Lieutenants Mc Call, Fogarty, and Roberts. However, with the unsettling new disclosure concerning the Confederate ram, the wives were informed that at the very first sign of danger they and their children would be sent east to the safety of Roanoke Island. However, two chose not to wait until such a time, with Mrs. Palmer leaving on March 12th, and Mrs. Mackey on March 20th. [8]

Dated April 12, 1864, Lieut. Charles Flusser wrote his penultimate letter to his young sister Fanny. At that time confidence permeated his words:

"The rebs promise to fight us this week, with the ironclad ram, for which I have been watching so long, and eleven thousand men, I wish our garrison was one-third as strong. I don't know whether the scamps will come or not, but will be prepared by day after to-morrow to give them a good fight so far as the boats are concerned. The long-shore people must look out for themselves while we afloat destroy the Sheep—the name we've given the ironclad because we thought it would not show fight. It will prove to be a formidable antagonist and we will have our hands full to whip it. Fortunately it will not be many minutes after her appearance before the result of the 'passage of arms' is known. I wrote the admiral to send me some good shot to penetrate her armor and I should need no more boats. Fact is I look on her as peculiarly mine own. I am prepared for a very desperate fight, and think unless Fortune frowns outrageously on me my arrangements will defeat her.

The plan to fight her was the result of long thought and some anxiety. While I was lying sick, abed, she was reported coming down the river. I was awake and trying to read, but was not satisfied with my preparations, and read without understanding, thinking all the while of her. At 4 o'clock in the morning I had found what I wanted, and turning to a friend who was smoking by my bedside, and who was formerly in the Navy, I gave him my plan. He expressed his delight and his entire confidence of success. The next day it was made known to several officers, and its advantages were so evident that all immediately approved. I feel gratified at having received the happy thought. I think there is no instance on record of a fight on the plan I intended to pursue.

In fifteen minutes after we get to close quarters my commission as commander is secured or I am a dead man." [9]

Two days later Captain Robert Davidson Graham of the 56th North Carolina Regiment wrote in his journal concerning the prelude to the battle:

"14 April. The 24th, 25th, and 56th N.C. State Troops, under Gen. M. W. Ransom, set out by rail and reported to Brig. Gen. R.. F. Hoke at Tarboro. The 49th was on outpost duty near Edenton, and its place was now supplied by the 8th from Clingman's brigade.

"15 April. The column, consisting of Hoke's N.C. brigade, under Col. Mercer, of the 21st Ga. Regiment, which was then with it; Kemper's Virginia, under Col. Terry, and Graham's Virginia, Miller's, Moseley's and Reade's batteries of artillery, belonging to Col. Dearing's command, and Dearing, battalion of cavalry, took up the line of march against Plymouth.

At Hamilton we were joined by the 35th N.C. Passing through Williamston and Jamesville, we reached the vicinity Sunday, the 17th, a little before nightfall. Immediately a strong line of skirmishers, including Co. I of the 56th, was thrown out from Ransom's brigade, under Maj. Graham, and pushed forward nearly to the entrenchments. A picket post of 11 men was surprised, 9 captured, one killed and one escaped.

A reconnaissance in force was made in front of Fort Gray, on Warrens Neck, between the mouths of two creeks emptying into the Roanoke, two miles west of Plymouth, and Dearing's artillery crippled one of the boats so that it sank on reaching the wharf. A redoubt was immediately begun on the Jamesville road leading south for our 32-pound Parrott gun. The iron-clad Albemarle, Capt. J. W. Cooke, was expected during the night. Fort Gray's armament was one 100-pounder and two 32-pounders." [10]

Meanwhile on April 15th Brig. General Montgomery D. Corse and his brigade, including the 17th Virginia Infantry, marched for New Bern, intending to fool the enemy; for the Rebels wanted the Yankees to concentrate on the defense of New Bern instead of sending reinforcements to Plymouth. Exactly according to plan when Corse's brigade returned to camp on April 17th, General Robert Hoke had successfully surprised the Yankee garrison at Plymouth. [11]

Charles Flusser's final letter to his sister Fanny was dated April 17, 1864. He must have written and posted it on that lovely spring Sunday morning. After receiving the letter, broken-hearted Fanny Flusser read her beloved brother's words that had been so optimistic:

> *"No fight yet and not likely now to be one soon. Guess I will get along without any for some weeks if not months."*[(12)]

However, at the very moment the letter was being penned, the dreaded ironclad *CSS Albemarle* already was making her way down the tenuous Roanoke River, well prepared to engage the Yankees garrisoned at Plymouth. As Charles Williamson Flusser was sealing the last letter he ever was to write home, his fate also was being sealed.

Fig. 30. The "Albemarle" Ready for Action
History of the 103rd Regiment

Chapter 13

A SURPRISE SUNDAY ATTACK

For the Federals garrisoned at Plymouth during the early spring of 1864, life had been quite dull, especially with the hours of daily compulsory military drilling for battles not happening. For neither during the second half of 1862, nor in all of 1863, did any large-scale battles take place in the Tarheel state. Therefore, the biggest problem experienced by the homesick soldiers from the North was just plain boredom.

In the words of Captain John Donaghy of the 103rd Pennsylvania Volunteers:

"At Plymouth we had no cares on account of our eating, for the machinery ran smoothly and our tri-daily meetings were very pleasant. We discussed the news—the great events of the war and their influence on our thoughts and actions and watched them with interest and often with anxiety. For all that we laughed when we could; and there were many opportunities. Laughter was encouraged, and the author of a good joke was deemed a public benefactor."[1]

So in order to maintain some degree of optimism the soldiers in their spare time would laze around, contemplating just when their promised furloughs might be granted; for they were expecting orders any day from headquarters in New Bern. The men of Co. H, 16th Connecticut Regiment Volunteer Infantry, however, were quite upset at being sent on the morning of April 17th to Roanoke Island instead of remaining with the rest of the regiment. However, unbeknown to the lucky number leaving, the Confederates' second attempt at occupying Plymouth was about to commence.

Sunday, April 17, 1864 was an exceptionally beautiful warm spring day in eastern North Carolina, and azaleas and dogwoods were in bloom. Everything appeared to be quite peaceful in the small town of Plymouth. However, conditions were soon about to change. The veteran brigades of Generals Hoke, Ransom, and Kemper had been alerted that the ironclad ram *CSS Albemarle* finally was ready for combat, and so over 10,000 Rebel soldiers were on the move. Commanded by Captain James Wallace Cooke, the *Albemarle* was on her way down the Roanoke River with stern foremost and a heavy chain dragging from her bow to combat steering problems due to the flood conditions and the strong current in the river.

General Robert Hoke had no doubt that he would be able to successfully attack the Yankees garrisoned in the forts at Plymouth when Captain Cooke kept his end of the bargain. The plan was that the Confederate *Albemarle* would successfully remove the four Union gunboats from the Roanoke River, after which time the greatly outnumbered Yankee land forces would be left totally unprotected. By carrying out such an ambitious strategy, the Confederate Army and Navy were cooperating in the manner prescribed by General Robert E. Lee when he addressed officers at Gloucester Point: *"In a war such as this, unanimity and hearty cooperation should be the rule."*

The collective Confederate forces preparing to attack the Federals garrisoned at Plymouth, North Carolina: [2]

ARMY
Ransom's Command- Brigadier General Matthew W. Ransom
    8th N. C. Infantry Regiment
    24th N. C. Infantry Regiment
    25th N. C. Infantry Regiment
    Co. F, 35th N. C. Infantry
Mercer's Command- Colonel John T. Mercer
    6th N. C. Infantry Regiment
    21st N. C. Infantry Regiment
    Co.'s B, H, & I, 43rd N. C. Infantry Regiment
    21st Georgia Infantry Regiment
Terry's Command- Colonel William R. Terry
    1st Va. Infantry Regiment
    3rd Va. Infantry Regiment
    Co. D, 7th Va. Infantry
    11th Va. Infantry Regiment
    24th Va. Infantry Regiment
Cavalry- Colonel James Dearing
    8th Confederate Cavalry
    Graham's Petersburg Va. Horse Artillery
Branch's Battalion- Lieut. Colonel James R. Branch
    Pegram's Va. Battery- Captain Richard Gregory
    Bradford's Mississippi Battery
Moseby's Battalion- Major Edgar Fearn Moseby
    Wilmington Light Artillery
    Montgomery (Alabama) True Blues
Gurion's Battalion- Lieutenant Colonel Henry T. Gurion
    1st N. C. Artillery composed of detachments from Co.'s B, G, & H,
    10th N.C. State Troops
Reed's Battalion
    38th Va. Battalion of Light Infantry composed of Faquier Artillery
    Richmond Fayetteville Artillery
    Lynchburg Artillery
    Miller's N.C. Artillery

NAVY
    Ram *CSS Albemarle*
    CSS Cotton Plant

W. H. Morgan of Kemper's Brigade, Co. C of the Eleventh Regiment, described the trying conditions through which the Confederates were forced to march in order to reach Plymouth:

"In places the roadbeds were worn down a foot or two; in rainy weather the roads would be full of mud and water half-leg deep through which we tramped for miles on a stretch, the roadside being closely bordered with thick-growing bushes and intertwining vines; it was impossible to avoid the slush and water...

Some of these marches were made in the night time when the men would splash and flounder along through the mud, some swearing, some laughing and cracking jokes, and ever and anon, the 'Bonnie Blue Flag,' 'Dixie,' or some other patriotic song would be started, when the woodland would ring for miles with the songs, and the echoes go rolling through the swamps and marshes.

In some sections the roads ran through high and dry lands, the roadbeds filled with loose, white sand, over which the marching was very laborious; sometimes through the long-leaf pine turpentine orchards, as they were called--great forests of tall pines, the bark from two sides of the trees being scraped off, with steel-bladed knives on long poles, many feet from the ground, so that when the sap rises it exudes freely, running down the trunks of the trees into deep notches near the ground, cut with long-bladed axes, made for the purpose, and then dipped out into buckets and conveyed to the turpentine distillery...

These high sandy roads traverse the country between Goldsboro, Kinston, and Tarboro.[3]

The following account concerning the surprise attack on the Yankees was written by Major John W. Graham, 56th North Carolina Regiment:

"...The Confederate forces had been collected rapidly at Tarboro, from which the expedition started on April 15, 1864, and arrived within five miles of Plymouth by 4 P.M. on Sunday, the 17th, capturing the pickets and routing a company of cavalry. The 1st Virginia Regiment, under Maj. Norton, was thrown forward as skirmishers, and Kemper's brigade, with Dearing's cavalry and two batteries of artillery under Maj. Reid, turned off on a road to the left leading to Warrens Neck, to threaten the town from that direction; and Gens. Hoke and Ransom, with their brigades, not following the direct road from Jamesville, as the bridge across the creek had been destroyed, turned to the right and, crossing the troops on a mill-dam, made a circuit around into the Washington road, a mile below its junction with the Jamesville road. Sending on a company of cavalry, two Yankees were killed of the picket at this post (Red Top), two only escaping.

Soon we hear the 'long roll' of the enemy, and our line is formed to receive a shelling. Gen. Hoke's brigade is some distance in advance and on both sides of the road, and Ransom's further to the right and along a road which goes perpendicular to the line of breastworks on the south of the town. Skirmishers are sent forward by both sides, the enemy also opening briskly with his artillery. Night soon comes on, and all is quiet on the part of the line except an occasional interchange of shots between the skirmishers." [4]

Captain Robert D. Graham, also of the 56th North Carolina, wrote concerning the initial steps of the four-day battle at Plymouth:

"A reconnaissance in force was made in front of Fort Gray, on Warrens Neck, between the mouths of two creeks emptying into the Roanoke, two miles west of Plymouth, and Dearing's artillery crippled one of the boats so that it sank on reaching the wharf. A redoubt was immediately begun on the Jamesville road leading south for our 32-pound Parrott gun. The iron-clad Albemarle, Capt. J. W. Cooke, was expected during the night. Fort Gray's armament was one 100 pounder and two 32-pounders." [5]

By deliberately choosing a Sunday for his attack, General Hoke was expecting to surprise the relaxing Yankees at Plymouth, which is exactly what he did. Some of the unsuspecting Federals waiting for the usual Sunday dress parade scheduled for 5:30 p.m. were lolling around their tents, day-dreaming of their long awaited furlough. Others were writing letters home or recording in diaries and journals, expecting soon to hear the artillery and cavalry bugles, as well as infantry drums sounding the call. Instead, at near 4:30 p.m. they were startled out of their reverie upon hearing unexpected firing by the pickets. Every soldier was well aware that picket shots at night might be caused by nervous trigger-fingers, but picket shots in the daytime were not to be taken lightly.

Corporal Luther Dickey of the 103rd Pennsylvania Volunteers recorded the activities of the pickets on duty:

"On the main approach to Plymouth, such as the Columbia, Lee's Mills and Washington roads, it was customary to post a sentinel some distance in advance of the post, the picket reserve being at these main posts, where another sentinel was always on guard during the night time. The sentinels at these points were relieved every two hours, as on camp guard." [6]

Several versions exist as to just when the battle actually began. In one instance eyewitness Second Lieut. B. F. Blakeslee of the 16th Connecticut Regiment Volunteer Infantry told of an early warning.

"On Saturday, April 16th, I was again officer of the picket on the Columbia road. The next morning (Sunday) at dawn, while asleep at the reserve post, I was awakened by the discharge of a musket by the picket at the bridge. Rushing to the spot, I found the picket to be William Maxwell, of Company A. He reported five or six scouts who had come to the edge of the woods suddenly, but fled on being fired at. I reported the fact to General Wessells, on being relieved at nine o'clock A.M. He seemed to think them guerrillas, but they proved to be advance guards, for in the afternoon when most of the soldiers were in church, the pickets were attacked by cavalry on the Washington and Lee's Mill roads simultaneously, and so sudden was the attack on the Washington road that the entire reserve picket were taken prisoners." [7]

To the recollection of Private George N. Lamphere of the 16th Connecticut, the battle began with a shot from a field gun. His regiment in dress uniform and already on the parade ground swiftly changed into their fatigues. Lamphere was one of the skirmishers sent out to meet the enemy. [8]

Capt. John Donaghy of the 103rd Pennsylvania Volunteers recollected:

"Then a company of cavalry was sent out to reconnoiter and we watched them as they rode gaily towards the woods nearly a mile away. Suddenly from the timber came a murderous volley, and some of the saddles were emptied. The squadron was momentarily thrown into confusion; then they turned and galloped back to camp." [9]

Soon after he heard the shots, Private Charles Mosher of the 85th New York learned what was happening when he questioned a returning squad of cavalrymen desperately attempting to keep the severely wounded Lieutenant Russell from falling from the back of his horse.[10] During the reconnaissance, Private Amos Fancher had been killed, the first casualty in the Battle of Plymouth.

Rushing back to his quarters, Mosher reported what he had just learned and the orderly, J. B. Robinson, immediately blew his whistle for the command, *"Fall in!"* [11]

"The Rebs are coming! The Rebs are coming!" was the terrified yell of Corporal George Wilcox [12] as his horse thundered to the 12th New York Cavalry's headquarters. Indeed, the Rebels were coming. General Hoke's forces were on the move. Traveling for seventy-five miles undetected, they had crossed swollen creeks, waded through treacherous swamps, and chopped away entangling vines and shrubs. The Rebels were determined to wrest Plymouth from the Yankee occupation, beginning with driving in the Union cavalry videttes and then capturing nine infantry pickets on the Washington Road outpost.

One of the captured pickets was First Lieut. Charles McHenry, Co. B of the 85th New York Volunteers. Sometime in the past he had declared that he would like to be on picket duty when the rebels arrived. He got his wish, for he was the first officer captured at the Battle of Plymouth. [13]

Surprised Federals at Fort Williams quickly scrambled to don their blue blouses and "kepis," grab the Springfield rifles that had been exchanged for Austrian rifles the prior August, add ammunition boxes, pack a supply of hardtack in their haversacks, and rush to defend their assigned positions at the fortifications. For the 85th New York, the general order was to form on the parade grounds and to remain there, awaiting further orders. Therefore, the six companies of the 85th already were in line before their officers even knew what was occurring. The four other companies of the regiment were elsewhere: Co. A on Roanoke Island, Co. K in Fort Wessells, Co.'s C and H at Fort Gray.

Captain John Donaghy of the 103rd Pennsylvania penned his version of the surprise Sunday attack:

> "It was now evident that the enemy had come in force. Companies of skirmishers were sent out and they engaged the enemy until dark. At night the campfires of our foes lighted up the sky nearly all around our front. Preparations were made for the morrow, which we knew would bring us serious work." [14]

Other skirmishers sent out to face the Rebels included Co. G of the 103rd Pennsylvania Volunteers commanded by Captain James J. Morrow, as well as details from several other regiments. The unrelenting cacophony from cannons, canisters, rifles, and grenades continued. Bullets and shells, especially, created a peculiar kind of music, so observed a soldier to the *Rebellion Record*:

> "I caught a pitch of a large-sized Minie [15] yesterday—It was a swell from E flat to F, and as it passed into the distance and lost its velocity, receded to D--a very pretty change.
>
> One of the most startling sounds is that produced by the Hotchkiss shell. It comes like the shriek of a demon. It is no more destructive than some other missiles, but there is a great deal in mere sound to work upon men's fears." [16]

Weary soldiers on both sides were directed that Sunday night to sleep in all of their clothes and accoutrements with rifles kept close by their sides. The specter of death loomed in the anxious faces of all of the troops at Plymouth. Many soldiers, whether Yanks or Rebs, desirous of having some type of identification on their bodies in case they were killed in battle, carefully wrote their names on handkerchiefs or scraps of paper to secure inside their uniforms. Or else, a piece of paper was pinned on the breast of a dead soldier, giving name, company, regiment, and perhaps the date of his death. [17] By use of those first "dog tags," identified bodies could be sent back home to their families for a proper Christian burial.

Immediately after the fray had begun, General Wessells issued the order for all noncombatants to leave for the safety of Roanoke Island. Panic stricken women pleaded with Amos S. Billingsley, the chaplain of the 101st Pennsylvania, to pray with them as they evacuated Plymouth, not knowing what was about to befall them or the men they were leaving behind.

So amid much clamor and confusion, terror stricken officers' wives and children hastily boarded the *Massasoit,* General Wessells' dispatch boat. Lieutenant George S. Hastings of the 24th New York Battery, recorded the following scene at the mail steamer's departure:

"All night long the heavy music of artillery and the bustle of hostile preparations continued. About midnight the steamboat 'Massasoit' left us, carrying to a safer point the 'impedimenta' of the garrison, consisting of women, children and the disabled. The writer still retains in vivid remembrance the hasty farewells then and there spoken (some of which were final), the pale faces of affrighted women and children, the groans of the sick and wounded and the bustle and confusion which, if reproduced, would form so striking and touching a picture of war.

He well recollects how proudly the gallant Flusser, the lieutenant commander of the little fleet of gunboats guarding the waters of the Roanoke, paced the decks of the 'Massasoit' with brave words like these: 'Ladies, I have been waiting two long years for the rebel ram. The navy will do its duty. We shall sink, destroy or capture it, or find our graves in the Roanoke.'"[18]

The *Miami's* logbook indicated that the *Massasoit* departed on April 18th at 12:05 a.m. and did not return to Plymouth until 5:30 p.m. Two trips were required to transport all of the officers' wives and children, as well as the wounded and other noncombatants, including a number of elderly blacks and families of "Buffaloes." On May 2, 1864 Chaplain A. S. Billingsley would submit to the *New York Daily Tribune,* *"The women children and our sick were sent to Roanoke Island on Sunday night, together with a schooner load of old Negroes. Another load went on Monday night."*

Rev. Horace James, Superintendent of Negro Affairs for North Carolina, in his annual report noted that on Sunday night many black women and children left Plymouth for Roanoke Island, perhaps as many as 500, forlorn and sick. An undetermined number of black men who were not soldiers remained in Plymouth, some willingly while others were dragooned. [19] For the return trip from Roanoke Island, a number of the 101st Pennsylvania Volunteers boarded the *Massasoit,* returning to reinforce the troops at Plymouth.

Earlier, just as Sunday's sun was about to set, Colonel Reed and Colonel James Dearing had opened fire at about fifteen hundred yards from Fort Gray, cutting down its flagstaff. The fort vigorously returned fire and after a few hours, the Rebels quieted, listening in vain for the arrival of the already tardy *Albemarle*, whose aid was so desperately needed if the Yankee gunboat protection on the Roanoke River were to be eliminated.

From aboard the *USS Ceres*, Acting Master H. H. Foster reported to Commander H. K Davenport, Senior Naval Officer, Sounds of North Carolina what had happened on the 17th:

> Sir:
> I have the honor to submit this following report: While at Plymouth, N.C. on the 17th instant, at 5:40 P.M., I was ordered by Lieutenant-Commander C. W. Flusser to proceed with the Ceres under my command to Broad Creek, Roanoke river, with dispatches for U.S. S. Whitehead. I immediately got under way. Before reaching the lower obstruction near Fort Gray I observed a battery of six guns, apparently 20-pounders, on the port hand of the river, which opened fire upon us, striking the vessel several times, destroying one of the boats and damaging the machinery, killing William Rose, first-class fireman; mortally wounding Samuel Pascall, ship's cook; dangerously wounding John Flynn, landsman; severely wounding George A. Dean, acting third assistant engineer; John Peterson, seaman; John Benson, landsmen; and slightly wounding James B. Hopkins, acting master's mate; John A. Frank, acting third assistant engineer, and J. R. Sherwood, acting third assistant engineer.
>
> I returned their fire from the two 20-pounder Parrott guns of the Ceres, and at 6:30 P.M. communicated with the Whitehead and delivered the dispatches. Got under way and proceeded down the river for Plymouth at 8:35 P.M. On getting in range of the battery above Fort Gray they again opened fire with artillery and musketry, doing no material damage. I returned the fire as we passed.
>
> I arrived alongside the Miami and reported to Acting Volunteer Lieutenant C. A. French. The surgeons of the Miami and Southfield came on board and attended to the wounded. On the morning of the following day, by order of Lieutenant-Commander C. W. Flusser, I sent the bodies of W. Rose, and S. Pascall on shore for interment, which I was unable to effect (leaving them in the basement of the quartermaster's building at Plymouth), as the services of the vessel were required. I also sent Mr. Dean, John Peterson, John Benson, and John Flynn to the post hospital. I was well pleased with the conduct of the officers and crew.
>
> The following amount of ordinance was expended, viz.: 14 5-seconds shells for 20-pounder Parrott and 14 cylinders of 2 pounds of powder each for the same.
> Very respectfully, your obedient servant,
> H. H. Foster, Acting Master, Commanding [20]

Soon afterwards, Fort Gray on Warren's Neck two miles above the town was completely cut off from the other forts. Nowhere was the battle at Plymouth going well for the Federals, neither on the land nor on the river. For early on Monday the 18th, shortly after having been disabled by a shot through her steam chest, the armed Federal transport *USS Bombshell* sank due to the damage caused by Colonel Terry's artillery. She had been carrying ammunition and supplies while relaying messages to Fort Gray. Upon reaching the safety of Plymouth the riddled *USS Bombshell* then sank at the dock. [21]

Private Warren Goss of the 2nd Regiment of Massachusetts Heavy Artillery described his dangerous trip to the fort:

"I passed safely through the town, and getting up steam on board the 'Dolly' was fortunate enough to get her, with rations to Fort Gray, much in want of supplies. A rebel battery, commanding the river, had made it difficult and dangerous to make the attempt. I was fortunate in escaping the attention of the rebel battery, and arrived with the dead from Fort Gray. That night, Sgt. Evans and myself buried the dead we had brought down..." [22]

★★★★

During Sunday night, Colonel Faison of the 35th North Carolina with his 250 troops and a gang of slaves completed erecting an earthwork near the Washington and Jamesville Roads. [23] From such a vantage point they could effectively bombard Fort Wessells (85th Redoubt) at the Sanderson house southwest of Plymouth.. All throughout Monday, sharp skirmishing took place on Washington Road, extending across fields, even almost reaching Acre Road. From Welch's Creek Swamp Hoke's and Kemper's Brigades waged a fierce fight in the direction of Fort Wessells. Colonel James Branch was the officer in charge of the Confederate artillery.

A Confederate description of the siege on Fort Wessells was as follows:

"That afternoon General Hoke determined to carry 'Fort Wessell' with his and Kemper's brigades, and the battery under Major Reid; he ordered Ransom, with his brigade and Branch, with fourteen pieces of artillery, to make heavy demonstration simultaneously with his attack.

Ransom's brigade, with the 8th North Carolina, was drawn up in the woods, facing the works on the Washington, Lee's Mill, and Bath roads. A heavy line of skirmishers was thrown out, and advancing rapidly with the peculiar gait of the sharpshooters, and the yell with which Confederate troops go to the charge, drove the enemy back into his works, and approached within two hundred and fifty yards of the fort, earnestly demanding to be led into the place. Meanwhile, Pegram's battery dashed forward at a run, supported by the infantry, and unlimbering, delivered a furious fire upon the devoted place. Three times the infantry advanced, each time nearer, until within good charging distance; but the artillery had it all to themselves. *The movement was merely a demonstration to call off the enemy's attention from Hoke's attack upon Fort Wessells.* "[24]

Lieutenant B. F. Blakeslee of the 16th Connecticut later was to describe:

"*It was regular artillery fight, and many old army officers said it was the handsomest artillery duel they ever witnessed*" [25]

While Ransom's Brigade was demonstrating at Fort Williams in order to focus the Yankees' attention there, Hoke's Brigade had been advancing stealthily and steadily through the darkness to be within 100 yards of the isolated Fort Wessells. At close to 10:00 p.m. Monday, Kemper's Virginia Brigade, led by Colonel Mercer, began its attack on the fort with a battery of twelve-pounder Napoleons and three twenty-pounder Parrotts. [26] The Yankees' earthen fortification was equipped merely with an armament of a light 32-pounder on a ship carriage and an old-pattern iron six-pounder field piece. [27]

Fort Wessells took a terrible beating; for in addition to the Confederate artillery's fierce pounding, misdirected fire from Federal gunboats on the river also struck the fortification. In the fort at that time were forty-two enlisted men of Co. K, 85th New York Volunteer and twenty-three enlisted men of Co. H, 2nd Massachusetts Heavy Artillery led by the following officers: Capt. N. Chapin, Lieut. L. A. Butts, Second Lieut. S. S. Peake, and 2nd Lieut. H. L. Clark.

General Hoke then ordered more artillery brought forward to be set up as an effective crossfire. Soon afterwards, percussion shells struck a small building in the corner of Fort Wessells, mortally wounding Captain N. Chapin. [28] At that time, Lieutenant L. A. Butts assumed command of the 85th New York.

One Confederate report described the action at Fort Wessells, a fortification surrounded by a deep ditch with a row of abatis:

"*When the regiment (8th N.C.) had advanced to within about one hundred yards of the fort the order to charge was given. The 'yell'* [29] *was raised and the regiment rushed forward to mount the fort. Just at the moment the 'yell' was raised, the enemy's infantry poured a destructive fire into the ranks of the regiment.*

Our artillery ceased firing as the regiment approached near the fort. The men rushed and leaped into the ditch and attempted to scale the fort. While the men were attempting to climb over the outside of the Fort the enemy threw hand grenades [30] *into the ditch. Those who were in the ditch had to get out of it.*" [31]

After fulfilling their duties, when entering the safety of Fort Wessells, weary Yankee skirmishers spotted a company of black recruits belonging to the 37th USCT. At that time no units of the United States Colored Troops were present at Plymouth. Exact numbers unknown, the black recruits were awaiting orders, expecting soon to be sent to Norfolk, Virginia, where they would be mustered officially into their regiment. Prepared to fight and to die for their freedom, if need be, the black men were standing eagerly, guns held ramrod straight with bayonets gleaming and readied. Both groups of men, black and white, greeted one another with optimistic smiles. (32)

Following four unsuccessful attempts in six hours, the Confederates finally were able to capture Fort Wessells, even while being repelled by hand grenades. At 11 o'clock p.m. when the Yankees in the fort were forced to surrender, the Rebels demanded that the whole town be surrendered, as well. However, they were peremptorily declined.

In his report on what occurred at Fort Wessells, Lieut. Butts' listed the following Federal casualties: (33)

85th New York Volunteers, Co. K:
    Captain N. Chapin mortally wounded
    1 sergeant killed
    3 enlisted men wounded, one mortally
2nd Massachusetts Heavy Artillery
    6 wounded, 2 mortally

Confederates reported the following as having been wounded: Lieut. Charles Wilson, Co. D of the 21st Georgia, and fourteen men of the 56th North Carolina. In addition, Colonel Mercer of the 21st Georgia was killed. (34)

General Robert Hoke had accomplished his goal. He was able to use Fort Wessells as the concentration point, turning its guns into the Federals' right flank. However, even though he just had experienced a great victory, the general still needed the aid of the *Albemarle* if he were to successfully oust the detested Yankees from the town of Plymouth.

Meanwhile at nightfall, in order to divert the Federals' attention while Hoke's Brigade engaged Fort Wessells, Ransom's Brigade had begun firing on the town from every direction. Their fire was answered by General Ira Sampson with the 24th New York Battery in Fort Williams, as well as by the four gunboats on the Roanoke. The intense battle lasted from 6 p.m. to nearly 10 p.m. (35)

Corporal Luther Dickey recalled the following incident:

"*A most distressing accident occurred to one of the gunners of the 24th New York Battery during this action—Wilbur M. Hoyt—who was number one, and whose duty it was to use the swab and rammer. His piece had been firing with great deliberation and effectiveness for some time, when orders were given to fire with more rapidity. As he was 'ramming a shell home,' No. 5, whose duty it was to keep the vent hole covered, became excited, and in turning around to give instruction concerning the ammunition, he uncovered the vent. A premature discharge immediately followed, and rammer, shell and all went through the arm of Hoyt. One arm was shot off, the other shattered, and his face and body blackened skin-deep with the burnt powder. He lingered, suffering greatly, until after Fort Williams surrendered, and died a prisoner of war, on April 26, and was buried in Plymouth.*" [36]

The *Daily Richmond Examiner* printed the following description of the sky at the time Ransom's Brigade was advancing to be within 800 yards of Fort Williams in the center of the town:

"*The action commenced about sunset, the night being perfectly clear with a full moon, every object was visible. The sight was magnificent—the screaming, hissing shells meeting and passing each other through the sulphurous air, appeared like blazing comets with their burning fuses, and would burst with frightful noise, scattering their fragments as thick as hail.*"

About 150 yards in front of the 8th North Carolina a missile from a gunboat (shot by Lieut. Flusser, according to Chaplain Billingsley) [37] hit the ground, bounced forward and exploded in the midst of Company H, leaving fifteen Rebels killed, wounded, or scattered along the battle line. During the fray, Fort Williams received little injury with only one man killed. Lieut. Zachariah M. Cline, Co. G of the 103rd Pennsylvania Volunteers, died from a fatal head injury. [38]

Chaplain A. S. Billingsley's letter in the *New York Daily Tribune* on May 2, 1864 described his observations on that fateful night of April 18th:

"*Just after dark, one of our gunboats opened upon them with a most galling fire. The conading now for more than two hours was most grand, awful, terrific and sublime. I stood upon the piazza of my own room with shells and balls dropping around me. Men who had been in the Peninsular campaign said they never saw anything to equal the firing here... About 9 o'clock all firing ceased, and the Rebels retired to the woods in front of Fort Williams.*" [39]

Chapter 14

THE REBEL GOLIATH

Much before the break of day on Tuesday, the 19th of April, the Rebels once again opened fire upon Fort Gray, this time, though, to create a diversion. Their strategy was to draw the Federals' attention from what was happening *on* the river; for at 3:00 a.m. under the bright moonlit sky, the brand new Confederate ironclad ram *CSS Albemarle* was steaming down the Roanoke. Despite the punishing heavy barrage that had been inflicted upon it up to that time, the Federal fortification, Fort Gray, had been able to remain intact.

Accompanying the Confederate ironclad ram was a smaller boat, the *CSS Cotton Plant*, on which Rebel troops were concealed behind rifle screens. Huge volumes of black pitch-pine smoke blew out of the *Albemarle's* stack, as stealthily she slipped by Fort Gray located two miles above her destination of Plymouth.

On Sunday, April 17th, Commander James Wallace Cooke had commissioned the brand new Confederate ironclad. She was so brand new that as she cast off to begin her voyage down the twisting Roanoke, the last of the thick iron plates still were being attached to her decks and deckhouse. Several mishaps, however, were to prevent the *Albemarle* from an uneventful journey downstream, a trip usually taking less than two hours from Hamilton to Plymouth under the most favorable conditions. The ironclad's trip was to take thirty-two hours.

Due to a broken rudder, followed by engine failure, the *Albemarle* was delayed for several hours before being able to continue. Then, when nearly three miles above Plymouth, she had to halt once more where the Federals had made an attempt to narrow the river with torpedoes and pilings, as well as with sunken old schooners and boats loaded with rocks. The time was nearly 10:00 p.m. on Monday, the 18th of April, and the *Albemarle* was already late.

Even though Commander Cooke was well aware that he had been expected on the 17th, he felt compelled to wait until morning when he would be able to see well enough to evaluate his options. Meanwhile, down the Roanoke River at Plymouth the anxious Rebel troops were eagerly anticipating the tardy *Albemarle's* appearance at any given moment.

One of the volunteers on board the *Albemarle* was the impatient young shipbuilder, Gilbert Elliott, who emphatically voiced his objections at waiting until morning. He requested permission to make his own reconnaissance that very night. After Cooke assented, Pilot John Luck and two other experienced seamen accompanied Elliott to take soundings.

Gilbert Elliott would write later:

"To our great joy, it was ascertained that there was ten feet of water over and above the obstructions. This was due to the remarkable freshet (overflow of a stream due to recent rains) then prevailing; the proverbial oldest inhabitant said, afterward, that such high water had never before been seen in Roanoke River." [1]

After the excited Elliott delivered this welcome news to the cautious Commander Cooke, immediately the *Albemarle* built up steam in order to pass Fort Gray at Warren's Neck. General Fisher's attempts from the fort to halt the *Albemarle* were futile, her thick iron skin protecting her well, even from a direct hit by a one hundred pound shell. Gilbert Elliott noted that shells bouncing off the iron sounded *"no louder than pebbles thrown against an empty barrel."* The *Albemarle* was unstoppable even as she passed Battery Worth where the rifled Parrott gun there, carrying a chilled end shot weighing two hundred pounds, failed to fire in time. [2]

Making an attempt at assessing the possible reason for the gun's failure to fire at Battery Worth, Private Charles Mosher of the 85th New York Infantry wrote in his diary dated April 18, 1864:

"When the ram came past Fort Worth (with its hundred pound rifled parrot gun) the ram was so close to the fort, our men could hear the rebels talking on her. The gunman in charge of that big gun, sung out, 'Number one, are you ready?' 'Yes' was the response. Then the Captain asked, 'What have you got her trained on, boys?' 'Why, the ram, of course,' was the reply.

Then the Captain gave the command not to fire, as that would draw the fire from the ram. That was what that fort was built there for. Just that ram and nothing else. Hard luck! The 2nd Mass. Heavy artillery had the full charge of that fort and its big gun. The enlisted men of that company were all right. The Captain had no sand..." [3]

Another explanation was that of Lieutenant Alonzo Cooper's:

"...But when the ram passed battery Worth, she was so low in the water and came down so still, and the night was so very dark, that the lookout at battery Worth failed to see her until she had passed the work, although the gunbot Whitehead, Capt. Barrett, dropped down just ahead of her, having been stationed up the river on picket, and notified Lieutenant Hoppins, who was in command of battery Worth, of the approach of the ram. Only one shot was fired at her, and this after she had passed the redoubt, but as she had got by, the aim of the gun was inaccurate, so she passed on uninjured." [4]

Another suggested that the gunners could not swing the cannon around because its tackle was fouled. [5] Still others hypothesize that the *Albemarle* may have passed by the battery totally undetected or that, perhaps in the darkness, she had been mistaken for a Yankee vessel. [6].

Years later W. H. Nott wrote to the editor of the *National Tribune Veteran Newspaper* to substantiate the latter supposition. A sergeant in Co. H of the 16th Connecticut and a survivor of Andersonville, Nott's speculation was that at the time, the sergeant whose duty it was to fire the gun insisted that the ram was approaching. However, Lieutenant Hoppin, who had charge of the gun, mistakenly insisted that the vessel was the *Bombshell* and, therefore, would not open fire. [7]

★★★★

Down river the prows of the flagship *USS Miami* and the *USS Southfield* had been shackled together by hawsers and chains, forming a "vee." Lt. Cdr. Charles Williamson Flusser, commander of the flagship, had hoped that the two gunboats together might be capable of entangling the rumored Rebel ironclad, if, indeed, she ever should materialize. Flusser was speculating that if the *Albemarle* could be immobilized, she would be a certain target for the guns positioned at both Fort Gray and Battery Worth.

At approximately 3:45 a.m., driven by the force of her two 200 horsepower engines with stern propellers, the Confederate ram *Albemarle* arrived at Plymouth. After having become cognizant of the Yankee trap set for him, Captain Cooke hugged the tree-lined northern shore of the Roanoke River. Then he ordered *"All ahead full!"* and deliberately plowed the *CSS Albemarle's* eighteen-foot metal prow more than nine feet into the *USS Southfield's* starboard quarterdeck, even into her fire room, thereby sinking the Federal gunboat and drowning many of her crew within minutes.

Afterwards, however, the Rebel ram was not able to immediately withdraw her armored prow from the *Southfield*, and so the two boats remained stuck, causing the *Albemarle* to begin sinking along with her quarry. To Captain Cooke's consternation his order of *"All systems full!"* did nothing to release his ironclad ram from the wooden gunboat. As the battle continued to rage, skirmishers on both vessels frantically fired at each other. To the amazement of the Yankees, shots hitting the ironclad ricocheted harmlessly off her well-protected metal-plated exterior. They glanced off *"like peas thrown against the round surface of a stove pipe,"* according to Lieutenant Alonzo Cooper of the 12th New York Cavalry. [8]

Except for the flagship *USS Miami*, the remaining Union wooden gunboats, *USS Ceres* and the tin-clad *USS Whitehead*, were forced to retreat to the safety of the Albemarle Sound. Meanwhile, while standing on the quarterdeck of the flagship *USS Miami* unchained from the sinking *USS Southfield*, Lieut. Cdr. Flusser attempted to shoot from a bow-mounted X1-inch Dahlgren gun a shell having a ten-second-fuse.

Disastrously, the shell ricocheted off the tough iron hide of the *Albemarle*. After exploding in the air above Flusser, deadly parts mercilessly tore into his unprotected body. With the lanyard of the gun still held tightly in his hand, Cdr. Charles Williamson Flusser collapsed to the deck of the *Miami* and died just before daybreak on Tuesday, April 19th. [9] Immediately, the undamaged flagship bearing her dead commander moved downstream to join the other wooden Union gunboats in the Albemarle Sound.

Meanwhile, just as the *USS Southfield* hit the bottom of the Roanoke River, she rolled slightly, just enough to release the *CSS Albemarle*. Free once again, she was ready then to attack the *USS Miami*. However, the sailors on the Rebel ironclad were met with disappointment because the Yankee flagship already had retreated at full speed to the safety of the Sound.

The Confederate strategy had worked as planned because minus the protection of the gunboats on the river, the Yankees now had no chance against General Hoke's 10,000 troops. Completely satisfied with his victory, Captain Cooke then ordered the *Albemarle* to anchor about a mile below Plymouth. Afterwards, the Rebel ram arrogantly sat downriver, thus preventing any reinforcements from being able to reach the isolated Federals at Plymouth.

Upon checking the ironclad for any damage she might have sustained, Captain Cooke found only nine plates fractured. There was only one Confederate casualty, and it had been due to curiosity. A crewman by the name of Harris had decided to take a quick peek from a gun post, a fatal mistake indeed. From the *USS Miami*, he immediately was sighted and killed by a Yankee with a very accurate aim. [10]

Following the end of the war Ex-Lt. Col. (CSA) Alfred M. Waddell made the following assessment of the *CSS Albemarle*:

> "This vessel stands alone in the history of naval architecture. She was the only vessel of war ever seen in the world whose keel was laid in a corn row on a river bank and which started without an experimental trip to attack a superior naval force...and hove in sight of the enemy...while workmen were hammering on her unfinished armor." [11]

Fig. 31. **CSS *Albemarle* attacks USS *Miami* and USS *Southfield***
From engraving by J. 0. Davidson, courtesy of Hampton Roads Naval Museum

Chapter 15

CAPTAIN JAMES WALLACE COOKE, CSN

A native of Beaufort, North Carolina, James Cooke was born in 1812. Unfortunately, both of his parents, Thomas and Esther Cooke, died at young ages, leaving orphaned a daughter and four-year old James. Reared by his uncle, Colonel Henry M. Cooke, the boy at the age of sixteen years entered the United States Navy in 1828 as a midshipman on the *USS Guerierre*. Thirteen years later in 1841 he had risen to Lieutenant, his same rank until the War Between the States erupted twenty years later.

In May of 1861 after having resigned his commission in the United States Navy, James W. Cooke immediately joined the Virginia State Navy. Very soon afterwards on June 11 he entered the Confederate Navy, still maintaining his rank of lieutenant. In the same year he was appointed official liaison between the Confederate Navy Department and North Carolina contractors involved with ship building. [1]

Later he was placed in command of a small iron hull tugboat, the *CSS Ellis*, captured on February 10, 1862 by the Yankees in a fight on the Pasquotank River. Lieutenant Cooke, even though badly wounded by both a bayonet and a musket ball, continued to fight fiercely until his enemies overpowered him. Fortunately, just as he was about to be shot and killed, he was recognized by a former shipmate, Lieutenant Charles Willliamson Flusser who luckily had appeared just in time to save his life. So instead of being killed, Cooke was taken prisoner on the *USS Commodore Perry* and a short time afterwards paroled. [2]

In January of 1864, James Wallace Cooke was assigned as the *CSS Albemarle's* commanding officer. [3] Three months later, very early on April 19th Captain Cooke was sailing the ironclad ram down the winding Roanoke River to the small town of Plymouth on the south bank. Unbeknown to him, he once again was to face in battle his former friend and shipmate, Lieut. Commander Charles W. Flusser.

CHAPTER 16

LIEUT. CMDR. CHARLES WILLIAMSON FLUSSER, USN

Second of the six children of Charles Thomas Flusser and Julianna (Waters), Charles Williamson Flusser was born on September 27th, 1832. Sometime later his lawyer father decided to move his family from their home in Annapolis, Maryland, to Vicksburg, Mississippi. There they remained until his death, after which time the family moved to Louisville, Kentucky where Charles attended the public schools.

At the age of fifteen he received an appointment to the United States Naval Academy and on October 15, 1847, was appointed Acting Midshipman aboard the USS Cumberland, flagship of the Home Squadron at Norfolk, Virginia. After the War Between the States erupted, Lieut. Flusser chose to remain in the United States Navy, even though the rest of his family's sympathies lay with the South. He was very close to his mother and so was disappointed when she did not share his loyalty to the Union. Then to his dismay, two of his brothers became Confederate soldiers, both later to be killed in battle. The oldest brother Ottakar served with the 4th Texas Infantry, Hood's Texas Brigade, and a younger brother Guy with the 4th Kentucky Cavalry Regiment. [1]

While serving as an instructor at the Naval Academy several years prior to the war, Lieut. Cdr. Flusser had been well known and well liked, remaining so until he chose loyalty to the Union. Consequently, he lost all of his old friends who chose the South's cause, declaring, as did Mrs. Flusser and her sons Ottakar and Guy, that the war was being fought over "states rights," while Charles agreed with the North's declaration that it was being fought "to preserve the Union."

Also while Flusser was at the Naval Academy, he had befriended a student, a brash young man with the reputation of being a prankster. Even so, Flusser had liked him and so tried to be of help when the boy got himself into some serious trouble. However, even the older man's friendship could not prevent the younger man's expulsion from the Academy just months before graduation. Unbeknown to both of them, however, that particular student, William Barker Cushing, would play a serious and defining role in the drama that would unfold at Plymouth, North Carolina, in April of 1864.

The young unmarried Flusser was accustomed to writing lengthy and descriptive letters home to his mother and his sister Fanny. In one dated April 25, 1863, when he was commanding the USS Commodore Perry, he described the paradox of friends, family, and acquaintances fighting on opposite sides of the rebellion:

"I went out the other day with a flag of truce and had a pleasant interview with a Lt. Colonel Townes of the 62nd Georgia. He knew some people in Louisville, was educated in Kentucky. I bantered him pleasantly, and he us. I gave up to him some good whiskey, and tolerable cigars. I told him that I knew he had nothing of the sort for a long time. From the way he took to them I think my surmise was correct...

Your affectionate son, Charles

Would that this horrid war was finished. God bless you." [2]

Following the war, Corporal Luther Dickey of the 103rd Pennsylvania Volunteers recorded the following correspondence of Mr. S. B. Spruill, an attorney at law and later Mayor of Plymouth in 1909. He describes a meeting between two Flusser brothers serving on opposite sides of the conflict:

"The Roanoke river and streams flowing into same were in the Federal lines, and all that Col. Flusser did was to employ a man who had a canoe and get him to carry him from what is known as Cashoke creek to the Roanoke river, and drop same to Admiral Flusser's flag ship. Col Flusser may have remained during his entire visit to his brother aboard Admiral Flusser's flagship and sent back same way, and no one would have known it. It is hardly possible for a brother of Capt. Flusser to have boarded the Miami without coming to the knowledge of the crew, especially if he remained on board several days. I am satisfied that Admiral Flusser did not allow his brother to visit the fortifications or learn anything about the Federal strength at Plymouth. Col. Flusser was a Kentuckian: what regiment he commanded I do not know. I carried him through the Confederate lines without any trouble, they knowing me, but I am satisfied his visit was only of a friendly nature. Col. Flusser stayed about three days according to my best recollection now." [3]

After the death of the young Federal naval officer Charles Flusser, the following letter of condolence was sent to his mother:

Mrs. Julianna Flusser
Louisville, Kentucky

Navy Department
Washington,
May 4, 1864

Madam:

It was with true grief that the Department received the report of the death of your son, Lieutenant Commander Chas. W. Flusser, of the Navy, who was killed on the deck of his vessel, the Miami, at Plymouth, N.C. on the 19th ultimo during the action with the rebel ironclad ram which came down to him.

But he did not dread or fear the combat; on the contrary, with the heart of a brave soldier, he rather courted it—feeling confident of his ability, with the force around him, to secure a victory. Had he not met with his death so early in the action, it is not impossible that his efforts would have been as brilliant as they had been on many previous occasions.

The career of Lieut. Commander Flusser in the Navy was most useful and honorable, and his record from the commencement of the rebellion to his last moments, has been marked by devotion to duty and to his country. Possessing superior intellect, and fine abilities, as an officer, he used them advantageously, and the service lost in him one of the bravest and best officers. Acting Rear Admiral Lee has very truly said, 'his patriotism and distinguished services had won for him respect and esteem of the Navy and of the Country. He was generous, good and gallant, and his untimely death is a real and great loss to the public service.'

The name of Lieutenant Commander Flusser is identified with the principal victories achieved in repossessing the Sounds of North Carolina—'Roanoke Island,' 'Elizabeth City,' 'New Bern,' 'Plymouth,'--and it was his lot to have been most prominent in maintaining the possession.

The Department sincerely sympathizes with you in your affliction, and considers it a duty to pay this feeble tribute to the worth of the late lamented Lieut. Comdr. Flusser.

Very respectfully,
Gideon Welles
Secretary of the Navy [4]

Fig. 32. **Lieut. Commander Charles W. Flusser, USN**

CHAPTER 17

ATTACKING THE FORTS

In April of 1864 Plymouth, North Carolina, had a population of only 250 persons, much less than the 650 listed in 1862. Yet upon that little town more than 18,000 [1] soldiers, Billy Yanks and Johnny Rebs, converged for four days in the month of April. An incredible number to conceive, considering that in the year 2003, the total population is fewer than 5,000 permanent residents. On Tuesday night, April 19th following the *Albemarle's* ridding the Roanoke River of the protection of the Yankee gunboats, Ransom's Brigade successfully crossed Coneby Creek under the mantle of darkness at the spot where it faced Columbia Road, the main approach from the east. Columbia Road ran parallel to the river, crossing Coneby Creek about a mile from town near where today the Riverside Baptist Church sits on East Main Street (formerly Columbia Road).

In that eastern area of the town, the fortifications had been the weakest due to the swamps and because of the Yankees' confidence in the Federal gunboat protection from the river. The bridge had been destroyed over Coneby Creek not fordable with the water level higher than usual. Therefore, General Wessells was not anticipating a Rebel move during the night. In fact, he was speculating on sending any necessary reinforcements to that side of town in the morning, if need be. However, he was very mistaken in his speculations.

A member of the 56th North Carolina Regiment described the secretive crossing of Coneby Creek as follows:

> "General Hoke ordered an assault from this (east) side by Ransom's Brigade. Accordingly that night our sharpshooters effected a crossing of Conaby creek on felled trees with some opposition. A pontoon bridge was laid and before the night was far advanced, the brigade was over." [2]

Lieutenant George S. Hastings of the 24th New York Battery described the surprise move by the Rebels:

> "About midnight of Tuesday, April 19, in the teeth of a sharp and destructive fire, they laid their pontoons across a creek intersecting the open ground lying just east of our left line." [3]

A member of the 56th North Carolina Regiment described the crossing of Coneby Creek as follows:

"In the last charge the Twenty-fourth went in abreast with us, having entered the town by the Columbia road, which leads into Second street, after crossing Conaby creek with a northwest trend and then midway changing to due west. While the Eighth and Thirty-fifth swung around to invest Fort Comfort, the Twenty-fourth overcoming all opposition before them at the Bateman and Latham redoubts, pushed forward and connected with our left flank as we struck the fortifications,--redoubt and entrenched camp." [4]

Then, accompanying Hoke's Brigade, Captain Joseph G. Lockhart and his men were ready to conquer the last Yankee fortification--the formidable Fort Williams located in the center of town. First, however, the exhausted Confederates lay on the hard ground to sleep soundly under a bright moonlit sky. [5]

Prior plans had been formulated that in the morning as soon as General Ransom's troops got into proper position for attack, a rocket would be shot as a signal to General Hoke. Therefore, at dawn on Wednesday, April 20th, General Matt Ransom was seated on the back of his horse in readiness, and so immediately after the rocket exploded, the general's voice rang out loudly, *"Attention, brigade!"*

Immediately the line of battle formed. *"Fix bayonets! Trail arms! Forward march!"* Then came General Ransom's final command. *"Charge, boys, and the place is yours!"* [6]

A member of the 56th North Carolina Regiment described the beginning of the attack:

"...*The alignment was as follows: The Fifty-sixth on the right, flanked by Company I, as sharpshooters, (resting on the Roanoke and near the 'Albemarle,' then engaged, as it has been at intervals through the night, with Battery Worth on the river face of the town), and Twenty-fifth, Thirty-fifth, Eighth and Twenty-fourth successively on to the left. On our part of the line a large drove of cattle was encountered and driven on as a living wall between us and the enemy until they reached the canal, down which they refused to plunge, or escort us further. Maddened by this strange spectacle of 'man's inhumanity to man,' they turned about, and 'with no reputation to lose,' dashing through our line, sought safety in flight...*"[7]

Lieutenant Bernard F. Blakeslee was on the skirmish line on the Columbia Road.

"...*At this hour* (four thirty a.m.) *a rocket was sent up as the signal for the attack, and a more famous charge we never witnessed. Instantly over our heads came a peal of thunder from the ram. Up rose a curling wreath of smoke—the batteries had opened, and quickly flashed fierce forks of flame—loud and earthshaking roars in quick succession. Lines of men came forth from the woods—the battle had begun...*"[8]

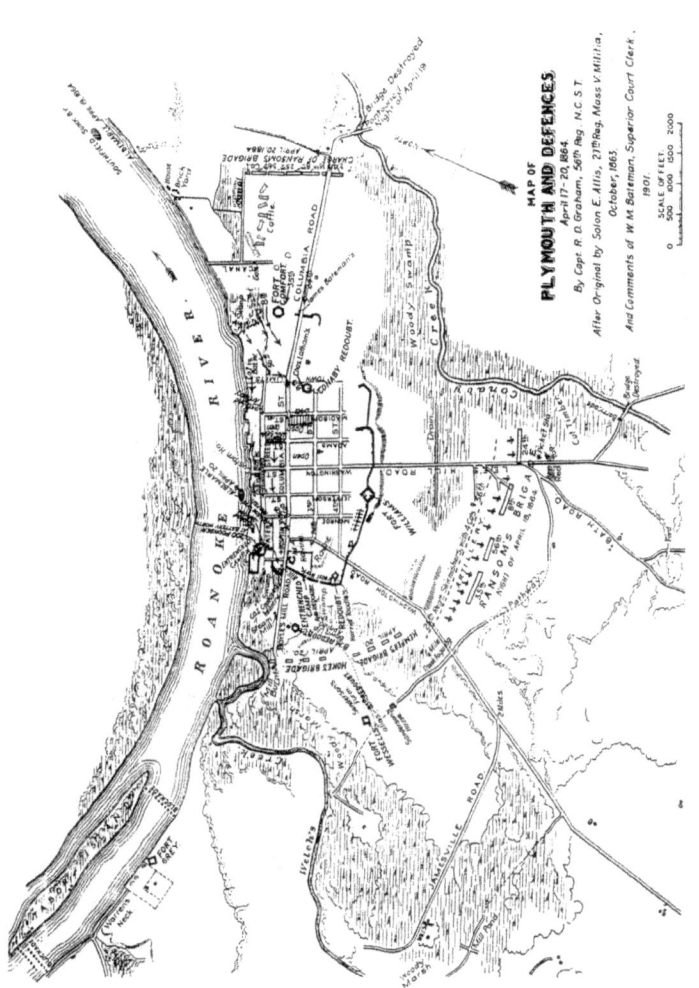

Fig. 33. *Battle of Plymouth, April 17-20, 1864*
"History of 103rd Penna. Regiment"

Chapter 18

GENERAL ROBERT HOKE, CSA

*B*orn in 1837, a native of Lincolnton, North Carolina, the ambitious Robert Hoke rose swiftly in the Confederate Army in twenty months. Originally, he had enlisted as a private in the 1st North Carolina Volunteers, amazingly rising to major very rapidly. In June of 1961 at the Battle of Big Bethel, Virginia, he first had the opportunity to demonstrate his combativeness. Later Hoke was promoted to lieutenant colonel of the 33rd North Carolina after its reorganization as the 21st North Carolina Regiment. In 1862 he proved himself in the Peninsula and Fredericksburg campaigns, earning the rank of general.

Robert Hoke was promoted to brigadier general on June 17, 1863, after he had proposed a plan to General Robert E. Lee for pushing the Yankees out of New Bern, North Carolina. Through no fault of Hoke's logic, the plan, however, failed under the command of General George Pickett. During the first week of July 1863, Hoke again met disappointment, having missed the Battle of Gettysburg in Pennsylvania due to a wound received during May at the Battle of Chancellorville in Virginia.

In the spring of 1864 he was given command of the very same forces that had failed under General Pickett at New Bern. However, instead of concentrating on New Bern as had Pickett. Hoke's strategy was to focus his attack on the small town of Plymouth located much closer to the Atlantic coast. After establishing his headquarters at Tarboro, North Carolina, fifty miles west of Plymouth, Hoke formulated his determined plan for returning the small town to Confederate occupation. Later on April 23, 1864, Confederate President Jefferson Davis would make Hoke major general as a reward for his success.[1]

*Fig. 34. **General Robert Hoke, CSA**
"Battles and Leaders of the Civil War"*

Chapter 19

YANKEE CAPITULATION

Even though the Johnny Rebs numbered approximately 10,000, the vastly outnumbered Billy Yanks determined to maintain their hold on the town, concentrating on trying to save their last remaining bastion, Fort Williams. However, they soon were forced to realize the futility of such a plan when Matt Ransom's Brigade came in full force from the east. Second Lieut B. F. Blakeslee of the 16th Conn. described it:

"...The conflict was bloody, short and decisive. The enemy was in such numbers we had to yield. There were in the fort at the time forty artillery men who fired grape and canister and forty-two of Co G, 16th Conn.; total loss, 82.

"The enemy then passed in the rear and on the bank of the river, to the right of town, and while part was on the right working towards the center, those on the left were doing the same. Every position was obstinately maintained. A squad of men here, and a squad there, the redoubts and forts were slowly captured. For three or four hours, Fort Williams, with guns turned, did murderous execution, nearly two hours of which was in the streets of Plymouth." [1]

Years later on September 19, 1889, George O. Brown, Co. G of the 2nd Massachusetts Heavy Artillery, would write a letter to the *National Tribune Veterans Newspaper* to complain that in a prior edition "Comrade" Slaybaugh had omitted mentioning the presence of the 2nd Massachusetts Heavy Artillery. Brown included also an additional story about the battle at Fort Williams.

"Private Jas. Smith, of Co. G, 2nd Mass. H. A., a half-breed Indian, from Webster, Mass., was No. 1 on one of the 32-pounder Columbiads. It was almost sure death on Wednesday morning, April 20, for a man to attempt to load a gun for in so doing he was obliged to expose his body in the embrasure and draw a shot from some of the swarm of sharpshooters lurking behind the stumps in front of the fort.

At about 10 a.m. on the day mentioned, as Smith was about to step in front of his gun to load it, a spent shell with fuse burning landed within five feet of him, and about the same distance from Serg't Benj. F. Baxter, of the same company, who is now dead. Baxter cried out quickly, 'Damn it, Smith, pick it up and throw it over!' and sure enough over it went, the shell exploding a second later, injuring no one.

Inside of an hour Smith was torn to pieces by a shell exploding in the mouth of his gun, and thus died as brave a man as ever drew breath..."

On Wednesday morning, April 20th, the fourth day of battle, the *Albemarle* was anchored off Jefferson Street where her gunners were exploding fused shells over Fort Williams. The young twenty-seven year old Confederate Brig. General Robert H. Hoke requested a personal meeting with the much older General Wessells to discuss negotiations for surrendering the garrison. A Hartford, Connecticut, newspaper article reported that instead of meeting with General Wessells, General Hoke met under a flag of truce with Colonel Francis Beach of the 16th Connecticut Volunteers, second in command. [2] As courteously as was possible under the circumstances, the Confederate general cited the impossibility of relief for the Federals because of the *Albemarle's* overwhelming success on the Roanoke River, the honorable defense that had already been made by the Yankees, and their untenable position.

General Hoke guaranteed an exchange of officers following the capitulation. However, not being satisfied with the inclusion of solely officers, Colonel Beach requested that the same treatment be extended for the rank and file. General Hoke refused the concession. According to the newspaper article, Colonel Beach then responded, *"Then you will have to come and take us."* [3]

Other reports make no mention of the presence of Colonel Beach, although as second in command, he most likely was present. In his final report General Wessells describes the scenario as if he were the negotiator, even though he had requested meeting with General Pickett, another West Pointer, rather than with the civilian general, Robert Hoke. The request was refused, and whether Wessells might have turned the negotiations over to Beach for that reason is speculative. What is true, however, is that the negotiators returned to their respective men waiting anxiously to hear the outcome. Subsequently, because General Wessells was not willing to surrender the garrison, hostilities quickly resumed, even though under the threat *"that further resistance might lead to indiscriminate slaughter."*[4]

For the next hour General Wessells deliberated with his officers in Fort Williams where his headquarters had been moved. Four-fifths of his men already were prisoners of the Rebels and no reinforcements were expected. By that time the other officers were ready to raise the white flag of surrender.

Regarding the capitulation on Wednesday morning, April 20th, Lieutenant George S. Hastings described:

"For nearly two hours did the fight go on in the streets of Plymouth, our forces surrendering only under stern military necessity and in small detachments. Fort Williams turned its guns upon the rebels, and did murderous execution for three or four hours. Finally, when every portion of that strong earthwork was covered by rebel sharpshooters, and the rebel artillery had been so disposed as to

143

send a concentric shower of shells within its parapets, Gen. Wessells accepted the situation and saved the garrison from certain sacrifice by a reluctant surrender." [5]

Following the severe wounding of his nephew and aide-de-camp, Lieut. Foot, [6] General Wessells finally made the heartbreaking decision to capitulate, as described by Captain John Donaghy:

"We were now subjected to a most furious bombardment. It was a hopeless struggle, but our men kept firing bravely. The rebels were amassing to the left and pressed too closely that the 101st Penna., that stood here, surrendered and marched out of the works of our regiment. That left but Capt. Mackey's company and mine outside the fort on that side. Mackey came over into my works and advised that we too should surrender. I agreed with him that our case was hopeless, but told him I did not want to give up as long as the fort held out. He then declared he would go into the fort and persuade the general to surrender.

I tried to dissuade him from the attempt, telling him that he would never reach the fort alive, as the ground was swept by sharpshooters, but he started and I expected to see him fall. He crossed the intervening space and disappeared around an angle of the fort. It was not long after Mackey left us till an enlisted man from within the fort mounted the parapet and waved as a flag of truce, a white woolen shirt fastened to a musket. The garrison flag, which hung by the upper corner alone, was hauled down and we were prisoners of war." [7]

The flag staff was shot away and replaced twice before General Henry Walton Wessells ordered Captain Ira B. Sampson, Chief of Artillery, Sub-District of the Albemarle, commander of Fort Williams, to have the garrison flag lowered. Rather than assign the odious task to someone else, Captain Sampson chose to carry out the order himself. [8]

Upon the raising of the white flag, three hundred men from the Union infantry and artillery were turned over then to Captain Joseph G. Lockhart. [9] Lieutenant Blakeslee concluded his observations with:

"We were prisoners, and as we marched out of the fort we could see at what a fearful cost it was to them. ...Our loss was one wounded, an artillery man, while the rebel loss...was five hundred killed. [10]

J. J. Broadwell, a Confederate soldier who following the war became a schoolteacher in Selma, South Carolina, described what he remembered about the battle at Fort Williams. However, his report of the number of Rebels killed was two hundred less than Blakeslee's.

"There was a large fort on the east side of the breastworks that ran all around the town. The soldiers in the fort were well prepared that dealt death to the Confederates. They say they were surrounded on all sides but kept on fighting after Hoke and his men were in the town.

The great Oak gate of the fort faced the river. There is a street that ran from the gate to the river. As they would not give up and lower the Stars and Stripes, the Albemarle moved up to the mouth of the street that ran to the gate and fired into the gate of the fort some of those 200-pound balls and shells. Old Glory slipped down the pole with alacrity and dispatch.

The firing ceased, 700 prisoners were taken, and from the fort a lot of rations were taken, salt, bacon, and spun cotton.... Our loss in killed and wounded was about three hundred." [11]

Confederate author Edward Pollard described that last hour of battle:

"The town was ours. But still Wessells, shut up in his stronghold, Fort Williams, refused to yield. A heavy cannonade was opened upon the fort, and the garrison was galled by our sharpshooters. At last some of the Confederates, creeping forward through the entrenchments, got an enfilading fire upon them, which soon brought them to terms, and hundreds of them rushed out of the fort without arms and surrendered. When the smoke cleared away, the hated flag was fluttering rapidly down to the ground." [12]

About the capitulation Private Charles Mosher of the 85th New York Infantry recorded in his diary:

"It did not take the rebels long after to get this place. Soon our company had to climb out of our hole with a white cloth in our hands. As we ran along out on top of the works those rebels kept up their firing on us. None of Company B got hit. When I got out into the open, I passed by a well and dropped my revolver into it for safekeeping. I did not want the rebels to take it away from me. I could have kept it, as we were not searched at all. About noon this 20th day of April 1864 every thing and every one had been captured except Fort Williams and its garrison. Brigadier General Henry W. Wessells surrendered. The Flag was lowered to the ground and Plymouth, N.C. was in the hands of the rebels." [13]

Sources vary concerning the actual hour when with waving colors the Yankees marched out of the Fort Williams garrison to ground their arms. General Wessells reported the time as 10:00 a.m. when he was forced to surrender approximately 3,000 men. According to his report, he relinquished to the victors 28 artillery pieces, 500 horses, forage, wagons, sutlers' stock, 5,000 stands of small arms, and a large supply of ammunition [14] In addition, over 200 tons of high quality anthracite coal from northeastern Pennsylvania was an added boon for the *Albemarle*, since only low quality bituminous [15] mined in western Virginia and Kentucky was being used by the Confederates.

A Confederate report, however, differed somewhat with the figures:

"The fruits of this capture were sixteen hundred prisoners, twenty-five pieces of artillery, vast quantities of commissary and quartermaster supplies, and immense ordnance stores." [16]

The *Richmond Examiner's* version differed, also, in the numbers it reported on April 24, 1864:

"The result of this most brilliant success was the capture of some 2,500 prisoners, 28 pieces of artillery, heavy and light, some 500 horses, 5,000 stands of small arms, 700 barrels of flour, with other commissary and quartermaster supplies, immense ordnance stores, and the strong position of Plymouth, which protects the whole Roanoke Valley, and furnishes a base for our iron-clad to drive out from Albemarle and Pamlico Sounds the large fleet of the enemy's gunboats, and open a large and right country from which we can obtain supplies." [17]

The penultimate scene of the tableau at Plymouth was the exchange between the victorious Confederate in gray and the defeated Federal in blue. Standing nearby was Private Norval D. Goe, a hospital steward from Co. A of the 103rd Pennsylvania Volunteers. He later wrote what he had observed.

"As the Confederate commander approached Gen. Wessells, the latter reached him his sword, saying: 'Gen. Hoke, this is the saddest day of my life.'

Gen. Hoke, as he received the sword, replied: 'General, this is the proudest day of my life.'

And then, as if impressed by the wonderful and quiet bearing of the defeated commander, he handed back the sword, saying: 'General Wessells, you are too brave a man to part with your sword: Take it back! Have you any request to make?'

'I have but one request to make, General, and that is that my men are not robbed.' A quick and sympathetic response came from the victorious commander: 'Your request is granted.' And be it said to the credit of the Confederate soldiers, both officers and men, whose duty it was to guard the captives, this promise of Gen. Hoke's was faithfully kept." [18]

When writing the history of the 56th North Carolina Regiment, Captain Robert D. Graham recorded his observations:

"The writer was near Gen. Hoke when he received Gen. Wessells, accompanied by his officers, as his prisoner. There was everything in his courteous and considerate bearing to lessen the sting of defeat. Dismounting from his horse and clasping the captive's hand, he assured him of his respect and sympathy, and added: 'After such a gallant defense you can bear the fortune of war without self-reproach.'" [19]

From reports of the 24th Regiment North Carolina, the summation of the capitulation was:

"The recapture of Plymouth, N.C. under the existing circumstances, was one of the most splendid victories achieved by Southern arms in this real contest, and about the only hard fought battle on North Carolina soil. At night, the troops were marched out of town and the dead buried with military honors. On the following day the Twenty-fourth Regiment was sent to garrison the town where we remained for a day or two, when we were relieved by the Fiftieth Regiment, North Carolina troops, and Ransom's Brigade sent to lay siege to Washington, N. C." [20]

Later a vote of thanks was passed from the Confederate Congress to both Commander James W. Cooke and General Robert Hoke, as well as to the officers and men under their commands. Due to the victory gained by the two men, North Carolinians loyal to the Confederacy became hopeful that very soon their state would be free of the "blue-belly" invaders. A sergeant in the 50th North Carolina Infantry sent this optimistic letter home to his family in Rutherford County, North Carolina:

Plymouth, N.C. May the 6th 1864

Dear sisters,

I take my seat to let you know that we was well, hoping this may find you the same. I read your letter yesterday. I was glad to hear that they was the same. We left Wilmington the other week. We came to Tarboro town on the steam train, then we made a long march about 75 miles. It wore all our feet out.

They have made a smash among the Yankees, they took Plymouth. That was one of the most complete victories that has been gained since the war commenced. They took about two thousand prisoners and a great many other things that I can't mention. They have all left Washington, it is in the hands of our men.

It is said they are leaving Newbern, if it is so they will be most off our soil. We are at this place. I don't know how long we will stay here, but I can't think long and I hope that you can write Tarboro. They will be sent to this Regiment. Here we are about 50 miles from the railroad. Here it is a bad place to stay. You must all do the (best) you can. We will have hard times summer, but I hope we will come out safe if we put our best on. The Lord help us at all times is my wish.

I am your brother,

E. Wilson [21]

★ ★ ★ ★

On April 20, 1864, all of the surviving Federals at Plymouth became prisoners of the Confederacy except for an undetermined number of "Buffaloes" and perhaps some blacks who had made their escape the night before, well aware of what might befall them if captured. Some of the North Carolinians fled in canoes, such as Corporal Nathaniel Miller, who was to remain concealed among cypress trees until the *USS Ceres* rescued him a week later. Private Laton Gardner hid in the water for two days and one night before wading more than ten miles to reach Union lines. First Sergeant James H. Mitchell hid in the swamps for ten hours before escaping to Washington, North Carolina. [22] Some other men desperately held on to floating logs to be carried downstream by the swift flowing current to the Sound where they were picked up by the Federal gunboats.

All of the members of the 103rd Pennsylvania Volunteers Regiment were forced to surrender except for a lucky few. That number included those who were hospitalized and those away on detached duties such as the men of Co. C who were to escape the disastrous battle at Plymouth because they, fortuitously, were garrisoned at Fort Reno on Roanoke Island. [23]

Captain Donaghy mentions one soldier in particular barely escaping the Battle of Plymouth:

"My old comrade Dill was ambitious to become a commissioned officer in the new colored regiments then forming at the north. I procured for him recommendations from most of our officers, and he secured an order to appear at Washington for examination before Casey's board. He passed for the rank of captain and then returned to his company to await his commission. It came in due time, and he was assigned to the 43rd Regiment Colored Troops then forming in Philadelphia. He left Plymouth on the morning of April 17, and it was lucky for him that he got off that day." [24]

On the 21st of April General Benjamin Butler being totally unaware that Plymouth was in Confederate control sent this ironical telegram message to Major Henry W. Halleck:

"They ought to hold out, and I have every confidence they will." [25]

Even though outnumbered five to one, the Union troops at Plymouth had fought gallantly. They might have been victorious if Lieut. Commander Charles W. Flusser had not died on the quarterdeck of the *Miami*. After the retreat of the gunboats into the Albemarle Sound, the Union soldiers were defeated soundly.

The report of casualties in the Union forces commanded by Brig. General Henry W. Wessells at Plymouth, N.C., April 17-20, 1864: [26]

Commands	Officers	Men	Total
Staff	10	0	10
16th Conn.	23	440	463
2nd Mass. Heavy Art'y, Cos. G & H	7	262	269
2nd N.C. Co.'s, B & F	4	162	166
12th N.Y. Cav. Co.'s A & F	3	118	121
85th N.Y.	26	518	544
24th N.Y. Battery	2	120	122
101st Penna.	27	382	409
103rd Penna.	24	461	485
Unattached recruits	1	244	245
Total Killed, wounded and missing	127	2707	2834

★ ★ ★ ★

The following telegrams were sent to Richmond, Virginia immediately following the capitulation of the Yankee forces:

Plymouth, April 21, 1864

Gen. Bragg, Richmond, Va.

I have stormed and captured this place, capturing 1 brigadier, 1,600 men, stores, 25 pieces of artillery.

R. F. Hoke, Brigadier-General [27]

★ ★ ★ ★

Plymouth, April 21, 1864

His Excellency President Davis, Richmond, Va.,

Heaven has crowned our efforts with success. Gen. Hoke has captured this point, with 1,600 prisoners, 25 pieces of artillery, and navy cooperation.

J. Taylor Wood, Colonel and Aide-de-Camp [28]

★ ★ ★ ★

Richmond, Va., April 23, 1864

Maj. Gen. Robert F. Hoke (Via Rocky Mount, N.C.):

Accept my thanks and congratulations for the brilliant success which has attended your attack and capture of Plymouth. You are promoted to be a Major General from that date.

Jefferson Davis [29]

★ ★ ★ ★

Casualties in General Robert Hoke's Command: [30]

	Killed	Wounded
Mercer's Brigade	48	100
Ransom's Brigade	96	377
Terry.s Brigade	7	25
Hoke's artillery units	2	27
Dearing cavalrymen	about 10	25
Totals	163	554

★ ★ ★ ★

On the day after the Confederates took the town, Benjamin G. Jones of the 21st Georgia Regiment sent the following message back home:

Fort Williams
April 21, 1864

My Dear Brother,

After eating a hearty supper such as sugared coffee, bacon and chicken and pushing back my plate and taking a light, I will tell you of our late battle at this place. On the 13th of this month we took the cars at Kinston. On the morning of the 14th we arrived at Tarboro and took up march for this place and on the 17th we reached their picket lines and took them on surprise. We captured some of them though the reserve made their escape and gave the alarm.

When we reached the town we formed a line of battle within one mile and a half of the town and lay quiet until the morning of the 18th when a severe artillery fight took place. The enemy were well fortified and had three forts built and three gunboats to support them and on the morning of the 19th our regiment and the 21th North Carolina was drawn up in line to charge one of the forts which had three siege pieces in it and a good many infantry. Our Colonel was acting Brigadier General- the charge was ordered and the men went like a thunder storm and yelling like so many wild beasts . They soon reached the fort through a storm of grape shots and cannister—the fort had brush around it and every limb sharpened and next to the fort a ditch was near ten feet deep which made the fort near twenty five feet high—the most of the boys made their way through the brush and got to the fort, but the ditch being so deep and the fort so steep not many men could reach the top. The enemy stopped firing of their guns but threw hand grenades over the fort which exploded very rapidly amongst the men—our flag reached the fort and was planted on it and they struck at it with their guns and tore it nearly in two. They finally surrendered. Our Colonel was killed, Colonel Mercer, and Wiley W. Carter of our company was mortally wounded who has died since, Milford Wiley very badly wounded in the shoulder and one or two slightly wounded.

Our gun boat ran down the river of the enemy and sunk one gun boat and one transport and came very near sinking two more. They went off in a sinking condition. We then had the enemy surrounded and commenced siege on the other two forts which they soon ceased to fire and surrendered. We took twenty five hundred prisoners and I think thirty pieces of artillery and enough commissaries to do us four or five months. All of their tents fell into our hands though they are badly torn up. The tent that I am in has more than a hundred holes in it. Our Brigadier General commanded the fight—we had only three Brigadiers.

This place had been a beautiful town though badly torn up now. The river is called Roanoke and is a very long river. Our Regiment is staying in the town and a portion of them in the fort. My quarters is within ten steps of Fort Williams. We are living fit now have most anything to eat that we want. I know not how long we will remain here but I suppose until we rest. Think as soon as we get well rested we will try a place near this called Washington and if we succeed we will have a fine time. I think we will soon have North Carolina cleaned of all Yankees.

I forgot to tell you the name of the place that is taken. It is Plymouth. ⁽³¹⁾

General Order No. 66

"With feelings of the deepest sorrow the commanding general announces the fall of Plymouth, N.C. and the capture of the gallant commander, Brig. H. W. Wessells, and his command. This result, however, did not obtain until after the most gallant and determined resistance had been made. Five times the enemy stormed the lines of the general, and as many times were they handsomely repulsed with great slaughter, and but for the powerful assistance of the rebel iron-clad ram and the floating iron sharpshooter battery, the **Cotton Plant**, Plymouth would still have been in our hands.

> For their noble defense the gallant Gen. Wessells and his brave band deserve the warmest thanks of the whole country, while all will sympathize with them in their misfortune.
>
> To the officers and men of the navy the commanding general tenders his thanks for their hearty co-operation with the army and the bravery, determination, and coolness that marked their part of the unequal contest.
>
> With sorrow he records the death of the noble sailor and gallant patriot, Lieut. Com. C. W. Flusser, U. S. Navy, who in the heat of battle fell dead on the deck of his ship, with the lanyard of his gun in his hand. The commanding general believes that these misfortunes will tend not to discourage but to nerve the Army of North Carolina to equal deeds of bravery and gallantry hereafter.
>
> Until further orders, the headquarters of the Sub-district of the Albemarle will be at Roanoke Island. The command devolves upon Col. D. W. Wardrop, of the 99th New York Volunteer Infantry.
>
> > By Command of Maj. Gen. John J. Peck
> > J. A. Judson, Assistant Adjutant General [32]

With the loss of Plymouth the Federals were forced to evacuate Washington, North Carolina. However, before they left, they deliberately torched the town on the 28th of April so there would be nothing left for the Rebels to confiscate.

Upon learning what his troops had done, General Palmer was dismayed, stating:

> "It is well known that the army vandals did not even respect the charitable institutions, but bursting open the doors of the Masonic and Odd Fellows' lodge, pillaged them both and hawked about the streets the regalia and jewels. And this, too, by United States troops! It is well known that both public and private stores were entered and plundered, and that devastation and destruction ruled the hour."
[33]

To the consternation of the North Carolinians loyal to the Confederacy, six months later the insufferable "blue-bellies" returned again to Plymouth, there to remain for the duration of the war, not only at that small river port, but also on Roanoke Island. Following the battle, the headquarters of the Sub-District of the Albemarle had been transferred from Plymouth to Roanoke Island. Colonel Theodore Lehmann of the 103rd Pennsylvania Volunteers with detachments of various state volunteer units plus two companies of the Rhode Island Artillery would occupy the Roanoke Island Post from January of 1865 until March of 1866.

Chapter 20

SACRED FLAGS

Due to poor visibility amid smoke and dust filled air, waving flags were essential for identifying each side during a battle. Since the din of blasts from rifles, cannons, and grenades easily might drown out any orders being shouted, the troops depended upon their flags for differentiating between friend and foe.

A flag, complete with staff and ornaments, was called "a stand of colors." The most valuable possession of a regiment, it always was carried by an unarmed bearer to whom the honor frequently spelled his death. Union regiments usually carried two flags, the Stars and Stripes and a regimental flag called the "regimental colors." A Union bearer was protected by a color guard composed of a sergeant and five to eight corporals who went into action at "shoulder arms," lowering them when resistance was met.[1]

The Confederates' method of carrying their flags differed from the Yankees'. Regarding his unit's flag at the Battle of Plymouth, a writer of the 56th North Carolina Regiment recorded:

> "The regimental colors were carried by a Sergeant, later given the rank of Ensign by the Confederate Congress, and he was supported by eight volunteer Corporals. This guard of three ranks in line of battle formed the extreme left of the right centre company..."[2]

In the attempt at creating a suitable flag for the Confederate States, the design of the Stars and Bars was changed three times during the war. In addition, a special flag was reserved just for battle.

Fig. 35. Confederate flags
"Personal Reminiscences of the War of 1861-5"

A second reason why flags were so important is that they served as representations of the troops' country or state, their beliefs, and their way of life. Third, a flag planted within enemy lines would denote victory while absence of the flag from view was a signal of defeat. Therefore, to be chosen to carry the flag was considered a great honor, whereas to have the flag captured by the enemy was considered a major disgrace. [3]

Such was the case at the surrender of Fort Gray. The Rebel "yell" went up three times three as the Stars and Stripes was being hauled down and a white flag of surrender run up in its place. [4]: In contrast, J. W. Merrill of the 24th New York Battery described his disheartened feelings upon observing the descent of the Stars and Stripes at Fort Williams:

" All loyal citizens of the United States have a pride in our beautiful national banner, and ever is it a pleasure to their hearts to see it fluttering to the breeze. As children we learn to love it, honor it and cherish it.

Two epochs in my life have been strongly marked by the sight of the 'emblem of the free.' First---when it was slowly lowered from the color staff of Fort Williams at Plymouth, and the Confederate colors replaced it. Second---when for the first time in seven months I saw it waving from the masts of the vessels that had come to take us from our horrid prison pens.

In experiencing the first, it was a sad sight to see our pride, our boasted 'Stars and Stripes' falling. We had fought for them, many of our comrades had died for them; but all was lost! Few of the many Union soldiers that stood around me had dry eyes as those colors fell...." [5]

★★★★

After acknowledging their defeat, the Yankees at Plymouth then needed to prevent their sacred flags from falling into the hands of the enemy. Conrad Petzinger of the 103rd Pennsylvania, for example, wrapped Company C's flag tightly around his body underneath his uniform. When Petzinger, with nearly 400 other members of the 103rd Pennsylvania Volunteers, entered the 26-acred stockade of Andersonville Prison, Georgia, Co. B's flag was still concealed beneath his clothing.

In 1861 when Co. B had been organized at Camp Orr near Pittsburgh, the wool bunting flag was hand stitched meticulously within three days by several girls of the Blaney School of Sugar Creek Township, Pennsylvania. Their former teacher James M. Carson was entrusted with the company flag. Unfortunately, he contracted typhoid fever, subsequently dying. The flag then was turned over to Conrad Petzinger for safekeeping. [6]

155

In December, 1864, when he was paroled from Andersonville Prison, Conrad Petzinger carried back to his home in Pennsylvania the flag he had successfully hidden for eight months. After being in the possession of the Petzinger family for many years, the flag was presented first to the Regimental Association, who in turn donated it to the Soldiers and Sailors Memorial Hall in Pittsburgh, Pennsylvania.[7]

Fig. 36. **Flag of Co. B, 103rd Penna. Volunteers**
History of the 103rd Regiment

So it would not get into the hands of their enemies, prior to their capture by General Matt Ransom's troops, the soldiers of the 101st Pennsylvania Veteran Volunteers buried their flag near Fort Compher. Following the war then, unlike other Pennsylvania units, the 101st did not have the opportunity to ceremoniously return state colors to Governor Andrew Gregg Curtin. Instead, their sacred flag was to remain buried forever in the soil of North Carolina. One hundred and thirty six years later on June 10, 2000, re-enactors symbolically returned the flag of the 101st Pennsylvania Veteran Volunteers to the state.

The same words used by General George Gordon Meade in Philadelphia on Independence Day, 1866, when Pennsylvania's battle flags were being returned to Governor Curtin were spoken in the 2000 ceremony. Colonel Wilson (portrayed by Dr. Dean Wilson, direct descendant of John Hays Wilson, brother of the Colonel) spoke the following words as the Regimental flag symbolically was presented to the Governor:

> *"Your Excellency, Governor Curtin: At the request of the descendants of the brave men who served with the 101st Pennsylvania Veteran Volunteer Infantry, and who on the field of battle represented our beloved State of Pennsylvania, I am here upon this occasion to present to you, Sir, a faithful likeness of their battle-stained banner. For four years it was carried by those noble men amidst the bullets and cannon roar, and in the face of the enemy.*
>
> *The war is long past and peace has returned to bless our happy land. It is altogether fitting that you should receive on this day, sacred to their memory, this flag, symbolic of the original color which our forefathers carried through the fiery ordeal. In the name of our ancestors who served proudly and faithfully in the 101st Pennsylvania Infantry, I present to you this flag. Its predecessor was borne through the war with honor by the soldiers we remember today. Receive it, Sir, as a memento of the prowess and deeds of valor of our ancestors, noble sons of Pennsylvania. Cherish it for all time and place it where our posterity for all generations may see it, to know what their forefathers did in the hours of trial."*

Governor Andrew Curtin'a response was as follows:

> *"On behalf of a grateful Commonwealth, I accept this flag. To your ancestors, the men who carried the steel, the musket and the sabre--to the private soldier, the unknown dead--I seek this day in vain to express all my gratitude. If there be men more distinguished than others, more entitled to our highest veneration, it is the private soldier of the Republic. If we follow him through all the sufferings and privations of the service, his long weary marches, his perils on the outposts, his wounds and sickness, even unto death, we trace him back to that sentiment of devotion to his country that led him to separate from home and its ties, and to offer even his life as a sacrifice to the Government his fathers gave him and his children.*

I cannot take back this likeness of the color committed to your ancestors' keeping without attempting to gather into my arms the full measure of the Commonwealth's overflowing gratitude and lay it at their feet. As their descendants, it is fitting that I present to you, in their stead, the thanks of your cherished mother, this ancient and goodly Commonwealth of Pennsylvania. And now, remembering your ancestors' sacrifice, and acknowledging your faithful performance of their final duty, I transfer possession of this symbol of their sacrifice to the official representative of the Commonwealth of Pennsylvania, the Honorable Gary Crowell, Secretary of the Interior." [8]

★ ★ ★ ★

In order to prevent its ever reaching the hands of the enemy, the 85th New York's regimental flag was torn into small pieces. Each man then received a scrap of the flag for safekeeping, with diarist Private Charles Mosher receiving a patch of red stripe six inches long by one inch wide. [9] As for the sacred flag of the 103rd Pennsylvania Volunteers, earlier in the spring it fortuitously had been sent north to Harrisburg in order to have battle honors added. Therefore, it was safe in Pennsylvania. Later it officially would be returned to the regiment during the 1866 ceremony. [10] At the present time the flag may be viewed by appointment in Harrisburg, Pennsylvania, through the Pennsylvania Capitol Preservation Committee.

The *Hartford Daily Times* reported the following information concerning the regimental flag of the 16th Connecticut Infantry:

"Corp. Lauren C. Mills of the color guard was fatally wounded, dying at Plymouth, April 28, 1864. The grape and canister attack was renewed by the rebels from the captured redoubt. It was at this juncture that the Conn. colors were stripped from the flag staff and saved. The eagle from the state colors had been shot from the staff and fallen at the feet of Color Sergeant William E. Bidwell of East Hartford." [11]

After the war was over, W. H. Nott of Bristol, Connecticut, wrote a letter to the Editor of the *National Tribune* about the ultimate fate of his regiment's flag:

"Some of the 16th Conn. seeing that they would be compelled to surrender, tore up the United States Flag and the State flag and wrapped the pieces around their bodies under their clothing and thus carried these pieces through Andersonville, and thence home to the State of Conn. They are now in the State Capitol, Hartford, Conn. being the center of a new flag." [12]

Today the flag can be viewed on the first floor in the Hall of Flags at the State Capitol, Hartford, Connecticut. Penned by Frank P. O'Brien was another story about a flag belonging to the 16th Connecticut. According to him, on April 20th he, G. M. "Mortie" Williams, and two other Confederates captured a Union bombproof and several 16th Connecticut Volunteers, including Major John H. Burnham, five lieutenants, and the color guard corporal who struggled to keep the regimental flag in his possession. Even so, it was wrested from his hands, so the story goes. Distraught over having to relinquish the flag, the color bearer pleaded for a piece of it. Private Williams complied by cutting off a corner and handing it to the defeated Yankee about to be sent to Andersonville Prison.

Shortly afterwards, Major Burnham was separated from his men and sent to Salisbury, North Carolina, there to be detained with other officers. However, that was not the end of the story of the flag. The next act in the drama unfolded some time later when Frank O'Brien was on a mission to capture the *Fawn*, a Yankee mail-boat on which the paymaster was sailing.

Even though the Rebels had formulated a well-thought-out plan, a serious mistake was made. A pistol was discharged too soon, thereby alerting the Yankees of the trap and providing enough time for the greenbacks to be burned before the Rebels could board the boat.

When finally he boarded the *Fawn* Frank O'Brien, was surprised to discover Major John Burnham who had been paroled following his capture at Plymouth. After reporting for duty at Norfolk, he had been granted a furlough due to his poor heath. However, before leaving the area Burnham wanted to visit some of his friends, a decision that was a huge mistake on his part.

Private Frank O'Brien continued his story by writing:

"Just here came a struggle between country and sympathy for the unfortunate soldier broken in health caused by confinement in prison, who had been looking for a speedy reunion with loved ones he had not seen in over two years. I would gladly have liberated him, but duty forbade, and poor Burnham was again an inmate of a Confederate prison."

That incident was not yet the end of the tableau involving Confederate Frank O'Brien and Federal John Burnham. According to O'Brien's story, twenty years later in another twist of fate, the two former enemies met again in New York City in July of 1884.

Former Alabama artillerist Frank O'Brien wrote that he was lunching with an old comrade at the Union Square Hotel café. Then another mutual friend joined them at the table. Meanwhile, a gentleman passing by stopped to greet the man who had just taken his seat. As introductions were being made, Frank O'Brien discovered the gentleman to be none other than his old enemy, John Burnham.

The first question Burham asked was, *"O'Brien, where is my flag? I would give a thousand dollars to get it back. Do you know what was done with it?"* The response was that, yes, O'Brien did know. He said that the flag was in the possession of its captor, Major Mortie Williams of Birmingham, Alabama.

O'Brien promised Burnham, "*The next time I see him I will tell of our meeting and of your great desire to obtain possession of the flag and I can safely say that he will send it to you.*"

So upon returning to the South, Frank O'Brien relayed the message from John Burnham to Mortie Williams who sent the pennant to Hartford, Connecticut. The *Hartford Times* reported:

"*Secretary McLean today received from General James of Montgomery, Alabama, one of the flags of the 16th Connecticut Volunteers, captured at the surrender of Plymouth, North Carolina 1864. The flag is not the United States flag furnished by the government to each regiment, nor the state colors furnished by Connecticut, but one of the guidons, and has been identified as the one presented to the regiment by the Hartford City Guards. It is about two by three and a half-foot in dimensions, of heavy blue silk. The state coat of arms and inscription, "16th Connecticut Volunteers," are embroidered in silk and the edges are trimmed with yellow silk fringe.*

The guidon is in excellent state of preservation and the colors almost as bright as when the flag was new; one corner was missing. Although this is not a battle flag, the good feelings of the Alabama veterans in returning it is greatly appreciated by the 16th as if it were a flag which had been torn by shell in the rage of battle. It is the fraternal feeling, not the flag alone, which is appreciated." [13]

Today, however, the guidon is nowhere to be found. According to Scott Holmes, historian of the 16th Connecticut, the curator of flags at the Connecticut State Capitol building said that he has searched for it and this particular guidon is not part of the capitol collection, nor does the state museum have it. Therefore, is the story true, and it if were, was the guidon actually returned? If so, where is it today? These are some of the questions concerning events occurring during the Civil War still unanswered.

Of paramount importance to the Yankees during the Battle of Plymouth was the thirty-starred United States flag that flew over the Customs House. It was the 1851 model, since flags manufactured during the years of 1856 and 1857 possessed thirty-five stars. Following the capitulation of the town, members of a Unionist family took down the Stars and Stripes. The flag then was carefully folded and placed on a high shelf of a closet for safe keeping.

At the turn of the twentieth century, the historical flag was donated to the Public Library in Plymouth, where, once again, it was kept on a shelf for some time. In the year 2003, however, fittingly, it is displayed prominently on a wall in the Port-O-Plymouth Museum on Water Street.

161

Fig. 37. *Port-O-Plymouth Museum*
From author's collection

Chapter 21

EYEWITNESS ACCOUNTS

Several versions exist concerning what happened on April 17-20, 1864, at Plymouth, North Carolina. Some accounts agree, while others drastically differ. According to Corporal Luther Dickey of the 103rd Pennsylvania Volunteers Regiment, the Union troops were in the following positions:

"Two companies of the 85th New York Vols., and a detachment of the 2nd Mass. Heavy Artillery in Fort Gray; Co. K, 85th New York, and a detachment of Co. H, 2nd Mass. Heavy Artillery, commanded by Capt. Chapin, Co. K, 85th New York, in Fort Wessells (redoubt); Companies E and G, 85th New York, on the extreme right, near Battery Worth; a detail from 16th Conn., commanded by Lieut. Hoppin, having charge of the 200-pounder; North Carolina troops, negroes and refugees in the fortification on the west side of the town; 24th New York Independent Battery at the Washington road, with a detachment of the 85th New York at its left; the 103rd Penna. in the center with Co. A, commanded by Capt. A. H. Alexander, and a detachment of the 24th Mass. Heavy Artillery, in charge of the guns in the redoubts."

The line of defense surrounding the town was divided into three nearly equal parts, the right commanded by Col. Fardella, the center by Col. Lehman, and the left by Col. Beach." [1]

On Monday: April 18, 1864 Private Charles Mosher of the 85th N.Y. Infantry recorded in his diary:

"Heavy firing up at Fort Gray last night. The boys on duty up there last night saw small boats in the river with lights on making sounding for that ram. Battery Worth on the river front with her hundred pound parrot gun is waiting for her.

We were up at three o'clock this morning and stood in line until day light. I was detailed for picket this morning. Lieut. Fay of Co. F is officer of the guard. Seven of us are on the ridge of sand between Fort Wessells and that morass. We have a good view of the whole field and woods in our front. The picket line has been drawn in half way between our old picket line and the works, in the slashing. We can see clear through the woods where the rebels are planting a battery. A shell from the 32 pounder in Fort Wessells goes right after it and makes it change its position very quick. When a shell from a 32 pounder explodes it kicks up a big dust. You bet.

A heavy skirmish line from the rebels make a drive across the open field. Our boys get after them and rush them back in a hurry. This is done many times. On the picket line to the right of Fort Wessells I saw one of our men crawl out over the open field to near the woods where the rebels opened fire on him when he run back to our lines. I don't know who he was, or what he was after. He was a brave and a bold fellow. Out on the picket line (our old picket line) near the reserve post stands a large pine tree. Behind it was a rebel soldier. Before this I had made me a cob house of pieces of rails to rest my gun on, as I lay down prone. Then when I saw that rebel away from his big tree, I banged away at him, how near I came to him I don't know. Then he discovered my whereabouts and returned the compliment. We had quite a duel there for a half hour more or less. He dropped a bullet about eight feet or so in front of me. He had a dead bead on me. It made me feel creepy. How near I got to him, I can't say.

Orders came for the pickets to cease firing. We stopped. It was quite sport. About dusk the rebels cut loose all their guns on the town, 30 in number and in different positions. Our picket line had orders to fall back. Most of the boys went by the Boyles Mills road. I went though the morass. I knew of a run way of single logs through it which I took. I had not gone a rod when a shell plunged in the mud near me (so it seemed then) I run faster, then another shell was after me. Of course the rebel gunner did not see me there. His shell was looking for me just the same, which answered every purpose. If I had by any means made a misstep or a shell had disabled me, I surely would nave been in a fix.

Those shells chased me clean through the morass. When I was through I was directly in front of our regimental lines. I ran up on our Col. (Fardella) he said stop here. I said no I will go to my company. I found them.

During the afternoon I had been in after more ammunition, so I knew their position at the works. The rebel artillery fire was so sharp and heavy that the gunboats Miami & Southfield *had to unshackle in order to be able to use their guns on the rebels, which they did with good effect. Between nine o'clock and ten o'clock the rebels captured Fort Wessells and turned the guns of the fort on the town."...* [2]

★★★★

A letter sent from Lieut. Commander Flusser to Acting Rear Admiral Samuel Phillips Lee, Comdg., North Atlantic Blockading Squadron, reported:

USS Miami, *Plymouth, N.C.*
April 18, 1864

Sir:
Here all day. About sunset the enemy made a general advance along our whole line. They have been repulsed. There is no firing now, 9:30 P.M. I am fearful our upper fort may be gone, but do not know anything certain about it. The

85th Redoubt repulsed three severe assaults, but the enemy still occupy a position near it.

The ram will be down to-night or to-morrow. I fear, for the protection of the town, I shall have to abandon my plan of fighting the ram, lashed to the Southfield.

The army ought to be re-enforced at once. I think I have force enough to whip the ram, but not sufficient to assist in holding the town, as I should like. I today gave to Fort Gray 100 projectiles for Parrott 100-pounder rifle. If the enemy should make frequent assaults I shall need a large supply of powder and projectiles for 100 pounder Parrott IX-inch Dahlgren, 24-pounder howitzers, and for the Ceres *four 20-pounder Parrott rifles.*

If we whip the ram the land force may retire. I have not heard of any casualties. In the action yesterday the Ceres *had 2 men killed and 7 wounded. Of the latter, four were officers, fortunately but one of them seriously hurt. Reports of killed and wounded will be forwarded at once, so soon as time is had to make them out. At present we are very busy, and the mail boat leaves in a few minutes* (3)

The following letter penned to Commander H. K. Davenport is believed to have been Lieut. C. W. Flusser's last. Presumably, it was written around ten o'clock on the night of the 18th.

Miami, Plymouth, N.C.
18th April, 1864

My dear Davenport:

The Army has been engaged with the enemy off and on all day. About sunset the rebs advanced along our whole line, but were driven back. They were obstinate and continued to fight till near 9 o'clock. The Southfield *and* Miami *took part and the General* (Wessells) *says our firing was admirable. I am fearful for Fort Gray. The enemy has established a battery of long range guns above it, with which they would sink all our boats if we went near enough to the fort to fire grape and canister into the enemy's infantry. They sunk the army steamer* Bombshell *to-day, temporarily under command of Ensign Stokes, who fought her well.*

I gave the army to-day 100 projectiles for 100-pounder Parrott. Please send powder, shot and shell, for that gun, for IX-inch and 20-pounder Parrott. The ram will be down to-night or to-morrow. She was just after daylight this morning foul of a tree 6 miles above Williamston. I think if she doesn't stay under cover of their battery established above Fort Gray, that we shall whip her. I had to destroy the obstruction in the Thoroughfare, as the Whitehead *was above, and could not run by the battery placed below her on the Roanoke.*

I have written the Admiral. The Eighty-fifth Redoubt repulsed three obstinate assaults, but the enemy remain near it.

In great haste,

C. W. Flusser [4]

★ ★ ★ ★

Skirmishing took place all throughout April 19th. Then during the night, the Rebels surreptitiously crossed Coneby Creek at the spot where it paralleled Columbia Road, the main approach from the east.

Lieutenant George Hastings wrote the following concerning the Rebels' successful advancement:

"...Crossing with two brigades of infantry and several pieces of artillery, they formed a new and strong line of battle, the right of which rested upon the Roanoke and the left swerving around to our front. At the same time, another force advanced against our right line. About three o'clock, on the morning of April 20th, the entire rebel force charged our extended and feeble lines, moving forward with loud and defiant yells.

Largely outnumbering our exhausted garrison, they were able to make a vigorous onset upon every portion of the defenses, and at the same time to send an independent column along the banks of the river into the heat of the town. The pieces of the 24th New York Battery were served double shotted with canister, hurling disorder and death into the ranks of the enemy; and not until the rebels seized the muzzle of the guns did the cannoneers fail in their work." [5]

Consequently, without the protection of the gunboats on the river, the Yankees were losing the battle, just as General Hoke had anticipated. By that time, all of the fortifications had been captured on the western side of the town, as well as Fort Gray isolated two miles up the river. On the eastern side of the town, Battery Worth already had been taken. The Yankees, however, still were making a last ditch attempt at preventing their enemies from reaching Fort Williams in the center of town.

Captain John Donaghy recorded his observations concerning the final defense of Fort Williams:

"The troops to the left of Fort Williams were ordered to unite in an effort to drive them (rebels) *out again. I called my company from the protection of the pits and bombproof and joined the others in the street leading back into the town. Lieut. Col. Maxwell was in command of our battalion. That we might face the enemy, he ordered us to charge front forward on the left company. I led my company to the position desired, which was along a drain which would serve as a line of rifle pits.*

The rebels were pouring on us a severe fire from buildings, and from behind any object that would conceal them. We saw but few of them, though the whizzing balls and white smoke from their weapons told us of their presence. As I stood on the flank of my company bringing it into line, a bullet went whizzing through the muscles of my thigh, giving me such a shock that I staggered and my sword dropped from my hand. Some of the men offered to assist me to the rear, but I declined their aid, sheathed my sword and limped back to the works, leaving Sergt. Armagroat to command the company, which was bravely fighting. The ball that struck me went through the muscles of one thigh and slightly wounded the other, and then fell into my boot. It was soon seen that our men could accomplish nothing where they were, so they came back to the works. Three others of my company were wounded—Corp. Benjamin Mortimer, and Privates Reed and Boyle, the first mortally. He was one of our best men.

He was carried into the bombproof on a stretcher. He looked at me and said reproachfully, 'Oh, Captain! Why did you take us out there?'

The enemy grew closer and kept up a harassing fire which our men returned when they could see a human target. As there was no moving about to be done by the company, I was enabld to resume command." [6]

An account of that final day of battle according to Rev. Amos S. Billingsley, Chaplain of the 101st Pennsylvania Volunteers, was published on May 7, 1864, in the *Buffalo Morning Express.*

"...Early on Wednesday morning, about daylight, the rebels, with five brigades, commanded by Gen. Ransom (a part of Stonewall Jackson's division), made assault after assault upon Confer (sic) redoubt on the left, in which we had about 200 men and four 32 pounders. Coming up with such an overwhelming force, they succeeded, with the loss of scores of killed, in taking this little fort, which let them into the town, up Main Street.

Shortly after their entrance into the town, about 300 of us were taken prisoners of war, and marched nearly two miles below town, leaving our beautiful flag still floating over Fort Williams with the brave Gen. Wessells, his staff, and some 200 men still holding out, and refusing to surrender until 10 a.m. on Wednesday." [7]

Lieutenant Alonzo Cooper of the 12th New York Cavalry described the final scene of the siege:

"This attack commenced at half-past four, and at half-past six a.m. of April 20th, I was a prisoner. As we marched past Compher redoubt to the Johnson farm, a mile to the south, we had an opportunity to witness the terrible slaughter the victory had cost the enemy.

Dead bodies of men and animals were strewn in every direction. Broken caissons and disabled cannon in front of these two redoubts showed plainly what a terrific struggle had been gone through with in their front.

The piteous cries for help of the suffering, the groans of the wounded that had not yet been removed (the ambulance corps not having yet been able to reach them) the roar of artillery and the rattle of musketry where the battle was still going on, the riding back and forth of mounted orderlies hurrying up re-inforcements, all served to make up a picture that I am unable to adequately describe. [8]

Chapter 22

THE FATE OF THE DEFEATED YANKEES

Following the capitulation of the garrison at Plymouth, North Carolina, the defeated Yankees became prisoners of war. Amos S. Billingsley, chaplain of the 101st Pennsylvania Volunteers, observed the *"wounded, dead and dying throughout the town, friend and foe alike being either treated for their wounds, waiting for death or burial. Throughout the town, where we cracked jokes and ate crackers, now lie rebels, bleeding soldiers, and heroic wounded patriots dying for their country."* [1]

The captives, including officers, spent the night of the 20th in an open field just outside of town. Wounded Yankees, however, were left behind in the care of the Confederate surgeon, as well as Surgeon Abraham P. Frick of the 103rd Pennsylvania who remained in Plymouth for three days to tend to the wounded before accompanying General Wessells and his staff to Libby Prison in Richmond, Virginia.

Diarist Private Charles Mosher penned concerning the capture of his regiment:

"We were treated very kindly. Not one of us insulted, nor molested. A few of our men, and only a few, had a cap or haversack taken. All of us were well clothed, each had his overcoat and blanket or blankets." [2]

In his book, *Life and Death in Rebel Prisons,* Sergeant Major Robert H. Kellogg recalled:

"I saw but one instance of robbery at the beginning, and that was by an officer, evidently in a state of intoxication. Riding up to one of our boys, he drew his sword and demanded his watch, using threatening and insulting language, and declaring he would split open his head if he refused. Of course, there was no way but to yield." [3]

Luther Dickey wrote about a similar incident occurring following the capitulation:

"A few minutes after the surrender, before the excitement following the final capitulation had subsided, Gen. Wessells noticed a Confederate soldier taking the hat from a captive; he immediately rushed toward the culprit and ordered him to return the hat, which was done without any more hesitation than if Gen. Wessells had been in supreme command." [4]

The next day captains and below (company grade officers) and the majority of majors and above (field grade officers) accompanied the enlisted men as they were forced to march seventy tortuous miles to the town of Tarboro where a train depot was located. General Wessells, however, was separated permanently from his troops. Under the guard of the 35th North Carolina he was retained at Plymouth with other high-ranking officers until April 23rd, later being transported by the *CSS Cotton Plant* to Weldon, North Carolina, a distance of one hundred and twenty-five miles. Afterwards some officers were sent by rail to Libby Prison in Richmond, Virginia, while others went to Morris Island outside of Charleston, South Carolina. Also retained with General Wessells were Colonel Lehmann of the 103rd Pennsylvania and Colonel Fardella of the 85th New York, as well as a number of surgeons and noncombatants that were soon released. Paroled on August 3, 1864, and returning to New York City on the 9th, General Henry Walton Wessells never again was to lead his men. [5]

After the Federal capitulation, the 166 "Buffaloes" at the Plymouth garrison knew they were in grave danger. The majority of them were native North Carolinians from nearby Bertie County, members of Companies B and E of the Second Regiment North Carolina Infantry. A number of the "Buffaloes" had deserted the Confederate Army to align themselves with the Federals.

The reasons for doing so varied. For one, "Buffaloes" generally were poor men who did not feel compelled to join forces with the rich plantation owners whose wealth was determined by the number of slaves they owned. Other North Carolinians were objecting to the "tax-in-kind" law requiring the payment of a tithe (one tenth) of their farm produce with the product itself. Since cotton was excluded, the poor farmers reached the conclusion that they were being unfairly taxed while the rich cotton planters were being unfairly favored.

Others resented the forced Confederate conscription. The Conscription Act enacted in April, 1862, by the Confederate Congress stated that all able bodied men between the ages of eighteen and thirty-five must serve in the military. Sometime later, however, the required ages were changed to be between seventeen and fifty. [6]

Still other "Buffaloes" may have been die-hard Unionists, sincerely desiring to preserve the Union, while others simply may have been lured by the tempting greenbacks being dangled in front of them. Confederate currency was rapidly becoming worthless due to unchecked inflation. For instance, the price of a pair of men's shoes had soared to $125. A supply of salt costing $1.25 in the North was being sold at $60 in the South. Eventually, prices would escalate by 9,000%, thereby converting Confederate money into worthless pieces of paper. [7]

In addition, many women and children were left at home without food and the wherewithal to grow any with their husbands, brothers, and fathers *in absentia*.

Consequently, the majority of the men simply wanted to remain close to their families in order to protect them from destitution and starvation. Food shortages already had led to rioting in some of the larger cities of North Carolina. Governor Zebulon Vance was being bombarded constantly with letters from farm-women begging for aid. [8]

While the battle at Plymouth was still raging, the "Buffaloes" were advised by their officers to quickly scatter among other regiments to assume the names of dead Yankees, or of those absent due to sickness, or away on detached duty. Privates William T. Cullipher and James Hassell, as well as Corporal Worley Butler, were among the number to change identities. [9]

Private Charles Mosher of the 85th New York Volunteers recorded in his diary on April 20, 1864:

"...The privates were very glad to change their names. They took the names of our men who were killed. Our (sic One?) little fellow, a drummer took the name of our Seymour Smith." [10]

Another possible name taken by a "Buffalo" may have been Barber Popple whom Charlie Mosher noted as having been killed at Plymouth. [11] However, there is a gravesite (#1830) at Andersonville for Private Barber Popple, Co. B, 85th New York, recorded as having died on June 11, 1864.

Officers of the "Buffaloes" doffed their identifying uniforms as well, donning that of a private. In addition, especially in grave danger were three visiting officers, Captain Hiram Leonard Marvin, and Lieut. Richard Bascome, recruiters for the United States Colored Troops and Lieut. George French, a recruiter for the Cavalry. [12]

Concerning two of those recruiters, Charlie Mosher's wrote:

"The Captain reduced himself to the ranks without a hint of a court-martial. It was Private Martin in a private's uniform. He did not wish to be known as an officer of colored troops. The lieutenant kept his rank and his uniform, and said that he was an officer of colored troops, and told the rebel officers he would not deny it, and they could do as they d__d pleased with him. The last we heard of him was that he was breaking stone on the streets of Raleigh, N.C. along with darkies. He is a plucky fellow." [13]

The men were all aware of the fate of the twenty-two "Buffaloes" captured at New Bern by Confederate forces under the command of Generals George E. Pickett and Robert F. Hoke. After having been court-martialed by seven Virginia officers, with General Montgomery Corse (17th Virginia Infantry) serving as president, the "Buffaloes" were executed in Kinston during February of 1864. [14] The pseudo-Yankees, therefore, knew that they, too, were in grave danger.

All of the unfortunate men who had gone to the gallows at Kinston were members of the Second North Carolina Infantry. Many of them originally had joined the state militia after being promised that they could stay near their families. However, when they began being sent away from the vicinity of their homes, they rebelled, siding then with the invading Federals.

At the same time, a number of North Carolinians had been acquitted at Kinston. General Corse would remember the execution of the twenty-two as the "most unpleasant duty of his life." [15] Concerning the men sent to the gallows, Confederate Colonel James T. Morehead of the 53rd North Carolina Regiment justified the executions in his report:

> "Among the prisoners 22 had formerly belonged to our army, and had gone over to the enemy and taken up arms against us. These prisoners were sent to Kinston, given a fair trial by court-martial, convicted of high treason, and duly executed by our brigade." [16]

After the war had ended, Union Commander Rush Hawkins made it his main purpose to prosecute Pickett for his act by charging him in Congress as a war criminal. However, before that could be accomplished, Pickett fled the country with his family to Canada. For several years afterwards Hawkins continued to push Congress. Finally, Pickett contacted the President of the United States, Ulysses S Grant, who had been his West Point classmate. President Grant addressed Congress, informing them that had he been in Pickett's shoes, he would have done the same thing. Afterwards, George Pickett was pardoned and he was able to return to the United States with his family. [17]

Following his capture the day before, on April 21st Private Charles Mosher recorded in his diary that the prisoners of war:

> "...drew four day's rations, forty hardtack and about one pound of pork each. I took my watch and hung it inside my boot-top...All of us stowed our valuables out of sight for fear the rebs would take them from us. But thus far none of us have lost anything, with the exception of a hat or canteen. There has not been any searching of our persons, no insulting language used to us; we have been treated in a soldierly manner, by men who are very gentlemanly in their conduct toward us." [18]

At the time he was chronicling that particular passage, Mosher was not cognizant of General Wessells' request of General Hoke asking that the Yankee prisoners not be robbed, and they had not been. Fortunately, too, the commissary and quartermaster stores were filled with an abundance of the supplies much needed by the Rebels. Also, what had been left behind in the deserted homes of the town provided plenty for the victors to confiscate. Fortunately for the Yankees then, their captors had no compulsion to steal from their captives.

The Yankees were herded for an extremely hard march to the small town of Hamilton thirty miles away, marching "up country " on deeply rutted roads and fording swollen creeks. Sometimes along the way compassionate southern women would provide fresh water for the weary northern soldiers. Finally, on Saturday, April 23rd the totally exhausted Yankees and their Rebel escorts arrived in Hamilton. There the detested "Buffaloes" were forced to pass between two lines of Confederates for identification by the 17th North Carolina or by former neighbors. Out of the total number of "Buffaloes," only six, however, were identified.

Modern researcher Gerald W. Thomas states in his book, *Bertie in Blue*:

"*Capt. Isaiah Conley of the 101st Regiment Pennsylvania Infantry saw the men whom the Rebels 'pulled out' of the ranks. He later wrote: 'I shall never forget the look of hopeless despair deputed on the countenances of those thus picked out.'*"
[19]

Subsequently, on April 24, 1864, at the Spring Green Church area of Hamilton, the six "Buffaloes" were hanged from trees by the roadside *"without even the ceremony of a drum-head court-martial."* [20]. According to Harry Thompson, curator of Port-O-Plymouth Museum, grave markers indicate the spot where the executed "Buffaloes" were buried.

★ ★ ★ ★

The name "Buffalo" originally had been applied to men specifically in the First and Second North Carolina Union regiments, the majority hailing from neighboring Bertie County. Soon afterwards, though, the derogatory appellation began being applied to any North Carolinian who had exchanged his Rebel cadet-gray for Yankee blue, regardless of where his home was located in the state. However, by the time of the battle at Plymouth in 1864, the term was being bestowed on any native North Carolinian with leanings toward the Union.

Just who then, were the men who became "Buffaloes?" One analysis was that they were mostly small non-slave holding farmers, fishermen, and artisans whose homes were in northeastern North Carolina. Generally illiterate, not only were they disdained by their southern neighbors, but they were scorned also by the northerners who called them "yokels" and "riff-raff." [21] Lieutenant Commander Charles Flusser commented that they were *"the strangest people in the world."* [22] Even so, the Federal officers would rather see those "country boys" who were such excellent shots serving on the Yankee side of the war. After the "Buffaloes" had determined that for them there was no advantage in serving the Confederacy, they decided to take their chances with the Federals who steadily were penetrating deeper and deeper into eastern North Carolina.

Additional explanations have been offered for the use of the term "Buffalo." John A. Hedrick, a port collector from Beaufort, North Carolina, suggested that the light blue pants and dark blue coats and caps made the soldiers appear so large that people began dubbing them "Buffaloes." *"They go around in gangs like herds of buffaloes."* He also added that he thought the men rather favored the appellation, even though used in a derogatory manner by the Confederates. [23]

In another context, a Raleigh newspaper in January of 1865 referred to Millard Fillmore's supporters in eastern North Carolina as "Buffalo Know Nothings." [24] Still others suggested that the name originally might have been attributed to a roisterous young Rebel deserter John Fairless, said to be *"as hard to rope as a wild buffalo."*

Having deserted from the Confederate Army, Fairless assumed command of Company E, First Regiment North Carolina Union Volunteers. With his motley group of marauders he roamed all over North Carolina, pillaging, burning, and wreaking havoc. In addition, his men informed slaves that they were free to leave the plantations and their masters. Consequently, "Buffaloes" were blamed for much of the vindictive violence inflicted upon their Rebel neighbors and so as local Unionists, they were held in the greatest of contempt.

★★★★

On Monday the 25th, after traveling "up country" to the bank of the Tar River, the Yankee prisoners bivouacked in sight of the Tarboro Bridge. There the Rebels provided a small kettle and some water for each prisoner to prepare his unappetizing meal consisting of a small supply of corn and small red cowpeas. The Yankees were not accustomed to such fare and so their digestive systems were disrupted terribly. Charlie Mosher called it "rank grub."

All week long until Friday the miserable Yankees remained corralled in the same spot where there was no sanitation and nothing at all provided to shield them from the elements. Charlie Mosher noted that out of curiosity *"the ladies of the place came out to see the 'yanks,' and said, 'What did you'uns come down here to fight we'uns for? You'uns critter backs.'* [25]

Sergeant Julian Wheaton Merrill, 24th NY Independent Battery Light Artillery, wrote the following letter to his father who resided in Perry, New York.

Tarboro
April 27th 1864

My dear father,

I was taken prisoner at Plymouth a week ago today, have marched over land sixty five miles, been here two days, stood the march capitally, am very well and hope to get out before long. May go to Americus, Georgia, to day. Shall keep up good spirits. Do you and mother and my dear sisters the same.

> *I am in the hands of a kind Providence who will protect me and if it is best will carry me through it all.*
>
> *I have plenty to eat & to drink. My clothing is warm & comfortable. I had on my working suit and it was all I saved. If I live to see you I shall have a long story to tell you.*
>
> *Your loving son,*
>
> *J. W. Merrill* [26]

However, the son was not telling the entire truth in his letter, as B. Conrad Bush, present historian of the 24th N.Y. Battery, explains:

> *"He fell out of the line of march and was helped by Hiram Buckingham, Quarter Master Sergeant with the 16th Conn. Infantry. Merrill was suffering from a rupture he had received in a fall from a horse shortly before as well as being ill with malaria and diarrhea. Buckingham had never met Julian before and befriended him and remained his tent mate (without the tent) until he got to Andersonville. This most probably saved his life. Julian's ability to make friends and his education would serve him well during his prison life."* [27]

The last sentence is substantiated in a deposition that was be written by a compassionate Confederate doctor, G. G. Roy, M.D., after the war had ended:

> *"...I was placed in charge of the enclosure known as prison hospital. There and then in the summer of 1864 I first met J. W. Merrill, a Federal prisoner, the beneficiary in this claim.*
>
> *In my efforts to organize a hospital corps I endeavored to select the most intelligent and trustworthy men I could get. I was struck with Merrill's appearance as an educated gentleman and more so with his enfeebled condition and wishing to lighten his burden and give him better sanitary surroundings, I asked him if he could fill the position of Chief Clerk. He said he would gladly undertake it.*
>
> *In this way I was thrown in daily contact with him and he gained my confidence & respect by the faithful efforts he made to discharge his duties and did discharge them as far as he was physically able. But he was then almost a physical wreck, from Rheumatism and Chronic Diarrhoea contracted in service and from that terrible Malarial fever which carried off so many at Andersonville. Besides these troubles he was ruptured while in service from which he suffered much as he could not get a suitable truss. His present condition in my judgement is due to diseases & injury received while in the service of the United States as a soldier and the late war...."* [28]

Finally, early on the morning of April 29th, the Federal prisoners were ordered to line up for the short march to the Tarboro railroad depot. Robert Black of the 103rd Pennsylvania Volunteers submitted to the *National Tribune Veterans Newspaper* the following amusing incident that had happened on the way to boarding the train:

> "*I recall that when passing on foot near Tarboro, N.C., a big, frowzy–headed woman, with a dozen or so of equally frowzy children about her, asked one of our guards where our ' horns' were. She had always believed the Yankees had horns, and was surprised to see we had none...*" (29)

When the battle began on the 17th, the Pennsylvania regiments had been attired in their dress uniforms and so were wearing the detested "Hardee" hats they had received new at the beginning of the year. The men much preferred their blue "kepis." The dress hats caused the Yankee soldiers to very much resemble the Massachusetts Mayflower Pilgrims of old. Consequently, when marching in formation through Tarboro on their way to board a southbound train, the soldiers were dubbed "Plymouth Pilgrims" by the curious townsfolk who gathered in a circus atmosphere to get a good look at the defeated Yankees.

The *Charleston Mercury* in South Carolina on April 26, 1864 was the first to put into print that appellation for the Yankee prisoners:

> "*THE PLYMOUTH PILGRIMS—We learn that the 2500 Yankee prisoners, captured by General Hoke's forces at Plymouth, left Wilmington last night, and may be expected to pass through Charleston this evening, on their way to the Prison Depot at Americus, Ga.*" (30)

Another explanation for the nickname came from Captain David Mullin, Co. G of the 101st Pennsylvania Volunteers. He said that as the defeated Yankees at Plymouth were marching single file to stack their arms, to the observant Confederates the slow and somber gait of the defeated Yankees was reminiscent of the Pilgrims of Plymouth, Massachusetts, on the way to church to present their monetary offerings. The Yankee offerings, however, were their precious rifles.

*Fig. 38. **A Plymouth Pilgrim in his Hardee hat***
"Andersonville, A Story of Confederate Military Prisons"

By the 50's and 60's the prisoners of war were herded into two-door fetid boxcars previously used for transporting cattle. First, after stopping at Goldsboro for rations consisting of three crackers and a small piece of bacon, the Yankees continued on to Wilmington where they crossed the Cape Fear River on ferryboats. Corralled again in oppressive boxcars, the Yankee prisoners arrived in Charleston, South Carolina, on Sunday, May 1st. Then, after only a few hours, they were forced once again to board another southbound train. That time, however, they were being transported on flatbeds open to intense heat and drenching rain as they traveled through the Georgia cities of Savannah and Macon. Unbeknown to the Yankees, they were on their way to Camp Sumter where the most infamous Confederate prison, Andersonville, was located: a lamentable stockade where during fourteen months nearly 50,000 pitiful Yankee prisoners would be crowded.

On the night of May 2nd between the hours of 9 and 10, the Yankee prisoners finally arrived at their destination. Totally exhausted by then, the men lay on the hard ground outside of the stockade to sleep. Among them was "the company of brothers," Co. D. of the 101st Pennsylvania Volunteers, that included the twenty-seven year old fraternal twins, Isaac and Abraham Rice, and three sets of Hanks brothers who were first cousins, being the sons of three brothers. [31]

The next morning the already incarcerated John McElroy, Co. C of the 16th Illinois Cavalry, described the incredible sight of the four hundred well-dressed "Plymouth Pilgrims" entering the Andersonville stockade through the open gates:

> "They were attired in stylish new uniforms, with fancy hats and shoes; the Sergeants and Corporals wore patent leather or silk chevrons, and each man had a large well-filled knapsack, of the kind new recruits usually carried on coming first to the front, and which the older soldiers spoke of humorously as 'bureaus.' They were the snuggest, nattiest lot of soldiers we had ever seen, outside of the 'paper collar' fellows forming the headquarter guard of some General in a large city. As one of my companions surveyed them, he said: 'Hulloa! I'm blanked if the Jonnies haven't caught a regiment of Brigadier Generals, somewhere.'" [32]

Soon, however, the cockiness of the "Plymouth Pilgrims" disintegrated as their eyes opened in sudden shock at viewing the inside of the stockade where not a tree was standing. Nothing at all was provided for shelter, only the makeshift "shebangs" [33] the prisoners had constructed with sticks, torn blankets, and rags. Captives were crowded haphazardly. Cleanliness and sanitation were nonexistent.

During Andersonville's fourteen lamentable months of existence, 49,484 captured enlisted Federals would be transported there. A number close to 13,000 would not survive their captivity due to diarrhea and dehydration, dysentery and typhoid fever, malaria and yellow fever, measles and smallpox, tuberculosis and pneumonia, scurvy, bronchitis, gastro-intestinal parasites, or simply from the ravages of starvation.

One of the "Plymouth Pilgrims" to succumb at Andersonville was Private Newton Leonard of Co. H, Second Massachusetts Heavy Artillery. His name is being recollected here because of the unique fact that his wife Margaret had accompanied him to the Andersonville Prison. [34]

Two 101st Pennsylvania "Pilgrims" were the twenty-seven year old fraternal twins Alexander and Isaac Rice, both fortunate enough to survive Andersonville. However, after they were transferred to Charleston, Isaac died on September 21, 1864, and was buried in the National Cemetery in Beaufort, South Carolina.

Other captives surviving the horrendous ordeal to tell their stories were Luther Dickey of the 103rd Pennsylvania Infantry and Charles Mosher of the 85th New York Infantry. The detailed diary kept by Mosher has proven invaluable, particularly the record of the 315 days he spent in captivity at Andersonville,

Silas G. Burdick, a member of the 85th N.Y., in later years became a member of the Dedication Commission for the monument erected at Andersonville by the state of New York. In 1914 Burdick stated in a dedication speech that of the 463 soldiers of his regiment who had entered Andersonville, 311 died, the largest number from any regiment. [35]

In the preface of the *History of the 103rd Regiment; Pennsylvania Veteran Volunteer Infantry 1861-1865*, Corporal Luther Dickey explained to readers why he felt compelled to write about his regiment:

> "With few exceptions no Pa. regiments have records less complete than the 103rd. Its regimental and company records were twice completely lost in battle, and under circumstances that made it impossible to have them fully replaced. The writer has spared no pains to get authentic histories of the various companies of the Regiment by correspondence with surviving members, writing to every one whose address he had." [36]

Not only were most of the 103rd's records lost by accident, General Wessells deliberately burned many of his papers so the Confederates would not be able to determine which "Buffaloes" had assumed Yankee names. So because of the lack of concrete evidence, two deaths sometimes were recorded for the same person: one presumed death at the Battle of Plymouth, but later recorded as dying at Andersonville Prison. [37]

Alonzo Cooper wrote about the officers' arrival at the Macon Prison:

> "Upon the arrival of new prisoners at the gate of the stockade, there would be a cry raised throughout the camp, commencing near the entrance, and spreading rapidly to the farthest extremity of the enclosure, of 'Fresh fish! Fresh fish!!' It was like the alarm of a fire in a city, and quickly collected a crowd, and as the numbers increased, the din became more deafening, and to the new comer who did not know what it meant, perfectly appalling
>
> I have seen prisoners come in who looked perfectly bewildered as they gazed upon the mob of ragged, shoeless, hatless, unshaven, long-haired, howling beings who confronted them, looking more like escaped lunatics than officers; when some one back in the crowd would sing out, give the gentleman air, don't take his haversack, keep your hands out of his pocket, don't put that louse on him, why don't some of you fellows take the gentleman's baggage, and show him to his room, Johnny show the gentleman up to No. 13." (38)

On March 9, 1864 General Ulysses Simpson Grant was commissioned lieutenant-general and assigned the command of the armies of the United States. Immediately he determined to make the Army of the Potomac his headquarters. One of his reasons was because he considered the Rebel force opposing the Army of the Potomac "...the strongest, the best led, and the best appointed" army in the Confederate service. (39)

One of Grant's very first policies was to have a disastrous impact upon the "Plymouth Pilgrims." He believed that the exchange of prisoners to that time had been a decided benefit to the Confederacy and not to the Union, claiming that upon release the Rebels were in good enough physical condition to immediately return to their posts. He felt that Yankee ex-prisoners of war often were too debilitated from the poor treatment they had received in Confederate prison camps to be able to rejoin their units promptly. Furthermore, he maintained that future exchanges during the campaigns of 1864 might possibly endanger General William Tecumseh Sherman's destructive and devastating march from Chattanooga, Tennessee eastward to Savannah, Georgia. (40)

The other problem with the exchange was the status of the colored soldiers. General Butler, a commissioner for exchange, determined that colored captives should receive the same treatment from the Confederacy as was given to white soldiers. Such an idea was refused by the Confederacy. Later, after General Grant had studied the problem thoroughly, he sent General Butler the following stongly worded message:

> "...No distinction whatever will be made in the exchange between white and colored prisoners; the only question being were they at the time of capture in the military service of the United States. If they were, the same terms as to treatment

while prisoners and conditions of release and exchange must be executed and had in the case of colored soldiers as of white soldiers. Non acquience by the Confederate authorities will be regarded as refusal to further exchange and will be so treated by us." [41]

On April 14, 1864, just four days before the Battle of Plymouth, Secretary Edwin Stanton had submitted a report to General Grant from General Butler who was concerned about the negotiation regulations with Robert Ould, the Confederate commissioner of exchange. Stanton requested that Grant send explicit instructions to Butler. Subsequently, Grant wired Butler: *"Until examined by me, and my orders thereon are received by you, decline all further negotiations."* [42]

Ironically, on April 20th, the very day of the Yankees' defeat at Plymouth, North Carolina, General Butler telegraphed General Grant:

"Instructions in regard to exchange of prisoners received and will be implicitly followed. I assume, however, that they are not intended to interfere with the special exchanges of sick and wounded prisoners on one side and the other now going on." [43]

General Grant's explicit reply was: *"Receive all the sick and wounded the Confederate authorities will send you, but send no more in exchange."* [44] So for the ill-fated "Plymouth Pilgrims" about to enter the deplorable Andersonville Prison, there was no hope for exchange. Instead intense heat, inadequate food, poor medical care, and disease would take the lives of 12,912 Yankee prisoners of war. [45]

Many wives, mothers, sisters, and even the sweethearts of missing soldiers chose to wear the black of mourning until their loved ones returned. Many, however, were to wait in vain. Among the relatives of the captive Yankees, exchange was a constant topic, and so numerous appeals were made to the Federal Government.

Likewise at Andersonville Prison, the subject of exchange was constant among the Yankees being held captive there. In August 1864, a committee was formed from the Union sergeants in charge of distributing daily rations. The committee's purpose was to convey an appeal to Washington for the reestablishment of prisoner exchange. Not in favor of the government's stand on exchange, the committee was in favor of adopting a cartel of exchange that would not consider the plight of the "Col'd" soldiers who had been captured. [46]

However, the 16th Connecticut Volunteers Regiment was not in agreement, maintaining that *"the negro soldiers in prison were entitled to the same consideration that was given to the white soldiers."* Outspoken twenty-one-year-old Sergeant Richard H. Lee of Co. E led the Connecticut men in forming their opinion, maintaining that the

United States Government was bound to protect *"the negroes as soldiers of the Union Army."* (47)

A number of other Yankees were not in agreement with the committee, either. They did not believe the prisoners of war should be pleading for exchange. Charlie Mosher of the 85th New York was one; for on July 20, 1864, he recorded in his diary:

"There is a good deal of excitement in here now about getting up a petition to our government, asking help [to] get us out of here. I think it shows a weak head and a cowardly crew. But I suppose they want to go home. Can't blame them for that. I want to go to [too], but I won't whine nor sign a paper." (48)

The delegation left Andersonville Prison intending to reach President Lincoln with an appeal for exchange. After being delayed several times before reaching Union lines, one delegate finally arrived at Hilton Head, South Carolina where he made an affidavit before Provost Marshall Hall on August 19, 1864, concerning the treatment of the Andersonville prisoners. Whether the information ever got to President Lincoln is not known. The last news heard about the delegation was in a statement dated August 19, 1864, asserting that four of the delegates had been exchanged and ordered back to their regiments. (49)

On October 1, 1864 General Robert E. Lee sent a proposition to General Ulysses Grant for a "man for man" exchange of prisoners belonging to the armies operating in Virginia. General Grant's reply was that he would agree to such an exchange of prisoners captured within the last three days and that should include black soldiers, as well. General Lee readily agreed to include all captured Federal soldiers under his control. However, known deserters from the Confederacy and Negroes belonging to Confederate citizens definitely would not be considered.

General Grant's prompt reply on the very same day was *"that the United States government was bound to secure to all persons received into its armies the rights due soldiers... This being denied by you, in the persons of such men as have escaped from Southern masters induces me to decline making the exchange."* (50) He was never to yield from that position.

However, the Confederacy was running out of space and resources to be able to continue taking care of prisoners of war. Therefore, enlisted men would be paroled if they would take the following oath:

"To The Authorities of the Confederate States of America:

We do solemnly swear we will not bear arms against the Confederate States of America, nor in any way give aid and comfort to the United States against the Confederate States, during the existence of the war between the said United States and Confederate States, unless we shall be duly exchanged for other prisoners of war, or until we shall be released by the President of the Confederate States. In consideration of this oath, it is understood that we are free to go whereever we may see fit." [51]

★ ★ ★ ★

Finally, on October 15, 1864 General Grant was given full authority to take steps to exchange prisoners. The first to exit Rebel prisons were officers released from Florence, South Carolina. The last to leave on April 28, 1865 would be those incarcerated in Andersonville, Georgia, with less than 4,000 prisoners making the exodus from the stockade

Twenty three-year-old emaciated and ill Robert J. Holmes, a musician in the 16th Connecticut Volunteers band, had been paroled on December 11, 1864, and, subsequently sent to Camp Parole in Annapolis, Maryland. The poet Walt Whitman was working there as a nurse. His observation about the returning prisoners of war was that "*probably no more appalling sight was ever seen on this earth.*" [52]

Another of the fortunate Yankees to be exchanged due to debilitating illness was Sergeant Julian Wheaton Merrill of the 24th N.Y. Independent Battery Light Artillery. He had survived seven months interment at Andersonville Prison, most likely due to the consideration of the kindly Confederate surgeon, Dr. G. G. Roy, a graduate of Virginia University and the Jefferson Medical College in Philadelphia, Pennsylvania. [53]

From Charleston Harbor Sergeant Merrill on December 8, 1864 wrote the following to the Editor of the *New Yorker*

"*...All the descriptions of horror and suffering that the Northern daily papers have furnished, are true. It is almost impossible to exaggerate statements concerning the treatment of prisoners incarcerated in their black and filthy pens. Men have died there at the rate of a hundred a day for a month at a time--their causes diagnosed "Chronic Diarrhea and Scurvy,"--which, truly defined, means "Exposure and Starvation."*

These words have a terrible meaning, and I know it--and know, too, what I say. I have seen men die from want of food and from want of clothing and covering to protect their emaciated bodies from the chilly, frosty atmosphere of the Autumn nights. We lived in an atmosphere of death. Men fell away like sheep with rot.

The Hospital was crowded. A hundred sick went in per day. A hundred dead went out. Medicine (the little that was furnished) was of no avail. The cry was for food. They responded only with promises. Their daily ration was half a pint of gruel, half pint of cooked rice, and a quarter of a loaf of corn bread-if I may be allowed so to title that unpalatable, indigestible conglomeration of corn cobs, corn husks, dirt, flies, &c. The rebel Surgeons, themselves in their official daily reports as "Officers of the day," complained bitterly of the diet, and appealed for a reform; but the higher authorities either for the sake of gain or for the want of humanity, refused to change or improve it..." [54]

A Waterloo, New York man not fortunate enough to return to his home was 3rd Sergeant Wyman Johnson. One hundred years after the Civil War on September 21, 1964, he was remembered still due to a bronze plaque being placed on a very special tree.

"Specie- Balm of Gilead

During the Civil War, James Wyman Johnson came from the field one morning, hung his scythe in the crotch of a small tree and said, 'Leave this scythe in the tree until I return.' He enlisted in the Union Army, Company G, 85th N.Y. Volunteers on October 29, 1861. He died from wounds received at Plymouth, N.C. in 1864.

His parents, refusing to believe the report, left the scythe in the tree where it remains today completely enveloped..." [55]

The Commandant of the hellish camp at Andersonville was Captain Henry Wirz, a native of Zurich, Switzerland. By profession a physician, he was a blustery man prone to profanity. Having enlisted in Louisiana as a private, Wirz served with the Confederate Army as an *aide-de-camp* to General Joseph Johnston. After his right arm was shattered at the Battle of Seven Pines, Virginia, Wirz was assigned the command of a prison at Tuscalossa, Alabama and later granted a leave of absence in order to regain his failing health. Upon returning to duty on March 27, 1864, he assumed the command of the deplorable Andersonville Prison. [56]

Three months later he submitted the following report concerning conditions at Andersonville:

Headquarters Commandant of Prison
Camp Sumter, Andersonville, Ga., June 6, 1864

Capt. H. D. Chapman, Acting Adjutant of Post:

I most respectfully call the attention of the colonel commanding post through you to the following facts: The bread which is issued to prisoners is of such an inferior quality, consisting fully of one sixth husk, that it is almost unfit for use and increasing dysentery and other bowel complaints. I would wish the commissary of the post be notified to have the meal bolted or some other contrivance arranged to sift the meal before issuing. If the meal, such as is now, was sifted the bread rations would fall short fully one-quarter of a pound.

There is a great deficiency of buckets. Rations of rice, beans, vinegar, and molasses cannot be issued to prisoners for want of buckets, at least 8,000 men in the stockade being without anything of the sort. If my information is correct, any number of buckets can be got from Columbus, Ga. if the quartermaster of the post would make the requisition for the same. Hoping that you will give this your attention as soon as possible, I remain,

H. WIRZ, Captain Commanding Prison[57]

Fig. 39. **Captain Henry Wirz, CSA**

After the war had ended, when Nurse Clara Barton visited Andersonville to have the dead identified and properly buried, she became outraged at what she beheld there. In righteous indignation she attempted to testify against Henry Wirz at his trial, but was not allowed to do so because of her gender. [58] Even without Clara Barton's testimony, though, Wirz was held responsible for the lamentable conditions at the prison that led to 12,912 deaths. Wirz, however, insisted that he was innocent. Regardless of his protestations, the United States Government declared him guilty.

The only Confederate officer executed for war crimes, Henry Wirz was hanged on November 10, 1865 before an audience of two hundred in the Old Capitol prison yard in Washington, D.C. The charges were: *"combining, confederating and conspiring—to injure the health and destroy the lives of soldiers in the military service of the United States, then held and being prisoners of war, and---murder in violation of the laws and customs of war."* [59]

For many years the controversy over whether he should have been convicted and executed have lived on. The question was and still is whether or not Captain Henry Wirz had been used as a scapegoat. According to Alan Marsh, Cultural Curator Specialist, Andersonville Historic Prison Site in 2003, there are those today, even, who feel that since someone had to be blamed for the atrocities at the prison, Wirz was the most obvious target.

"Whether the terrible conditions were a result of incompetence, circumstances, or cruelty, those who had suffered at Andersonville blames Captain Wirz and felt that his command had been a 'crime against humanity.' Citizens in the North wanted and expected revenge." [60]

Luther Dickey wrote that the total number of Yankees confined at Andersonville Prison from the date it had been established during the last week of February 1864 until the war ended was 45,613, of whom 12,912 perished and were buried there. [61]

Chapter 23

ESCAPEES FROM REBEL PRISONS

Several soldiers from the regiments garrisoned at Plymouth, North Carolina, by twists of fate were saved from participating in the battle. For instance, some weeks prior to the battle, Sergeant William S. Camp and Corporal S. A. Stoddard of the 24th New York Battery had left Plymouth journeying to Washington, D.C. They went to the capitol to take an examination to determine their fitness for receiving commissions to lead black troops. However, upon arrival they were disappointed to learn that Major General Silas Casey's Board of Examination was not granting commissions in artillery; therefore, they were ordered to return immediately to their company at Plymouth.

Expecting to board a boat at Norfolk, Virginia, for the trip through the Chesapeake and Albemarle Canal, the two men, however, arrived too late, for their boat already had departed. Consequently, they were forced to wait at Norfolk for the next southern-bound vessel scheduled to leave on Sunday, April 17th. Instead of sailing to their original destination, they were taken to Roanoke Island where they were learned about the catastrophe at Plymouth. [1] If William Camp and S. A. Stoddard had not missed their boat, and if perchance they had survived the four-day battle at Plymouth, they, too, would have been captured on the 20th to be taken to Andersonville Prison along with their unfortunate comrades.

Another lucky Yankee was Francis M. Alburty, also of the 24th New York Battery. He was delayed by illness from returning to Plymouth after members of his regiment had been granted their veteran furlough, [2] veterans being those soldiers who had re-enlisted on January 1, 1864.

In another twist of fate, one company of the 16th Connecticut Volunteers led by Captain Joseph Barnum was sent to Roanoke Island on the morning of April 17th, just hours before the battle erupted. As well as those lucky soldiers, another from Connecticut fortunate to escape the battle at Plymouth was Sergeant John Gemmill of Co. A. Having been on recruiting service in Hartford, he was on Roanoke Island, preparing to return to his regiment at Plymouth the very next day. [3]

Among the unlucky captives were twenty-five men who had been transferred to the 85th New York Infantry from the 16th New York Battery just a week before the battle. On April 15th Charlie Mosher had mentioned them in his diary:

"...Capt. Aldrich of our company, Lieut. Fay of F Co. and Capt. Cartwright of Company I came in from recruiting service and in nearly 100 new men. I feel sorry for them, they are so green." [4]

Among the Yankees captured at Plymouth, many were to die within just days of their arrival at the Rebel prisons. However, some, even with emaciated bodies, merely walking skeletons, persevered to survive until the end of the war. Unfortunately, only five of those unlucky men transferred to the 85th survived the ravages of prison life. [5]

Still others refused to accept their lot as prisoners of war, all of the time planning and plotting until they were able to make their escape. A small number of officers were successful in reaching Federal lines while others, unfortunately, were caught and remanded once again to their living nightmare.

One successful escapee was Lieutenant John A. Lafler of the 85th New York Infantry, the great-grandfather of the present day historian of the regiment, John Ball. During the battle of Plymouth, Lieutenant Lafler acted as company commander before being captured when Fort Wessells fell. Provided with rations expected by the captors to last the captives four days (a pound of pork and forty hardtack crackers), he dejectedly marched out of Plymouth with the other prisoners of war. [6]

Because they had not wanted to incarcerate the officers with the men of the ranks, a problem arose for the Confederates. For when the train made its frequent stops for rations and water at Wilmington, North Carolina; Charleston, South Carolina; Savannah and Macon, Georgia, the guards were unable to find cooperative authorities willing to take the Yankee officers. Therefore, a number of officers, including Lieutenant John Lafler, accompanied their men for the ride south. [7]

Two ironical incidents occurred while the prisoners were en route to their final destination—Andersonville Prison. One was that the 85th New York crossed a repaired bridge previously burned by them in 1862. The second was, that to the shock and consternation of the Yankees, the Confederate railroad engineer had been born in Penn Yan, New York, the very same northern town in which Lieutenant John Lafler and some of the others had enlisted into the Union Army. [8]

Upon arriving at Andersonville, the Plymouth Pilgrims were informed by Captain Wirz, the commandant, that he had no facilities for the officers. Consequently, Lieutenant John Lafler with the other officers were taken to Camp Oglethorpe in Macon, Georgia, another lamentable prison where over fifteen hundred Federal officers eventually would be incarcerated.

As would future prisoners of war in German stalags of World War II, the officers were determined to escape by tunneling out of Camp Oglethorpe. They were spurred on by a story related by prisoners arriving from Libby Prison in Richmond.

From there one hundred and nine prisoners had escaped on February 3, 1864, with fifty-nine successfully reaching the safety of Union lines. [9]

Lieutenant George Hastings described how the Yankee prisoners attempted to escape:

"...Tunnels were dug again and again, but were uniformly discovered before completion,--as the axes and shovels were removed from camp before night, our mining companies were obliged to resort to primitive inventions. The tunnels were generally commenced from 12 to 20 feet inside the dead line [10] under some bank. A hole about three feet square and five feet in depth was first dug and then the underground work commenced. The work was done by means of a hinge or knife; a pan with cord attached being used to remove the earth to the opening, where it was emptied into haversacks and carried to the sinks or into the main building.

This process was of course painfully slow and laborious. As the work proceeded the air became damp and foul, and it was impossible for the person digging to remain in the tunnel for upwards of half an hour. From three to six feet a night might be the usual advance in these excavations. During the day these tunnels would be carefully closed and could be discerned only by the most minute examination.

At one time four were in progress, varying from 20 to 80 feet in length. Just as one of these was completed and tunnel stock commanded a premium, the rebels discovered them, capturing and confiscating the valuable machinery. Tunnels were declared unconstitutional and subversive of Southern Institutions, and a full excommunication pronounced against those who had the temerity to dig. The result was renewed attempts with stricter precautions, but Rebel vigilance was an overmatch for Yankee cunning in this particular. [11]

Lieutenant John A. Lafler's story is not of just a single attempt at escape, but of four. The first three unsuccessful, he was returned to prison thrice. Undaunted, however, he continued trying until finally he met success.

"You cannot imagine what joy filled our bosoms as we thought of being free men once more, after suffering and enduring almost everything except death while in the hands of the Rebels." [12]

As one reads of Lieutenant John Lafler's attempts at escape from Rebel held territory, certain parallels emerge between the desperate flight for freedom of a white Yankee POW and that of a fugitive slave. Similarities include being directed by total strangers sympathetic to the escapee's cause, being secreted in woods, barns, sheds, and root cellars during the day where they were nourished and protected, and even to being guided by the stationary North Star as they ran at night. [13]

White "conductors" on the Underground Railroad were willing to risk their reputations and some even their lives to aid fugitive blacks. One such "conductor" was James Fulton whose nephew, William Fulton, was in Co. F of the 103rd Pennsylvania Volunteers garrisoned at Plymouth, North Carolina. James Fulton, a staunch abolitionist, was a member of the Associated Seceder Church, a branch of Presbyterians. Even though being aware that the penalty for helping runaways was the astronomical fee of $1000 and six months in jail, from 1847 to 1855 he had taken the risk with other ministers of his denomination. They passed two to seven men at a time along the Railroad from Virginia and north to Lake Erie where they could cross the border into Canada. [14]

Private William Allison Fulton, ancestor of the present day 103rd Pennsylvania historian Ruth Fulton, however, was not one of the lucky escapees from the Rebel prisons in Andersonville, Charleston, or Florence. The men most able to escape were officers confined in the less fortified prisons. Due to ill health, Fulton was paroled on February 27, 1865 at Northeast Ferry, moved to the hospital at Annapolis, Maryland, and finally to Jarvis Hospital in Baltimore where he remained until his discharge. [15].

★ ★ ★ ★

Seemingly, many blacks still in bondage, as well as those having been manumitted, were willing to risk their lives for the "saviors from the North." On March 25, 1864, when writing a letter home, Joseph E. Fiske of the 2nd Massachusetts Heavy Artillery garrisoned at Fort Gray, Plymouth, had stated:

"...I wish you could be here when some of the refugees and escaped prisoners come in. Four came in a few days since who had escaped from the cars while on the way to Georgia from Richmond. They were a whole fortnight in the woods and, what is now agreed upon by all, they testified that every negro they saw was faithful to them, that when they found they were Union soldiers they would feed them and conceal them, act as their guides and risk their lives for them..." [16]

In his memoirs Lieutenant John A. Lafler of the 85th New York Volunteers described the aid he had received from blacks while making four different attempts at escape:

"Soon after we came onto the road in the evening, we met a Negro with a bag of corn on his back. We soon learned he was a friend to Yankees. He took us to his home and made a fire for us to sit by while they prepared some corn bread and sweet potatoes for us.

We got a good supply of rations and were ready to start again about two o'clock. He went with us about two miles to a secluded place where he thought we could remain in safety until the next night. We did not get much sleep as we needed to keep moving to keep warm.

After dark the Negroes came and brought us some rations. One of them went with us about two miles to assist us in finding the right road. Here we stopped at a house occupied by Negroes who were very kind to us—some of them acting as pickets while we warmed ourselves..."[17]

Later Lieutenant Lafter wrote of another similar incident occurring during another one of his attempts to reach Union lines:

"*...We discovered some Negroes at work in a mill and, after some difficulty, we succeeded in calling the attention of one of them who came to our assistance. He informed us that his wife lived on the other side of the river and that he was allowed to go and see her occasionally. He had a canoe at the river which he used to carry himself across. He told us to come to the mill after dark. He would meet us there and convey us across the river in his canoe...*"[18]

On his final attempt to reach the Federals, Lieutenant Lafter described the following assistance he had received:

"*...We had some difficulty in finding the road as the night was very dark and cloudy and we were unable to direct our course by the stars. After we had walked a few miles we called on some Negroes who informed us that we were going too far south. They advised us to wait until the next night when they would direct us to the road. In the meantime, they would procure some rations for us.*

We secreted ourselves in the woods until the following evening when we came to the house of our colored friends again. After receiving our rations, we started with one of the Negroes who acted as our guide."[19]

Fig. 40. **Lieut. John Lafter**
*(age 54 in 1895
Courtesy of John Ball*

Some other escaping Yankees related similar stories, as well. For instance, Captain Langworthy and Captain Aldrich of the 24th New York Battery credited their success to the assistance they had received from Negro slaves. [20]

★ ★ ★ ★

According to Captain George Hastings of the 24th New York Battery, the Rebel vigilance was so good that even though many officers escaped the stockade at Macon, Georgia in the guise of laborers or in gray jackets fashioned from blankets, only one escape actually succeeded in reaching the Union lines. [21] However, more officers were able to make their escape from Camp Sorghum, Columbia, South Carolina, than from any other prison. One officer was Captain Hastings, who escaped on October 10, 1864, after he had been moved from Macon to Columbia. [22] Nearly four hundred other Yankee officers were as successful, and perhaps more would have been if they had adequate footgear. [23]

Captain John Donaghy of the 103rd Pennsylvania Volunteers described his successful escape from Camp Sorghum.

"Before it was quite dark we tied up and went on another hunt for food. Two miles from the river we saw a house, and making a detour came to negro quarters. I crept up to one of the buildings just as a woman came out with a blazing torch in her hand. Not wishing to stand in its bright glare, I walked into the house before I spoke to her. She turned and surveyed me with a look of distrust till I uttered the magic words, 'I am a Yankee.'

Her manner changed at once, and pushing an old arm chair before the fire, said, 'Sit down, Massa; you shall have the best in the house.' She went out, promising to soon return and I brought in my companions. While we were waiting for her we could not help thinking she might betray us, but she returned, bringing with her men, women and children, and their friendly manner banished all doubt. They gave us a supper of sweet potatoes and hoe cake..." [24]

Captain L. A. Cady of the 24th New York Battery escaped while en route from Charleston to Columbia. He finally reached the Union lines at Strawberry Plains in East Tennessee, sixteen miles east of Knoxville, but his health was so impaired from traversing the difficult southern swamps, forests, and mountains that, unfortunately, he died very soon after the war ended.

Luther Dickey recorded other Plymouth Pilgrim officers also making successful escapes from Rebel prisons:

Capt. Adams	85th New York Volunteers
Capt. Alvin Alexander, Co. A	103rdPennsylvania Volunteers
R. G. Beggs, Co. A	103rd Pennsylvania Volunteers

Capt. Alphonzo Cartwright, Co.	85th New York Volunteers
James Cooper, Co.A	103rd Pennsylvania Volunteers
Capt. Eli Cratty	103rd Pennsylvania Volunteers
Norval D. Goe, Co. A	103rd Pennsylvania Volunteers
Daniel Huddleson, Co. H	103rd Pennsylvania Volunteers
Lieut. W. H. Kiester, Co. I	103rd Pennsylvania Volunteers
Peter Klingler, Co., H	103rd Pennsylvania Volunteers
Serg't Daniel Krug, Co. K	103rd Pennsylvania Volunteers
Capt. James Morrow	103rd Pennsylvania Volunteers
Lieut. Pierson	85th New York Volunteers
Lieut. George Pitt, Co. E	85th New York Volunteers
Robert Reardon, Co. H	103rd Pennsylvania Volunteers
Corp. John F, Rupert, Co. A	103rd Pennsylvania Volunteers
John Hilbert, Co. I	103rd PennsylvaniaVolunteers
George Shaffer, Co. H	103rd Pennsylvania Volunteers
Lieut. Terwilliger, Co D	85th New York Volunteers [25]

Charlie Mosher included in his diary a report stating that during the month of August 1864, thirty men successfully escaped from Andersonville Prison. Eleven left while on "parole of honor." Even though they had sworn not to attempt escape while working outside the stockade, when the opportunity presented itself, they could not resist taking it. The other nineteen bribed the sentinel with greenbacks, while still others walked off at night when they were returning tools. During that particular month, more prisoners attempted escape, but were caught by vicious baying, bloodhounds. [26]

During his escape, Captain Aldrich lost his diary in which the names of those escaping were listed, as well as all of the events occurring since the escape. Found and returned to the Columbia prison, it was used as a deterrent against any future escapes. At roll call the officer in charge informed the remaining prisoners that the five men who had made their escapes on October 3rd had been found. He concluded his intimidation by saying that since the Yankees had refused to surrender, they all had been shot and killed.

Of course, the successful escapees knew nothing at all about the fabrication until after the war had ended. Captain Langworthy who had escaped with Captain Aldrich would write about a paroled lieutenant who had wanted to pay his respects to Captain Langworthy's bereaved family. What a pleasant shock the young man received when greeted by the captain himself, who had no idea that he was supposed to be dead. [27]

Fig. 41. **Officer escapees from Columbia, Georgia Prison**
*Left to right: Lieut. Terwilliger, Capt. Aldrich, Capt. Langworthy,
Lieut. Hastings and Capt. Starr
From "Tracing Your Civil War Ancestor"*

Chapter 24

BLACKS DURING THE BATTLE

More than 200,000 black men enlisted in the Union Army, the majority assigned to the 166 regiments of the United States Colored Troops (USCT). When the battle commenced on April 17, 1864, there were no USCT units garrisoned at Plymouth, North Carolina. However, a number of recruits for the 2nd United States Colored Cavalry, 10th and 37th Regiment USCT were present. [1]

Even though expected to enroll solely in colored regiments, a number of black soldiers enlisted in white regiments. At Plymouth, North Carolina three such units were the 103rd Pennsylvania Volunteers, the 24th New York Battery, and the 85th New York Infantry. Following the capitulation of Plymouth, in gravest danger were those particular soldiers since some Confederate regiments went into battle waving a black flag signifying the "no quarter" policy towards black soldiers. For instance, an unidentified member of Ransom's brigade that fought at the Battle of Plymouth, wrote to the *Charlotte Daily Bulletin* on March 18, 1864:

"...Ransom's brigade never takes any negro prisoners. Our soldiers would not even bury the negroes—they were buried by negroes..." [2]

Even though they had enlisted in the Union Army in order to fight for their freedom, most black soldiers mustered into white regiments were allotted only menial jobs such as cooks. Therefore, the majority of blacks were segregated within white regiments by the tasks to which they were assigned. Since no set policy had been established by the Federal Administration, each commander could use his own discretion concerning what to do with black soldiers. For instance, in the 8th Connecticut Volunteers, William Johnson, a black from Norwich, did not serve as a menial, but fought alongside white solders at Antietam (Sharpsburg) on September 17, 1862. [3] That was even before Abraham Lincoln issued the Emancipation Proclamation on January 1, 1863 and, therefore, before the USCT was organized.

When the Battle of Plymouth erupted, the following "Col'd" privates were known to have been present:

Nelson Sheppard	24th N. Y. Battery
George Washington	24th N.Y. Battery
Henry Pugh	85th N.Y. Infantry
John Rolack	85th N.Y. Infantry
Alec Johnson (waiter)	85th N.Y. Infantry

George E. Freeman	103rd Penna. Volunteers.
Dolphus Garrett	103rd Penna. Volunteers
Samuel Granville	103rd Penna. Volunteers
Titus Hardy (aka Titus McRae)	103rd Penna. Volunteers
Richard West	103rd Penna. Volunteers [4]

Those particular colored soldiers at Plymouth were in grave danger because of the Rebel policy toward any blacks wearing the blue uniform of the North. "No quarter" meant indiscriminate killing without any mercy shown. Such a horrendous occurrence already had taken place a mere eight days prior to the Battle of Plymouth. It was on April 12, 1864, at Fort Pillow, Tennessee. *"Blacks who were there were not permitted to surrender; they were shot, and some were burned alive."*[5]

Two eyewitness reports concerning the "no quarter" policy demonstrated in that battle led by Major General Nathan Bedford Forrest state:

"...We arrived at Ft. Pillow and attacked the same early in the day. The Fort was defended by about 450 blacks and 250 whites. We captured about 40 Blacks and 100 Whites and killed the remainder. We demolished the place."

W. R. Dyer, CSA

★ ★ ★ ★

{I} saw the bodies of 15 negroes, most of them having been shot through the head. Some of them were burned as if by powder around the holes in their heads, which led me to conclude that they were shot at very close range. One of the gunboat officers who accompanied us asked General Chalmers if most of the negroes were not killed after they [the Confederates] had taken possession. Chalmers replied that he thought such a hatred for the armed negro that they could not be restrained from killing the negroes after they had captured them.

Captain John G. Woodruff[6]

★ ★ ★ ★

Before the battle had erupted at Plymouth several officers were recruiting refugees for black regiments, and so a number of recruits were awaiting orders to join their units, including the 37th USCT Infantry with headquarters in Norfolk, Virginia. Reports conflict as to how many black troops actually were present at the Battle of Plymouth, the numbers varying from 40 to as much as 300.

Reports also vary as to what happened to those black troops after the Yankees were defeated. One black soldier known to have been captured, but not killed, was Private Nelson Sheppard, a cook in the 24th New York Battery who had enlisted on

May 11, 1863, at Plymouth in accordance with General Order No. 73 Act 7, Section 10 of the War Department orders for 1863. [7] After being taken prisoner on April 20, 1864, he was beaten severely for several consecutive days because he had acted as a guide on Yankee raids. Then he was put in a gang, fettered with ball and chains, and sent to Tarboro. Eventually, he was relieved of the ball, later being sent to Weldon where he worked on the fortifications there. Eventually, Private Sheppard was able make his escape, and on February 8, 1865, he rejoined his regiment reconstituted on Roanoke Island. [8]

Private George Washington was mustered into the 24th New York Battery under the same order as Sheppard. Somehow during the Battle of Plymouth, he was able to make his escape before the capitulation, later to become a cook in the 23rd New York, Light Artillery garrisoned in New Bern, North Carolina. [9]

Another black cook captured on April 20th was Private Richard West, a twenty-one-year-old runaway from Bertie County. He had been attired in his civilian work clothes when the garrison in Fort Williams was forced to surrender. So Private Richard West of the 103rd Pennsylvania Volunteers, looking not at all like a soldier, was enslaved once again. Put to work by his captors for nine months and eight days to repair the breastworks at Rainbow Bluff located upriver from Plymouth, he bided his time, waiting for just the opportune moment to escape. Familiar with the local terrain, Private Richard West was able to make his way with frostbitten feet, taking five days to reach Plymouth that once again was under Yankee occupation. [10]

The following information about a runaway from Chowan County is recorded on the roster of the 103rd Pennsylvania Volunteers:

"Pacien, Crowder, Private, Company C. Mustered age 18, April 4, 1864-June 24, 1865. Cook, colored, apparently escaped capture following Battle of Plymouth, North Carolina, April 20, 1864." [11]

After learning of the Federals' defeat at Plymouth, one might wonder how he was able to escape when most of the other Federal troops were reported captured, missing, or killed. The answer is readily explainable. For on January 2, 1864, the very day after Crowder Pacien had enlisted at Plymouth, the company to which he was assigned (Co. C), fortuitously was sent to Roanoke Island. [12]

The official policy was that one company of the 103rd would always be on Ronoake Island, there blocking the entrance to the Atlantic Ocean in order to prevent the Confederates from exporting cotton and importing arms with Europe, as well as cutting off their supply of salt for producing gunpowder. The other nine companies of the 103rd were garrisoned inland at Plymouth.

Fortunately for Private Crowder Pacien, when the battle was taking place in Plymouth on April 17-20 he was with Co. C safely garrisoned on Roanoke Island. This information is not recorded on the roster.

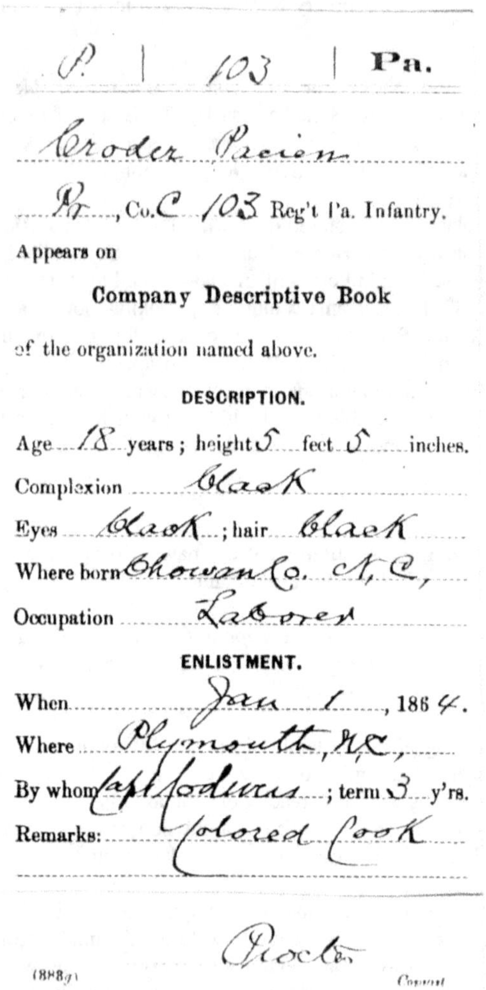

P | 103 | Pa.

Croder Pacien

Pr., Co. C /03 Reg't Pa. Infantry.

Appears on

Company Descriptive Book

of the organization named above.

DESCRIPTION.

Age 18 years; height 5 feet 5 inches.
Complexion Black
Eyes Black; hair Black
Where born Chowan Co. N. C.,
Occupation Laborer

ENLISTMENT.

When Jan 1, 1864.
Where Plymouth, N.C.,
By whom Capt Roderus; term 3 y'rs.
Remarks: Colored Cook

Procter

Fig. 42. Private Crowder Pacien's enlistment record
From author's collection

Another cook in Plymouth at the time of the battle was a runaway from Tyrrell County, Private Titus Hardy (alias Titus McRae) of the 103rd Pennsylvania Infantry. Captured and returned to his master, he was to remain in bondage until the war ended. [13] Eighteen-year old Private Henry Pugh, a black cook of the 85th New York Infantry, originally was reported missing, but later rejoined his unit, perhaps because he was able to escape easily from the isolated Fort Gray where his company had been sent. [14]

Twenty-one-year-old Private John Rolack, also of the 85th New York, a light-skinned, hazel-eyed mulatto, most likely passed for white, [15] because after his capture he was sent to Andersonville Prison, the only runaway slave reported confined in a Confederate prison. There he died on September 23, 1864, from the ravages of dysentery and scurvy and lies in grave #9549. [16] Privates Samuel Granville and Dolphus Garrett of the 103rd Pennsylvania, both natives of neighboring Bertie County, were officially recorded as missing. [17]

Records of other black soldiers who were at the Battle of Plymouth are available at the National Archives in Washington, D.C. For example, Private John Ward, a Bertie County recruit of the 37th USCT, survived because he "played dead" after having been injured. Private George Burdin, also from Bertie County, was remanded to slavery after his capture. Privates Madison Miller and John Burdin somehow were able to make their escape from Plymouth. [18]

Corporal Owen Brown of the 10th USCT was taken prisoner and later paroled. Other unnamed black soldiers managed to survive the battle, as well; just how many, however, were not reported. Private Frederick Burrows, Private George Drummer, and several others were reported as having been taken prisoner, but later dropped from the rolls by order of the War Department when their whereabouts were not known.

By intent, newspapers reported nothing concerning the fate of blacks at Plymouth. Fearful of the Federal reaction to captured black soldiers and sailors being returned to their masters rather than being treated as prisoners of war, President Davis had directed North Carolina's Governor Zebulon Vance to make certain that such information would never reach the newspapers.

General Braxton Bragg sent the following dispatch to Governor Zebulon Vance, discussing the situation of black soldiers being returned to their former masters rather than being treated as prisoners of war:

> "The president directs that the negroes captured by our forces be turned over to you for the present, and he requests of you that if, upon investigation, you acertain that any of them belong to citizens of North Carolina, you will cause them to be restored to their respective owners. If any are owned in other states, you will please communicate to me their number and the names and places of residence of

their owners, and have them retained in strict custody until the President's views in reference to such may be conveyed to you.

To avoid as far as possible all complications with the military authorities of the United States in regard to the disposition which will be made of this class of prisoners, the President respectfully requests Your Excellency to take the necessary steps to have the matter of such disposition kept out of the newspapers of the State, and in every available way to shun its obtaining any publicity as far as consistent with the proposed restoration." [19]

His directions having been followed explicitly, no records like those pertaining to the "Buffaloes" can be found concerning the blacks present during the Battle of Plymouth, neither of civilians nor of soldiers. However, several accounts circulated concerning their fates, even to allegations of a "massacre." One man identifying himself as Serg't. Samuel Johnson, Co. D, 2nd U.S. Colored Cavalry, [20] stated that he had been assisting in the recruitment of "contrabands" for the cavalry when the battle began. Immediately, he said, he changed into civilian clothing, well aware that he had better not be captured in his blue Union uniform. Therefore, when Fort Williams fell, Serg't Johnson was remanded into slavery.

After finally finding a way to escape, Serg't. Johnson swore on July 11, 1864, in an affidavit that the following information was true:

"I am orderly sergeant of Co. D, 2nd U.S. Colored Cavalry. In about April last I went to Plymouth, N.C. in company with Sergt. French, a white man, who acted as a recruiting officer, to take charge of some recruits, and was there at the time of the capture of Plymouth by the rebel forces. When I found that the city was being surrendered I pulled off my uniform and found a suit of citizen's clothes, which I put on, and when captured I was supposed and believed by the rebels to be a citizen.

After being captured I was kept at Plymouth for some two weeks and was employed in endeavoring to raise the sunken vessels of the Union fleet. From Plymouth I was taken to Weldon and from thence to Raleigh, N.C. where I was detained about a month, and then was forwarded to Richmond with Lieut. Johnson, of the 11th N.C Regiment, as his servant, to Hanover Junction. I did not remain there over four or five days before I made my escape into the lines of the front of Petersburg.

Upon the capture of Plymouth by the rebel forces all the negroes found in blue uniform, or with any outward marks of a Union soldier upon him, was killed. I saw some taken into the woods and hung. Others I saw stripped of all their clothing and then stood upon the bank of the river with their faces river ward, and there they were shot. Still others were killed by having their brains beaten out by the butt-end of the muskets in the hands of the rebels. All were not killed the day of *the capture. Those that were not were placed in a room with their officers, they (the officers) having previously been dragged through the town with ropes around their necks, when they were kept confined until the following morning, when the remainder of the black soldiers were killed. The regiments most conspicuous in these murderous transactions were the 8th N.C., and, I think, the 6th N.C."*

Samuel (his X mark) Johnson

*Witnessed by John I. Davenport, lieutenant and acting aide-de-camp
Sworn and subscribed to before me this 11th* (21)

Upon receiving a copy of Serg't. Johnson's affidavit, the indignant response by Robert Ould, Confederate commissioner of prisoner exchanges, was as follows:

"This is a villainous lie, and badly told at that. Samuel Johnson is a bad affidavit man, whatever may be his other excellencies. If the truth is wanted, let inquiry be made of Col. Beach, or other captured officers, always excepting the chaplains." (22).

There were other witnesses relating similar undocumented stories, as well. Lieutenant Alonzo Cooper of the 12th New York Cavalry reported:

"While at the Johnson farm we could hear the crack, crack, crack of muskets, down in the swamp where the negroes had fled to escape capture, and were being hunted like squirrels or rabbits. The Johnnies themselves laughingly said, They'd been out gunning for niggers.

"The negro soldiers who had surrendered were drawn up in line at the breastwork and shot down as they stood. This I plainly saw from where we were held under guard, not over five hundred yards distant. There were but few who saw this piece of atrocity, but my attention was attracted to it and I watched the whole brutal transaction, when the company of rebels fired, every negro dropped at once, as one man." (23)

Second Lieut. B.F. Blakeslee, Co. G of the 16th Connecticut Volunteers wrote:

"The rebels raised the 'black flag' against the negroes found in uniform and mercilessly shot them down. The shooting in cold blood of three or four hundred negroes and two companies of North Carolina troops who had joined our army, and even murdering peaceable citizens (as I have the personal knowledge of the killing with the butt-end of a musket of Mr. Spruell, the man whom I boarded with and, by the way, a secessionist of objecting to the plundering of a trunk which he had packed), were scenes of which the Confederates make no mention, except the

hanging of one person, but of which many of us were eye-witnesses, was but the Fort Pillow massacre re-enacted." [24]

On April 21, 1864, Private Charles Mosher of Co. B, 85th New York Volunteers entered the following into his diary:

> "Last evening the Rebs went gunning for the colored troops, who, when the 'jig was up' with us, broke over the works and took to the woods. They were shot down at sight. It was a massacre." [25]

Amos S. Billingsley was the chaplain of the 101st Pennsylvania Volunteers, having arrived at Plymouth on December 19, 1863. Five months later he would write a letter that was published in the *New York Daily Tribune*. His words on May 6, 1864 were: "*They shot a great many blacks after the fight was over—some say 150."* [26]

Robert P. Black, Co. E of the 103rd Pennsylvania Volunteers, sent his recollections to *The National Tribune*:

> "...Of the negroes who were captured with us here a part had enlisted, but I think had not been mustered into the United States service, but were intended as recruits for some colored regiments. These were taken out the next morning to the edge of the woods, in plain sight of us all, and shot down like so many cattle. There must have been from sixty to eighty of them. It looked rough to see those poor colored men shot down in cold blood, and we unable to save them. Surely their blood cries from the ground..." [27]

Expectedly, newspapers in the North were swift to report "a massacre of blacks and 'Buffaloes.'" Articles appeared in the *New York Herald*, the *New York Daily Tribune*, as well as the *Philadelphia Inquirer* that printed:

> "...Two full companies belonging to the 2nd North Carolina Union Volunteers were among the captured at Plymouth, the most of whom were taken out and shot by the enemy after our forces had surrendered. All the negroes found in uniform were also shot..." [28]

Confederate newspapers such as the *Wilmington Journal* insisted that the allegation was a "*ridiculous falsehood*," and the *Raleigh Daily Confederate* called the *Philadelphia Inquirer* report "*A Specimen of Yankee Lying."* [29]

However, the *North Carolina Times* of New Bern may have been alluding to such an occurrence when on April 27th it reported:

"On the surrender of the place the colored soldiers and 2nd Loyal North Carolina stampeded for the swamps. Most of the negroes, we regret to hear...have been barbarous in the extreme..." (30)

On April 29th, the *Daily Richmond Examiner* denied the atrocity charges by stating:

"The strict laws of civilized warfare acknowledge the power of the victor to put all to the sword in such cases. However, severe as such an example might seem, it would strike a salutary terror in the Yankees, which will be useful to them in the end....". (31)

However, on the very next day the same newspaper reported:

"It is positively affirmed that the rebels in taking possession of Plymouth, ordered out the North Carolina (Union) troops, who formed part of the garrison, and shot them; and that all negroes found in uniform were murdered. We presume the account is correct, and it only proves that what was supposed to be an exceptional barbarity at Fort Pillow, has been adopted as the deliberate policy of the rebels. As the issue is to be made it must be met." (32)

The following was published on May 3rd in the *Richmond Dispatch*:

"...Between 300 and 400 negro women and children, who had been taken from their legal owners, were recaptured at Plymouth. The men were either killed in battle or made their way to the swamps or forests. Many of the later will no doubt be taken. A Yankee Lt., who was in command of the Negro forces has, by order of Gen. Hoke, been confined with the Negro women and children." (33)

Allegations of a massacre were refuted by the Federal Government as exaggerations, contending that if such atrocities had really occurred, surely surviving blacks like Private Richard West of the 103rd Pennsylvania Volunteers would have complained. However, complaining was not something blacks instinctively would have done, fearing that they had no one to whom they could complain. Also, illiterate slaves, not having been allowed to learn to read or to write, were not penning letters, keeping diaries, or organizing their thoughts in journals to be read at some future date. Therefore, little can be found to indicate what those particular ex-slaves actually had been thinking or feeling, barring the disputed sworn affidavit of a man calling himself Serg't. Samuel Johnson, the very existence of such a soldier by that name being questionable since no records can be found for him. (34) Just who was the man then?

Even as late as 1909 such massacre allegations at Plymouth would still be debated. At one of the meetings of the 103rd Pennsylvania veterans they were in agreement that many blacks had been killed, but not "massacred." Following that meeting, Luther Dickey decided to write to Robert Hoke and Walter Clark, Chief Justice of the North Carolina Supreme Court, regarding the issue. Perhaps, the matter could be cleared up, once and for all. However, Dickey received no response from Hoke who, following the war, refused to discuss anything about it, even to disposing of all of his personal papers.

Judge Clark, however, replied to Dickey by writing: *"No armed prisoners of any color were killed at Plymouth."* Then he turned the matter over to Major John W. Graham of the 56th North Carolina Regiment whose reply was as follows:

"I have no hesitation in saying that the reputed killing of any colored troops the day after the capture of Plymouth, N.C., April 20, 1864, is entirely untrue. I heard of nothing of the kind at that time nor have I ever heard of it since until the receipt of your letter." [35]

As a result of that correspondence, Luther Dickey concluded:

"When the writer began this investigation it was with the expectation of, in a measure, verifying the affidavit of the negro, Sergeant Johnson. It was not with the motive of doing justice, especially to the victorious Confederates of Plymouth, but merely to tell the whole truth bearing on the battle of Plymouth, in which he knew his Regiment had done its full duty. In his careful research for the truth he became fully convinced that an injustice had been done the Confederates who had captured his Regiment, and that as an impartial historian, these facts should be recorded in this volume." [36]

In addition, many other eyewitnesses who had kept diaries, journals, and who had written letters and reports, never mentioned a massacre. Neither did General Wessells allude to one in his reports. He did state, however, that a number of Union North Carolinians had left their companies without permission during the battle. Indeed they had, being well aware of what would befall them if captured, especially those who had deserted from the Confederate Army. The general made no mention of whether "Col'd" soldiers may have been among that number. [37]

Confederates, likewise, declared such stories of a massacre as blatant lies. Admittedly, though, they did not refute the allegation that while attempting escape, many of the blacks, as well as native North Carolinian "Buffaloes," were deliberately killed by Confederates vowing "no quarter."

One Confederate veteran, however, Frank O'Brien, Alabama artillerist and scout, reported in his post-war account of the battle:

"About 800 (blacks) made a break through our lines on the western (eastern) side and tried to reach the thickly wooded swampy ground in the direction of

Little Washington. Dearing's cavalry and a detachment of the 25th North Carolina resisted the effort successfully but this was attended with great slaughter as but few reached the swamp alive. Those who were successful in gaining refuge there were afterward killed or died of starvation...It is a well known fact that for three weeks after the place was captured negro (sic) bodies were seen floating out of the swamp into the river. The sight was sickening. Our General (Hoke) and other officers could not be blamed for this. While it is true the rules of civilized warfare did not countenance such terrible retribution let those who might condemn, put themselves in the position of a large body of men who made up that attacking force, and see what they would have done under like circumstances." [38]

Contemporary researchers Weymouth Jordan and Gerald Thomas consider the large number of blacks suggested by O'Brien an exaggeration, as well as the large numbers reported by other post war accounts. [39]

W. H. Morgan, the orderly sergeant of "The Clifton Grays," (Company C), Eleventh Regiment of Kemper's Brigade wrote in his memoirs:

"It was said that there were some negro soldiers at Plymouth, who took to the swamps, were pursued by Dearing's Cavalry and left in the swamp, dead or alive; none of them were taken prisoners, or brought out of the swamp. Some of the prisoners captured were identified as deserters from the Confederate service; a court-martial was convened later, and several of them were hung. These men were North Carolinians. [40]

At Plymouth Colonel James Dearing won his brigadier-generalship, being put in command of the artillery and cavalry. Described in the eyes of his Confederate comrades:

"...He was a dashing officer, and in this battle performed his part with great skill and bravery, charging a fort with artillery, running the guns by hand right up to the fort, pouring shot and shell into it until the white flag was sent up.

The first day he surprised, by a quick dash with his troopers and artillery, another fort running in on the Yankees so suddenly that they had no water to cool their guns, and could only fire a few rounds, when they sent up a white flag...." [41]

The question of whether there had been a "massacre" of blacks and "Buffaloes" at Plymouth remains an issue even in the year 2003; for what is meant by a "massacre" may vary with individuals. Both Federals and Confederates, however, did acknowledge that when the blacks, especially, tried to escape to the swamps, they were "pursued."

In the opinion of Weymouth T. Jordan and Gerald Thomas, indeed a "massacre" did take place at the Battle of Plymouth because *"there can be no justification for the killing of blacks and Buffaloes, uniformed or otherwise, after the battle had ended."* They conclude by stating that *"the episode remains in many respects an enigma."* [42]

Chapter 25

PROPERTIES SURVIVING THE BATTLE

Confederate J. H. Broadwell described the destruction of Plymouth:

"The pocasin between the two rivers is two miles across. The gun boats in Middle River filled the town with great 200-pound shells. Before that the houses in town had from one to ten cannon balls shot through them. Most of them were shot through by our artillery in the spring when our troops captured the town." [1]

Before noon on April 20, 1864, the cannons, rifles, and grenades finally had ceased their din. Then following Lieut. Colonel John C. Lamb's torching of the garrison headquarters, as well as the majority of buildings on Main Street, the town of Plymouth, once quite lovely, was left with only seven buildings standing. Fortunately, they were in fairly good condition, albeit bullet riddled.

One was the "T" shaped home on the corner of Washington and Third Streets, known as the Windley-Ausbon House. The neat building, today painted white and trimmed with green shutters, is listed on the National Register of Historic Places. Situated on the north side of the lot, the two-roomed house on Lot # 48 was built sometime in the 1830's or 1840's, thereby making it one of the oldest homes within the town of Plymouth.

Originally, Arthur Rhodes had sold the half-acre lot to Caleb Bembridge for the sum of five pounds. Eleven years later Seth Hardison purchased the property for twenty pounds. Following Hardison's death in 1805, ten members of his family jointly inherited the property. After the passage of two years, one of the heirs, a house builder by the name of Ezekial Hardison, bought out his relatives for the sum of eighty pounds. Some sources imply that he may have built the frame house on Lot # 48, but there is no proof. Following the death of Ezekial Hardison, in 1834 Edmon Windley purchased the property. Differing sources suggest that Windley was the builder of the original part of the "T" shaped house. [2]

Windley died in 1848, after which time the house was to change hands three more times before being deeded to Mary Pettijohn Keith and her husband James. In 1855, the property passed to Mary Keith from her father John C. Pettijohn. Therefore, at the time of Colonel John C. Lamb's 1862 punitive raid on Plymouth, the house was in the possession of the Keiths.

At the time Mary Keith took possession she received from her father not only the house, but also a slave girl and any of her offspring, since colored children always took the legal status of their mother. According to hearsay, Mr. and Mrs. James Keith probably were not in residence during the war. Town records indicate that the house may have been used by a physician, as well as by occupying Federals and Confederates using it for officers' quarters. [3]

During the first of the three battles for the occupation of Plymouth, one writer wrote about a Rebel sniper who was targeted by the Yankees on December 10, 1862:

"There was sharp fighting. In the second floor of this house was a Confederate sharpshooter, who fired from a window. With him was an officer named Barnard. As the Federal troops advanced the officer warned the sharpshooter that he had better get out; that the attackers would locate him, but he stayed.

Barnard wisely ran across the street and hid in the cellar under a dwelling. In a few minutes, there was heavy rifle fire on the house. The sharpshooter was shot several times, crawled out of the room and downstairs and was found dead in the lower hall." [4]

Today thirty bullet holes still remain on the exterior of the house by the window from which the sniper had been firing. Another eight holes are found in the interior wall behind the window. [5] Because the sharpshooter's blood had not been wiped up immediately, the stain on the wide floorboards of the bedroom became impossible to remove, and so it remains, never able to hold a paint finish, instead being hidden by carpeting.

Folklore abounding from that period of history alludes to another residence having stood directly across the street, as well as to a small schoolhouse set between that particular house and the Roanoke River. If so, during the April 17-20, 1864 battle, somehow shellfire from the river would have had to miss both of those two buildings in order to score direct hits on the house situated on Lot #48. Proof of those hits can be seen upstairs even today where the original banisters and doorframes were riddled with minie balls, leaving several grooves and one three-inch shell. They never have been removed, only covered by paint. Also, remaining still is a large hole in the north chimney. [6]

Unfortunately, after the war ended, even more sadness was to be associated with the house on Lot #48; for by 1869 the two minor children of the Keiths (Joseph and Jeanette) would become orphans and, thereby, heirs of the property. However, in order to provide for the children's expenses, their guardians were forced to use the house as collateral. After having accrued a great deal of debt over the years, it was auctioned off in 1880 when Jeanette Keith was married. Following two more owners, Mrs. Priscilla N. Ausbon purchased the house on March 10, 1885. Thenceforth, 302 Washington Street became known as the Ausbon House.

Until her death in 1995, the owner of the antebellum house with wide floorboards and original pressed glass in the windowpanes was Mrs. Hermine Ausbon Ramsey. Born in 1902, she enjoyed recounting important Plymouth happenings and recorded many of them.[7] At the present time, the lovely restored home is owned by Mrs. Ausbon's niece, Nee Humphrey with her husband Charles.

*Fig. 43. **Ausbon House, Plymouth, N.C.**
From author's collection*

Also left standing after the Battle of Plymouth was the large house located at 233 Main Street, built in 1850 by a well-to-do northern-born lawyer, Charles Latham. His lovely Greek Revival-style antebellum home was intended to reflect both his wealth and position as Washington County's representative in the Legislature and Senate, as well as serving as County Sheriff.[8]

Interesting is the fact that the first three feet of the foundation of the Latham House is composed of ballast rocks that had been used to secure stability in ships sailing to the Port of Plymouth, North Carolina. The rocks had arrived in the holds of empty ships sailing from Plymouth, Massachusetts, perhaps, or even from as far away as Falmouth, England. Before a cargo could be put on board for the return trip, the rocks would be unloaded and since there was no further use for them, they were discarded, oftentimes used to cobble the dusty dirt roads of Plymouth.

*Fig. 44. **Latham House, Plymouth, N.C.**
Courtesy of John Ball*

Some fascinating folklore has been associated with Charles Latham and his role in the drama at Plymouth in April 1864. A story told and retold is that when the battle began, several frightened citizens sought the Latham residence for protection, desperately huddling in the basement while right outside on the wide, park-like lawn Ransom's Brigade was battling with the Yankees. According to town legend, a cannon ball crashed through a basement window. Immediately, so "they say," Charles Latham picked up the ball and threw it back out before it had a chance to explode. Maybe that is a true anecdote and then again, maybe it is not. A known fact, however, is that the house did take direct hits as evidenced by visible holes from musket balls, one having penetrated both the front and rear doors. [9]

As Ransom's men pressed towards Fort Williams, all the while tearing down fences and hedges, they also left sprawled on the Latham lawn a slew of dead troops, both Yanks and Rebs. So upon exiting his home after hearing the final shots, Unionist Charles Latham was fearful to discover lying among the blue and gray dotting his lawn one of his Rebel soldier sons. However, he was relieved to find that not one of his three boys was there. All had survived the battle fought in their own front yard, and all would survive the bitter war that pitted a Plymouth Unionist father against his Confederate sons.

Until the year 1981 the Latham home was thought to be the only antebellum house in Washington County having been resided in by a continuous procession of its builder's descendants. After that date, however, the home was sold to the Latham Foundation. Then in 2001 with intentions "to restore it to its original beauty and grace," Joseph and Susan Pate from Indianapolis, Indiana purchased the spacious Latham House. [10]

★★★★

The edifice of the Episcopal Church located at 107 Madison Street was another building still standing following the destructive battle. In January 20, 1842, worshippers had elected a vestry and selected a name for the church they were planning to build. They called it Grace Episcopal. Later, in March of 1842, the vestry voted to purchase a lot for $175.00 and then proceeded to erect a modest wooden building for the sum of $300.00.

On January 11, 1859, rather than repairing their old wooden church, the vestry voted $6,000 for the building of a new brick edifice, the amount being increased to $7,000 on August 6, 1860. The eminent architect Richard Upjohn was hired to design the church and soon afterwards construction of the new Episcopal Church commenced. Twelve shady sycamores, each named for a disciple of Jesus, were planted around the perimeter and all were standing in 1861. None, however, are surviving today.

The building could not be completed as expected because the War Between the States limited the necessary supplies. For instance, northern slate for the roof was impossible to procure, so cypress shingles had to be used on a temporary basis. Sadly, the church, "*long the symbol of prestige among wealthy merchants and ship owners of the day*," [11] suffered considerable damage from the shelling of the town, as well as from the destructive occupation by the careless invaders. Wood from the massive pews bearing the names of prominent families, as well as wood from the gallery, was cut up to build coffins for dead Yankees. [12]

The following article written by Mary Cotton Davenport appeared in the *Roanoke Beacon*:

"In the town of Plymouth on the south bank of the Roanoke stands an old ivy-covered Episcopal Church surrounded by the graves of generations of its worshippers. Standing sentinel over the dead up to a few years ago were twelve sycamores named for the brave apostles. Eleven of them were straight and beautiful. The twelfth, which by a queer coincidence was named Judas, was crooked and malformed. When the wind blew from the north and the Roanoke was muddy and sullen the trees flung their giant arms to the sky and bowed their mighty heads remembering.

They whispered together of the evil days that once beset the church and spoke among themselves of a day in the summer of 1861 when crowds of excited men, weeping women, and wide-eyed children gathered there to ask divine blessing upon the cause of the Confederacy and to pray that success attend the undertaking of two sons of the Confederacy, Captain N. J. Whitehurst and Stuart L. Johnston. As these two young men knelt at the altar for the blessings of The Reverend Houghton little did they think that the two companies of volunteers that they led away so hopefully to the defense of Roanoke Island would spend two years in a Federal prison in Boston and that the Union troops would be quartered in the church.

But the walls soon rang to the heavy boots of the Yankee soldiers who occupied Plymouth from 1862 to 1864. A Freedman's bureau was set up and the church served as an asylum for the motley crew that hovered around the bureau like birds of prey.

Fat back and flour were passed out across the chancel rail and Edward Stanley, military governor of the state, bitterly denounced from the pulpit the rebels who once worshiped at the altar..." [13]

An unidentified chaplain serving under General Wessells was appalled by the Yankee vandalizing of the church. So after the war had ended, through his concerted efforts, funds were raised for replacing the broken pulpit, altar, pews, furniture, and windows. [14]

Fig. 45. **Grace Episcopal Church**
Courtesy of John Ball

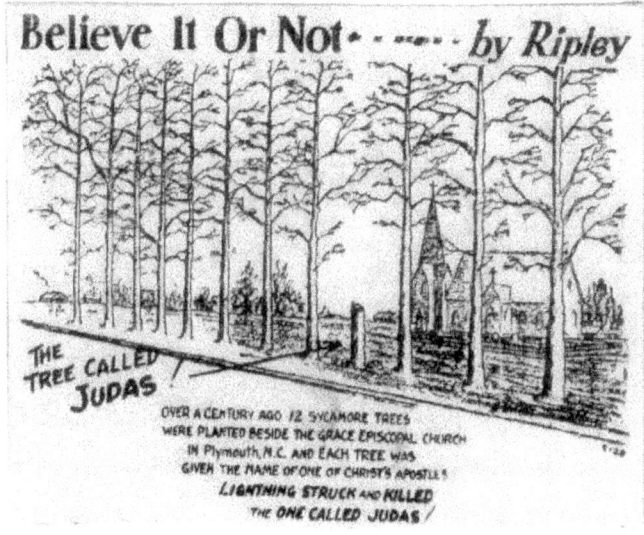

Fig. 46. "Ripley's Believe It Or Not"
Courtesy of Washington County Historical Society

Fig. 47. **Photograph of Methodist Episcopal Church, April 2002**
Author's Collection

219

At 109 East Third Street stands the oldest church in town. Plymouth United Methodist occupies four of the original town lots: # 45, #46, #21, and #22. [15] In the church cemetery, shaded by tall century-old cedars, are buried many past residents of Plymouth, including prominent Charles Latham and his four wives.

Originally, in 1827, the congregation of the Methodist Episcopal Church had worshipped at the Morratock Primitive Baptist Church, two miles southwest of town. The second oldest church in Washington County, it had been established in 1785. [16] In 1832 for $40.00 the first lot was purchased by the Methodists on which a small wooden-framed church was built. [17] Today above the front door of the present edifice is a commemorative stained glass window with the year 1832 inscribed on it.

Mention of the Methodist Church can be found in several documents penned by northern soldiers garrisoned at Plymouth. David L. Day, a member of the 24th Massachusetts Volunteer Infantry recorded on March 29, 1863:

"Church service today for the first time in several weeks; we occupied the Methodist church. The house was well filled with soldiers and the galleries running around three sides of the house were filled with darkies, who somewhat resembled an approaching thunder squall." [18]

Corporal John F. Rupert of Co A 103rd Pennsylvania Volunteers recorded in his diary:

Thursday, Nov. 26. "National Thanksgiving day. At 11 A.M. a small number met at the church where Lieut. Col. Taylor, 101st Penna. Vols. and 1st Sergt. Stoddard of 24th N.Y. Battery, made addresses." [19]

Sergeant Julian Wheaton Merrill of the 24th N.Y. Independent Battery Light Artillery wrote on January 26, 1864, to the editor of the *New-Yorker*:

"For recreation, music of all sorts has been generally adopted among us. During the winter Corporal E. T. Hurlbut of our battery...has had a course of singing classes at the Methodist church, and at the close gave a concert. His school was well attended by soldiers belonging to all of the different regiments in town, as well as in the battery.

Friday eve. The Concert passed off. The house was crowded, overflowing full."
[20]

Corporal Luther Dickey of Co C, 103rd Pennsylvania Volunteers wrote about an occurrence at the Methodist Church on January 29, 1864:

"On the evening of Jan. 29, there was a vocal and instrumental concert given by amateurs in the Plymouth Methodist Church, and the house was crowded. I was there

with some of our officers, and the performance was not half over when we observed Gen. Wessells and Commander Flusser of the navy climb out of a window near the stage. Presently some one announced that the adjutants of our brigade were wanted and some more figures went out of the window. Our party surmised that 'something was up.' By and by word came to me that I was wanted in camp, and I displayed my coat tails going out of the window...." [21] A raid on Windsor, North Carolina was about to commence.

Amos Billingsley, Chaplain of the 101st Pennsylvania Infantry, wrote about a sermon he had preached on the first Sunday evening after his arrival. At that time he was announcing that the next week he would preach a Christmas sermon.

"At the hour appointed, the large Methodist church, seating some eight hundred, was crowded to overflowing: hundreds, they said, had to go away for want of room..." [22]

He recorded that prior to the battle two other chaplains were conducting services at the Methodist Church, also: Chaplain Dixon of the 16th Connecticut Volunteers and Chaplain John H. Rowlings, the third chaplain to serve with the 103rd Pennsylvania Volunteers. Chaplain Billingsley noted that the Methodist Church was being used by different denominations for their respective religious services.

Also Chaplin Billingsley recorded the following:

"The colored people had preaching or prayer-meeting in the same house every Sabbath afternoon, and a flourishing Sabbath-school, conducted by a sergeant of the New York Battery." [23]

On January 20, 1864, in a letter to his brother Dan, Sergeant Ed Boots of the 101st Pennsylvania Regiment mentioned the same activity:

"...I have read my testament through four times & the Book of Psalms once since I have been in the Army. I hope you read your testament. I wish that you could see the negro sabbath school that is in operation here, and how anxious the poor ignorant negroes are to learn about Jesus..." [24]

Prior to the battle commencing on April 17, 1864, the Methodist Church had to have been intact; for on the night of April 16th the band of the 16th Connecticut rendered a concert of rousing martial music. [25] Customarily, in the evenings the musicians would give concerts. A flautist in Co. B was Robert J. Holmes, great-great grandfather of Scott Holmes, present historian of the 16th Connecticut Regiment. [26]

The musicians played an important role to the regiments because the daily routine of the soldiers was regulated by fife, bugle, and drum calls. In the field, commanders were alerted to proceed by the long roll of drums. Spirited cadences and songs helped to raise the morale, as well as to help the troops march in step. Musicians played for guard mount, general inspections, and ceremonial occasions such as funerals, parades, mustering in, and drumming out of soldiers. [27].

Although considered noncombatants, musicians were trained in the use of firearms. Oftentimes during a battle as they were performing their duties, they, too, came under fire. Most often, though, during a battle they would serve as stretcher-bearers or assistants to the surgeons in field hospitals. [28] After the battle erupted on the 17th of April, the Methodist church's frame building, with its narrow balcony extending across the back and partly down each side, became one such emergency hospital. [29]

In the June 13, 1890, issue of the *Roanoke Beacon,* W. Fletcher Ausbon, under the pseudonym of "Flipp," wrote the following concerning the church:

"...but during the war this town being destroyed, the churches received their share of the ill fate. The Methodist Church was torn down and its timbers used for firewood or to make coffins for the dead soldiers who fought and died under its shadows. The records were destroyed and the members scattered far and near, some of which never returned, therefore the records are silent as to its history."[30]

According to Harry Thompson, curator of the Port-O-Plymouth Museum, the church building, in all probability, was totally destroyed in the two naval bombardments of October 30-31, 1864, when the Federals recaptured Plymouth. No documentation seems to exist denoting exactly when the Methodist Church of Plymouth was rebuilt. However, when it was, the enormous spire was 105 feet tall.

Records indicate that in April, 1896, two workmen had painted the spire in half a day, together being paid $1.25, the current day's wage. Sometime shortly after 1906, a violent storm blew down the steeple. Its replacement, however, was not nearly as tall. [31]

★ ★ ★ ★

One of the oldest surviving houses in Plymouth is the Clark House built on Lot #77 circa 1811 and located at 219 Jefferson Street. [32] No one can say exactly when and to whom that lot first was sold, since no records exist in either Washington or Tyrrell Counties. No deed has been found for the sale from the original trustees of the town. Rather, the very first sale ever recorded was that of David Clark of Halifax County to Levi Fagan in 1811 for the sum of $1000.00.

David Clark who owned forty or fifty other lots in Plymouth most likely never lived on Lot #77. After having been sold to a series of owners, the property was purchased in 1848 by Joseph A. Spruill for $500. However, no record has been located conveying the property to the next owner who possibly might have neglected to record the deed.

No records have been found, either, to identify the occupants of the Clark House during the Civil War. In the main portion of the house there were once visible bullet holes and other scars; however, they are now concealed with putty. In 1880, the property was sold to Joseph S. Chesson, the father of Mrs. Gary (Lillian) Campbell, owner of the property in 1979. [33]

Fig. 48. *Clark House, Plymouth, N.C.*
Courtesy of Washington County Historical Society

On Arthur Rhode's Lot # 104, located at the corner of Main and Monroe Streets, stands a large house today painted white and trimmed with green shutters. In 1814 a physician, Dr. Julian Picot, purchased the property for $100. In February of 1832 Peter O. Picot paid the sum of 10 schillings for the property on which he built the house. Preceding the Civil War it was to change owners several times. [34]

Prior to the Civil War, the property at 302 West Main Street had been owned by Robert Armistead, a wealthy New England shipowner and trader. During the war the house served as a hospital. Originally, the wide building had a 49-foot front porch that was removed in 1976. Also, a kitchen area was built completely separate from the house, customary in antebellum homes so that if the kitchen were to catch on fire, the main house would be spared. Fortunately, the house did escape being burned or disastrously shelled during the war. Only a single shell hole can be found on the upper right-hand corner of the large house.

The 16-roomed house was well constructed of plaster over peg and mortice, with the windowsills and wide-slatted floorboards made of light wood. A unique and interesting feature of the large house was the existence of two trap doors. The one located in the entrance hall led down into the basement, referred to as the "fort" by Nancy Coffey Pettiford, one of the later owners.

Located in the front room, a second trap door allowed any person who might be hiding in the "fort" to come up into the house to get warm by the fireplace. In earlier years a tunnel ran diagonally across the street from the Armistead House to the home of Mrs. Ayers, a milliner, and then on to the river. Today the spot is a vacant lot behind the offices of *The Roanoke Beacon*. Legend says the tunnel may have been used as an Underground Railroad station for escaping slaves waiting for northern ships. If that were true, the slaves easily could have run swiftly through the tunnel to the river and their freedom when a ship was about to depart for the North.

In 1914 a successful black brick mason, Reuben Pettiford from Warrenton, North Carolina, purchased the house. According to several local octogenarians who know some of the Pettiford family history, the house served as a boarding house for blacks in need of lodging. The Armistead-Pettiford House became the possession of Gladys Pettiford Staplefoote after the death of her parents. [35]

Mrs. Gladys Staplefoot-Whitley died in 2000, and the present owners of the Armistead-Pettiford House are James and Velma Braye, residents of Tuskegee, Alabama. Recently, Mrs. Braye, surrogate daughter of the last owner, stated:

"We want people to know about the Armistead people who bought the house and know how it became part of African-American history and part of the Pettiford legacy."

Because of those intense feelings, the Braye family has *"agreed to lease the Armstead-Pettiford House for twenty years while the North Carolina Division of Archives assists them in researching and developing the history of the house, concentrating on its black history."*[36]

Perhaps with the help of Underground Railroad experts, the intriguing mystery surrounding the two trapdoors and the tunnel in the Armistead-Pettiford House will be solved at last.

*Fig. 49. **Armistead-Pettiford House, Plymouth, N.C***
Courtesy of John Ball

The spacious house built circa 1830 on Lot # 12 still was standing following the devastating 1864 battles. Adolph Stubbs, born in 1890 on Winesett Circle, recalled the following:

> *"It was the only house there; the rest was farmland where we grew peanuts, cotton, corn, sweet potatoes. Nobody grew much tobacco then. The war? No, my mother disliked the war, but we found some cannon parts once. She wouldn't let us talk about it much."* [37]

The hand-hewn foundation beams made of heart of cypress were held together by large pegs; however, throughout the rest of the house square iron nails were used. Today original hand-blown glass windowpanes still can be found in some of the windows. Downstairs, a wide hallway runs the length of the house, a typical feature of antebellum houses. Possessing the low ceiling characteristic of old eastern North Carolina houses, a small bedroom on the second floor exhibits the original architecture. At one time the house was equipped with two-deck porches on both front and back. However, they were removed during later renovations.

Throughout the years the property was owned by several prosperous men, including Caleb Walker, ship builder and master of his own vessels. In addition, he was a merchant, as well as a farmer, owning a significant number of slaves. Unfortunately, business reversals forced Walker to borrow heavily. In July, 1850, his holdings were transferred to Lawyer Charles Latham and Hezikiah G. Spruill, who served as trustees to assume Walker's debts.

Soon afterwards, Louis Picot bought the house, as well as twenty-five acres of the surrounding land, all for the sum of $2000. Then on the very same day, he sold his acquisition to Hezikiah G. Spruill for exactly the same amount of money. It was an interesting transaction, since the purchaser was one of the trustees who had ordered the property sold. Then a few weeks later on February 1, 1852, Hezikiah Spruill, for a $200 profit, sold the property to Dr. Warren M. Ward who may later have used his residence as a hospital during the Civil War. Totally out of range of the Yankee gunships moored in the Roanoke River, the house on Lot # 12 would have made an ideal hospital.

The farm was sold several more times until purchased by W. H. Stubbs on September 17, 1886. Years later on December 29, 1919, his widow sold the home, and from then on it was in the possession of several families until 1956 when Selby O. Price became the owner of the Stubbs House. [38]

★★★★

Even though not the owner of a large antebellum house, the name of Harriet Toodle appears on an 1864 map drawn to describe the Battle of Plymouth. Her property is labeled as a spot where the Yankees built a redoubt. The name of Harriet Toodle is mentioned also in a report from the 56th North Carolina Regiment:

> *"At Boyle's steam mill near the road entering Second street from the west was another redoubt outside the entrenchments, and within the southwest angle still another at Harriet Toodle's."* (39)

Later in the battle, the same writer recorded:

> *"The redoubt at Boyle's steam mill on the road on this side of the town, appears to have been blown up by a shell entering its magazine, and so it offered no resistance to our infantry, while that at Harriet Toodle's, about the southwest angle, and the intervening entrenched camps were taken with the connecting breastworks."* (40)

Harriet Toodle, a " free woman of color," was not listed in the 1860 United States census for Plymouth, North Carolina. However, a 22 year-old free man by the name of William Tuttle, a day laborer, was listed as "head of household." If a man were living in a house, automatically he would be the one listed. What the relationship was between Harriet and William is not known. The difference in the spelling of the surnames perhaps may be due to the census taker's interpretation of what he heard, since most likely neither Harriet nor William could spell their names.

Prior to the Civil War, only free blacks were listed by name in Federal censuses. Slaves were not citizens; they were chattel and, as such, could not own property. Ten years later on the 1870 census, a 70 year-old "head of household" appears as Harriet Tuttle. Recorded residing with her, were four other persons: Louisa (15), Mary (19), Pros (18), and Romulus Webb (70). (41)

However, the name of William Tuttle was not recorded as residing in Plymouth when the 1870 census was taken. Interestingly, the name of William Toodle had appeared in a letter written at Roanoke Island in December, 1867. The correspondence was to Colonel Charles Benzoni, commanding officer at Plymouth. Members of the then defunct Freedmen's Colony were being evicted from Roanoke Island after the land was returned by the United States Government to the antebellum owners. In the letter the black men were requesting permission to remain on the island until the following spring. (42) One of the men marking his "X" was William Toodle.

Registered in 1847, three different deeds passed the ownership of several lots in Plymouth from Alfred Winchell and Sheriff Charles Latham to Harriet Toodle for the total of $90. (43) Who Harriet Toodle was and how she came about purchasing land is a mystery lost in time. Interesting, though, is the fact that a woman named Edy Toodle was recorded as being "head of household" in Plymouth's 1830 census. Residing in her home were the following unnamed persons: one boy and four girls under 10 years of age, one female between 10 and 24, a woman between 36 and 55, and one woman between 55 and 100 years.[44] Harriet, born in 1800 would have been the right age to be the second eldest. Perhaps the children were hers. However, there is nothing on the census report to prove that hypothesis since names were not recorded, except the "head of the household," Edy Toodle.

Today the same Toodle property is occupied by a funeral home located at 305 Wilson Street, behind which a wide tree shaded cemetery is filled with the remains of many generations of blacks, even of many who had migrated from Plymouth. Merion Baker Anderson, a neighbor who had grown up in the neighborhood, states that her mother told her years ago white strangers quite often walked through the cemetery. She had no idea why they would be there. However, upon being informed that during the Civil War a Federal redoubt had been on the property of Harriet Toodle, the daughter today understands that the visitors were searching for spent shells or any other Civil War artifacts they could find.[45]

Even 139 years later in the year 2003, new and interesting facts are being uncovered still about the long ago, mostly forgotten Battle of Plymouth.

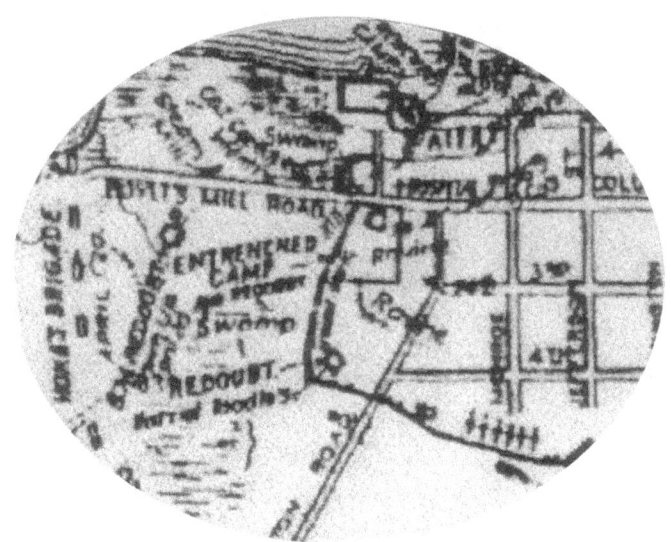

*Fig. 50. **Harriet Toodle's property***
From map of the Battle of Plymouth, April 17-20, 1864

Chapter 26

THE DROWNING OF A LEVIATHAN

On May 5, 1864, the formidable Rebel ironclad *Albemarle,* accompanied by two smaller boats, was about to enter the Albemarle Sound from the Roanoke River. Aboard the *CSS Cotton Plant* were troops being shielded by bales of cotton, while aboard the *CSS Bombshell* were critical supplies of coal and food. [1] Unbeknown to him at the time, Captain James Wallace Cooke was soon about to make naval history. It happened when the *CSS Albemarle,* equipped with only two rifles, went up against seven Union gunboats with the combined armament of 34 guns.

The drama commenced at about 2:00 p.m. as the three Confederate boats were making their way to New Bern, confidently steaming toward the Albemarle Sound in order to enter the mouth of the Tar River. The objective was to support the Rebel troops who were strategizing an attack on the Yankees garrisoned at New Bern. The Rebels soon discovered, though, three heavily armed Federal gunboats guarding the mouth of the Roanoke River. Yankee sailors from the *Commodore Hull,* the *Ceres,* and the *Whitehead,* all under the command of Captain Melancton Smith were attempting to position two lines of mines called torpedoes across the river. Accompanying the three large gunboats was the smaller transport *Ida May* which immediately upon her crew's spotting the approach of the Rebel ships sped ahead to warn the rest of the Union fleet twenty miles down the Sound. [2]

With utmost assurance that the Yankee wooden gunboats could be of no threat to his invincible ironclad ram, Cooke followed the vessels as they swiftly steamed into the safety of the Sound. Unknowingly, however, Cooke was about to be confronted by four very large double-ended gunboats: *Miami, Wyalusing, Sassacus,* and *Mattabesett.* Unfortunately for the Rebel captain, he was without necessary backup; for the *Cotton Plant* already had retreated to Plymouth as she had been ordered. The *Bombshell,* though, had not left yet, and so during the ensuing battle she was seized with all of her crew being placed in double irons, and her officers held under sentry. [3]

Commencing close to 5 o'clock p.m., an improbable confrontation occurred between seven wooden-hulled Union gunboats and a *single* ironclad in the Battle of Bachelor's Bay. The number of gunboats, seemingly, meant nothing for the ram; for neither the 9-inch solid shot nor the 100-pound rifled projectiles had any effect on her exterior.

Each of the Union vessels, including the *USS Miami* commanded by Acting Lieut. Charles A. French, had the option of ramming the *CSS Albemarle.* Not one, however, was capable of penetrating her tough shield. Therefore, they were unable to stop her as she attempted to ram the Yankee *Sassacus* commanded by Lieutenant Commander Francis A. Roe. However, due to the *Albemarle*'s slow speed she was not successful. She was successful, though, at disabling the *Sassacus* when a 100-pound Brooke rifle shot passed through one of the boilers. As a result, many of the crew got scalded mortally, including William Sutherland, first-class fireman.

> *"The beak of the* Sassacus *tore over the bow of the* Albemarle. *As it did, the ram's effective forward gun fired a telling shot. It tore into the side-wheeler's overcharged boilers. With a shrill scream that drowned the noise of battle, the boilers discharged their super-heated steam. Men with scalded flesh cried in torment. The Sassacus listed to port. The* Albemarle's *crew prepared to board her, but rifle fire held them off.*
>
> *For 13 terrible minutes, the two ships were interlocked. One vessel of the Federal squadron signaled mistakenly, that she was sinking. The guns of the others, perhaps in fear of hitting the* Sassacus, *were silent. Then the ironclad and the wooden vessel parted. The wounded* Sassacus *limped away..."*[(4)]

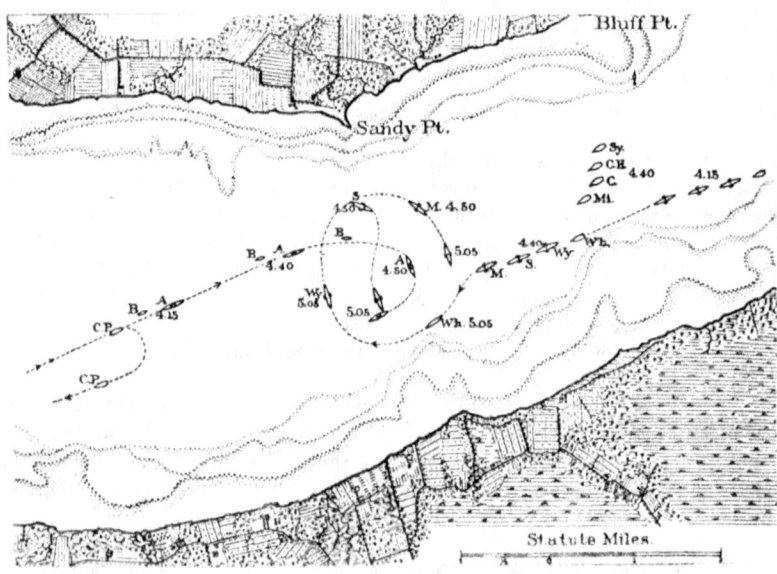

Fig. 51. **Chart of engagement in Albemarle Sound, May 5, 1864**
"Century Magazine, 1888"

Fig. 52. **USS Sassacus *attempting to ram* CSS Albemarle**
U.S. Naval Historical Center

IV

Very soon afterwards, the *CSS Albemarle* ran out of fuel and luckily for the Confederates, fate intervened. As soon as Captain Cooke realized what a perilous situation he was in, he ordered his crew to burn anything combustible. Even after they had, Cooke still was not able to raise enough power because he had no draft. Shells had punctured the *Albemarle's* smokestack. *"The vulnerability of their funnels was one of the weakest points of Confederate ironclads,"* stated Raimondo Luraghi, foremost European historian of the American Civil War. [5]

Then someone ingeniously suggested burning the large supply of fatty hams, slabs of bacon, and tubs of lard that had been stored on board the ironclad. Amazingly, the fire provided heat enough to raise the steam pressure. So the *Albemarle* fortuitously escaped towards the Roanoke River after having been hit over 280 times and with some of her iron plates torn away. In addition, her stern gun's muzzle had been destroyed and her steering mechanism damaged.

Just before 7 o'clock p.m. the flagship *USS Mattabesett* hoisted the "Cease Fire" signals, and the battle ended in a tactical draw. [6] Interestingly, both captains were claiming the victory. The irony of the matter was that the Federals incorrectly had perceived the ironclad as being too well protected for them to continue fighting, not being cognizant of her desperate fuel emergency.

During the ferocious confrontation between the seven Union gunboats and the single Rebel ironclad, the Federal ships with their eight types of guns, sixty in total, had expended 557 shots, while the *Albemarle* with her two guns had expended only 27. [7] The Federals had used every method in their power in the attempt to destroy the formidable ironclad, but to no avail. In addition, during the fray one Federal gunboat was completely disabled and three others damaged severely. Four Federal crewmen were killed and twenty-five wounded.

Afterwards, the *CSS Albemarle* steamed defiantly into the mouth of the Roanoke River where she was moored at Plymouth. There she remained a threat to the Yankees still, even though desperately in need of repair. One positive outcome of the battle for the Union forces was the retrieval of their steamer *Bombshell* that the Rebels had raised only the month before following her sinking during the Battle of Plymouth.

Secretary Mallory's theory had been validated. An ironclad fleet certainly would prove invaluable to the Confederate Navy, just as he had predicted. However, Commander Cooke's biggest problem was that his Rebel ironclad was much too slow and cumbersome to be able to catch and destroy the faster and more maneuverable Yankee wooden gunboats, especially the double-enders.

Even so, because of his efforts, Commander James Wallace Cooke on June 10th received the following notification from Secretary of the Navy Mallory:

"You are hereby informed that the president (Davis) has appointed you by and with the advice and consent of the Senate as Captain in the Provisional Navy of the Confederate States, for gallant and meritorious conduct on the 19th, 20th, and 21st days of April 1864 in attacking the enemies ships and batteries and in cooperation with the army in the capture of the town of Plymouth NC, and in the action of the 5th of May, 1864 between the sloop Albemarle under your command and nine of the enemies gun boats in Albemarle Sound...." [8]

Until the war's finale, Cooke was in charge of Confederate forces on North Carolina's internal waters. The final scene of the drama at Plymouth, however, did not unfold until November of 1864, six months following the Yankee capitulation. Due to the daring of a 21-year old lieutenant by the name of William Barker Cushing, the Union Navy was able to retake the town, thereby ushering in Plymouth's third and final military occupation.

Since September 1864, plans for destroying the *CSS Albemarle* had been in the making. *"At all hazards the ram must be destroyed,"* was the order of Rear-Admiral Samuel Phillips, commander of the North Atlantic Squadron.

After having engaged the seven Yankee gunboats in May, the Confederate ironclad was still capable of wrecking havoc on the Federal fleet. Proof enough was when the wooden *Sassacus* had made her attempt to destroy the *Albemarle*, but instead ended up being damaged herself. Subsequently, because the United States Navy had no ironclad capable of crossing the Hatteras Bar to enter the Sound, the *Albemarle* was able to arrogantly anchor at the wharf in Plymouth

Lieut. William Barker Cushing, a personal friend of the late Lieut. Commander Charles W. Flusser, was determined to find a way to destroy the Rebel ironclad. After having submitted several proposals to Admiral Lee, Cushing concluded that the best plan for success involved the use of a small, low-pressure steamer armed with a torpedo. A single howitzer (a short cannon for high-angle firing of shells at low velocities) would also be part of the necessary equipment.

At the Brooklyn Navy Yard, Cushing, for the sum of four thousand dollars each, purchased and outfitted two fast 30-foot-long open steam launches (whaleboats) equipped with small engines propelled by a screw. *"Each craft had a boiler amidship, a steam engine mounted between the boiler and stern. They were fitted with tanks, pumps, condensers, small coal bunkers, a cockpit, and a small deck forward on which to mount the twelve pound Dahlgren boat howitzer. Each craft was driven to great speeds up to seven knots by a single propeller and steered by a simple rudder and tiller, by a helmsman who sat in the cockpit at the stern."* [9]

Finally, each launch was outfitted with a Woods-Lay torpedo fastened to the starboard side. A "torpedo" at that time was what would be considered a mine today, being *"merely a can of 150 pounds of black powder, air and a gravity operated detonator consisting of a common percussion cap and a large ball bearing."*[10]

Another definition is: *"The torpedo was a copper capsule holding 50 lbs. of powder perhaps with percussion caps on the front and standing out like frog eyes ready to be exploded by the first thing they came in contact with."*[11]

In addition, a 12-power howitzer was fitted to the bow of each launch and a 14-foot torpedo hook securely bracketed to the side. The Hudson River served as the testing place for the torpedo boom. *"Each (launch) has a long boom swiveled to the bow. It could fold sternwise. Primed for attack, the launches were designed to swing their booms directly forward. The vessel's momentum gave the torpedoes their impetus. The jerk of a line as they reached their target detonated the torpedoes."*[12]

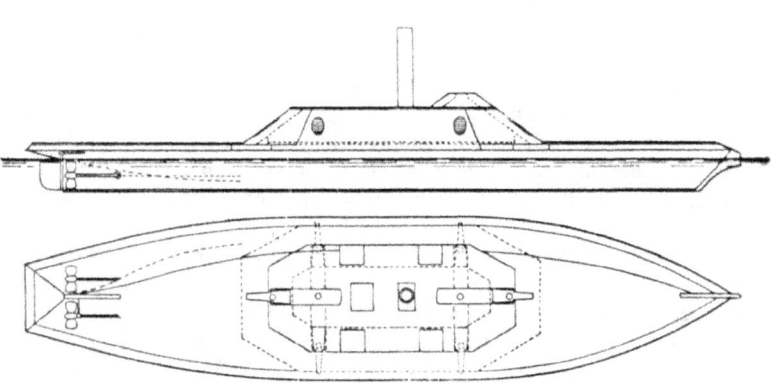

Fig. 53. ***Cushing's launch***

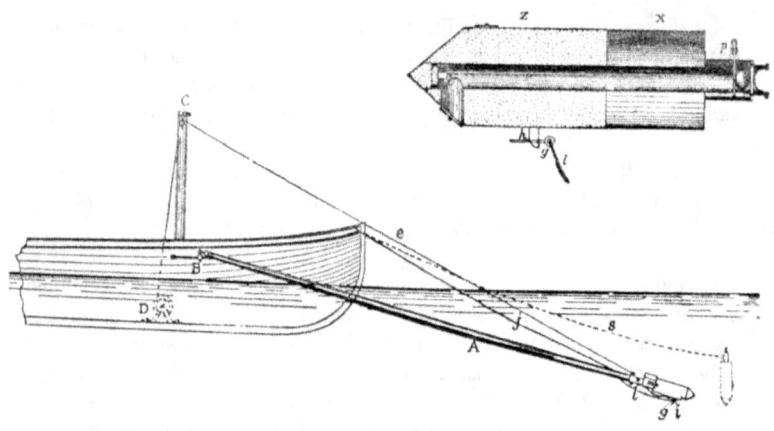

Fig. 54. Cushing's torpedo

Ironically, during the second year of the war, a Confederate shipbuilder, Theodore Stoney, had designed a similar small craft armed with a spar torpedo capable of carrying 100 pounds of explosives. Nick-naming the vessel, "David," the Rebels likened it to the Old Testament story of little David and the giant Goliath.[13]

After gaining possession of the launches and being confident that they would suffice, Cushing formulated plans for getting the two safely to North Carolina. However, during the journey, one of the vessels was lost. *Picket Boat Number Two* with Acting Ensign Andrew Stockholm in charge was captured by Confederate troops in Wicomico Bay, Virginia while en route to Fort Monroe.

Unfortunately, mechanical troubles had forced the launch to pull ashore for much-needed repairs. Meanwhile, a body of Confederate guerillas attacked the Yankee crew. After making a futile attempt at fighting them off, and upon realizing that he was going to lose the effort, Stockholm made the decision to burn the launch and to destroy all of his supplies.

Upon learning of Stockholm's desperate actions, Cushing was irate over what he considered the unnecessary loss of one of his boats. Unsympathetically, he expressed his ire:

"...I forget the name of the volunteer ensign to whom care was entrusted, but am pleased to know that he was taken prisoner. I trust that his bed was not of nor his food that of princes while in rebel hands."[14]

October 27, 1864, was a rainy night with the temperature registering 68 degrees and rapidly dropping. Protected by a mantle of dense fog, Lieut. Cushing set into action his clandestine plan for reaching the *CSS Albemarle* without being seen. Accompanied by a cutter carrying twelve men and with thirteen others with him in *Picket Boat Number One*, Lieut. Cushing planned to sneak up to the *Albemarle*, whose captain was then Lieut. Alexander Warley. Cushing's intention was to explode a charge under the metal protection of the *Albemarle's* hull, just at water level in order to create a hole large enough to drown the leviathan. By using a spar torpedo, Cushing was confident he would be able to sink the formidable ironclad to deck level.

He was well aware that his plan, although well thought out, was suicidal. In the first place, in order to be successful he would have to get past the vigilant guards on the shore. Second, he would have to get past the disabled *USS Southfield* being guarded by Rebels. Third, in order to detonate the torpedo by hand he would have to get extremely close to the well-guarded *CSS Albemarle*.

Professor J. R. Soley later would write about the danger involved:

"...When it is reflected that Cushing had attached to his person four separate lines, via, the detaching lanyard, the trigger-line, and two lines to direct the movements of the boat, one of which was fastened to the wrists and the other to the ankle of the engineer; that he was also directing the adjustment of the spar by the halliar; that the management of all these lines, requiring as much exactness and delicacy of touch as a surgical operation, where a single error in their employment, even a pull too much or too little, would render the whole expedition abortive, was carried out directly in front of the muzzle of a 100-pounder rifle, under a fire of musketry so hot that several bullets passed through his clothing, and carried out with perfect success, it is safe to say that the naval history of this world affords no other example of such marvelous coolness and professional skill as were shown by Cushing in the destruction of the Albemarle." [15]

★ ★ ★ ★

Cushing had no trouble at all in soliciting volunteers for his dangerous mission because his reputation was well known and his daring legendary. The young officer was highly respected within the Navy. Therefore, more than enough men volunteered, even though at first, they were not aware of the nature of the actual goal or of the extent of the danger involved. Cushing was speculating that he, as well as the other men involved, in all probability would not be able to escape, and so he did not brief the men until almost the actual moment for proceeding. At that time he offered them the option of turning back. No man did.

On the night of October 26th, Cushing tested the eight-mile run to the *Albemarle* in order to try out the feasibility of his daring idea. He was detected quickly; Federal pickets could have fired on him easily, making him realize that *Picket Boat Number*

One was much too noisy. So on the next day he had her engine enclosed in a wooden box and then covered with a heavy tarpaulin in order to muffle the engine's sound.

*Fig. 55. **"Picket Boat Number One"**
Courtesy of U.S. Naval Historical Center*

Among the men accompanying Cushing in *Picket Boat Number One* were two old friends, Acting Master's Mate John Woodman, and Acting Master's Mate William Howorth. [16] Even though the night was moonless, from the light of Rebel fires on the shore Cushing and his men could make out the dark looming form of the *Albemarle*. As the crew stealthily approached the anchored ironclad, they saw a large protective boom--a cordon of single cypress logs chained together--extending out nearly thirty feet from the ironclad's base.

Even though the crew of the *Albemarle* numbered only sixty, they were keeping a diligent watch on her deck. With the rumor of a launch having been seen just the night before on October 27th, Lieut. Warley had requested assistance from Rebel troops nearby; a picket of twenty-five soldiers equipped with rockets and a field piece had been dispatched as backup. The extra men had positioned themselves strategically on a schooner anchored just below the *Albemarle*.

Nevertheless, due to the dense fog *Picket Boat Number One* with her engine's throb muffled by the heavy tarpaulin, was able to steal unseen past the schooner. Then, by keeping close to the riverbank and without a sound being uttered, the launch passed within twenty feet of the well-guarded *Southfield*. Lieut. Cushing positioned his launch approximately 100 yards from the ironclad. Then at full speed he deliberately steered *Picket Boat Number One* into the protective log boom.

Upon hearing the noise, the Rebels immediately opened heavy fire from the *Albemarle*, as well as from the shore. Miraculously, throughout the shelling no one was injured, even though Cushing's coat was torn away by buckshot, and the sole of one of his shoes ripped off.

Captain Maffitt yelled down loudly from the *Albemarle*, demanding to be informed of the identity of the enemy. Cushing's prompt response was a shot from his launch's canister. Then immediately afterwards, he slid *Picket Boat Number One* over the slick barrier, getting stuck a distance of ten feet from the ram. Carefully then, Cushing lowered the torpedo into the water, and upon its release waited anxiously for it to settle under the *Albemarle*. Only when he was certain it was in place did he detonate the mine.

At that very same instant the *Albemarle* fired one hundred pounds of grape shot at ten-foot range, failing, however, to hit the small launch. Instead, an enormous geyser of water thrown out by the torpedo's explosion crashed soundly into *Picket Boat Number One*.

241

*Fig. 56. **"Cushing's Daring and Successful Exploit"***
Courtesy of U.S. Naval Historical Center

Fig. 57. **Lieut. Cushing's torpedo boat sinking the Albemarle on Roanoke River, N.C., October 27, 1864**
Courtesy of U.S. Naval Historical Center

Shouting, "*Men, save yourselves,*" Cushing with the other Yankees quickly dove into the frigid water. Two were drowned: Samuel Higgins, First-class fireman; and Cushing's good friend, John Woodson. Eleven were captured. The only two able to make their escape were Lieut. William Cushing, and Ordinary Seaman Edward Houghton, later to be awarded the Medal-of-Honor.

Among the Rebels, one man only was killed in the fray: Acting Master's Mate James Charles Hill. When the torpedo from *Picket Boat Number One* exploded, a hatchway fell on the very spot where Hill was sleeping. He died from the severe injuries he sustained. [17]

After being unsuccessful in his attempt to save John Woodson's life, Cushing swam to shore. Totally exhausted, he lay half-frozen on the riverbank, not knowing whether or not he had been successful in destroying the *Albemarle*. However, hearing a positive report delivered by a black man Cushing had paid to investigate the matter, the lieutenant was optimistic.

Upon awakening at daybreak, he soon realized how dangerously close he was to a Confederate picket station. Even so, he was able to steal a small skiff armed with a paddle, proceeding then to row for ten grueling hours in order to cover the eight miles separating Plymouth from the Albemarle Sound. Fortunately, he was traveling downstream with the current and the last four hours were, as Cushing described, spent "*asleep with exception to my arms and brain.*" [18]

Finally, near midnight he reached the picket-vessel *USS Valley City*. The sailors aboard the boat thought Cushing had perished the evening before. So at first they would not respond to his pleas for help, thinking that it might be part of a Confederate ruse. Consequently after they finally responded, they were astounded upon discovering that the exhausted man in the skiff was none other than the hero instrumental in drowning the Confederate leviathan. Only then did Cushing know with certainty that he had been successful in his mission. The abominable *CSS Albemarle* had been destroyed.

In his personal account of the encounter, former Confederate soldier J. H. Broadwell wrote a somewhat differing account, not mentioning the successful escape of Edward Houghton:

"*None of those that volunteered to destroy the Ram escaped except Lieut. W. B. Cushing himself. He had nine men besides himself and two were killed, with our field guns. The second shot shattered their little boat that bore the torpedo that sank our boat. Seven of the men climbed out and surrendered. One history says there were fourteen men while another history says there were eight men. It is not so. There were only ten men and only Cushing escaped.*" [19]

However, the following fifteen officers and men on *Picket Boat Number One* were recorded officially [20]:

Lieut. William B. Cushing, Commander	*Monticello*
William L. Howorth, Master's Mate	*Monticello* [22]
John Woodman, Acting Master's Mate	*Commodore Hull*
Francis H. Swan, Acting Assistant Paymaster	*Otsego*
Thomas S. Gay, Acting Master's Mate	*Otsego*
William Stotesbury, Acting Third Assistant Engineer	Picket-boat
Charles Steever, Acting Third Assistant Engineer	*Otsego*
Samuel Higgins, First class fireman	Picket-boat
Richard Hamilton, Coal heaver	*Shamrock*
William Smith, Ordinary seaman	*Chicopee*
Bernard Harley, Ordinary Seaman	*Chicopee*
Edward J. Houghton, Ordinary seaman	*Chicopee*
Lorenzo Deming, Landsman	Picket-boat
Henry Wilkes, Landsman	Picket-boat
Robert H. King, Landsman	Picket-boat

With *the Albemarle's* protection finally removed from the Roanoke River, on the very next day, October 29, 1864, at 11:15 a.m. Commander Macomb of the *USS Valley City* got under way with plans to immediately retake Plymouth. Union ships in his expedition included: [21]

Double-enders:	
Shamrock	Commander W. H. Macomb
Ostego	Lieutenant Rufus K. Duer
Wyalusing	Lieutenant-Commander Earl English
Tacony	Lieutenant-Commander W. T. Truxton
Ferryboats:	
Commodore Hull	Acting Master Francis Josselyn
Gunboat:	
Whitehead	Acting Master G. W. Barrett
Tugs:	
Belle	Acting Master James G. Green
Bazley	Acting master Mark D. Ames

Soon the expedition arrived at the spot where the wreck of the *USS Southfield* still lay. While exchanging shots with the lower batteries, Commander Macomb discovered that the Rebels had obstructed the channel with schooners sunk deliberately alongside the *USS Southfield*. Subsequently, the Union expedition was not able to continue upriver to Plymouth as planned.

Commander Macomb was forced then to formulate a new plan. On the next day, after ascertaining from a reconnaissance by the *USS Valley City* that the Middle River was clear, he determined to approach Plymouth by an alternate route. [22] As the expedition carefully threaded the narrow channel, it shelled Plymouth across the woods on the intervening neck of land. After reaching the head of the Middle River, the Union boats safely passed into the Roanoke River where they anchored, there to remain until morning.

At 9:30 a.m. the line was formed. The *USS Commodore Hull* was placed in advance since she was a ferryboat whose construction enabled her to fire ahead. The gunboat *USS Whitehead*, having arrived with stores just before the attack, was lashed to the *USS Tacony*, and the two tugboats, *Bazley* and *Belle*, to the double-enders *USS Shamrock* and *USS Otsego*, respectively, in order to furnish motive power in case the machinery were to become damaged.

An hour later after receiving and returning sharp fire of grape, shell, and canister, the *USS Shamrock* successfully planted a shell in an ammunition magazine. Immediately, the explosion caused the Confederates to hastily abandon their works, and Plymouth once again was in the possession of the Union forces. The third battle for Plymouth had ended, and until the conclusion of the war, the Yankees would remain in possession of the small town on the south bank of the Roanoke River.

Regarding Lieutenant William Barker Cushing, President Abraham Lincoln sent the following message to both the Senate and the House of Representatives:

"In conformity to the law of July 16, 1862, I most cordially recommend that Lieutenant William B. Cushing, United States Navy, receive a vote of thanks from Congress for his important, gallant and perilous achievement in destroying the rebel ironclad steamer Albemarle *on the night of the 27th of October, 1864 at Plymouth, N.C. The destruction of so formidable a vessel, which had resisted the continued attacks of a number of our vessels on former occasions, is an important event touching our future naval and military operations, and would reflect honor on any officer, and redound to the credit of this young officer and the few brave comrades who assisted in this successful and daring undertaking."* [23]

Lieutenant William Barker Cushing received congratulations from the Navy Department, the thanks of Congress, and a promotion to lieutenant-commander. [24] In his "Note on the Destruction of the Álbemarle," the ironclad's captain, A. F. Warley, later would report: *"That is the way the Albemarle was destroyed, and a more gallant thing was not done during the war."* [25]

Ironically, the type of launch the Confederates had dubbed "David" was the very same kind Cushing had chosen. So, a David (*Picket Boat Number One*) once again defeated a Goliath (*CSS Albemarle)*.

With casualties amounting to six killed and nine wounded, Plymouth once again was in possession of the Union forces for the third and final time. The Confederate ironclad, *Albemarle*, was destined to scrape the bottom of the Roanoke River until her raising by Union forces in 1867.[26]

And so the final curtain fell on the drama entitled "The Battle of Plymouth."

Fig. 58. ***Sunken "CSS Albemarle"***
Engraving from photograph by J. O. Davidson
N.C. Division of Archives and History

Chapter 27

FINAL REPORTS ON THE DESTRUCTION OF THE CSS ALBEMARLE

Report of Lieutenant Warley, C. S. Navy, commanding the CSS Albemarle

Honorable S. R. Mallory
Secretary of the Navy

Sir:
    The night of the 27th instant, a dark, rainy night, I had the watch on board doubled and took extra precaution. At or about 3 o'clock a.m. on the 28th, the officer of the deck discovered a small steamer in the river, hailed her, received an unsatisfactory answer, rang the alarm bell and opened fire on her with the watch. The officers and men were at their quarters in as quick time as was possible, but the vessel was so near that we could not bring our guns to bear, and the shot fired from the after gun loaded with grape, failed to take effect. The boat running obliquely, struck us under the port bow, running over the boom, exploded a torpedo, and smashed a large hole in us just under the water line, under a heavy fire of musketry. The boat surrendered and I sent Lieutenant Roberts to take charge of her. Manned the pumps and gave the order to fire up, so as to use the donkey engine. The water gained on us so fast that all exertions were fruitless, and the vessel went down in a few moments, merely leaving her shield and smokestack out.

    In justice to myself I must say the pickets below gave no notice of her approach, and the artillery which was stationed by the vessel for a protection, gave us no assistance, manning only one piece at too late a time to be of any service.

    Having condensed this report as much as I could, I respectfully request a court of inquiry, to establish on whose shoulders rests the blame of the loss of the Albemarle.

    I am, respectfully, your obedient servant.

                        A. F. Warley,
                        Lieutenant, Commanding, C. S. Navy [1]

★★★★

Report of Lieutenant William Barker Cushing, U.S. Navy

Rear-Admiral D. D. Porter
Commanding North Atlantic Squadron

Albemarle Sound, North Carolina, October 30, 1864
Sir:
I have the honor to report that the rebel ironclad Albemarle is at the bottom of the Roanoke River. On the night of the 27th, having prepared my steam launch, I proceeded up toward Plymouth with 13 [2] officers and men, partly volunteers from the squadron.

The distance from the mouth of the river to the ram was about 8 miles, the stream averaging in width some 200 yards, and line with the enemy's pickets. A mile below the town was the wreck of the Southfield, surrounded by some schooners, and it was understood that a gun was mounted there to command the bend. I therefore took some of the Shamrock's cutters in tow, with orders to cast off and board at that point if we were hailed. Our boat succeeded in passing the pickets, and even the Southfield, within 20 yards, with our discovery, and we were not hailed until by the lookouts on the ram. The cutter was then cast off and ordered below, while we make for our enemy under a full head of steam.

The rebels sprung their rattle, rang the bell, and commenced firing, at the same time repeating their hail and seeming much confused. The light of fire ashore showed me the ironclad made fast to the wharf, with a pen of logs around her about 30 feet from her side.

Passing her closely, we made a complete circle so as to strike her fairly, and went into her bows on. By this time the enemy's fire was fairly severe, but a dose of canister at short range served to moderate their zeal and disturb their aim. Paymaster Swan, of the Otsego, was wounded near me, but how many more I know not. Three bullets struck my clothing, and the air seemed full of them.

In a moment we had struck the logs, just abreast of the quarter port, breasting them in some feet, and our bows resting on them. The torpedo boom was then lowered and by a vigorous pull I succeeded in diving the torpedo under the overhand and exploding it at the same time that the Albemarle's gun was fired. A shot seemed to go crashing through my boat, and a dense mass of water rushed in from the torpedo, filling the launch and completely disabling her.

The enemy then continued his fire at 15 feet range, and demanded our surrender, which I twice refused, ordering the men to save themselves, and removing my own coat and shoes. Springing into the river, I swam, with others, into the middle of the stream, the rebels failing to hit us.

The most of our party were captured, some were drowned, and only one escaped besides myself, and he in another direction. Acting Master's Mate Woodman, of the Commodore Hull, I met in the water half a mile below the town, and assisted him as best I could, but failed to get him ashore.

Completely exhausted, I managed to reach the shore, but was too weak to crawl out of the water until just at daylight, when I managed to creep into the swamp, close to the fort. While hiding a few feet from the path, two of the Albemarle's officers passed, and I judged from their conversation that the ship was destroyed.

Some hours traveling in the swamp served to bring me out well below the town, when I sent a negro in to gain information and found that the ram was truly sunk.

Proceeding through another swamp, I came to a creek and captured a skiff, belonging to a picket of the enemy, and with this, by 11 o'clock the next night, had made my way out to the Valley City.

Citing master's Mate William L. Howorth, of the Monticello, showed, as usual, conspicuous bravery. He is the same officer who had been with me twice in Wilmington harbor. I trust he may be promoted, when exchanged, as well as Acting Third Assistant Engineer Stotesbury, who, being for the first time under fire, handled his engine promptly and with coolness. All the officers and men behaved in the most gallant manner. I will furnish their names to the Department as soon as they can be procured.

The cutter of the Shamrock boarded the Southfield, but found no gun. Four prisoners were taken there.

The ram is now completely submerged, and the enemy have sunk three schooners in the river to obstruct the passage of our ships.

I desire to call the attention of the admiral and Department to the spirit manifested by the sailors on the ships in these sounds. But few men were wanted, but all hands were eager to go into the action, many offering their chosen shipmates a month's pay to resign in their favor.

I am, sir, very respectfully, your obedient servant,

W. B. Cushing
Lieutenant, U.S. Navy [3]

Chapter 28

LIEUT. WILLIAM BARKER CUSHING, USN

In October, 1864, when Confederate Colonel John N. Whitfield of the 67th Regiment assumed command of the Plymouth garrison with the express purpose of guarding the *Albemarle,* rumors were circulating, suggesting that the Yankees were about to make a move. Therefore, in anticipation, Confederate Captain Lee had moved several artillery pieces to the banks of the Roanoke adjacent to the ironclad.

Indeed, such plans were in motion, and they were about to be implemented by the dauntless and determined twenty-one-year-old, Lieut. William Barker Cushing. His parents' fifth child, "Willie" was born in 1842 in a Delafield, Wisconsin log cabin. However, he grew up in Fredonia, New York, because in 1845 his physician father contracted pneumonia while traveling in Ohio in an attempt to improve his failing health. So following the death of her husband, Mrs. Cushing took her seven children back to her home in Cautauqua County, New York, where two Cushing ancestors, Hezekiah Barker and Zattu Cushing, originally had settled. There in Fredonia, William's mother opened a school in order to support herself and her large family. [1]

Always considered a brash young man, William Barker Cushing is credited with achieving the most daring venture of the Civil War; he destroyed the Confederate ironclad, *CSS Albemarle*. Well known for his love of adventure, Cushing was just the man to embark upon such a task. His high spirited personality did not always keep him in good stead, however, because after his appointment at the United States Naval Academy at Annapolis, he often got himself into trouble. Although at first his antics were not considered serious infractions, they were, however, enough to nearly give fifteen-year old "Willie" an early expulsion.

Even though a mediocre scholar and one inclined to be a prankster, Cushing was able to survive at the Academy to his fourth year. However, when he began playing jokes on his Spanish teacher, he also began his downward slide to disgrace. "The straw that broke the camel's back" came when Willie rigged a tub of water to pour down on the professor upon opening the door. In addition to carrying out that prank, Cushing also drew an uncomplimentary caricature of the professor, then passing it around to the amusement of his classmates. So after receiving a failing grade in Spanish, he was deemed by that time too disruptive and too disrespectful to be allowed to continue at the Academy. Therefore, on March 23, 1861 the shocked William Barker Cushing was forced to resign, mere months before his anticipated graduation. [2]

Crushed by the unexpected enforced resignation, young Cushing traveled to Washington, D.C., to stay for a while with Commodore Smith who had befriended the young man. For weeks, he wandered through the streets of the capitol while contemplating his unpromising future. Often he would meet with former fellow midshipmen, all sympathetic to their friend's plight and making attempts at offering counsel. Even so, Cushing could see nothing positive in his future since a career in the Navy always had been his goal. Then came the Confederates' firing on Fort Sumter, igniting the War Between the States, and thereby changing the fates of thousands, including that of young William Barker Cushing.

Because he was southern born, Cushing was offered the opportunity to join the Confederates. After refusing, he presented himself to Gideon Welles, the Secretary of the Union Navy, ironically the very man who had informed "Willie" of his dismissal from the Naval Academy. As Cushing was requesting an opportunity to serve in the United States Navy, Welles was impressed by the young man's sincerity. So William Barker Cushing was given the opportunity to redeem himself, being appointed an Acting Master's Mate in the United States Volunteer Navy, assigned to the *USS Minnesota*. [3]

Quickly proving himself, Cushing on June 1, 1861, was warranted as a midshipman, exactly what he would have been had he graduated from the Naval Academy with his class. At that time, due to an Act of Congress on July 16, 1862, many opportunities for promotion were becoming available. During the next month nineteen-year-old William Barker Cushing was promoted two grades to Lieutenant, being assigned to the *USS Commodore Perry* commanded by Cushing's Academy teacher, friend, and mentor, Charles Williamson Flusser. [4]

Even by his physical appearance young Cushing could be thought of as a nonconformist. At that particular time in history, men were quite proud of their elaborate goatees, beards, and fancy whiskers, such as General Burnside's "mutton chop" sideburns. However, William Barker Cushing, however, almost in defiance, was clean shaved and wore his sandy-colored hair in a "page-boy" style, as contrasted to the styles so popular at that time. [5]

As Cushing's reputation for daring grew, volunteers, admiring the seemingly invincible young man, were hopeful of serving with him on dangerous raids. For instance, when he planned attacks on Rebel salt works, he had no trouble at all with securing enthusiastic recruits.

Another of his daunting missions took place in May of 1864 when he was assigned the task of ascertaining the disposition of the *CSS Raleigh*. Taking with him two cutters of sailors, he was able not only to ascertain the abandonment of the *Raleigh*, but was able to accomplish several other daring feats as well. Within the duration of one day he evaluated the weakness of the Confederate fleet, stole the CSA mail, and evaded eight guard boats. In the meanwhile, he appropriated two skiffs, pilfered one set of civilian clothing in order to buy from a general store dinner for nineteen sailors, borrowed a horse in order to spy on a camp of 1300 Rebel infantrymen, cut a telegraph line, and all before capturing ten prisoners.[6]

During his naval career Cushing was given commands of the following ships: the *USS Commodore Barney*, the *USS Shokoken*, and the *USS Monticello*.[7] It was from that last gunboat he was summoned to meet with Rear-Admiral Samuel Phillips Lee who proposed that William Barker Cushing lead and expedition against the *CSS Albemarle*.

Fig. 59. **Lieut. Commander William Barker Cushing, USN**
Courtesy of U.S. Naval Historical Center

Chapter 29

DEMISE OF THE SHIPS OF WAR

The clash between the two ironclads on March 9, 1862 brought about what experts insist changed naval warfare. The battle between the *CSS Virginia* (*Merrimac*) and the *USS Monitor* marked a whole new era of naval history; for with that one pivotal confrontation wooden vessels became obsolete.

The two mighty ironclads never again were to meet in combat; for after the single encounter with the *CSS Virginia* (*Merrimac*), the *USS Monitor* experienced only limited action. Then, on December 31, 1862, while headed toward a new blockade duty assignment at Beaufort, North Carolina, the *USS Monitor* ran into a fierce storm and sank off Cape Hatteras. Sixteen crewmen unfortunately drowned while desperately attempting to climb into lifeboats.

For ninety-one years the *USS Monitor* would lay undetected, rusting on the bottom of the Atlantic Ocean. In September of 1951, the United States Navy officially would list her as "out of commission." Years later in 1973, scientists aboard Duke University's research vessel *Eastward* would locate the *Monitor* approximately sixteen miles off Cape Hatteras, lying more than 220 feet down. Even though the ship would not in good enough condition to be raised, experienced skin divers would be allowed to get close enough to study her. [1]

Information about the ship lost 140 years ago has been in the news recently. On August 6, 2002, the *Monitor's* 150-pound revolutionary revolving gun turrett was recovered, and on August 10th, removed to the Mariner's Museum in Newport News, Virginia. There it will remain in a conservation tank for the next twelve to fifteen years, after which time it will go on display at the USS Monitor Center, expected to open in 2007. [2]

★ ★ ★ ★

The mighty *CSS Virginia* (*Merrimac*) was afloat a mere two months because the Confederates chose to scuttle her near Craney Island in order to avoid her capture by the Federals. Prior to that, she had been either in dock or getting repaired, not fighting on the high seas.

The *CSS Virginia* (*Merrimac*) had three commanders during her brief life, the first being former Union naval officer Franklin Buchanan, who lasted but three days before he was wounded. [3] Buchanan was convinced that his ironclad had mortally damaged his enemy's boat, while Captain John Worden on the *USS Monitor* believed the same about his ironclad. [4] However, neither boat had been damaged to any degree.

Historians categorize the commanders' conclusion as *"one of history's curious cases of mutual misrepresentation."*

After the sinking of the *CSS Albemarle*, the United States Navy purchased her for $79,944.00, but had no plans for rebuilding. [5] The *Albemarle's* final fate was to be towed by the *USS Ceres* to the Norfolk Navy Yard where she would sit deteriorating for the next sixteen months. Finally, in October of 1867, following her $2500.00 sale at the Navy auction, the once feared ironclad ram became just a pile of junk, leaving behind only her battered funnel that can now be viewed at the North Carolina Hall of History in Raleigh, North Carolina. [6]

The fate of the ironclads, in general, was a dismal one. Secretary of the Navy Mallory initially had envisioned a small, but unconquerable fleet of formidable Rebel ironclads against the larger fleet of Federal gunboats. He felt that ironclads had the advantage over the wooden hulled gunboats, and rightly so. However, only twenty-two Confederate ironclads ever were launched. Of those, some became waterborne and unusable, while others were destroyed deliberately by their commanders in order to avoid leaving them to the Yankees. Only four actually got into the hands of the enemy. [7] Of the seventy-six Union ironclads begun a mere forty-two were commissioned.

Although not an ironclad or even a boat of any great size, measuring only about 100 tons, the *Ellis* played an important role in the lives of three naval officers involved in the last two battles for the occupation of Plymouth. Initially, she had been a Rebel side wheel steamer.

During the Pasquotank River battle, the *CSS Ellis* was captured by the United States Navy and assigned to the North Atlantic Blockading Squadron. On November 25, 1862 after grounding above the river's mouth at New Bern and not being able to be set afloat, she was torched by the Federals and completely demolished by the explosion of her magazine. That was just another illustration of self-destruction by fire in order to keep something of value from getting into enemy hands.

The most interesting and intriguing fact about the small boat was that she was associated with the following three seamen who played roles in the Plymouth drama:

> Charles Williamson Flusser USN who early in the war saved the life of the commander of the *CSS Ellis*, James Wallace Cooke CSN. At that time the boat fell into Federal hands.

> James Wallace Cooke CSN who later became commander of the ironclad CSS Albemarle. Because of the Rebel ram, Charles Williamson Flusser who had saved Cooke's life, lost his.

William Barker Cushing USN who was commander of *CSS Ellis* in 1862 when she was demolished by the explosion of her magazine. Because of his fast friendship with the deceased Flusser, Cushing destroyed the *CSS Albemarle* in 1864.

Chapter 30

THE WAR'S FINALE

Charleston, S.C., July 1, 1864

Maj. Gen. J.G. Foster, Comdg. Dept. of the South, Hilton Head, S.C.:

General: The journals of this morning inform us, for the first time, that five general officers of the Confederate service have arrived at Hilton Head with a view to their being subjected to the same treatment that we are receiving here. We think it is just to ask for these officers every kindness and courtesy that you can extend to them, in acknowledgement of the fact that we, at this time, are as pleasantly and comfortably situated as possible for prisoners of war, receiving from the Confederate authorities every privilege that we could desire or expect, nor are we unnecessarily exposed to fire.

Respectfully, General, your obedient servants,

H. W. Wessells, Brig. Gen., U.S. Vols.
T. Seymour, Brig. Gen., U.S. Vols.
C. A Heckman, Brig. Gen., U.S. Vols.
Alexander Shaler, Brig. Gen., U.S. Vols.
Prisoners of War [1]

Hdqrs. Dept. of the South, Hilton Head, S.C., July 29, 1864

Gen. Wessells:
My dear General:

I have just received authority to exchange the prisoners in my hands, rank for rank, or their equivalents, according to the cartel. I send an **aide-de-camp** to make arrangements for the exchange.

Yours truly, J. G. Foster [2]

Hdgts., Dept, of the South, Hilton Head, S.C, Aug. 4, 1864

Maj Gen. H. W. W. Halleck, Chief of Staff, Washington, D.C.
General:

I have the honor to acknowledge the receipt of your letter of the 12*th* (ultimo), authorizing me to exchange the prisoners of war now in my hands, and to report that I made such exchange yesterday in Charleston Harbor, and that our released officers, comprising 5 generals and 45 field officers, will proceed North on the steamer Fulton, under command of Brig. Gen. Wessells, who has orders to report to the Adjutant General of the Army from Fort Monroe, and also from New York, if no orders are received before their arrival in the latter city. Three line officers that escaped from the railroad train en route to Charleston are sent with the other officers.

I have the honor to be, very respectfully, your obedient servant,

J. G. Foster, Maj.-Gen. Commanding [3]

★ ★ ★ ★

War Dept. Adjt. General's Office, Washington, Sept. 12, 1864

General Orders, No. 255.

The following named officers and enlisted men of the U.S. Army, having been duly exchanged as prisoners of war by an agreement entered into between Maj. Gen. J. G. Foster, commanding Department of the South, and Gen. S. Jones, commanding the city of Charleston, are hereby declared so exchanged: Brig. Gen. H. W. Wessells,...Col. T. F. Lehmann,...Lieut. Col. W. C. Maxwell..., .The officers...whose exchange is announced above will proceed to join their respective regiments and commands at the expiration of the leaves of absence which may have been given.

By order of the Secretary of War: E. D. Townsend, Assistant Adjutant General

[4]

★ ★ ★ ★

Finally during the early months of 1865, the disastrous War Between the States was reaching its finale. The end was near, even as the exchanged Colonel Theodore Lehmann returned to duty. The original commander of the 103rd Pennsylvania Volunteer Regiment when it had been organized in 1861, Lehmann was given command of the Sub-District of the Albemarle in December of 1864, with headquarters on Roanoke Island. [5]

After the fall of Plymouth, Captain Thomas Cochran was in command of the 103rd Pennsylvania Veteran Volunteers Regiment. [6] He requisitioned a copy of the last muster roll staff and field, as well as the names of the nine companies captured at Plymouth. Due to their being at Fort Reno on the island since January 2, 1864, the tenth, Co. C, fortunately, had been spared the fate of the others disastrously garrisoned at Plymouth.

Army regulations required daily and quarterly returns, muster rolls of field and staff, as well as bi-monthly rolls for counting every man in each regiment. Therefore, the names of all members of each company were called, including those having been taken prisoner by the Confederates. The absent men were recorded as "Captured at Plymouth, N.C., April 20, 1864." Captain Cochran also compiled a muster roll for the detachment consisting of the four members who, fortunately, were absent from the captured companies during the battle. [7]

One evening, after their numbers had reached the necessary one hundred for filling a company, the ex-prisoners of war appeared as a detachment at dress parade, not having drilled or executed the manual of arms for nearly a year. With great pride Corporal Luther Dickey recorded the moving scene:

"Without any preliminary practice, whatever, they executed the manual of arms, as if it were done by one man. No company of the Regiment, at any time in its history, ever surpassed this detachment in the manipulation of arms, as it was executed on this occasion." [8]

Captain Thomas Cochran, well respected by his men, had been with the 103rd Pennsylvania Volunteer Regiment ever since its organization, having risen steadily in rank until becoming captain. Daily more officers and men were returning to the regiment being reconstituted on Roanoke Island; so when Captain Cratty arrived with more seniority, Captain Cochran no longer was the officer in command. [9]

Eight companies, accompanied by commissioned officers, arrived on the island for consolidating with the 103rd, as well as an equal number with the 101st. By that time, though, the troops wanted nothing more than to return home, some having been away for nearly four years. After experiencing such a horrific war, the Yankees were of the mind that even the northern coal mines, factories, mills, and farms, from which they had so eagerly escaped, would look good to them. However, the war had not ceased and so they could not depart just yet for home; but they were sensing that the end was very near.

All reports at that time, official as well as unofficial, were indicating that the Federals were the victors, and so, understandably, the war-weary men were beginning to become quite restless. In the spring of 1865 Army discipline on Roanoke Island was not as tight as it was elsewhere. Because of the severe deprivations the men had suffered as prisoners of war, they were allowed much more freedom than they would have been accorded under any other circumstances. Scuppernong wine was quite plentiful on the island, and various social activities were being held, such as lively dances arranged by the Terpsichoreans and various Unionists living on the island. Due to being granted more liberties than the other troops, and also being exempted from duty, the laxity of discipline got a number of the ex-prisoners of war into a great deal of trouble.

Since government food rations never had been what the soldiers considered satisfactory, they were accustomed to supplementing their meals by foraging the surrounding areas for decent food. So under the cover of darkness, some of the ex-prisoners of war had begun skulking around, stealing chickens from the "contrabands" who, in turn, protested to Colonel Lehmann. Even though subsequently being given strict orders to remain in their quarters at night, the soldiers paid little attention, stubbornly continuing to poach. When a number of new troops arrived on the island, Colonel Lehmann ordered them to patrol the island both day and night in order to keep the ex-prisoners of war in their quarters unless they were given special permission to leave. However, in spite of the order, the new guards allowed the men to come and go at will.

One night about twenty-five ex-prisoners of war decided to sneak out to a dance being held at a nearby home. When Colonel Lehmann was made aware that his order to remain in quarters was being disobeyed so flagrantly, he was furious, immediately issuing an order that the revelers be arrested and padlocked in the log guardhouse until morning. One soldier was to remain on duty all night, standing guard in front of the only door. At dawn Colonel Lehmann planned to put in his appearance and to mete out an appropriate punishment.

A highly disciplined soldier, the 53 year-old German-born colonel expected his men to be likewise, and when they failed, he was known to become quite angry. So at the break of day as he was approaching the guardhouse, he already was in a foul mood, spouting denunciations peppered with expletives. After the soldier on duty was ordered to open the guardhouse door, it swung open to reveal nothing but emptiness. All of the men were gone!

Unbeknown to the soldier guarding the door in front, during the night, surreptitiously, the prisoners had dug themselves a tunnel that allowed them to crawl out through the rear of the guardhouse. If at all possible, the Colonel was more furious than he had been before.

Even before reveille was bugled, he stormed the quarters demanding that the culprits step forth. Of course, no man did. The Colonel then resorted to fabrication by saying that he knew exactly who they were, and that it would go much easier on them if they confessed then. However, the miscreants were well aware that the Colonel did not know their identities, and so they all stood as one. Consequently, the enraged Colonel meted out a severe punishment to the whole detachment, to the innocent as well as to the guilty, ordering it into exile. All of the men were to be sent to a bleak place called Coynjack, located on the Dismal Swamp Canal, there to be totally isolated from civilization.

Fortunately for everyone concerned, the war was at its finale. So instead of going into isolation, the men were going home. Sometime at a future reunion Colonel Lehmann would find it possible to laugh heartily with some of those same men, because by that time he, too, would consider it a funny war anecdote. [10]

★ ★ ★ ★

On June 27, 1865 the surviving 187 members of the 85th New York Volunteers were mustered out at New Bern, North Carolina. Some of the originals had been mustered out previously in scattered places due to the fact that the majority had been in prisons. Silas G. Burdick was an ex-member of the 85th New York Volunteers and a member of the Dedication Commission for the state of New York's monument at Andersonville. He stated in a recorded dedication speech that of the 463 soldiers from the regiment entering Andersonville Prison, 311 had died there, the largest number from any Union regiment. According to John Ball, present historian of the 85th New York Volunteers Regiment, of the 986 men originally enrolled, 399 died between October of 1861 and June of 1865. [11]

When the 16th Connecticut Regiment was mustered into service on August 24, 1862, the number had been 1,007. However, on June 24, 1865, when they were mustered out at New Bern, North Carolina, the number had dwindled to a mere 131. Assembling in Hartford, Connecticut, on August 24, 1865, the men received their final pay as Union soldiers. Officers, however, were not paid until the final returns had been made and all property accounted for. [12]

Robert Holmes, an original member of the 16th Connecticut, was not among that number gathering at the state capitol. Rather, he had been furloughed in December, 1864, and sent home to recuperate. His orders were to return to duty on January 25, 1865. However, Dr. George W. Samford stated in a medical certificate:

" *(I) find he is suffering by reason of eight month (the actual number of months was seven) of cruel treatment in a Rebel Prison which has caused great emaciation, general debility, a bad cough, pain in the side, chronic diarrhea and in my opinion is unable to travel and will be unfit for any duty for twenty days from the expiration of his present furlough.*"

On July 7, 1865, twenty-four-year-old Robert Holmes was discharged from the Army after having spent six months in the U.S. Army General Hospital. [13] After settling in Avon, Connecticut, he was chosen to serve at the Constitutional Convention of 1902. For services rendered he was presented with an oak sapling that he, in turn, gave to the people of Avon. One hundred years later the tree is still standing at the corner of Route 44 and Avon Old Farms Road.

*Fig. 60. **Robert Holmes' 100 year old oak tree, 2002***
Courtesy of Scott Holmes

*Fig. 61. **Marker for centennial Holmes oak tree***
Avon, Conn.

According to his descendant Debra Miller Felice, historian of the 101st Pennsylvania Volunteers, Abraham Rice returned alone to his home in Rainsburg, Pennsylvania, leaving behind his twin, Isaac, buried in South Carolina. Abraham Rice adopted the children of his fallen comrade, Benjamin Hanks, one of four Hanks brothers who died at Andersonville Prison. [13] Originally, in addition to the Rice twins, there had been three sets of Hanks' brothers serving in the 101st Pennsylvania Regiment, giving it the moniker of the "Brothers' Regiment."

The 103rd Pennsylvania Regiment was ordered to New Bern for its mustering out of the Army on June 25, 1865. Sadly, at that time only eighty-one of the original almost 1000 members of the regiment were present. A greater percentage of the original organization of the "Hardluck Regiment" had died than that of any other regiment. [14]. However, from New Bern the Pennsylvanians were not yet free to leave for home because their final pay would not be issued until their formal discharge at Harrisburg, Pennsylvania, on July 13, 1865.

From the period of time in 1861 when Co. C of the 103rd Pennsylvania Volunteers had been organized near Pittsburgh and until the end of the war, the total enrollment was 128. However, of the original number of enlistees, only 36 were recorded as being mustered out because of death, wounds, disease, transfers, and desertions. [15] One of the survivors was William Allison Fulton who returned to his home in Clarion County, Pennsylvania where he married the sister of his best friend, Frank Mahoney, who had died in Andersonville Prison.

Interestingly, also being discharged in Harrisburg, Pennsylvania [16] far from his birthplace in Chowan County, North Carolina, was nineteen-year-old Crowder Pacien, great-grandfather of the author. He was not an original member of Co. C. Rather, he was an ex-slave, a runaway who had enlisted as a private on January 1, 1864 in the 103rd Pennsylvania Regiment when it was garrisoned at Plymouth, North Carolina. [17]

Surviving the war to become a lifelong member of the GAR, he lived in Pennsylvania for the remainder of his life. Every Decoration Day (Memorial Day) he would be found proudly marching, and in later years, riding in the annual parade originated to honor Union veterans. Crowder Pacien (Patience) died in 1930 at the age of 83 years, one month and five days, and was buried in the cemetery at West Pittston, [18] a small borough in the anthracite coal mining region of northeastern Pennsylvania. By his distinctively shaped Civil War gravestone is the GAR stanchion and a fresh American flag replaced annually.

*Fig. 62. **Crowder Patience (aka Pacien), aged 74 in 1922***
West Pittston, Pa.

*Fig. 63. **Tombstone of Crowder Patience, Co. C 103rd Penna. Vols.**
West Pittston Cemetery, West Pittston, Pa.*

CHAPTER 31

General Wessells Reports on the Battle of Plymouth [1]

Cooperstown, N.Y., August 18, 1864

General:

 I have the honor to inform you that on the 20th of April last I was compelled to surrender the post of Plymouth, N.C. to a superior rebel force, and now report to you the circumstances, as follows:

 For some months previous to the date above mentioned, I felt satisfied from information derived from various sources, that a vigorous effort on the part of the enemy would be made to wrest the State of North Carolina from our possession. This opinion was expressed to you in frequent communications, with the hope that the military force would be strengthened, and that at least one iron-clad gunboat would be added to the naval squadron for the protection of the sounds and rivers. My expectations were fully confirmed by the movement of General Pickett upon New Bern in February, and although this attempt resulted in failure, the enemy well remained in strong force along the line of the Neuse evidently with further designs.

 During the month of April conflicting reports were brought as to the movements of the enemy. At one time he was said to be concentrating on the Roanoke, at another on the Tar River, threatening both Plymouth and Washington, when, on the 13th, my information was so positive as to the former that I at once requested from department headquarters direct a re-enforcement of 5,000 men, believing they could not be spared from the North Carolina stations.

 On the 16th the gun-boat Tacony, Lieutenant-Commander Truxton, arrived from New Bern and having in the meantime learned that no considerable force of the enemy was on the Roanoke, but rather threatening Washington from some point on the Tar River, I permitted her to return on the following morning, April 17, and this decision is to be regretted. At 4 o'clock of that day the extreme mounted patrol on the Washington road was captured by an advanced guard of the enemy's cavalry, and the cavalry outpost dispersed and driven in, a re-enforcement, under Lieutenant Russell. Twelfth New York Cavalry, was also compelled to retire, bringing away that officer severely wounded. The infantry outposts were at once strengthened, and the enemy soon began to appear on the Washington road in great force, having made a forced march of near 30 miles in hopes of making a complete surprise. This design failed, as our line of skirmishers remained steady. Fort Gray, 2 miles above and on the river bank, was assailed at the same time, sustaining until dark a heavy connanade.

The garrison, composed of detachments of Eighty-fifth New York Volunteers and Second Massachusetts Heavy Artillery, Captains Brown and Fiske, though much annoyed by sharpshooters, returned the fire of the enemy with great vigor, and, with the exception of a few casualties, no impression was made on the work. The line of defense extended from Fort Gray to the crossing of Coneby Creek, below the town, a distance of 2 and ½ miles, the former being a detached work, separated from the main line by Welch's Creek and its marsh.

The garrison was distributed along this line, and composed as follows: Sixteenth Connecticut Volunteers Col. Francis Beach 400 effective men, Eighty-fifth New York Volunteers, Col. E. Fardella, 450; One hundred and first Pennsylvania Volunteers, Lieut. Col. A. W. Taylor, 300; One hundred and third Pennsylvania Volunteers, Col. T. F. Lehmann, 400; Twenty-fourth New York Independent Battery, six guns, Captain Cady, detachment from Companies A and F, Twelfth New York Cavalry, Captain Roche, and two companies Second Massachussetts Heavy Artillery, under Captain Sampson, the latter being distributed in small detachments in the several earth-works.

There were also present portions of two companies Second North Carolina Volunteers, native troops, under Captains Johnson and Hoggard. [2] The naval force at that time consisted of the gun-boats **Miami**, Lieut. Commander Charles W. Flusser, U.S. Navy one of Kentucky's most noble and chivalrous sons, **Southfield**, Lieutenant French, volunteer service, with the smaller boats, **Whitehead** and **Ceres**, the whole under the direction of Captain Flusser.

For several months previous it had been well understood that iron plated boats for operations in the sounds were in course of construction near Halifax on the Roanoke, and Kinston on the Neuse, to move down those rivers at the proper time in conjunction with a land force. Work on the former had been so often delayed for want of plates and other causes that its completion at times seemed doubtful, but was too well watched for me to obtain positive and reliable information. On the 10th of April, however, it was generally believed that the **Albemarle**, though not entirely covered with plating, had been floated down as far as the enemy's works at Rainbow Banks.

It was the design of Captain Flusser to fight this formidable antagonist in the river with his own boat lashed to the **Southfield**, running in at close quarter, whilst the **Whitehead** was to use every effort to disable her propeller, and great confidence was felt as to the result of this plan.

The line of defense surrounding the town was divided into three nearly equal portions, the right commanded by Colonel Fardella, the center by Colonel Lehmann, the left subdivision being under the direction of Colonel Beach. Eighty-fifth Redoubt, so named from the regiment by which it was constructed, was a small detached work in front of the right, garrisoned by detachments of Second Massachusetts Heavy artillery and Eight-fifth New York Volunteers, commanded by Captain Chapin, of the latter regiment. *The attacking force, as was subsequently ascertained, consisted of Hoke's Ransom's and Kemper's brigades (the latter commanded by Colonel Mercer), all veteran regiments, mostly from Virginia and North Carolina. This division was accompanied by several formidable field batteries and a suitable force of cavalry. Until dark of the 17th sharp skirmishing was kept up on the Washington road, extending across the fields nearly to the Acre Road, but without any important result, and the light was passed in comparative quiet. The enemy was too strong to attempt a sortie with any hope of success.*

On the following morning at daylight a severe connade was opened against Fort Gray, resulting in some fatal casualties, but the garrison remained firm, replying vigorously to the enemy's fire. The 200-pounder in Battery Worth was also brought to bear in that direction, but without any decided effect. The armed transport Bombshell, *in communicating with Fort Gray, received several shots below her water-line, being barely able to return to town, when she sank at the wharf.*

The transport Massasoit *made two trips to Roanoke Island, carrying away a large number of women and children, contrabands, and other noncombatants. The gun-boat* Ceres, *being above Fort Gray at the time of its investment, passed down the river under a destructive fire and rejoined the squadron, with a loss of 9 men killed and wounded. During the whole of this day incessant skirmishing was maintained along and between the main approaches in front of the town, at a distance of 1,200 yards from the line of defense, but soon after sunset the enemy advanced his batteries, supported by an over whelming force, and appearances indicated a general attack.*

Our line of skirmishers fell back firing and in good order, and the enemy under cover of darkness opened a furious cannonade upon the town in every direction. This fire was replied to by Captain Sampson from Fort Williams with great coolness and precision, inflicting heavy damage and loss upon the enemy. Finding our front too well prepared for an assault, the attack was discontinued at about 8 o'clock, and the attention of the enemy directed toward Eighty-fifth Redoubt. This work, after a desperate resistance, was surrendered, and, as I have understood, under a threat of no quarter. It's gallant commander, Captain Chapin, Eighty-fifth New York Volunteers, fell nobly at his post, and Colonel Mercer, commanding the attacking column, was killed. No report has been received in regard to this transaction, and I am therefore unable to detain the circumstances attending either the attack or surrender. A demand was then made for the surrender of the town, which was declined.

On the following morning, April 19, at 3 a. m., the enemy again opened upon Fort Gray, and soon after, under cover of night and shadow of the trees on the opposite bank, the iron-plated ram Albemarle *passed down unnoticed and without injury from the 200-pounder in Battery Worth. She was immediately engaged by the* Miami *and* Southfield. *I have no particulars in regard to this conflict, but the* Southfield *was sunk by the collision, and Lieutenant-Commander Flusser fell on his own quarter-deck with a lanyard in his hand. In the death of this accomplished sailor* the Navy has lost one of its brightest ornaments, and he will be long remembered by those who knew and loved him for his intellectual worth, his social qualities, and manly bearing.

The wooden gun-boats, being unable to contend with an antagonist so securely mailed, moved down the river, leaving it in full possession of the enemy. He was now on every side of the town, and this unlooked-for disaster created among the troops a moral effect of the most discouraging character. Hitherto every hardship and exposure had been met with cheerfulness and confidence. A series of covered excavations had been constructed along the line, affording shelter under the heavy fire, causing my loss to be comparatively slight. During this day the enemy planted a battery near the Eighty-fifth Redoubt, and, partly covered by that work, opened fire upon the town. The Albemarle *also opened from below*, both were returned from Fort Williams and Battery Worth, but without effect.

The enemy was very active, moving in different directions, withdrawing most of his force from the vicinity of Fort Gray, and apparently making a serious demonstration on my right. Skirmishing was severe in that quarter, and many casualties occurred on both sides. This state of things continued until dark, when the enemy in strong force succeeded in effecting the crossing of Coneby Creek below the town, and massed his column on my left. This disaster is unexplained, and placed me in a most critical position. Some changes were made during that night in the disposition of the troops, and arrangements made to repel attack both on the right and left.

At daylight of the following day, April 20, while my right and front were seriously threatened, the enemy advanced rapidly against my left, assaulting and carrying the line in that quarter, penetrating the town along the river, and capturing Battery Worth. A line of infantry was formed from the breast-works perpendicularly toward the river, in hopes of staying the advance. This effort succeeded for a time, but the troops seemed discouraged, and finally fell back to the entrenchments.

At the request of General Hoke, commanding the rebel forces, a personal interview was granted, at which a surrender was demanded in consideration of my untenable position, of the impossibility of relief, and that the defense had been highly honorable to all concerned. In failure of this, indiscriminate slaughter was intimated. The bearing of General Hoke during his interview was courteous and soldier-like. His demand was refused, and preparations were made to renew the contest.

I was now completely enveloped on every side, Fort Williams, an enclosed work in the center of the line, being my only hope. This was well understood by the enemy, and in less than an hour a connaded of shot and shell was opened upon it from four different directions. This terrible fire had to be endured without reply, as no man could live at the guns. The breast-height was struck by solid shot on every side, fragments of shells sought almost every interior angle of the work, the whole extent of the parapet was swept by musketry, and men were killed and wounded even on the banquette slope.

A covered excavation had been previously constructed, to which the wounded were conveyed, where they received efficient medical attention.

This condition of affairs could not be long endured without a reckless sacrifice of life, no relief could be expected, and in compliance with the earnest desire of every officer I consented to hoist a white flag, and at 10 a.m. of April 20 I had the mortification of surrendering my post to the enemy with all it contained. It is to be remarked that during the siege and in the night a considerable number of North Carolina soldiers (many of them deserters from the enemy, and all of them fearing bad treatment in the event of capture) left their companies without authority, escaping in canoes, being picked up, as I have understood, by our boats in the sound.

The foregoing statement is made, after an interval of four months, entirely from memory not having received a single report from my subordinate officers. Most of them are still in captivity, and the others scattered over the country beyond my control; in fact, they have had no opportunity until now to perform this duty. Myself and officers were plundered of all our effects except such as were on our persons; in other respects I was treated by General Hoke and his officers with kindness and courtesy.

For the reason stated above I am unable to report the losses on either side, but I have reason to believe that my own casualties did not exceed 150, while from information derived by medical officers, who remained in Plymouth, the lowest loss of the enemy in killed and wounded is given at 850, many believing it to be far greater.

With my personal staff I was at once separated from the troops, and on Saturday, the 23rd, I was conveyed to Richmond via Weldon and Petersburg, and then confined in Libby Prison April 26. The enlisted men, with the regimental officers, were marched to Tarborough, and thence by rail to Macon and Andersonville, Ga. On the 7th of May, in company with 850 captive officers, I was conveyed to Danville. Leaving that place on the 12th I was taken to Macon, and there confined until the 10th of June. On that day 50 senior officers, including myself, were ordered to proceed east, and passing through Savannah arrived in Charleston on the 12th. At this place the party was confined in the city under the fire of the batteries at Morris Island. No inconvenience, however, was experienced from this unusual proceeding. On the 3rd of the present month an exchange was effected under the direction of Major-General Foster, commanding Department of the South, and with the whole party I arrived in New York on the 9th.

It may be proper to state that a few days prior to the completion of this exchange a detachment of officers, prisoners of war, numbering 600, arrived in Charleston from Macon and were confined in the city jail and its yard. I visited them in the evening of the 2nd, and found them very uncomfortable, being much crowded and poorly sheltered. I was assured, however, by the rebel authorities that this condition was only temporary, and that they should be soon removed to more suitable quarters.

As soon as sub-reports are received and examined they will be forwarded as accompaniments to this statement.

Very respectively, your obedient servant.

H. W. Wessells,
Brigadier-General, U.S. Volunteers [1]

★ ★ ★ ★

Maj. Gen. J. J. Peck, late Commanding Dist. of N.C.

Note—In the foregoing report have neglected to state that on the morning of the 19th, subsequent to the marine disaster, Capt. H. I. Hodges, assistant quartermaster of volunteers, in endeavoring to communicate with the gunboats, was accidentally drowned by the upsetting of a canoe. No further information in regard to his fate has ever reached me. I should also add that on the following day, during the bombardment of Fort Williams, Capt. Coats, of 85th N.Y. Vols., acting as assistant inspector general of the district, was severely wounded in the face by a fragment of shell. It is difficult for me at this time, without the aid of subordinate reports, to detail with accuracy all the incidents of the siege, and other important omissions may have been made.

H. W. W.

CHAPTER 32

MAJOR JAMES F. MACKEY'S DIARY: APRIL 16 TO MAY 1, 1864

The following events were recorded in the diary of Major Mackey, 103rd Pennsylvania Volunteers, at the actual time they were occurring and so are considered trustworthy. [1]

April 16   Morning cool and cloudy. Went to ordnance office. Got receipt for one gun (unserviceable) also two blank requisitions. Came back to quarters where I remained all day. Got $120 from Daniel Huddleson. Paid Lieut. Spence $50 and A. Krebs $70 that I had borrowed from them. Looked anxiously forward for a letter from wife, but was disappointed. Wrote one to her. Rained some today All quiet here yet.

April 17   Morning pleasant. Being marked off duty did not go on Sabbath morning inspection. Wrote a letter to Helmbold Chemist. Paid for medicine. Sent it and $5, and a letter to wife with Capt. Dill. [2] *Feeling dull and lonesome. Stayed in quarters until 4 p.m. when the Rebs made an attack on us. Heavy firing. Kept up until 8 P.M. At 10 P.M. I lay down. Slept until 3 A.M., when we formed line at breast works.*

April 18   Got up at 3 A.M.. At 5 A.M. the ball opened again. Constant firing on the picket line. Rebs made an assault on Fort Gray. Bombshell sunk at sundown. Our pickets were driven in. Eighteen pieces opened on us a brisk fire for two hours. We silenced them. All quiet balance of night.

April 19   Morning cool and windy. Rebel ram came down at 3 A.M. After a short fight sunk the Southfield. Miami *escaped. Loss of life not known. After daylight went to work and built bomb proofs. Fort Wessells taken at daylight. Capt. Chapin killed. Cannonading going on all day. The loss on our side very light. There was but little firing from dark until 12 P.M.*

April 20   At 1 A.M. the enemy crossed at the bridge on the Columbia road and planted their artillery and commenced shelling. Then crossed their infantry and commenced advancing at 3 A.M. They were repulsed at daylight. We fought desperately, but were overpowered by numbers. Gen. Wessells surrendered at 11 A.M. [3] *All we had but what was on our backs fell into the enemy's hands. They marched us out one mile from town and encamped us on the ground, some having blankets; some none.*

April 21, one mile from Plymouth, N.C. –Being very cold, got up from my ground bed before day and started to build a fire to get warm by. At 8 A.M. drew rations from the rebels that they captured with us. Got for four days what we gave our men for one. Col. Tate's regiment guarded us. At 9 A.M. we were all searched. At 2 P.M. took up our march, guarded by 35th N.C. Regt., Col. Jones. Marched 16 miles and encamped for the night. Had a very hard march.

April 22, four miles from Jamesville, N.C--Felt well, but some sore, not being used to marching; got to Williamston, N.C., by 12 M. Rested one hour and then marched six miles and camped in a nice grassy field. Marched today sixteen miles; was very tired. Many of our poor men were nearly done out. There were over 2,000 of us. We were guarded by two pieces in front, a regiment on each side, and one brigade in rear. It seemed hard to be deprived of our liberty.

April 23, fifty miles from Hamilton, N.C.--Got up from the ground pretty early. Ate our bite of grub and again started on our way. Arrived at Hamilton, N.C., at 11 A.M. Were marched into a large yard all worn down, many hardly able to walk with blistered feet. We had to remain there in the sun all day and at night lay down on the sand with one blanket over us. A hard life, this.

April 24, Hamilton, N.C.--Sabbath morning after getting up, washed ourselves, and ate our little bite, and at 11 A.M. took up our march for Tarboro, N.C., guarded by the Holcomb Legion alone; Lieut. Col. Crawley commanded. Marched twelve miles, and again encamped for the night in a pine woods. Rained some during the night.

April 25 Got up early, after eating a few hard tack, and resumed our march. Got to near Tarboro between 11 A.M. and 12 M. Encamped near the bridge on the banks of the Tar river and in sight of town. Drew a meat ration at dark. Had hard living. Boys paid fabulous prices for a little bite to eat, fearing that their money would be taken from them. On Sabbath I wrote a letter to wife. Lieut. Johnson said that he would have it sent.

April 26, in sight of Tarboro, N.C. Got up pretty early and had a little bite to eat. Then drew a ration of corn cake such as we would not eat at our own loved homes. At 11 A.M. we marched through the town and were put on poor, filthy old cars for Charleston, S.C., guarded by the 17th S.C. Regt. Arrived at Goldsboro, N.C. at sundown. Left at dark and traveled by rail all night. The country swampy and thinly settled. Had a hard night of it.

April 27, Wilmington, N.C. Arrived here at daylight and marched down to depot. Drew rations, then crossed Cape Fear river. Saw several blockade runners. Saw a large amount of cotton and corn. Saw but little of the city. Judge it to be a nice place. Re-entered a filthy old car and proceeded for Charleston. We arrived at 10 P.M. at Florence, S.C., and changed cars. Remained until morning.

April 28, Florence, S.C. Left again for Charleston, S.C. at 8 A.M. where we arrived about midnight. Changed cars and remained in them until 8 A.M. Passed many rebel fortifications today. Crossed the Pedee, Santee and Savannah rivers today. Saw some rice plantations. The country is generally swampy and not fit for farming purposes. Would rather be at home than in prison.

April 29, Charleston, S.C. Left Charleston at 3 P.M. Could see none of the city being shut up in close cars. Arrived at Savannah, Ga., at about 3 P.M. gave two dollars to a black man to get me something to eat. He brought it. The officers would not let him give it to me so I lost my money. Left Savannah at 5 P.M. in close cars and very much crowded and traveled all night.

April 30, near Grisswold, Ga. Passed through Macon and several other towns today. Arrived at Andersonvile at about 3 P.M. and got off the miserable old cars. Our poor boys were put into the stockade. The officers put into a large church. Took a good bath, felt well, but much exhausted. Rested well through the night.

May 1, Andersonville, Ga...Sabbath morning very pleasant. Got up feeling very well considering the circumstances we are placed in. Slept in a church all night. The guard stole my blouse. Had a sermon preached by the chaplain of the 16th Conn. Regiment at 8 A.M. Received two days' rations at 9 A.M. and then left for Macon, Ga, where we arrived at 5 P.M.—Rained some today. In camp for the night in Camp Oglethorpe. Got new tents. [4]

After ten months of captivity, near Wilmington, N.C. at 10 a.m. on March 1, 1865 Major James F Mackey and other officers were exchanged. *"We passed into our line, the happiest day of our lives."* [5]

CHAPTER 33

A SURVIVOR'S STORY TWENTY YEARS LATER

May 1, 1884

To the Editor National Tribune,

In a late number of your valuable papers I notice a call from one of Wessells' brigade for a description of the battles at Plymouth, N.C., April 17-20, 1864.

I never have seen or heard of a description of these battles in print, (and I do not think they were ever written up for publication), and as I was one of the unlucky participants in them, as well as a victim of the long imprisonment which followed, I will give you as full a description as I can.

The town of Plymouth lies on the right bank of the Roanoke River, about seven miles from its mouth, where it empties into the Albemarle Sound. The Dismal Swamp crosses the Roanoke River close below Plymouth, and runs up into a kind of lagoon for perhaps a mile from the river. Before the war Plymouth had a population of from 800 to 1,000. There was a great deal of tar, turpentine, corn, pork, shingles, lumber, cotton, fish, canes etc., shipped from there to Baltimore and other ports. The soil is a sandy loam, with some gravel, and swamps are numerous. As I said, one swamp ran out nearly a mile from below the town, bending slightly up. Another ran out above the town about the same distance, bending down. A corduroy road crossed the latter at the river.

Further up the river –perhaps three-quarters of a mile—on a knoll, were the camp, fort, and works occupied by the 96th [1] New York Infantry. Just below this swamp, and running out from the river, was a series of works that passed in a semi-circle around the town to the lower end, near the swamp referred to. About one-fourth of the way from the river above was Fort Williams. From the river to Fort Williams was stationed the 85th Pennsylvania [2] volunteers.

The fort was occupied by company A, 103rd Pennsylvania volunteers; to their left the works was occupied by the remainder of the 103rd (except one company—company C—who were on detached duty on Roanoke Island, N.C.). Next to the 103rd lay the 16th Connecticut volunteers; to their left, the 15th Connecticut volunteers. These completed the front line. On their left the 101st Pennsylvania volunteers completed the semi-circle to or near the river. In front of Fort Williams about half a mile, was a small fort with one swivel gun; also, some works held by the 85th New York light artillery [3] had placed a gun on our line of works in the semi-circle. There was also a water battery, with a 200-pound gun on the wharf nearly opposite Fort Williams. On the river were four wooden gunboats—the Miami, Southfield, Whitehead, and another, whose name I have forgotten, as also two companies of the 12th New York cavalry, two parts of companies of colored troops, some loyal North Carolina volunteers [4] —or "Buffaloes," as the rebs called them,---and some heavy artillery [5] —in all about 1,600 to 1,800 men fit for duty.

THE REBEL ATTACK

The most of us had re-enlisted as veterans, and were daily expecting to be relieved to go home on furlough, and, indeed, the heavy artillery had come as a part of our relief, when, on Sunday evening, April 17, 1864, our cavalry pickets came in on the run, with the news that the rebs were coming in full force and had driven in our picket line. A strong support was at once sent out, but we had to come in faster than we went out, as we met a line of battle, four deep, backed up with two batteries of artillery. This was at dark, and for nearly three hours a perfect storm of shot and shell flew over us. The earth fairly shook, and the screaming of shot and shell (many of the latter bursting over us) was deafening. The rebs finally withdrew, and, in doing so, had to bring up their spare horses to get the only two whole guns left out of the two eight-gun batteries that came into line and opened on us three hours before. Their loss was terrible; ours, only trifling in wounded—none killed or missing so far as I know.

The next morning, about an hour before daylight, they again charged our lines, and took the 85th New York prisoners and turned their swivel gun on us. They took the 96th [6] New York about the same time, but the guns at the latter place did not do so much harm, owing to their peculiar position. There was steady picket firing all day, and another heavy charge on our lines after dark; which was met by us and repulsed with slight loss. The next morning (Tuesday) the rebel ram Albemarle came down the river and was on us before we knew it, sinking the gunboats Miami and Southfield, [7] and driving the others down the river towards Albemarle Sound.

The channel on the river had been obstructed with torpedoes, but owing to the high water the ram passed safely over them on its way down. In the sinking of our two boats, the gallant Captain Flusser, of the Miami, lost his life by a rebound of a piece of one of his own shells. Had he lived, it is very probable we would never have been taken prisoners, or the rebs have succeeded so well at that time. They were now in possession of our front, right and rear.

It was said that the wharf or water battery never fired a shot at the ram as it came down the river. Why, I could never learn. That forenoon (Tuesday) we were formed and charged the rebs time and again, but each time we were driven back, and the 85th Pennsylvania [8] was captured by piecemeal. At each charge we lost ground, were driven back, and a few more prisoners fell into the enemy's hands. Night came on with our position entirely surrounded, and during the night the 101st Pennsylvania lost, as the 85th had during the day, a few of its men at a time.

GENERAL WESSELLS SURRENDERS

At daylight the 16th Connecticut was also "gathered in," and the sun rose over about as helpless and forlorn a situation for the rest of us as can well be imagined. Our nearest forces were sixty miles distant, and the country between held by the enemy. Our commanding general, Brig. Gen.. H. H. Wessells, hoped against hope, and refused to surrender, as there was still a bare possibility of re-enforcement coming up the river to our relief. The enemy had by this time got into houses in the town behind us and compelled us to fight them from the front of our works.

We had constructed underground bomb-proofs, and while inside of them we were tolerably safe, but could do no fighting back. The swivel gun on the 85th New York's works (which they kept busy) annoyed us fearfully, doing us more harm than all the others. It killed Sergeant Logan, took Corporal Burtner's foot off, grazed my cap and ruptured my left forearm with a single shell. I have less than one-half the use of that arm today; but a generous Government allows me the magnificent sum of $2 per month for the loss I sustained.

My other disabilities—the result of scurvy, exposure, typhoid fever, and starvation—the Pension Office has declared "removed." I often wonder how they know? It seems to me I am very forcibly reminded of it every hour in the day, and often in the night, too. The examining surgeon could see and feel my arm; but, because he could not thrust his hand into my lame back and benumbed right thigh and feel the pain there, he was faithless—not believing. Still there are, no doubt, greater cripples than I who are today unrecognized by the Government that once promised to care for them.

But to my story. The 16th Connecticut were taken, a few at a time, early in the morning; the few that were left of us fought from the wrong side of our works until about 11 a.m. when Gen. Wessells, seeing that further resistance was useless—as only about one hundred men were left to him—permitted the flag on Fort Williams to be lowered. It was said by those present at the time that he wept like a child when the flag came down. We all realized that we were in a sad fix.

Our captors, commanded by Brigadier General Ransom and Major-General Hoke, allowed us to take our clothing and private property, but a little sneak of a reb, spying my watch chain, and being at some distance from his superiors, declared that if I did not give it up he would shoot me. That reb got the best watch in the regiment. It was an English open face, cap, lever, full jeweled, gold hands, and No. 669. It had my mark inside, near the balance wheel. If he has it still I wish he would return it. "No questions asked." As soon as we surrendered we were placed under a strong guard and ordered to "fall in" by company and regiment, and were marched out to the woods, or near them, on the road leading up the river, and in sight of our late camp.

Here all the prisoners were assembled and searched by the 35th North Carolina for deserters from their regiment. One of these same deserters stood at my elbow and was passed and re-passed by his cousin, yet not recognized. A roll was taken of all our names, with rank, company and regiment.

Of the negroes who were captured with us here a part had enlisted, but I think had not been mustered into the United States service, but were intended as recruits for some colored regiments. These were taken out the next morning to the edge of f the woods, in plain sight of us all, and shot down like so many cattle. There must have been from sixty to eighty of them. It looked rough to see those poor colored men shot down in cold blood, and we unable to save them. Surely their blood cries from the ground yet against General Hoke or General Ransom for vengeance! Yet, if I am not mistaken, this same General Ransom now represents his State in the United States Senate!

The next morning we were placed under the care of the 35th North Carolina to be sent on our way "up the country" as prisoners of war, and to many—very many--of us it meant a slow torture by starvation, sickness, exposure and inhuman treatment until death finally brought relief. We were surrendered on April 20, 1864, and from that time until May 3 we were in transit to Andersonville, Ga. Old prisoners will readily recall the arrival of the "Plymouth Pilgrims," as we were called.

A great many incidents happened on the way that amused us. I recall that when passing on foot near Tarboro, N.C. a big, frowsy-headed woman, with a dozen or so of equally frowzy children about her, asked one of our guards where our "horns" were. She had always believed the Yankees had horns, and was surprised to see we had none. I also remember that the hardtack we got at Goldsboro, N.C. was round and full of bedbugs. Still, hunger made them sweet to the taste—after we had picked the bugs out.

When we crossed the Cape Fear River at Wilmington, N.C., we were ferried over on an old tub of a ferryboat that could carry only about 250 at a time. While the last squad was crossing one of the guard took three of us back of an old cotton shed, and one of company K (103rd Pennsylvania volunteers) boys—Mort Jones, I think—stopped close to me while the other and the guard passed on a few steps. Jones was smoking a pipe, and, reaching through the shed, he got a handful of cotton and set it on fire with his pipe. He then rolled it up and shoved it through the crack in the shed. We soon after left Wilmington and when a few miles off saw a large light behind us. The next day—or rather that evening, at Charleston—we saw an account of a big fire at Wilmington that same morning, and loss of more than a million dollars' worth of cotton belonging to the Confederate government. We quietly smiled to ourselves but concluded to say nothing. This was May 1, 1864.

Robert P. Black
Co. E, 103rd P.V.V (Plymouth Pilgrim)
Parker's Landing, Armstrong Co., PA.

CHAPTER 34

"Ram Albemarle Sunk 110 Years Ago"

A Confederate Soldier's Personal Account

For old time and memory's sake I ask you to publish a few lines in regard to the capture and re-capture of the town of Plymouth in Washington County on the Roanoke River at or near the Albemarle Sound. I have seen the historical account in two or three histories and the account is not right.

I know the Federal troops were in possession of the town in 1863 and till late in April 1864. In the fall and winter of 1863 and 1864 the Confederates built in the Roanoke at Halifax a vessel called the Ram, *but the name was the* Albemarle.

When the vessel was completed and ready for battle General Hoke with a land force marched on Plymouth while the Ram *went down the river. Hoke's army and the Ironclad made connection and while Hoke attacked from land the* Ram *attacked from water.*

General Wessells, the Federal general, had a good army and gun boats all of wood. The two that were sunk were the Bombshell, *which was sunk right by the wharf, and the* Southfield, *three quarters of a mile down the river.*

The Albemarle *rammed the* Southfield *amid ships, tearing a great hole and drowning all on board. The town was not yet captured. The* Ram *went back up the river and went to pouring 200-pound shot and shell into every quarter of the town. Hoke kept closing in with his land forces.*

There was a large fort on the east side of the breast-works that ran all around the town. The soldiers in the fort were well prepared that dealt death to the Confederates. The way they were surrounded on all sides but kept on fighting after Hoke and his men were in the town.

The great oak gate of the fort faced the river. There is a street that ran from the gate to the river. As they would not give up and lower the Stars and Stripes, the Albemarle *moved up to the mouth of the street that ran to the gate and fired into the gate of the fort some of those 200-pound balls and shells. Old Glory slipped down the pole with alacrity and dispatch.*

The firing ceased, 700 prisoners were taken, and from the fort a lot of rations were taken, -salt, bacon, and spun cotton.

J. B. Stallings, of Clayton and myself were put out in a house on the breastworks with the spun cotton and salt to trade it with the citizens for more bacon.

The Albemarle had such good luck in the fight, that in three or four days she took a notion to have another fight so she ran boldly into a whole fleet of Union gun boats twelve or fourteen miles down the Sound and the fight lasted all day.

I could not see the fight, but could hear every pop. Go look in the Hall of History at that old smoke stack and you will find proof of what I say. A man who was in the fight and the guns of the Union fleet struck our boat 1560 foul hits; not a single shot went through. The thing was built of sills two feet by two feet and covered with six inch wide iron doubled. When it started, or before it started into the fight, it was thoroughly greased all over. The balls and shells would glance every way when they hit it on its greasy sides that were shaped every way.

In the beginning of the fight one of the Ram's guns was dislodged by a Union ball shot into the port hole when the door was drawn up for the gun to run out and fire. The Ram only carried two 200-pound guns. The one left got in sixty shots in the day.

The Union troops tried to get hold of it with chains and grabs, but could not. It was battered so bad and the smoke stack was so riddled that it would not draw smoke so it could get up steam.

At dusk it quit the fight and started for Plymouth. The Federals did not follow as they could not get up stream on account of the smoke stack. They threw ten day's rations of bacon for seventy men into the fire, and the greasy bacon made a quick blaze and got up steam enough to get back to Plymouth after dark. It took a whole month to repair the damage.

Hear the rest of my story. It never ventured out to fight any more, but lay at the wharf all the summer. I myself stood guard many a night down the river to keep watch for any foe that might come up the river to destroy the thing that was such a menace to the Union fleet.

But the day of doom for the Ram was fast approaching. Lincoln offered $150,000 in species to any man or set of men that would take their lives in their hands and destroy the hated monster. On the fourth day of July 1964 I with others were on guard down the Sound. The flags of the fleet were flying. We saw six men lower a boat, get in and row up the river. That was about eight o'clock in the morning. Two o'clock came and they had not returned; five o'clock and no sign of men or boat.

Ten men lowered another boat and went up the river. They came back with the six men and the boat. Twenty men about sundown lowered another boat, were gone a short while and came back as they went without their comrades.

Captain Hopkins, our Albemarle *pilot, had suspected that the Yanks would be out spying that day. He took another man and each slipped down the river about a mile, hid in the bushes and watched.*

Pretty soon the old pilot and his mate saw six men slipping along up the river in a row boat pulling along by the bushes. The old captain jumped up, pointed his six-teen shooter in the men's faces crying out, "Throw them guns in the river or I will blow your brains out!" Saying "Rally reserves," the other man jumped up with his gun.

The Yanks' guns were in the river so they both got in and made their prisoners row them up to town. Our officers let them sit out before the jail door in the day and stay in jail in the night.

But about October 20, 1864 Lieutenant W. B. Cushing with nine more men volunteered to go up in the face of death and blow up the Albemarle *on the 26th night between twelve and one o'clock. He slipped up the river on the off side from town and out boat. When far enough he turned down the river, ran his little boat over the fort of logs that surrounded our boat, led down a torpedo that was fastened to the end of a pole, and ran it under the water against the boat with all the power his little boat had.*

It exploded leaving a hole in our boat six feet by eight feet. The men ran out in their night clothes to keep from drowning. Two of Cushing's men were killed, seven climbed on the wharf and surrendered to our men. Cushing swam to the other side of the river.

After reaching the farther side of the river he waded down about three fourths of a mile in the edge of the water, jumped in the river again, swam to the side the town was on, went to an old negro man's house, called him out and told him to go up to town and see if the boat was blown up while he waited in the fork of a sugar-berry tree that stood in the negro's yard. The old man was soon back. He said, 'Boss, she blowed up, sho.'

Cushing slipped down out of the tree and handed the old man a handful of silver. While everything in town was in confusion, Lieutenant Cushing was going down the riverbank looking for a skiff which he found tied to a tree. He loosed it, got in and paddled down to his own ship, the Monticello. *He had lost his hat, coat and shoes, and was so benumbed and exhausted that when they pulled him on board he fainted. They poured some brandy in him and he was soon revived. He signaled the rest of the fleet to prepare for action.*

The rebel Ram *was dead. They made ready all that day for the battle and next morning at four o'clock they started up the river. A part of the river runs around a pocosin on the north and runs in again at the head of the Sound. Some of the gun boats went up what was called the middle river and some straight up the river to the town.*

The pocasin ⁽¹⁾ *between the two rivers is two miles across. The gunboats in the Middle River filled the town with great 200-pound guns. The shot from the gun boats disrupted our guns in the forts. Our troops were helpless against those great guns on the boats in the river. As our troops retreated the guns of the Yankee fleet poured grape shot and canister into every road that led from town.*

That evening the town was full of Federals. They could not come while our Ironclad was afloat. Soon as they sunk it, it was no job to retake the town.

This is a true story of our capture of the town by General Hoke and the Albemarle--the Ram, *and the destruction of the boat on the night of October 26, 1864 by Lieutenant Cushing, commander of the Union gun boat, the* Monticello. *None of those that volunteered to destroy the* Ram *escaped except Lieut. W. B. Cushing himself. He had nine men besides himself and two were killed, with our field guns. The second shot shattered their little boat that bore the torpedo that sank our boat. Seven of the men climbed out and surrendered. One history says there were fourteen men while another history says there were eight men. It is not so. There were only ten men and only Cushing escaped."*

Published in the *Smithfield Herald* on March 18, 1924, the above article was written by J. H. Broadwell of Selma, North Carolina. [2]

EPILOGUE

At the sacrifice of over 600,000 men, the Union was preserved and, even though not the original intent, slavery in this country was abolished forever. The word "freedom" then was to take on a new meaning in the United States of America.

The main actors participating in the drama at Plymouth were forced to begin new lives, some as the victors and others as the defeated. To be able to return to their homes was the goal of most of the men, regardless of their physical or mental condition. However, that was not to be an option for General Robert E. Lee; for immediately after he had resigned from the Union Army, all of his family's property situated on the western bank of the Potomac River at Arlington, Virginia, was confiscated by the Federals.

Actually, Lee had never been the owner of the land inherited by his wife, Maryann Parke Custis, great-granddaughter of Martha Washington. Following the death of his father-in-law and prior to the onset of the Civil War, Robert E. Lee was managing the land intended to be the inheritance of his eldest son upon the death of Maryann Custis Lee. Instead, during the war, the property was turned into a Federal graveyard, Arlington Cemetery. Following the war, George Washington Lee sued the Federal government for having confiscated his family's property. Eventually, he won his case in court, thereby forcing the United States Government to pay him for the land.

The four-year Civil War, The War of the Rebellion, The War Between the States, or by whatever else it was called officially ceased on April 9, 1865, when General Robert Edward Lee surrendered his Confederate troops to General Ulysses Simpson Grant. That history-making event took place at Appomattox Courthouse, Virginia in a small brick house owned by Wilmer McLean.

Ironically, four years earlier when he had owned a farm near Bull Run (Manassas), McLean had fled from the war to settle in a spot *"so remote from the struggle that 'the sound of battle would never again reach him and his family.'"* However, the *"man of peace"* suddenly was thrust again into the affairs of war when he was ordered by the Federal Government to vacate his home temporarily so it might be used for the surrender ceremonies. [1]

On Palm Sunday afternoon, April 9, 1865, General Robert E. Lee had attired himself immaculately in his dress uniform and somberly mounted his gray horse Traveler, aware that he was about to meet his fate and that of the Confederacy. While awaiting the appearance of the commander of the Confederate Army, the stocky, bearded Union General Ulysses S. Grant, had not time to change out of his dusty field clothes into his dress uniform.

Having no desire to further humiliate his defeated enemy and out of respect for the man who had fought so valiantly, General Grant did not accept General Lee's sword, the customary manner for surrendering. Oftentimes, an untrue anecdote has been related, depicting General Lee as having surrendered his sword to General Grant. However, present in the room to witness the formal proceedings was Charles Horton, a black man from Long Ridge Road in Washington County. The body servant of Capt. H. G. Lewis, Horton in a newspaper article refuted such a story, maintaining that General Grant did not ask for, nor did he receive General Lee's sword. [2]

In General Order No. 9 dated April 10, 1865, General Robert E. Lee's final words to his troops were:

"...You will take with you the satisfaction that proceeds from the consciousness of duty faithfully performed; and I earnestly pray that a merciful God will extend to you His blessing and protection.

With an unceasing admiration of your constancy and devotion to your Country, and a grateful remembrance of your kind and generous consideration of myself, I bid you all an affectionate farewell." [3]

The displaced Robert Edward Lee, whose carefree boyhood days had been spent in Alexandria, Virginia; who graduated from West Point Academy; who managed a prosperous antebellum plantation on the Potomac River; and who was the respected leader of a massive army, became president of Washington College (later Washington-Lee) in Virginia. On the other hand, the political star of Lee's Yankee counterpart rose steadily until Ulysses Simpson Grant was elected to serve as the eighteenth president of the United States of America.

Fig. 64. ***General Robert E. Lee, CSA***
"Harper's History of the Great Rebellion"

Fig. 65. **General Ulysses S. Grant, USA**
Courtesy of Virginia Room, Fairfax Library, Fairfax, Va.

Captain James Wallace Cooke, CSA
(1812-1869)

On June 17, 1864, an order was issued from the Navy Department in Richmond relieving Captain James Wallace Cooke of his command of the *CSS Albemarle* due to his poor health. However, once he felt that he had recovered sufficiently, Cooke applied for reassignment to duty, requesting command of the Halifax Navy Yard. The Office of Orders and Detail in Richmond denied his request, responding with," *There is no place for you at present, but you will be placed on duty as soon as possible.*" [4]

Finally on September 13th, Captain James Cooke received the following welcome dispatch:

"Proceed to Halifax, N.C. without delay, and relieve Captain Robert F. Pinkney, Provisional Navy C.S., of is present duty, commanding naval defenses, etc.

By command of the Secretary of the Navy." [5]

Unfortunately, during November of 1864, ill health again plagued Captain James Cooke, prematurely ending his career in the Confederate Navy. Just a few years later in 1869, he died at Portsmouth, Virginia.

Lieutenant William Barker Cushing, USN
(1843-1875)

William Barker Cushing was the only non-flag officer of the Civil war to be officially thanked by Congress. After the Civil War ended, he served in the Pacific and Asiatic Squadrons, as ordinance officer in the Boston Navy Yard, and even later as commander of the *USS Maumee*. On January 3, 1872, Cushing was promoted to the rank of commander, becoming the youngest man to attain that rank in the Navy.

As he continued his naval career, Cushing's last command was the *USS Wyoming*. After the ship's breakdown and while she was under repair, Cushing's health suddenly began to deteriorate. He constantly was in severe pain, the result of the numerous serious injuries sustained during his years in the Navy, most likely beginning with his miraculous escape during the sinking of the *CSS Albemarle*.

The week after Thanksgiving in 1874, due to the excruciating pain he was experiencing, William Cushing had to be sent to a mental hospital where he could be administered enough morphine to keep him sedated. Unfortunately, on December 17, 1874, the brave former naval officer died at the young age of thirty-two, leaving his mother, his wife Katherine, and their two daughters, Marie Louise and Katherine

Abell. William Barker Cushing was buried on January 8, 1875 at Bluff Point at the Naval Academy Cemetery in Annapolis, Maryland. [6]

William's brother, Colonel Alonso H. Cushing, was a graduate of West Point. While serving with the 4th U.S. Artillery, he was wounded four times during Pickett's Charge at the Battle of Gettysburg. At the age of twenty-two he died during the first week of July in 1863, as a result of his wounds and was buried at the West Point Academy Cemetery. [7]

The two Cushing brothers, both having fought in the Civil War, were buried in the two national military cemeteries. A memorial to honor the memories of Mary Barker Smith Cushing and her two sons, William and Alonzo, can be found at the Forest Hill cemetery in Fredonia, New York where they all had formerly resided.

Following the end of the Civil War, a younger Cushing son, Howard, joined the 4th U.S. Artillery. Unfortunately, in 1871 he, too, was killed. It happened near Tuscon, Arizona, where he died in an ambush of Apache warriors led by Cochise. [8]

★★★★

Lieutenant Gilbert Elliott, CSA
(1843-1895)

Immediately following the end of the war, on April 13, 1865, Gilbert Elliott married Lucy Ann Hill. Later they became the parents of one son, Gilbert Elliott III, and four daughters. After returning to the practice of law and moving his family to several different localities, Gilbert Elliott finally settled in New York City where in 1893 he and his son, Gilbert III, opened a law practice. Unfortunately, just two years later at the age of fifty-one, Gilbert Elliott II died during a bout with erysipelas, a streptococcal infection of the skin almost impossible to cure in that time in history before the discovery of antibiotics.

The famed builder of the *CSS Albemarle* was buried in the Green-Wood Cemetery, Brooklyn, New York. His grave is identified with a Confederate Veteran's marker, placed there in 1987 by a proud collateral descendant, Robert G. Elliott, great grandson of Gilbert's older brother Peter. [9]

Lieutenant Commander Charles Williamson Flusser, USN
(1832-1864)

Killed on the quarterdeck of the flagship *USS Miami,* Charles W. Flusser's body was transported by the *USS Ceres* to New Bern. The *Manufacturers and Farmers Journal* on Thursday, April 28, 1864 reported:

"NEWBERN, April 26

...The obsequies of Commander Flusser took place here on the 23d inst. It was the most affecting and imposing demonstration of the kind witnessed in North Carolina. The city was draped in mourning and all business suspended. His remains were interred in Newbern with distinguished honors. " [10]

Later the body of Charles Flusser was reburied in the United States Naval Academy Cemetery in Annapolis, Maryland. However, both of his Confederate brothers were buried where they had fallen in battle. Ottakar, the eldest of the three Flusser sons, was killed in action on September 17, 1862, near the Miller cornfield at Manassas (Sharpsburg), Maryland where he was serving with the 4th Texas Infantry, Hood's Texas Brigade. [11] The younger brother, Lieut. Guy Flusser of the 4th Kentucky Cavalry Regiment, died on June 9, 1864, in a battle at Mt. Sterling, Kentucky. [12]

A memorial headstone honoring the three Flusser sons killed during the Civil War rests on the family plot in Louisville, Kentucky.

General Robert Frederick Hoke, CSA
(1827-1912)

In 1864 President Jefferson Davis rewarded Major General Robert Hoke by giving him command of a full division known as Hoke's Brigade, composed of several brigades of the Army of Northern Virginia. Then, after returning to his home state of North Carolina, he fought at Wilmington and Bentonville, later being put in command of a division of General Joseph E. Johnston.

At the end of the war on April 26, 1865, General Robert F. Hoke surrendered with General Joseph Johnston at Durham Station. Following his discharge, Hoke was involved in a number of business enterprises, one of which was mining gold and iron in Lincoln County, North Carolina. Later he served as president of the Georgia, Carolina & Northern Railroad Company Railroad Company for eight years. When the Cuban War broke out, he was asked by President McKinley to become a major general of volunteers, but Hoke declined the commission. [13]

The 31st Regimental Reunion of the 101st Pennsylvania Volunteers and the 103rd Pennsylvania Volunteers was held on September 16, 1909, at Foxburg, Pennsylvania, a large estate located on the banks of the Allegheny River at the confluence of the Clarion River. Following the reunion, Luther Dickey, author of *History of the 103rd Regiment Pennsylvania Veteran Volunteer Infantry, 1861-1865*, wrote to Robert Hoke requesting information regarding the alleged "massacre" of blacks at Plymouth. Dickey received no reply from the general.

A very private man, Hoke was not involved with any veteran organizations after the war and left behind no writings about his war career, all of his personal papers having been burned. Determined to put the war behind him, Hoke refused even to visit the Confederate Old Soldier's Home near his residence in Raleigh. [14]

Later in his life, Hoke became a director of the North Carolina Railroad Company, a position he was appointed to by Zebulon B. Vance, former governor of North Carolina. An active businessman until diabetes killed him on July 3, 1912, nine years before the discovery of insulin in 1921, the seventy-one year old Robert Hoke had named the Lincoln Lithia Water Company in Lincoln County. [15]

Robert Hoke was held in such high esteem in North Carolina that a county was named in his honor. Also, among many other honors, a Liberty Ship was christened in his name during World War II.

★★★★

General Henry Walton Wessells, USA
(1809-1889)

General Wessells was promoted lieutenant colonel in the regular army on February 16, 1865 and brevetted colonel from April 20, 1864, "for gallant and meritorious services during the Rebel attack on Plymouth, North Carolina." After his subsequent return to New York City following the Battle of Plymouth, on November 11, 1864, he was appointed by the Secretary of War to be Inspector and Commissary-General of Prisoners for the country east of the Mississippi River with headquarters in Washington, D.C. After assuming that position on November 15th, he held it until the end of the war. [16]

On March 13, 1865, as a brevetted brigadier-general of the regular army, Wessells was assigned to command the Hart Island Prison in Long Island Sound in the juncture of the East River twenty miles north of New York City. Originally, the island had served as a draft rendezvous camp for that particular area of New York. Approximately 3,000 Rebel prisoners suffered there in a stockade enclosure of four acres for three and a half months until the end of the war. The number of Rebel prisoners-of-war held there was 3,413, with 235 perishing from the ravages of prison life. Smallpox, diarrhea, scurvy, and pneumonia killed them, as well as exposure to the unaccustomed intense cold of the North. [17]

Following the Civil War, Wessells was assigned to duty at the northwest frontier until his retirement from the army on January 1, 1871. He then returned to his native state of Connecticut, where he resided until his death. While visiting Dover, Delaware, General Henry Walton Wessells died on January 12, 1889, at the age of 80 [18] and was buried in Arlington Cemetery.

BIBLIOGRAPHY

Advance the Colors! Pennsylvania Capitol Preservation Committee. Harrisburg, Pa.

Alderman, John Perry. *29th Virginia Infantry*. Lynchburg, Va.: H. E. Howard, Inc., 1989.

Arms, Karen and Camp Pamela S. *Biology*. Philadelphia: Saunders College, 1982.

Ball, John. *Escape from Dixie: The Experiences of Lt. John Lafler, 85th N.Y. Civil War POW*. Williamsville, N.Y: Goldstar Enterprises, 1996.

Barefoot, Daniel W. *General Robert F. Hoke: Lee's Modest Warrior*. John F. Blair: Winston Salem, N.C., 1996.

Barrett, John Gilchrist. *North Carolina as a Civil War Battleground 1861-1865*. Raleigh: Division of Archives and History, N.C. Dept. of Cultural Resources, 7th printing, 1987.

Bates, Samuel P. *History of Pennsylvania Volunteers, 1861-65*. Harrisburg, Pa.: B. Singerly, State Printer, Vol. 3, 1869-1871.

Battles and Leaders of the Civil War: The Way to Appomattox: Being For the Most Part Contributions by Union and Confederate Officers. Based upon "The Century War Series." Edited by Robert Underwood Johnson and Clarence Clough Buel of the Editorial Staff of the *Century Magazine*, New York: Thomas Yoseloff, Vol. IV, 1956.

Billingsley, Amos S. *From the Flag to the Cross: Scenes and Incidents of Christianity in the War*. New World Publishing Co., 1872.

Blakeslee, Bernard F. *History of the 16th Connecticut Volunteers*. Hartford, Conn.: Case, Lockwood and Brainard Co., 1875.

Boatner, Major Mark M. *Military Customs and Traditions*. New York: David Company, Inc.

Bright, Leslie, William H. Rowland, and James C. Bardon. *CSS Neuse: A Question of Iron and Time*.

Catton, Bruce. *The American Heritage: New History of the Civil War*. New York: Viking, 1960.

Cecelski, David S. *The Waterman's Song: Slavery and Freedom in Maritime*

North Carolina. Chapel Hill: The University of North Carolina Press, 2001.

Chaitin, Peter M. *The Civil War: The Coastal War.* Alexandria, Va.: Time-Life Books, 1984.

Clark, Walter. (ed.) *Histories of the Several Regiments and Battalions from North Carolina, in the Great War 1861-'65.* 5 Vols., Raleigh: State of N.C., 1901.

Click, Patricia C. *Time Full of Trial: The Roanoke Island Freedmen's Colony 1862-1867.* Chapel Hill: The University of North Carolina Press, 2001.

Cooper, Alonzo. *In and Out of Rebel Prisons.* Oswego, N.Y.: R. J. Oliphant Job Printers, 1888.

Crabtree, Beth Gilbert and Patton, James. (eds.) *Journal of a Secesh Lady: The Diary of Catherine Ann Devereux Edmondson, 1860-1866.* Raleigh, N.C.: Division of Archives and History, 1979.

Davis, Burke. *The Civil War: Strange and Fascinating Facts.* New York: Crown Publishers, 1982.

Davis, Kenneth C. *Don't Know Much About the Civil War.* New York: Avon Books, 1996.

Denny, Robert E. *Civil War Prison and Escape: A Day by Day Chronicle.* N.Y.: Sterling Publishing Co., Inc., 1993.

Dickey, Luther S. *History of the 103rd Regiment: Pennsylvania Veteran Volunteer Infantry 1861-1865.* Chicago, Illinois: L. S. Dickey, 1910.

Donaghy, John. *Army Experience of Capt. John Donaghy: 103rd Penna. Vols., 1861-1865.* Deland, Florida: E. O. Painter Printing Company, 1926.

Durrill, Wayne K. *War of Another Kind: A Southern Community in the Great Rebellion.* New York: Oxford University Press, 1990.

Dyer, Frederick H. *A Compendium of the War of the Rebellion, Compiled and Arranged From Official Records of the Federal and Confederate Armies, Reports of the Adjutant Generals of the Several States, the Army Regiments, and Other Reliable Documents and Sources.* Des Moines: Dyer Publishing Co., 1908.

Elliott, Robert G. *Ironclad of the Roanoke; Gilbert Elliott's Albemarle.* Shippensburg, Pa: White Mane Books, 1999.

Foote, Shelby. *The Civil War: A Narrative: Red River to Appomattox.* New York: Random House, 1958.

Gancas, Ron. Research by Jack Blair and Dick Dougan. *The Hardluck Regiment: The Pennsylvania One Hundred and Third.*

Garrison, Webb. *Civil War Curiosities: Strange Stories, Oddities, Events, and Coincidences.* Nashville: Rutledge Hill Press, 1994.

Goss, Sergeant Warren Lee. *The Soldier's Story of His Captivity at Andersonville, Bell Isle, and Other Rebel Prisons.* Boston: Lee and Shepard Publishers, 1866.

Groene, Bertram H. *Tracing Your Civil War Ancestor.* Winston-Salem, N.C.: John F. Blair.

Hinds, John W. *Invasion and Conquest of North Carolina: Anatomy of a Gunboat War.* Shippensburg, Pa.: Beidel Printing House, Inc., 1923.

Kellogg, Robert N. *Life and Death in Rebel Prisons.* Hartford, Conn.: L. Stebbins, 1865.

Langworthy, D. A. *A Prisoner of War and His Escape.* Minneapolis, Minn.: Byron Printing, Co., 1915.

Mahood, Wayne. (ed.) *Charlie Mosher's Civil War: From Fair Oaks to Andersonville with the Plymouth Pilgrims.* Hightstown, N.J.: Longstreet House, 1994.

____. *The Plymouth Pilgrims: A History of the Eighty-Fifth New York Volunteer Infantry.* Hightstown, N. J: Longstreet House, 1991.

Marlow, Clayton Charles. *Matt W. Ransom: Confederate General from North Carolina.* Jefferson, N.C.: McFarland & Co., Inc., 1996.

McElroy, John. *Andersonville: A Story of Rebel Prisons.* Toledo: D. R. Locke, 1879.

Mc Pherson, James M. *Battle Cry of Freedom: The Civil War Era.* New York: Oxford University Press, 1988.

Morgan, W. H. *Personal Reminiscences of the War of 1861-5.* Lynchburg, Va.: J. P Bell Company, Inc., 1911.

Moss, Juanita Patience. *Created to Be Free.* Westminister, Md.: Willow Bend Publishers, 2001.

Pictorial History of the Civil War in the United States of America. Philadelphia: G. W. Childs, 1868.

Pollard, Edward. *Southern History of the War.* The Fairfax Press, 1866.

Ray, Delia. *Behind the Blue and Gray: The Soldier's Life in the Civil War.* N.Y.: Lodestar Books, 1991.

Records of the 24th Independent Battery, N.Y. Light Artillery U.S.V. Compiled by J. W. Merrill. Published for the Ladies' Cemetery Association of Perry, N.Y., 1870.

Redkey, Edwin S. *A Grand Army of Black Men.* Cambridge: Cambridge University Press, 1992.

Reed, John A. *History of the 101st Regiment Pennsylvania Veteran Volunteer Infantry, 1861-1865.* Chicago: L. S. Dickey and Co., 1910.

Roberts, Robert B. *Encyclopedia of Historic Forts: The Military, Pioneer, and Trading Posts of the United States.* New York: Macmillan Publishing Co., 1988.

Robertson, James I. *Virginia, 1861-1865: Iron Gate to the Confederacy.* Richmond, Va.: Official Publication, Virginia Civil War Commission, 1961.

Silverstone, Paul H. *Warships of the Civil War Navies.* Annapolis: Naval Institute Press, 1989.

Southern Generals: Who They Are, and What They have Done. New York: Charles B. Richardson, 1865.

The War of the Rebellion: A Compilation of the Official Records of the Union and Confederate Armies. 128 Volumes, Washington, D.C.: Government Printing Office, 1880-1891.

Thomas, Gerald W. *Bertie in Blue: Experience of Bertie County's Union Servicemen During the Civil War.* Plymouth, N. C.: Bacon Printing, Inc., 1998.

Trotter, William R. *Ironclads and Columbiads: The Civil War in North Carolina: The Coast.* Winston-Salem: John F. Blair, 1989.

Under Both Flags: A Panorama of the Great Civil War. Written by celebrities of both sides. San Francisco: The Whitaker & Ray Company, 1896.

Wallace, Lee A. *17th Virginia Infantry.* Lynchburg, Va.: H. E. Howard, Inc., 1990.

War of the Rebellion, O. R. of Union and Confederate Armies. Series 2, Vol. 7. Published under the direction of the Hon. Russell A. Alger, Sec'y. of War, Brig. Gen. Fred C. Ainsworth, Chief of the Record and Pension Office, War Dept. and Mr. Joseph W. Kirkley, Washington, D. C.: Government Printing Office, 1899.

Ward, Geoffrey C., with Richard and Ken Burns. *The Civil War: An Illustrated History.* New York: Alfred A. Knopf, Inc., 1990.

Warner, Ezra J. *Generals in Blue.* Baton Rouge: Louisiana State University Press, 1964.

____. *Generals in Gray.* Baton Rouge: Louisiana State University Press, 1959.

Welles, Edgar. *Diary of Gideon Welles: Secretary of Navy Under Lincoln and Johnson.* Boston & New York: Houghton Mifflin Co., Vol. 1, 1861-March 30, 1864.

ARTICLES

"A History of Grace Episcopal." *The Roanoke Beacon Living History,* Plymouth, N.C., 1998, p. 7.

"A Letter by Edward Nicholas Boots." *The Roanoke Beacon.* Plymouth, N.C., 1995, p 3.

"Ausbon House: One of Five to Pre-date Civil War." *The Roanoke Beacon Living History,* April 18, 2001, p. 8.

Ballard, Michael. "The 1864 Siege of Plymouth: A Good Time to Pray." *Civil War Times Illustrated,* p. 16, filed at Washington County Public Library, Plymouth, N.C.

"Battle Scars Can Still be Seen at Ausbon House." *The Roanoke Beacon Living History,* Plymouth, N.C., 1998, p. 4.

Black, Robert P. "Plymouth Pilgrims and How They Came to be Captured—A Survivor's Story." *Now and Then,* May 1, 1864.

Breiseth, Christopher N. "Lincoln and Frederick Douglass: Another Debate." *Journal of The Illinois State Historical Society,* Vol. LXV II, No. 1, February, 1975, pp. 9-20.

Broadwell, J. H. "Ram Albemarle Sunk 110 Years Ago, Confederate Soldier's Personal Account of 1864 Battles." *Smithfield Herald*, March 18, 1924. (Filed at Washington County Library.)

Brown, Jacob D. "Battle of Plymouth." *National Tribune Veterans Newspaper*, October 3, 1889.

Browning, Judkin Jay. "Little Souled Mercenaries? The Buffaloes of Eastern North Carolina During the Civil War." *North Carolina Review*, Vol. LXXVII, No. 3, July 2000.

"Capture of Plymouth." *National Tribune Veterans Newspaper*, Library of Congress Newspaper Room, October 8, 1914.

Cimprich, John and Mainfort, Robert. "Fort Pillow Revisited: New Evidence About an Old Controversy." *Civil War History*, 1982, pp. 293-306.

"Confederate Forces Capture Plymouth, Battle of Plymouth-April 17-20, 1864." (Filed at the Washington County Public Library, Plymouth, N.C.)

"Dedication of the Monument at Andersonville, Georgia, October 23, 1907." Hartford, Conn., 1908.

Dill, Lon. "Albemarle Scatters Fleet." *The Roanoke Beacon*. Plymouth, N.C., August 1968. (Filed at Washington County Public Library, Plymouth, N.C.)

_____. "Confederate Ram Albemarle Scattered Whole Fleets But Lost to Tiny Launch," *The News and Observer*. Raleigh, N.C., Sunday morning, October, 26, 1947, p. IV-3. (Filed at Washington County Public Library)

"From Bondage to Liberty." *National Tribune Veterans Newspaper*. Library of Congress Newspaper Room, January 9, 1902.

"History Lesson." Harry L. Thompson, curator of Port-O-Plymouth Museum.

Jordan, Weymouth T., Jr. and Gerald W. Thomas. "Massacre at Plymouth; April 20, 1864." *North Carolina Historical Review* 72, April 1995.

Langley, Harold D. *"The Image of War: 1861-1865," Fighting For Time*, Vol. IV.

Kirk, James B. "Treatment of Prisoners," *National Tribune Veterans Newspaper*, November 5, 1891.

"Life and Death of The Ram 'Albemarle,'" *Historic Washington County*, Compiled and published by Washington County Historical Society, Plymouth, North Carolina.

McPherson, James. "A War That Never Goes Away," *American Heritage*, March 1990, p. 41.

"Mission Impossible," *Sea Classics*, Vol. 3, No. 4, July 1970, p. 14.

Neff, Liz. "From Hartford to Andersonville," *Avon Life*, Avon, Conn., May-August '02.

Nelson, Sharlene P. "The Battle of Plymouth Reported 106 Years Ago." (Filed at the Washington County Public Library.)

"North Carolina's Second Largest Battle," *The Roanoke Beacon Living History*, Plymouth, N.C., 1998, p. 4.

Patterson, Gerald A. "Hangman Pickett," *America's Civil War*, November 2002, pp. 39-44.

Phelps, Shirley. "Ausbon House Dates Back to 1830's or 40's," *The Roanoke Beacon,* Plymouth, N.C., 1995, p. 7.
Pierce, Annette. "Polishing a Historic Gem," *The Roanoke Beacon,* Plymouth, N.C., April 2001.
"Plymouth Again," *National Tribune Veterans Newspaper,* Library of Congress Newspaper Room, September 19, 1889.
"Plymouth Last Major Victory For South in the War," *The Roanoke Beacon Living History,* April 18, 2001, p. 6.
"Plymouth--101 Pa.," *National Tribune Veterans Newspaper,* Library of Congress Newspaper Room, August 1, 1889.
"Plymouth Pilgrims," *National Tribune Veterans Newspaper,* Library of Congress Newspaper Room, May 1, 1864.
"Plymouth Pilgrims and How They Came to be Captured—A Survivor's Story," *The National Tribune Veterans Newspaper* Washington, D.C.
Reed, John A. "Union North Carolina Soldiers," *National Tribune Veterans' Newspaper,* June 8, 1911.
Sayers, Richard A. "Advance the Colors," *Now and Then,* p. 356.
Slaybaugh, George, H. "Battle of Plymouth," *National Tribune Veterans Newspaper,* August 22, 1889.
___ "How Cushing Destroyed the Albemarle," *National Tribune Veterans Newspaper,* August 19, 1926.
"South Captures 2,500 Union Troops in Battle," *The Roanoke Beacon Living History,* April 18, 2001, p. 9.
"The Capture of Plymouth," *Buffalo Morning Express,* p. 1, May 7, 1864. Courtesy of B. Conrad Bush.
"The Destruction of the 'Albemarle,'" *Harper's Weekly,* Vol. VIII, No. 412, New York, Saturday, November 19, 1864.
"The 1864 Siege of Plymouth, Civil War—A Good Time To Pray." *Roanoke Beacon,* Plymouth, N.C., August 6, 1986, p. 20, (Filed at Washington County Library.)
"The Fall of Plymouth 44 Years Ago To-Day," *The Hartford Daily Times,* Hartford, Conn., Monday, April 20, 1908, (Filed at Washington County Public Library.)
"Torchlight Tour to begin at the Methodist Church," *The Roanoke Beacon Living History,* Plymouth, N.C., 1998, p. 11.

ELECTRONIC SOURCES

"101st Pennsylvania: Return of the Colors."
http://home.att.net~edboots/colors.nun

"Accounts of the Actions at Fort Pillow, 1864."
http://members.aol.com/GnrljSB/FtPillowacc.html

"B. F. Blakeslee, History of the 16th Conn. Regiment Volunteer Infantry."
http://members.aol.com/SHolmes/hist16ct.htm

Black Sailors Database
http://www.izd.nps.gov/cwss/sailors_index.html

"The Story of William Barker Cushing."
http://cushingassociation.tripod.com/wbcush.htm

"Lieutenant Commander Charles Williamson Flusser, United States Navy."
http://members.aol.com/SHolmes54/Flusser.html

"Generalizations Regarding the U.S. Army Uniform of the Civil War."
http://members.tripod.com/howardlanham/general.html

"Report of Major General Benjamin Huger Concerning the Battle of the Monitor and Merrimac."
http://www.civilwarhome.com/huger.htm

Roster of the 36th USCT.
http://www.rootsweb.com/~ncusct/usct.htm

"Roster of the 103rd Pennsylvania Regiment"
http://users.aol.com/EvanSlaug/rostp.html

"The Soldier's Story of His Captivity at Andersonville, Belle Isle, and Other Rebel Prisons."
http://home.att.net/~CWppds/goss.htm

"U.S. Colored Troops Formed in North Carolina."
http://www.rootsweb.com/~ncusct/usct.htm

LETTERS

"Quartermaster Edward Boots' Letters." (Courtesy of Edward Boots, historian of the 103rd Pennsylvania Volunteer Regiment.)

Commander Charles Williamson Flusser's Letters to His Mother and Sister. (Courtesy of Harry Thompson, curator of Port-O-Plymouth Museum and Scott Holmes, historian of the 16th Connecticut Volunteers.)

Sergeant Julian Wheaton Merrill's Letters. (Courtesy of B. Conrad Bush, historian of the 24th N.Y. Independent Battery Light Artillery.)

"A. E. Wilson to his sister." (Courtesy of B. Conrad Bush.)

NEWSPAPERS

Avon Life. May 2002.
Buffalo Morning Express. May 7, 1864.
Harper's Weekly. November 19, 1864.
"Living History Weekend." Supplement to the *Roanoke Beacon.* April 21, 2001, April 19-21, 2002.
National Tribune Veterans Newspaper. May 1, 1864, August 1, 1889, September 19, 1889, January 9, 1902.
Roanoke Beacon. May 5, 1995; April 1998; April 17, 2002.
Smithfield Herald, March 18, 1924.
The Hartford Courant. April 13, 1907, April 15, 1907.
The Hartford Daily Times. September 3, 1907, October 15, 1907, April 20, 1908.

END NOTES

ACKNOWLEDGEMENTS

1. *The Roanoake Beacon*, April 19-20, 2002, p. 9.
2. *The Roanoke Beacon*, "Living History," April 18, 2001, p. 4.

CHAPTER 1 A Nation Divided

1. Geoffrey C. Ward with Richard and Ken Burns, *The Civil War: An Illustrated History*, (New York: Alfred A. Knopf, Inc., 1990), p. 2.
2. James M. McPherson, *Battle Cry of Freedom: The Civil War Era*, (New York: Balantine Books, 1988), p. 297.
3. *Ibid.*
4. James M. McPherson, "A War That Never Goes Away," *American Heritage*, March 1990, p. 42.
5. Harry Thompson, Curator of Port-O-Plymouth Museum, "Unionism in North Carolina and Washington County," *History Lesson*, 2001.
6. *Historic Washington County*, Compiled and Published by Washington County Historical Society, Plymouth, N.C., Revised in April 1979, p. 135.
7. McPherson, "A War That Never Goes Away," p. 44.
8. *Ibid.*, p. 46.
9. *Ibid.*, p. 47.
10. *Ibid.*, p. 44.
11. *Ibid.*, p. 46.
12. John Hope Franklin and Alfred A. Moss, Jr., *From Slavery to Freedom: A History of African Americans*, 7th Edition (New York: McGraw-Hill Inc., 1994), p. 196.

Scott vs. Sanford: "Dred Scott was a Missouri slave whose master had first taken him to live in free Illinois and subsequently to a fort in the northern part of the Louisiana purchase, where slavery had been excluded by the Missouri Compromise. Upon his return to Missouri, Scott sued for his freedom on the ground that residence on free soil had liberated him. The majority of the Court held that Scott was not a citizen and therefore could not bring suit in the courts. Chief Justice Roger B. Taney, speaking for the Court, added that since the Missouri Compromise was unconstitutional, masters could take their slaves anywhere in the territories and retain title to them. The decision was a clear-cut victory for the South...."

13. McPherson, "A War That Never Goes Away," p. 46.
14. Mc Pherson, *Battle Cry of Freedom*, p. 281.
15. McPherson, "A War That Never Goes Away," p. 44.
16. Robert G. Elliott, *Ironclad of the Roanoke: Gilbert Elliott's Albemarle*, (Shippensburg, Pa.; White Mane Publishing Co., Inc., 1999), p. 183.

17. John Hope Franklin, *From Slavery to Freedom: A History of Negro Americans*, Fourth Edition, (New York: Alfred Knopf, 1947), p. 228.
18. Webb Garrison, *Civil War Curiosities*, (Nashville, Tennessee: Rutledge Hill Press), p. 161.
19. *Ibid.*, p. 162.
20. Major Mark M. Boatner, III, *Military Customs and Traditions*, (New York: David McKay, Company), pp. 88-89.
"The American Army started lettering its companies in 1816. Since the script 'J' looked so much like 'I' the letter J was not used. (J is the most recent addition to our alphabet and when first adopted was used interchangeable with I. Remember also that the Army of that day relied entirely on handwritten orders and correspondence which made the likelihood even greater than the I's and J's would be confused.)"
Courtesy of the U.S. Army Military History Institues, Carlisle, Pa.
21. Edgar Welles, *Diary of Gideon Welles: Secretary of Navy Under Lincoln and Johnson,* (Boston & New York: Houghton Mifflin Co.,) Vol. 1, p. 544.
22. Joseph P. Reidy, "Black Men in Navy Blue During the Civil War," Prologue: Quarterly of the National Archives and Records Administration, Fall 2001, Vol. 33, No. 3.
23. *Ibid.*, from muster Rolls, *USS Miami,* RG24, NAB.

CHAPTER 2 A Small North Carolina Town

1. *Historic Washington County*, p. 14.
2. Luther Dickey, *History of the 103rd Regiment: Pennsylvania Veteran Volunteer Infantry 1861-1865*, (Chicago, Illinois: L .S. Dickey, 1910, p. 256). From a descriptive write-up of the town by Edward L. Conn that appeared in the *Raleigh News and Observer,* June 11, 1909.
3. *Ibid.*, p. 257.
4. *Ibid.*, p. 255.
5. *Ibid.*, p. 256.
6. *Ibid.*, p. 257.
7. *Ibid.*
8. Dorothy Spruill-Redford, *Somerset Homecoming*, (Chapel Hill: The University of North Carolina Press, 1988), quoting Edmund Ruffin, magazine editor who reported on the Somerset estate in 1839, p. 68.
9. "No Lake Phelps Resort Locality," Washington County Library files, Plymouth, N.C.
10. "Weyerhaeuser Company," Tacoma, Washington, May 1963, p. 8.
11. *Ibid.*
12. Thompson, "Unionism in North Carolina and Washington County," *History Lesson,* 2001.
13. *Ibid.*
14. Dickey, *History of the 103rd Regiment,* p. 256.
15. Thompson, *History Lesson,* 2001.

CHAPTER 3 **Yankee Invasion of Plymouth**

1. Dickey, *History of 103rd Penna. Regiment*, p. 255.
2. Mc Pherson, *Battle Cry of Freedom*, p. 372.
3. John W. Hinds, *Invasion and Conquest of North Carolina: Anatomy of a Gunboat War*, (Shippensburg, Pa.: Beidel Printing House, 1998), p. 96.
4. *Ibid.*, p. 100.
5. Dickey, *History of 103rd Penna. Regiment*, Map of the Operations at Roanoke Island, N.C., from the official record.
6. O. R. Army Series 1, Vol. 9, p. 188.
7. Elliott, *Ironclad of the Roanoke*, (Shippensburg, Pa.: White Mane Publishing Co., 1999), p. 122.
8. Dickey, *History of the 103rd Regiment*, p. 47.
9. Ron Gancas, *The Hardluck Regiment: The Penna. 103rd*, p. 13.
10. Samuel P. Bates, *History of Pennsylvania Volunteers, 1861-65*, (Harrisburg, Pa.: B. Singerly, State Printer, Vol. 3, 1869-1871), pp. 698-699.
11. Dickey, *History of the 103rd Regiment*, p. 256.
12. *Roanoke Beacon Living History '98*, p. 9.
13. Weymouth T. Jordan and Gerald W. Thomas, "Massacre at Plymouth," *The North Carolina Historical Review*, Vol. LXXII, April 1956, p. 127.
14. Thompson, "Unionism in North Carolina and Washington County," *History Lesson*, 2001.
15. "Feeding an Army," Fort Ward Museum, Alexandria, Virginia.
16. Dickey, *History of the 103rd Regiment*, p. 49.
17. *Ibid.*, p. 51.
18. Merrill, *Records of the Twenty- Fourth New York Battery*, p. 141. [In Albany fifty-six men from Perry, N.Y. came under the leadership of Major Thomas W. Lion, an ex-English army officer. Having invented a fire-rocket, he wanted to form a battalion to use the rocket in the field. The battalion was formed with other recruits making up two companies, Co. A with Captain A. Ransom and Co. B whose captain was Jay E. Lee. The rocket, however, turned out to be a failure.]
19. "Civil War Letters of Sergeant Julius W. Merrill to the Editor of the New Yorker," January 26, 1861. Courtesy of B. Conrad Bush, historian of the 24th Independent Battery B New York Veterans Light Artillery.
20. Bernard F. Blakeslee, *History of the 16th Connecticut Volunteers*, (Hartford, Conn.: Case, Lockwood and Brainard Co., 1875), p. 52.
21. Dickey, *History of the 103rd Regiment*, p. 49.
22. *Ibid.*, p. 352
23. *Roanoke Beacon Living History*, April 18, 2001, p. 8.
24. *Ibid.*
25. Courtesy of Scott Holmes, historian of the 16th Connecticut Volunteers Infantry.
26. Elliott, *Ironclad of the Roanoke*, p. 85.
27. Dickey, *History of the 103rd Regiment*, p. 256.

28. Robert Roberts, *Encyclopedia of Historic Forts: The Military, Pioneer, and Trading Posts of the United States*, (New York: Macmillan Publishing Company, 1988), p. 612.
29. Dickey, *History of the 103rd Regiment*, p. 255.
30. *Ibid.*, p. 52.
31. *Ibid.*, p. 255.
32. *Ibid.*, p. 258.
33. *Ibid.*
34. Walter Clark, (ed.) *Histories of the Several Regiments and Battalions from North Carolina, in the Great War 1861-'65*, 5 Vols., (Raleigh: State of N.C., 1910), p. 353.
35. Dickey, *History of the 103rd Regiment*, p. 258.
36. [Captain Compher recruited Co. D in Rainsburg, Pa. He was married to Barbara Mills, great-great aunt of Debra Miller Felice, one of the present historians of the 101st Penna. Volunteers.]
37. "Living History," *Roanoke Beacon*, April 19-21, 2002, p. 10.
38. Clark, *Histories of the Several Regiments and Battalions from North Carolina Troops, in the Great War, 1861-65*, p. 346.
39. Dickey, *History of the 103rd Regiment*, p. 51.
40. *Ibid.*, p. 258.
41. J. W. Merrill, *Records of the 24th Independent Battery*, (edited by B. Conrad Bush, published for the Ladies' Cemetery Association of Perry, N.Y., 1870), p. 64.
[Andrew T. Ferguson was a musician. After the capture, Merrill wrote: "Ferguson's music, which was always such a pleasure to the Battery boys, charmed even those Southern beasts and an occasional desire among the Reb officers to hear a tune, put him in favor with them."]
42. *Ibid.*
43. Wayne Mahood, *The Plymouth Pilgrims*, (Hightstown, N.J.: Longstreet House, 1989), p. 172.
44. Uniform information courtesy of Ed Boots, one of the 101st Penna. historians.
45. "Generalization Regarding the United States Army Uniform in the Civil War."
  http://members.tripod.com/howardlanham/general.html
46. Wayne Mahood, ed., *Charlie Mosher's Civil War: From Fair Oaks to Andersonville With the Plymouth Pilgrims*, (Hightstown, N.J.: Longstreet House, 1994), p. 137.
47. Dickey, *History of the 103rd Regiment*, pp. 53-54.
48. Merrill, *Records of the 24th Independent Battery*, p. 211. [Lieutenant Cady received a commission to replace Captain Lee in Co. B. on June 13, 1863.]
49. *Ibid.*
50. Mahood, *Charlie Mosher's Civil War*, pp. 184-185.
51. Courtesy of Scott Holmes

CHAPTER 4 **The "Contraband" Problem**

1. Jordan and Thomas, "Massacre at Plymouth," p. 127.
2. The 8th Census: U. S. Census taken in 1860.
3. *Washington County Genealogical Society Journal*, (Vol. 5, No. 2, Aug. 1997), p. 24.
4. Mahood, *Charlie Mosher's Civil War*, p. 193.
5. Thompson, "Black Participation in the Civil War," Battle of Plymouth.
6. Roster of the 36th USCT.
   http://www.rootsweb.com/~ncusct/usct.htm
7. Black Sailors Database
   http://www.izd.nps.gov/cwss/sailors_index.html
8. Information acquired from conversation with several black citizens of Plymouth.
9. *Historic Washington County,* Washington County Society, Plymouth, N.C., Revised, April 1979, p. 28.
10. From written information shared with author by Plymouth resident, Helen Collins McNair, a direct descendant of Annie Norman.
11. *"Historic Plymouth Walking Tour,"* # 4.
12. Courtesy of Helen Collins McNair.
13. Courtesy of John Ball.
14. *Ibid.*
15. Courtesy of Ed Boots.
16. *Ibid.*
17. Jordan and Thomas, "Massacre at Plymouth," p. 125.
18. Sergeant Warren Lee Goss, *The Soldier's Story of His Captivity at Andersonville, Bell Isle, and Other Rebel Prisons,* (Boston: Lee and Shepard, 1866.)
   http://home.att.net/~CWPPDS/goss.html
19. Franklin and. Moss, *From Slavery to Freedom: A History of African Americans*, 7th Edition, p. 199.
20. *Ibid.,* p. 118.
21. *Ibid.,* p. 200.
22. *Ibid.,* p. 82.
23. *Records of the 24th Independent Battery*, p. 210. [However, Sergeant Warren Lee Goss in *The Soldier's Story of His Captivity at Andersonville, etc."* stated that the Freemans were from Milford, Mass.]
24. Patricia Click, *Time Full of Trial: 1862-1867*, (Chapel Hill: The University of North Carolina Press, 2001), p. 85.
25. *Ibid.,* p. 40.
26. *Ibid.,* p. 55
27. *Ibid.,* p. 82.
28. Letters of J. W. Merrill, courtesy of Conrad Bush.
29. *Ibid.*
30. *Ibid.*
31. Click, *Time Full of Trial: 1862-1867,* p. 191.

32. *Ibid.,* p. 199.

CHAPTER 5 Birth of the Ironclad Rams

1. Elliott, *Ironclad of the Roanoke,* p. 14.
2. *Ibid.*
3. Archibald D. Turnbal, *John Stevens: An American Record,* N.Y., 1928.
4. Webb Garrison, *Civil War Curiosities,* p. 121.
5. Ibid., p. 122.
6. Garrison, *Civil War Curiosities,* p. 208; Elliott, *Ironclad of the Roanoke,* p. 15.
7. *Ibid.*
8. John Ericsson, "The Building of the Monitor," *Battles and Leaders of the Civil War,* Robert U. Johnson and Clarence C. Buel, editors, 4 Vols., N.Y., 1884-1888.
9. Garrison, *Civil War Curiosities,* p. 167.
10. *Ibid.,* p. 166.
11. *Ibid.,* p. 161.
12. Lon Dill, Jr., "Confederate Ram Albemarle Scattered Whole Fleets But Lost to Tiny Launch," *The News and Observer,* (Raleigh, N.C., October 26, 1947), p. IV-3.
13. Report of Maj. Gen. John E. Wool, U.S. Army, commanding Department of Va., concerning the Battle of the Ironclads from Fort Monroe, Va., March 9, 1862, written to Major General George B. McClellan, commanding the Army, Washington, D.C. and to the Secretary of War.
14. "Report of Maj. Gen. Benjamin Huger concerning the Battle of the *Monitor* and *Merrimac.*"
     http://www.civilwarhome.com/huger.htm
15. Report of Flag-Officer Franklin Buchanon, CSN Naval Hospital, Norfolk, Va., March 27, 1862, written to S. R. Mallory.
16. Elliott, *Ironclad of the Roanoke,* p. 15.
17. George M. Brooke, *John. M. Brooke: Naval Scientist and Educator,* University Press of Virginia, 1980.
18. *Ibid.*

CHAPTER 6 Ironclad Threat to Plymouth

1. Dickey, *History of the 103rd Regiment,* p. 55.
2. [Double-enders were used because large boats could not turn in the river. The double-ender *Miami* had a paddle in the center with rudders on both sides. Double-enders could go forward or backward, not needing to turn around.]
3. Elliott, *Ironclad of the Roanoke,* p. 106.
4. Lon Dill, Jr., "Confederate Ram Albemarle Scattered While Fleets But Lost to Tiny Launch," *The News and Observer,* (Raleigh, N.C., Sunday morning, October 26, 1947).

5. Elliott, *Ironclad of the Roanoke*, p. 118.
6. Lon Dill, Jr., "Albemarle Scatters Fleet," (*Roanoke Beacon,* Plymouth, N.C., August 1968).
7. Elliott, *Ironclad of the Roanoke*, p. 87.
8. *Ibid.,* p. 151.
9. *Ibid.,* p. 129.
10. *Ibid.,* p. 136.
11. *Ibid.,* p. 117.
12. Dill, "Albemarle Scatters Fleet," *Roanoke Beacon,* Plymouth, N.C., August 1968.
13. *Confederate Military History,* Extended Edition, Wilmington, N.C., p. 223.
14. *Ibid.*
15. Elliott, *Ironclad of the Roanoke,* p. 164, (with added information).

CHAPTER 7 Lieutenant Gilbert Elliott, CSA

1. Elliott, *Ironclad of the Roanoke,* p. 9.
2. *Ibid.,* p. 58.
3. *Ibid.,* p. 135.

CHAPTER 8 A Comedy of Errors

1. Dickey, *History of the 103rd Regiment,* p. 256.
2. *Ibid.*
3. *Ibid.*
4. Jordan and Thomas, "Massacre at Plymouth," p. 194.
5. *Ibid.*
6. *Ibid.*
7. Dickey, *History of the 103rd Regiment,* p. 257.
8. Jordan and Thomas, "Massacre at Pymouth," p. 194.
9. Daniel W. Barefoot, *General Robert F. Hoke: Lee's Modest Warrior,* (Winston- Salem, N.C.: John F. Blair, 1996), p. 129.
10. Jordan and Thomas, "Massacre at Plymouth," p. 194.
11. Dickey, *History of the 103rd Regiment,* p. 257.
12. Jordan and Thomas, "Massacre at Plymouth," p. 129.
13. *Ibid.,* p 194.
14. Mahood, *Charlie Mosher's Diary,* p. 193.
15. Jordan and Thomas, "Massacre at Plymouth," p. 194.

CHAPTER 9 General Henry Walton Wessells, USA

1. Dickey, *History of the 103rd Regiment,* p. 273.
2. *Ibid.*
3. *Ibid.,* p. 267.
4. *Ibid.,* p. 272.

5. Jordan and Thomas, "Massacre at Plymouth," p. 155.

CHAPTER 10 Yankees Garrisoned at Plymouth

1. Edward Boots' letter to his mother, October 11, 1863, the possession of great-nephew Edward Boots.
2. Karen Arms and Pamela Camp, *Biology*, (Philadelphia: Saunders College Publishing, 1982), p. 208.
3. *Ibid.*
4. Jacob D. Brown, "What Our Readers Have to Say About Their Old Campaigns," *The National Tribune*, Washington, D.C., October 1889.
5. Dickey, *History of the 103rd Regiment*, p. 258.
6. *Ibid.*, p. 257.
7. Mahood, Charlie Mosher's Diary, p. 204.
8. Jordan and Thomas, "Massacre at Plymouth," pp. 133-134.

CHAPTER 11 A Union Soldier's Letter to His Mother

1. Published in the *North Carolina Historical Review*, April 1959, stored at the Port-O-Plymouth Museum at Plymouth, N.C.; previously published in *The North Carolina Historical Review*, April 1959.

CHAPTER 12 Just Before the Battle

1. Michael Ballard, "The 1864 Siege of Plymouth, A Good Time to Pray, Confederate Victory in North Carolina," *Civil War Times Illustrated*, p. 16.
2. *Ibid.*
3. Dickey, *History of the 103rd Regiment*, p. 317.
4. B. F. Blakeslee, *History of the 16th Connecticut Volunteers*, p. 49.
5. Barefoot, *General Robert F. Hoke*, p. 105.
6. *Ibid.*, p. 108.
7. *Ibid.*, pp. 123-124.
8. Dickey, *History of the 103rd Regiment*, pp. 318-319.
9. Flusser, *Officers' Letters of the U.S. Navy*.
10. Dickey, *History of the 103rd Regiment*, p. 260.
11. Lee A. Wallace, Jr., *17th Virginia Infantry*, 1st edition, (Lynchburg, Va.: H. E. Howard, Inc., 1990), pp. 58-59.
12. Flusser, *Officers' Letters of the U.S. Navy*.

CHAPTER 13 A Surprise Sunday Attack

1. "Captain John Donaghy's Army Experience," *History of the 103rd Regiment*, p. 55.
2. Jordan and Thomas, "Massacre at Plymouth," p. 133.
3. W. H. Merrill, *Reminiscences of the War of 1861-5*, (Lynchburg, Va.:

J. P. Bell Company, Inc., 1911), pp. 178-179.
   4. Dickey, *History of the 103rd Regiment*, p. 259.
   5. *Ibid.*, p. 260.
   6. *Ibid.*, p. 50.
   7. Bernard F. Blakleslee, *History of the 16th Conn. Volunteers*, pp. 54-55.
   8. Jordan and Thomas, "Massacre at Plymouth," p. 135.
   9. Dickey, *History of the 103rd Regiment*, p. 59.
   10. Alonzo Cooper, *In and Out of Rebel Prisons*, Oswego, N.Y.: R. J. Oliphant, 1888, p. 14. [Russell was not wounded fatally because Alonzo Cooper lists Russell as being a prisoner of war at Macon Prison, p. 317.]
   11. Mahood, *Charie Mosher's Civil War*, p. 193.
   12. Gancas, *The Hardluck Regiment: The Pennsylvania One hundred and Third*, p. 10.
   13. John Ball, *Escape From Dixie: The Story of Lt. John Lafler (85th NY) Civil War POW*, (Williamsville, NY: Goldstar Enterprises, 1996), p. 33.
   14. Dickey, *History of the 103rd Regiment*, p. 59.
   15. [Minie balls were shot from muskets.]
   16. Garrison, *Civil War Curiosities*, p. 115.
   17. Dickey, *History of 103rd Penna. Regiment*, p. 105.
   18. *Ibid.*, p. 260.
   19. Jordan and Thomas, "Massacre in Plymouth," p. 157.
   20. Dickey. *History of the 103rd Regiment*, p. 261.
   21. *Ibid.*, p. 263.
   22. Goss, *The Soldier's Story of His Captivity at Andersonville, Belle Isle, and other Rebel Prisons*, (Boston: Lee & Shepard Publishers, 1866).
              http://home.att.net/~CWppds/goss.htm.
   23. Clark, *North Carolina Troops in the Great War, 1861-64*, p. 338.
   24. Pollard, *Southern History of the War*, Fairfax Press, p. 263.
   25. Blakeslee, *History of the 16th Connecticut Volunteers*.
             http://members.aol.com/SHolmes54/hist16ct.html
   26. Pollard, *Southern History of the War*, Fairfax Press, p. 263.
   27. Mahood, *Charlie Mosher's Civil War*, p. 195.
   28. Dickey, *History of 103rd Penna. Regiment*, p. 264.
   29. Garrison, *Civil War Curiosities*, p. 117. [General Ben McCulloch said the "Rebel yell" was first heard during an early engagement at Springfield, Missouri *"...still our men pushed onward and with one wild yell, broke upon the enemy."* Confederate Colonel Keller Anderson described the yell as he heard it at Chickamauga: *"Then arose that do-or-die expression, that maniacal maelstrom of sound; that penetrating, rasping, shrieking, blood-curling noise that could be heard for miles and whose volume reached the heavens—such an expression as never yet came from the throats of sane men, but from men whom the seething blast of an imaginary hell would not check while the sound lasted."* Colonel J. Harvey Dew of the Ninth Virginia Cavalry likened it to *"a well-known fox-hunter's yell, prolonged on the high note and more continuously repeated."*]

30. *Ibid.*, concerning hand grenades, p. 144. [*"Soldiers who may or may not have heard of the Ketchum grenade or the Excelsior sometimes improvised similar weapons. At Vicksburg, Confederates in Louisiana units struck short, lighted fuses into 6 and 12 pounder shells, then rolled them into ranks of Union sappers."*]
31. Pollard, *Southern History of the War*, p. 263.
32. Dickey, *History of the 103rd Regiment*, p. 262.
33. L. A. Butts, 1st Lieut., 85th N.Y. Vols. Written to the late Commander of the District of the Albemarle, N.C., Brig. Gen. H. W. Wessells, O. R. Series I, Vol. XXXIII, pp. 301-302.
34. Pollard, *Southern History*, p. 264.
35. Clark, *North Carolina Troops in the Great War*, p. 338.
36. Dickey, *History of 103rd Penna. Vols.*, p. 262.
37. "Battle of Plymouth 106 Years Ago," from files at the Washington County Library, Plymouth, N.C.
38. Dickey, *History of 103rd Penna Regiment*, p. 60.
39. "Battle of Plymouth 106 years Ago," from files at Washington County Library, Plymouth, N.C.

CHAPTER 14 The Rebel Goliath

1. Gilbert Elliott, article, "The Career of the Confederate Ram Albemarle," *Century Magazine*, July 1888, pp. 442-423.
2. Elliott, *Ironclad of the Roanoke*, p. 177.
3. Mahood, *Charlie Mosher's Civil War*, p. 197.
4. Alonzo Cooper, *In and Out of Rebel Prisons*, (Oswego, N.Y.: R. J. Oliphant, 1888), p. 20.
5. Ball, *Escape from Dixie*, p. 39.
6. Jordan and Thomas, "Massacre at Plymouth," Appendix B, p. 195.
7. George O. Brown, Co. G, 2nd Mass. H. A., "Plymouth Again," *National Tribune*, Sept. 19, 1889.
8. Jordan and Thomas, "Massacre at Plymouth," Appendix B, p. 195.
9. Dickey, *103rd Penna. Regimental History*, p. 276.
10. Elliott, *Ironclad of the Roanoke*, p. 183.
11. Wayne Mahood, *The Plymouth Pilgrims: A History of the Eight-Fifth New York Infantry in the Civil War*, (Hightstown, N.Y.: Longstreet House, 1989), p. 170.

CHAPTER 15 Captain James Wallace Cooke, CSN

1. Elliott, *Ironclad of the Roanoke*, p. 65.
2. Scott W. Holmes, "Lieutenant Commander Charles Williamson Flusser," p. 19.
    http//members.aol.com/SHolmes54/Muster.html
3. Elliott, *Ironclad of the Roanoke*, p. 139.

CHAPTER 16 Lieutenant Commander Charles Williamson Flusser, USN

1. Holmes, "Lieutenant Commander Charles Williamson Flusser," p. 4.
2. Flusser's Letters, *Officers' Letters of U.S. Navy*.
3. Holmes, "Lieutenant Commander Charles Flusser, USN," p. 14.
4. Dickey, *History of the 103rd Regiment*, p. 271.
5. Holmes, "Lieutenant Commander Charles Williamson Flusser, USN," p. 19.

CHAPTER 17 Attacking the Forts

1. *Roanoke Beacon*, April 18, 2001, p. 6. [The number is excessive since Hoke had 10,000 troops and there were less than 3000 Yankees at Plymouth at the time of the battle.]
2. Clark, *North Carolina Troops, in the Great War, 1861-'65*, Vol. 5, p. 339.
3. Dickey, *History of the 103rd Regiment*, p. 265.
4. Clark, *North Carolina Troops, in the Great War, 1861-'65*, Vol. 5, p. 339.
5. *Ibid.*, p. 340.
6. *Ibid.*
7. *Ibid.*
8. Dickey, *History of the Penna. Regiment*, p. 265.

CHAPTER 18 General Robert Hoke, CSA

1. Jordan and Thomas, "Massacre at Plymouth," p. 143.

CHAPTER 19 Yankee Capitulation

1. Dickey, *History of 103rd Penna. Regiment*, p. 265.
2. "The Fall of Plymouth 44 years ago Today," *Hartford Daily Times*, Monday, April 20, 1908. [Col. Beach, a native of Hartford, Conn., was a West Point graduate, class of 1857. He was brevetted Lieutenant Colonel in the regular army for gallantry at Plymouth.]
3. *Ibid.*
4. Dickey, *History of the 103rd Regiment*, p. 61.
5. *Ibid.*, p. 266.
6. Cooper, *In and Out of Rebel Prisons*, p. 30.
7. Dickey, *History of the 103rd Regiment*, p. 266.
8. Elliott, *Ironclad of the Roanoke*, p. 185.
9. Clark, *North Carolina Troops, in the Great War, 1861-'65*, p. 342.
10. Blakeslee, *History of the 16th Conn.*, p. 59.
11. "Ram Albemarle Sunk 110 years Ago: Confederate Soldier's Personal Account of the 1864 Battle" was first published in the *Smithfield Herald*, March 18, 1924, now on file at the Washington County Public Library, Plymouth, N.C.
12. Pollard, *Southern History of the War*, pp. 262-266.

13. Mahood, *Charlie Mosher's Civil War*, p. 199.
14. O. R. Ser. I, Vol. XXXXIII, p. 293.
15. Elliott, *Ironclad of the Roanoke*, p. 185.
16. Pollard, *Southern History of the War*, p. 265.
17. *Roanoke Beacon*, "Living History," April 19-21, 2002, p. 12.
18. Dickey, *History of the 103rd Regiment*, p. 267.
19. *Ibid.*
20. Clark, *North Carolina Troops, in the Great War, 1861-'65*, p. 284.
21. Courtesy of B. Conrad Bush, historian of the 24th Independent Battery New York Veteran Light Artillery.
22. Thomas, *Bertie in Blue*, p. 31.
23. Bates, *One Hundred and Third Regiment*, reprint, (Wilmington, N.C.: Broadfoot Publishing Company, 1993), p. 700.
24. Dickey, *History of the 103rd Regiment*, p. 55.
25. Jordan and Thomas, "Massacre at Plymouth," p. 194.
26. Dickey, *History of the 103rd Regiment*, p. 279.
27. Ibid., p. 360.
28. *Ibid.*
29. *Ibid.*
30. Jordan and Thomas, "Massacre at Plymouth," pp. 146-147.
31. Ball, *Escape From Dixie*, pp. 105-106.
32. Dickey, *History of the 103rd Regiment*, p. 279.
33. *Confederate Military History*, p. 225.

CHAPTER 20 Sacred Flags

1. Garrison, *Civil War Curiosities*, p. 174.
2. Clark, *North Carolina Troops in the Great War, 1861-1864*, p. 346.
3. "Flags of the Civil War," Courtesy of the U.S. Dept. of Interior, National Park Service.
4. W. H. Morgan, *Personal Reminiscences of The War of 1861-5*, Lynchburg, Va.: J. P. Bell Company, Inc., 1911, p. 186.
5. Merrill, *Records of the 24th Independent Battery*, p. 229.
6. Richard A. Sauers, *Advance the Colors: Penna. Civil War Battle Flag.*
7. *Ibid.*
8. "101st Pennsylvania Veteran Volunteer Infantry's Colors returned to Harrisburg."
    http://home.att.net~edboots/colors.nun
9. Mahood, *Charlie Mosher's Civil War*, p. 198.
10. Dickey, *History of the 101st Penna.*, p. 118.
11. *The Hartford Daily Times*, "The Fall of Plymouth 44 Years Ago To-day," Monday, April 20, 1908.
12. Letter to the Editor of the *National Tribune* from W. H. Nott, "The Capture of Plymouth: The Little Garrison Made a Stubborn Resistance Against Overwhelming Numbers," Oct. 8, 1914.

13. Frank P. O'Brien, "The Battle Flag of the 16th Conn. Captured in Plymouth," *Under Both Flags: A Panorama of the Great Civil War*, Boston: J. S. Round Co., 1896.

CHAPTER 21 Eyewitness Accounts

1. Dickey, *History of the 103rd Regiment*, p. 261.
2. Mahood, *Charlie Mosher's Civil War*, pp. 195-196.
3. Dickey, *History of the 103rd Regiment*, p. 263.
4. *Ibid.*
5. *Ibid.*, p. 265.
6. *Ibid.*, p. 266.
7. Billingsley's account courtesy of B. Conrad Bush, historian of the 24th N.Y. Independent Battery B, New York Veteran Light Artillery.
8. Cooper, *In and Out of Rebel Prisons*, p. 32.

CHAPTER 22 Fate of the Yankees

1. *Roanoke Beacon*, May 1995, p. 1.
2. Mahood, *Charlie Mosher's Civil War*, p. 199.
3. Dickey, History of 103rd Penna. Regiment, p. 267.
4. *Ibid.*, p. 268.
5. *Ibid.*
6. Browning, "Little Souled Mercenaries," *Historical Review* (Vol. LXXVII, No. 3, July 2000), p. 337.
7. Downe, Giese, Metalk, *U.S History: In the Course of Human Events*.
8. Browning, "Little Souled Mercenaries."
9. Thomas, *Bertie in Blue*, p. 31.
10. Mahood, *Charlie Mosher's Civil War*, p. 205; correction courtesy of John Ball.
11. *Ibid.*, pp. 304 and 307.
12. Jordan and Thomas, "Massacre at Plymouth," p. 154. [Lieutenant Bascombe may have been the officer being described by the *Fayetteville Weekly Intelligence* of May 10, 1864:
"*A Yankee Lieutenant who was in command of the negro forces, has, by order of Gen. Hoke, been confined with the negro women and children. He is said to present a most abject, hang dog appearance and has requested to be sent off with the other prisoners of war, but as he preferred the company of negroes previous to the capture of Plymouth, General Hoke determined not to separate him from them now.*" Lieutenant Bascombe was paroled on March 1, 1865, at North East Ferry, N.C. and mustered out on March 26th to accept a promotion as 2nd Lieutenant in the 38th USCT. p. 196.
Capt. Hiram L. Marvin, formerly a Sergeant Major in the 85th N.Y. Infantry

was paroled on Feb. 25, 1865, from the prison at Goldsboro, N.C. after which time he resigned on May 13 due to impaired health and was discharged on June 3rd. p. 197.

Lieut. George French identified himself as a member of the 12th N.Y. Cavalry and was sent to Andersonville where he died on July 3, 1864. p. 197.]

13. Mahood, *Charlie Mosher's Civil War*, p. 205.
14. Lee A. Wallace Jr., *17th Virginia Infantry*, (Lynchburg, Va.: H. E. Howard, 1990), p. 58.
15. *Ibid.*
16. Dickey, *History of the 103rd Regiment*, p. 266.
17. Information courtesy of Harry Thompson, curator of Port-O-Plymouth Museum.
18. Mahood, *Charlie Mosher's Civil War*, p. 205.
19. Thomas, *Bertie in Blue*, p. 33.
20. *Ibid.*
21. *Ibid.*, p. 7.
22. *Ibid.*
23. Browning, " Little Souled Mercenaries."
24. Thomas, *Bertie in Blue*, p. 1.
25. Mahood, *Charlie Mosher's Civil War*, p. 206.
26. Letters of J. W. Merrill, courtesy of B. Conrad Bush.
27. *Ibid.*
28. *Ibid.*
29. Robert Black, Co. E, 103rd Penna. Veteran Volunteers, "Plymouth Pilgrims and How they Came to be Captured—A Survivor's Story." (The *National Tribune*, Washington, D.C., May 1, 1884).
30. *Charleston Mercury*, April 26, 1854.
31. Courtesy of Debra Miller Felice.
32. John McElroy, *Andersonville: A Story of Rebel Prisons*, p. 186.
33. Liz Neff, "From Hartford to Andersonville, Part III, *Avon Life*, July 2002, p. 44.
34. Sergeant Warren Lee Goss, *The Soldier's Story of His Captivity at Andersonville, Belle Isle, and Other Rebel Prisons*, (Boston: Lee & Shepard Publishers, 1866).
   http://home.att.net/~CWPPDS/goss.html
35. Courtesy of John Ball.
36. Dickey, *History of the 103rd Regiment*, Preface.
37. Jordan and Thomas, "Massacre at Plymouth," p. 170.
38. Cooper, *In and Out of Rebel Prisons*, p. 72.
39. Dickey, *History of the 103rd Regiment*, p. 282.
40. *Ibid.*, p. 283.
41. "Grant's Treatment of Colored Troops," *Hartford Courant*, April 15, 1907.
42. Dickey, *History of the 103rd Regiment*, p. 282.
43. *Ibid.*, p. 282-283.
44. *Ibid.*, p. 283.

45. Dickey, *History of 103rd Penna. Regiment,* p. 283.
46. "Exchange of Prisoners," *Hartford Daily Times,* Tuesday, October 15, 1907.
47. *Ibid.*
48. Mahood, *Charlie Mosher's Civil War,* p. 239.
49. "Exchange of Prisoners," *Hartford Daily Times,* Tuesday, October 15, 1907.
50. "Grant's Treatment of Colored Troops," *Hartford Courant,* April 15, 1907.
51. Liz Leff, "From Hartford to Andersonville," *Avon Life,* July '02.
52. *Ibid.*
53. Letters of J. W. Merrill, Charleston Harbor, Dec. 8, 1864, courtesy of B. Conrad Bush.
54. *Ibid.*
55. Mahood, The *Plymouth Pilgrims,* p. 233.
56. *Ibid.,* p. 199.
57. Dickey, *History of the 103rd Regiment,* p. 294, O. R. Ser. II, Vol. VII, p. 207.
58. Kenneth C. Davis, *Don't know Much About the Civil War: Everything You Need Know About America's Greatest Conflict But Never Learned,* New York, (Avon Books, 1996), pp. 434-435.
59. Liz Neff, "From Hartford to Andersonville," pp. 45-46.
60. *Ibid.*
61. Dickey, *History of 103rd Penna. Regiment,* p. 283.

CHAPTER 23 Escapees From Rebel Prisons

1. J. W. Merrill, *Records of the 24th Independent Battery, N.Y. Light Artillery, U.S.V,* (published by Ladies' Cemetery Association of Perry, N.Y., 1870), p. 125.
2. *Ibid.,* p. 31.
3. *The Hartford Daily Times,* Monday, April 20, 1908, "The Fall of Plymouth 44 Years Ago To-Day."
4. Mahood, *Charlie Mosher's Civil War,* p. 192. [In *Diary of Albert H. Bancroft,* p. 610, the author notes thirty-seven recruits, from notes of Mahood, *Charlie Mosher's Civil War,* p. 342.]
5. New York State Adjutant General's Report, Vol. 30, Albany, N.Y., 1902.
6. Ball, *Escape from Dixie,* p. 46.
7. *Ibid.*
8. *Ibid.*
9. *Ibid.,* p. 59.
10. [Mahood described the "dead line" as *"poles or narrow strips of boards nailed to stakes driven into the ground on a line seventeen feet inside the stockade. Anyone who ventured too close was the object of target practice for the unseasoned guards." Plymouth Pilgrims,* p. 202.]
11. Merrill, *Records of the 24th N.Y. Battery,* Appendix, p. 26.
12. Ball, *Escape From Dixie,* p. 86.
13. Merrill, *Records of the 24th Independent Battery,* p. 29.
14. Courtesy of Ruth Fulton.

15. *Ibid.*
16. Ball, *Escape From Dixie*, p. 100.
17. *Ibid.*, pp. 71-72.
18. *Ibid.*, p. 72.
19. *Ibid.*, p. 81.
20. *Ibid.*, p. 77.
21. Merrill, *Records of the 24th Independent Battery*, Appendix, pp. 26-27.
22. *Ibid.*, Appendix, p. 36.
23. Ball, *Escape From Dixie*, p. 77.
24. Dickey, *History of the 103rd. Regiment*, p. 117.
25. List compiled from Dickey, *History of the 103rd Regiment*, "Prison Life," pp. 104-118.
26. Mahood, *Charlie Mosher's Civil War*, pp. 250-251.
27. D. A. Langworthy, *A Prisoner of War and His Escape*, Minneapolis, Minn.: Printing Co., 1915.

CHAPTER 24 Blacks During the Battle

1. Jordan and Thomas, "Massacre at Plymouth," p. 155.
2. *Ibid.*, p.153.
3. Edwin S. Redney, *A Grand Army of Black Men*, Cambridge University Press, 1992, p. 10.
4. Jordan and Thomas, "Massacre at Plymouth," p. 155. [Crowder Pacien was not at Plymouth. Fortunately, he was on Roanoke Island with Co. C of the 103rd Pennsylvania Volunteers at the time of the battle.]
5. Franklin and Moss, *From Slavery to Freedom: A History of African Americans*, (7th edition, N.Y.: McGraw-Hill, Inc.), p. 216.
6. http://members.aol.com/GnrlJSB/FtPillowacc.html
7. *Records of the 24th Independent Battery, N.Y. Light Artillery, U.S.V.*, (compiled by J. W. Merrill, published for the Ladies' Cemetery Association of Perry, N.Y., 1870), p. 119.
8. *Ibid.*
9. Information courtesy of B. Conrad Bush.
10. Deposition reproduced at the National Archives for the Bureau of Pensions, March 11, 1902, courtesy of Harry Thompson, curator of Port-O-Plymouth Museum, Plymouth, N.C.
11. Roster of the 103rd Pennsylvania Regiment
    http://users.aol.com/EvanSlaug/rostp.html
12. Dickey, *History of the 103rd Regiment*, p. 51.
13. Jordan and Thomas, "Massacre at Plymouth," p. 155.
14. *Ibid.*
15. Ball, *Escape From Dixie*, ["The regiment hired two Negro cooks, one of whom was so light skinned that he was occasionally mistaken for Caucasian."], p. 24.

16. Information courtesy of Alan Marsh, Cultural Curator Specialist, Andersonville Historic Prison Site.
17. Jordan and Thomas, "Massacre at Plymouth," p. 175
18. Thomas, *Bertie in Blue*, p. 64.
19. Jordan and Thomas, "Massacre at Plymouth," p. 175.
20. Ibid., p. 165.
21. Dickey, "*History of 103rd Penna*. Regiment, pp. 268-269.
22. *Ibid.*, p. 269.
23. *Ibid.*
24. B. F. Blakeslee, *History of the 16th Connecticut Volunteers*, 1875.
25. Mahood, *Charlie Mosher's Civil War*, p. 205.
26. "The Battle of Plymouth Reported 106 Years Ago," on file at Washington County Library, Plymouth, N.C.
27. *National Tribune*, Washington, D.C., May 1, 1884.
28. Jordan and Thomas, "Massacre at Plymouth," p. 166.
29. *Ibid.*, pp. 167-168.
30. *Ibid.*, p. 167.
31. *Ibid.*, p. 269.
32. *Richmond Examiner*, April 30, 1864, quoted in *History of the 16th Connecticut Regiment* by Blakeslee.
33. *Richmond Dispatch*, May 3, 1864, filed in Library of Congress, courtesy of Ruth Fulton.
34. Jordan and Thomas, "Massacre at Plymouth," p. 185.
35. Dickey, *History of the 103rd Regiment*, p. 270.
36. *Ibid.*
37. *Ibid.*, p. 277.
38. Jordan and Thomas, "Massacre at Plymouth," p. 160.
39. *Ibid.*, p. 183.
40. Morgan, *Personal Reminiscences of The War of 1861-5*, p. 187.
41. *Ibid.*
42. Jordan and Thomas, "Massacre at Plymouth," p. 192.

CHAPTER 25 Properties Surviving the Battle

1. J. H. Broadwell, "Ram Albemarle Sunk 110 Years Ago."
2. *Roanoke Beacon*, "Living History," Plymouth, N.C, April 18, 2001, p. 8.
3. *Roanoke Beacon*, Plymouth, N.C., August 11, 1976, p. 7.
4. *Historic Washington County*, p. 11.
5. *Roanoke Beacon*, "Living History '98," p. 4.
6. *Historic Washington County*, p. 11.
7. *Roanoke Beacon*, May 1995. p. 7.
8. *Historic Washington County*, p. 13.
9. *Ibid.*
10. *Roanoke Beacon*, September, 2001.
11. *RoanokeBeacon*, "Living History," April 19-21, 2002, p. 11.

12. *Roanoke Beacon*, "Living History '98," "A History of Grace Episcopal," p. 7.
13. *Roanoke Beacon*, August 1968, from files at Washington County Library, Plymouth, North Carolina.
14. *Roanoke Beacon*, "Living History 98", p. 7.
15. United States Dept. of Interior, National Park Service, *National Register of Places*, Section 7, p. 37.
16. *Historic Washington County*, p. 16.
17. "Brief History of Plymouth United Methodist Church," from files at the Washington County Library, Plymouth, N.C.
18. "National Register Historic Places," United States Department of the Interior, National Park Service, Section number 7, p. 37.
19. Dickey, *History of the 103rd. Regiment*, p. 58.
20. "Letters of J. W. Merrill," courtesy of B. Conrad Bush.
21. Dickey, *History of 103rd Penna. Regiment*, p. 54.
22. Amos Billingsley, Chaplain of 101st Penna. Vol. Infantry, *From the Flag to the Cross: Scenes and Incidents of Christianity in the War*. New World Publishing Co., 1872, p. 19.
23. *Ibid.*
24. Information courtesy of Ed Boots.
25. Mahood, *Charlie Mosher's Civil War*, p. 193.
26. Information courtesy of Scott Holmes.
27. Displays at Fort Ward Museum, Alexandria, Virginia.
28. *Ibid.*
29. *Roanoke Beacon*, "Living History, '98," p. 11.
30. *National Register of Historic Places*, Section 7, No. 53, p. 37.
31. *Historic Washington County*, p. 23.
32. *Ibid*, p. 9.
33. *Ibid.*
34. *Ibid.*, p. 12.
35. *Ibid.*
36. *Roanoke Beacon*, June 5, 2002, courtesy of Merion Baker Anderson, Plymourh, N.C.
37. *Historic Washington County*, p. 14.
38. *Ibid.*, p. 15.
39. Clark, *North Carolina Troops, in the Great War*, p. 339.
40. *Ibid.*
41. 9th United States Census taken in 1870.
42. Patricia C. Click, *Time Full of Trial: The Roanoke Island Freedmen's Colony, 1862-1867*, (Chapel Hill: The University of North Carolina Press, 2001), p. 227.
43. Plymouth Courthouse, Office of Deeds, J 378, J 387, J 403.
44. 6th United States Census taken in 1840.
45. Information shared with the author by Merion Baker Anderson.

CHAPTER 26 **Drowning of a Leviathan**

1. [The *CSS Bombshell* had been the *USS Bombshell* prior to April 18, 1864, when she sank at the Plymouth wharf.]
2. Elliott, *Ironclad of the Roanoke*, p. 194.
3. *Ibid.*
4. Dill, "Confederate Ram Albemarle Scattered Whole Fleet But Lost to Tiny Launch," *The News and Observer*, (Raleigh, N.C., October 26, 1947), in Washington County Public Library files.
5. Raimondo Luraghi, *A History of Confederate Navy*, written in Italian.
6. Elliott, *Ironclad of the Roanoke*, p. 209.
7. *Ibid.*, p. 212.
8. *Ibid.*, p. 228.
9. "Mission /Impossible," *Sea Classics*, Vol. 3, No. 4, July 1870, 1864, p. 48, filed at Washington County Library, Plymouth, N.C.
10. *Ibid.*
11. Port-O-Plymouth Museum caption in front of a torpedo display.
12. Dill, "Confederate Ram Albemarle Scattered Whole Fleet But Lost to Tiny Launch."
13. Garrison, *Civil War Curiosities*, p. 166.
14. "Mission Impossible," *Sea Classics*, p. 48.
15. J. Russell Soley, p. 637.
16. "Battles and Leaders of the Civil War: The Way to Appomattox," Vol. IV, (edited by Robert Underwood Johnson and Clarence Clough Buel of the Editorial Staff of the *Century Magazine*, N.Y.: Thomas Yoseff, 1965), p. 641.
17. Elliott, *Ironclad of the Roanoke*, p. 257.
18. "Battles and Leaders of the Civil War," p. 640.
19. J. H. Broadwell, "Ram Albemarle Sunk 110 Years Ago: Confederate Soldier's Personal Account of 1864 Battles," *Smithfield Herald*, March 18, 1924.
20. "Battles and Leaders of the Civil War," p. 640-641.
21. *Ibid.*
22. Thomas, *Bertie in Blue*, p. 81.
23. "The Story of William Barker Cushing,"
   http://cushingassociation.tripod.com/wbcush.htm
24. "Battles and Leaders of the Civil War," p. 641.
25. *Ibid.*, p. 642.
26. Elliott, *Ironclad of the Roanoke*, p. 272.

CHAPTER 27 **Final Reports on the Destruction of the CSS Albemarle**

1. O. R. Series 1, Vol. 10, p. 624.
2. [Cushing records the number as 14 men, including himself. The Offical Records lists a total of 15.]
3. *Ibid.*, pp. 611-613.

328

CHAPTER 28 **Lieutenant William Barker Cushing, USN**

1. http://cushingassociation.tripod.com/wbcush.htm   p. 1
2. "Mission /Impossible," p. 19.
3. http://cushingassociation.tripod.com/wbcush.htm   p. 3.
4. *Ibid.*
5. "Mission Impossible," p. 17.
6. *Ibid.,* p. 18.
7. "Journal of Civilization," *Harper's Weekly*, N.Y., Vol. VII, No. 412, Saturday, Nov. 19, 1864.

CHAPTER 29 **Demise of the Ships**

1. Garrison, *Civil War Curiosities*, p. 203.
2. "The Mariner's Museum- *USS Monitor* Discovery/Recovery."
   http://www.**monitor**center.org/discovery/expedition_2002.html
3. Garrison, *Civil War Curiosities*, p. 168.
4. *Ibid.*
5. Elliott, *Ironclad of the Roanoke*, p. 274.
6. *Ibid.*, p. 276.
7. *Ibid.,* p. 70.

CHAPTER 30 **The War's Finale**

1. O. R. Ser. 1, Vol XXXXV, part II, p. 163.
2. O. R. Ser. I, Vol XXXV part II, p. 199.
3. O. R. Ser. I, Vol. XXXV, part II, pp. 212-213.
4. O. R. Ser. II, Vol. VII, pp. 805-806.
5. Dickey, *History of 103rd Regiment*, p. 65.
6. *Ibid.*, p. 64.
7. *Ibid.*, p. 65.
8. *Ibid.*
9. *Ibid.,* p. 65.
10. *Ibid.,* pp. 65-66.
11. Courtesy of John Ball.
12. Courtesy of Scott Holmes.
13. Courtesy of Debra Miller Felice.
14. Gancas, *Hardluck Regiment,* p. 13.
15. *Ibid.*
16. Dickey, *History of the 103rd Regiment*, p. 84.
17. "Muster and Descriptive Roll of the 103rd Pennsylvania," quoted by Juanita Patience Moss in *Created to Be Free*, p. 99.
18. Death Certificate Registered at Luzerne County, Pennsylvania, in 1930, now in author's possession.

CHAPTER 31 General Wessells Reports on the Battle of Plymouth

1. Dickey, *History of the 103rd Regiment*, p. 314.
2. [Captain Donaghy's friend who left on the morning of the 17th to command colored troops.]
3. Dickey, *History of the 103rd Regiment*, pp. 320-321.
4. *Ibid.*, p. 321.

CHAPTER 32 Major James F. Mackey's Diary

1. O. R., Ser. I, Vol. XXXIII, pp. 296-300.
2. [General Wessells does not mention the 37th USCT recruits, originally the 3rd Regiment North Carolina Colored Infantry; neither does he include the recruits of the 10th U.S. Colored Infantry, nor the 2nd U.S. Colored Cavalry.]

CHAPTER 33 A Northern Survivor's Story Twenty Years Later

[The incorrect material contained in this letter has been changed by the historian of the 103rd Pennsylvania Volunteers, Ruth Fulton.]

1. 85th New York Infantry.
2. [15th Connecticut had been in Plymouth in January 1864, but returned to New Bern. For a reason unknown even today, 12 men were sent back to Plymouth.]
3. 85th New York Infantry. [The *Bombshell*, operated by the Quartermaster of the Army, not by the Navy, had 22 men from 3rd Penna. Heavy Artillery Regiment manning its guns.]
4. Two companies of 2nd North Carolina Infantry (Union).
5. Cos. G and H of te 2nd Massachusetts Heavy Artillery.
6. 5th New York Infantry.
7. The *Bombshell*. The *Southfield* sank later. The *Miami* did not sink at all.
8. 85th New York Infantry.

CHAPTER 34 A Confederate Soldier's Personal Account

Smithfield Herald, submitted in 1924 by C. L. Batten of Elm City, grandson of Mr. Broadwell, article found in the files at the Washington County Library in Plymouth, N. C.

EPILOGUE

1. Garrison, *Civil War Curiosities*, pp. 191-192.
2. Thompson, "Unionism in North Carolina and Washington County," *History Lesson*, p. 1.
3. Davis, *Don't know Much About the Civil War*, p. 405.

4. Elliott, *Ironclad of the Roanoke*, p. 241.
5. *Ibid.*, p. 245.
6. http://cushingassociation.tripod.com/wbcush.htm, p. 7.
7. *Ibid.*
8. *Sea Classics*, Vol. 3, No. 4, July 1970, p. 16.
9. Elliott, *Ironclad of the Roanoke*, p. 284.
10. *Manufacturers and Farmers Journal*, Vol. XLIII, No. 34, (Providence: Knowles, Anthony and Danielson, Office No. 6, Washington Buildings, April 28, 1864.)
11. http://members.aol.com/Sholmes54/Flusser, p. 11.
12. *Ibid.*, p. 18.
13. Barefoot, *General Robert F. Hoke*, p. 356.
14. Jordan and Thomas, "Massacre at Plymouth," p. 169.
15. *Ibid.*
16. Dickey, *History of the 103rd Regiment*, p. 274.
17. *Ibid.*

INDEX

101st Pennsylvania Volunteers, 34, 47, 52, 60, 62, 77, 96, 97, 99, 100, 115, 143, 156, 167, 169, 173, 176, 179, 180, 206, 219, 220, 261, 267, 281, 282, 296

103rd Pennsylvania Volunteers, 34, 35, 41, 42, 44, 48, 52, 62, 93, 96, 97, 105, 107, 109, 112, 113, 114, 120, 130, 137, 145, 147, 148, 151, 154, **155**, 157, 163, 169, 170, 176, 180, 192, 194, 195, 199, 200, 201, 203, 206, 207, 219, 220, 260, 261, 267, 270, 281, 284, 296

8th North Carolina Infantry, 110, 117, 120, 205

10th North Carolina State Troops, 110

10th USCT (United States Colored Troops), 203

11th Virginia Infantry, 110

12th New York Cavalry, 34, 97, 113, 123, 148, 167, 205, 282, 323

14th Amendment to the Constitution, 62

16th Connecticut Volunteers, 42, 97, 101, 109, 112, 113, 118, 123, 141, 142, 148, 157, 158, 159, 163, 175, 182, 184, 189, 205, 220, 263, 279, 281, 283

1st North Carolina Infantry, 37

17th North Carolina Regiment, 7, 43, 80, 85, 86, 173

17th South Carolina Infantry, 278

17th Virginia Infantry, 106, 171

18th Army Corps, 29, 49

1st North Carolina Artillery, 110

1st North Carolina Union Volunteers, 139, 174

1st North Carolina Cavalry, 37

1st North Carolina State Troops, 110

1st Virginia Infantry, 110

7th Virginia Infantry, 110

21st Georgia Volunteers, 106, 110, 119, 149

21st North Carolina Infantry, 110, 139

23rd New York Light Artillery, 201

24th Massachusetts Heavy Artillery, 163, 219

24th North Carolina Infantry, 106, 110, 146

24th New York Independent Battery, 34, 41, 49, 51, 59, 93, 97, 115, 119, 120, 135, 148, 154, 163, 166, 174, 175, 184, 189, 194, 199, 200, 201, 219

24th Virginia Infantry, 110

25th North Carolina Infantry, 106, 110

2nd Massachusetts Heavy Artillery, 118, 119, 122, 141, 148, 163, 192

2nd North Carolina Union Vol., 97, 148, 206, 330

2nd USCC (United States Colored Calvary), 93, 199

33rd North Carolina Regiment, 139

35th North Carolina. Infantry, 47, 106, 110, 117, 170, 278, 284

35th USCT, 56

36th USCT, 56
37th USCT, 56, 93, 97, 119, 200, 203, 330
38th Virginia Battalion, 110
3rd Massachusetts Infantry, 37
3rd Virginia Infantry, 110
43rd North Carolina Infantry, 110
50th North Carolina Regiment, 146
56th North Carolina Infantry, 91, 106, 111, 112, 119, 135, 136, 145, 153, 208, 226
62nd Georgia, 130
6th North Carolina Infantry, 110
85th New York Volunteers, 47, 52, 90, 92, 93, 95, 96, 97, 99, 113, 114, 118, 119, 122, 144, 148, 157, 163, 170, 171, 180, 183, 185, 189, 190, 192, 194, 195, 199, 203, 206, 263, 276, 281, 282, 283
85th Redoubt (Fort Wessells), 47, 117, 165
8th Confederate Cavalry, 110
8th Connecticut Volunteers, 199
8th North Carolina Infantry, 110, 117, 118, 120, 205
92nd New York Infantry Volunteers, 34
96th New York Infantry Volunteers, 34, 47
Acre Road, 19, 44, 77, 117, 274
Adams, Captain USA, 194
Ague (malaria, the "shakes"), 95
Albemarle Sound, 20, 29, 37, 62, 123, 124, 148, 229, 230, 234, 243, 248, 281, 282, 285
Alburty, Francis M. USA, 189
Aldrich, Captain USA, 190, 194, 195, **197**
Alexander, Alvin H., Captain USA, 163, 194
Allen, Nathaniel, 23
Ames, Mark D., Acting Master USN, 244
Anderson, Merion Baker, 227
Andersonville Prison, Georgia (Camp Sumter), 1, 52, 64, 100, 123, 154, 155, 157, 158, 171, 175, 177, 179, 180, 182, 183, 184, 185, 187, 189, 190, 192, 195, 203 263, 267, 275, 279, 284
Anopheles gambiae, mosquito, 63, 95
Antietam, 1, 199
Appomattox Courthouse, Virginia, 289
Arlington Cemetery, 289, 297
Armistead-Pettiford House, 223, **224**
Armistead, Robert, 223
Army of the James, 49
Army of the Potomac, 91, 181
Ausbon, W. Fletcher, 221
Ausbon, Priscilla, 212
Ayers, Mrs., milliner, 223

Ball, John, 85th N. Y. historian, 190, 263
Barnum, Joseph, Captain USA, 189
Barrett, George W., Acting Ensign USN, 98, 122, 244
Barton, Clara, nurse, 187
Bascome, Richard, Lieutenant USA, 322
Bateman's Farm, 47
Bateman Redoubt. 136
Battle of Bachelor's Bay, 229
Battle of Hampton Roads, 67, 71, 73
Battle of Plymouth, 1, 3, 52, 60, 64, 100, 113, 137, 147, 153, 159, **163**, 180, 182, 190, 199, 200, 201, 203, 204, 208, 210, 214, 225, 227, 233, 271, 296
Baton Rouge, Louisiana, 44
Battery Worth, 47, 77, 122, 123, 136, 163, 166, 273, 274
Beach, Francis, Colonel USA, 97, 142, 163, 205, 272, 320
Beasley, Edmund, USCT, 56
Beggs, R. G., USA, 194
Bell, Abram, USCT 56
Bembridge, Caleb, 211
Benson, John, landsman USN, 116
Bentonville, North Carolina, 7, 295
Benzoni, Charles, Captain USA, 226
Bermuda Hundred, Virginia, 88
Bertie County, North Carolina, 37, 41, 60, 170, 173, 201, 203
Billingsley, Amos S., Chaplain USA, 115, 120, 167, 169, 206, 220
Biner, Jacob, USCT, 56
Black, Robert, USA, 176
Black sailors from Plymouth listed, 15
Blakeslee, Bernard F., 42, 112, 118, 136, 141, 143, 205
Blaney School, Pennsylvania, 154
Boots, Ed, 101st Pennsylvania Volunteers' historian, **50**
Boots, Edward Nicolas, Quarter-Master Sergeant 60, 99, 100, 220
Boots, Samuel, 60
Boyle, Private USA, 167
Boyle's Mill Road, 164
Boyle's Stream, 226
Bradford's Mississippi Battery, 110
Bragg, Braxton, General CSA, 148, 203
Branch, James, Lieutenant Colonel CSA, 110, 117
Braye, Velma (Mrs. James), 223
Breckinridge family, 3
Brick House Plantation, 19
Broadwell, J. H., 143, 211, 243, 288
Brooke rifle, 74, 230
Brooke, John Mercer, Commander CSN, 74
Brooklyn Navy Yard, 234

"Brothers' Regiment," 267
Brown, Allen, USCT, 56
Brown, Captain USA, 272
Brown, George O. USA, 141
Brown, John, abolitionist, 33
Brown, Owen, Corporal USCT, 203
Buchanan, Franklin, Captain CSN, Flag Officer of *CSS Virginia*, 67, 255
Buckingham, Hiram, Quarter Master Sergeant USA, 175
"Buffaloes," 101, 115, 147, 170, 171, 173, 174, 180, 204, 206, 208, 209, 210, 282
"Buffalo Know Nothings," 174
Bull Run (Manassas), 1, 289
Bunch, Joseph, USCT, 56
Burdick, Silas G. USA, 180, 263
Burdin, George, Private USCT, 203
Burdin, John, Private USCT, 203
Bureau of Colored Troops, 56
Burnham, John, Major USA, 97, 158, 159
Burnside, Ambrose E., Major General USA, 29, **31**, 33, 48, 78, 253
Burnside's Expedition, 29, 78
Burrows, Frederick, Private USCT, 203
Bush, B. Conrad, 24th New York Volunteers' historian, 175
Butler, Benjamin F., Major General USA, 3, 29, 42, 61, 66, 67, 87, 88, 89, 90, 96, 147, 181, 182
Butler, Worley, Corporal USA, 171
Butts, Lieutenant USA, 118, 119
Cady, L. A., Captain USA, 51, 97, 194, 272
Cameron, Simon, Secretary of War, 25
Camp Oglethorpe (Macon Prison), 190, 279
Camp Orr, Pennsylvania, 154
Camp Sumter (Andersonville Prison), 179, 185
Camp, William S., Sergeant USA, 189
Campbell, Lillian, 222
Canandaigua, New York, 52
Carson, James, USA, 154
Cartwright, Alphonzo, Captain USA, 190, 195
Casey's Division, 91
Casey, Silas, General USA, 147, 189
Cashie River, 29
Cashoke Creek, 130
Chancellorsville, Virginia, 1, 139
Chapin, N., Captain USA, 118, 119, 163, 272, 273, 277
Chapinville, New York, 52
Chapman, H. D., Captain CSA, 185
Charleston, South Carolina, 3, 10, 25, 170, 176, 179, 180, 184, 190, 192, 194, 259, 260, 275, 278, 279, 284

Charlestown Mercury Newspaper, 176
Chesson, Joseph S., 222
Chickawanga, 1
"Chimerical absurdity," 80
Chowan County, North Carolina, 201, 267
Chowan River, 29, 33, 43
Clark, H. L., 2nd Lieutenant USA, 118
Clark, David, Halifax County, 221
Clark, General CSA, 37
Clark House, 221, **222**
Clark, Walter, Chief Justice of the N.C. Supreme Court, 208
Clay, Henry, 3
Cline, Zachariah M., Lieutenant USA, 120
Cochise, 294
Cochran, Thomas, Captain USA, 48, 260, 261
Collins, Josiah, 23, 41, 55, 61
Columbia Road, 19, 20, 47, 112, 135, 136, 166, 277
Compher, Alexander, Captain USA, 47, 313
Compher (Comfort) Redoubt, 77, 156, 168
Coneby Creek, 20, 135, 166, 272, 274
Coneby Redoubt, 47, 77
Conley, Isaiah, Captain USA, 173
Constitution of the United States of America, 8, 62
Conteras, Mexico, 91
"Contrabands," 8, 15, 42, 61, 63, 93, 95, 204, 262, 273
Cooke, James Wallace, Commander CSN, 3, 78, 79, 80, 81, **82,** 83, 85, 86, 89, 104, 106, 107, 109, 112, 121, 122, 123, 124, 127, 146, 184, 229, 233, 234, 256, 293
Coombs, Mrs., teacher, 63
Cooper, Alonzo, Lieutenant USA, 122, 123, 167, 181, 205, 318
Cooper, Adjutant and Inspection General USA, 73
Cooper, James, USA, 195
Corse, Montgomery, General CSA, 106, 171, 172
Coynjack, 262
Craney Island, 255
Crater at Petersburg, Virginia, 1
Cratty, Eli, Captain USA, 195, 261
Crittenden, John, 7
CSS Albemarle, 10, 74, **75,** 78, 79, 80, 81, 83, 85, 86, **107,**109, 110 121, 123, 124, 125, 127, 229, **231,** 233, 234, 237, 243, 245, **246,** 247, 248, 249, 251, 254, 256, 257, 293, 294
CSS Beaufort, 67
CSS Bombshell, 98, 117, 123, 165, 229, 233, 273, 277, 285, 327, 330

CSS Cotton Plant, 110, 121, 150, 170, 229
CSS Ellis, 127, 256, 257
CSS Jamestown, 67
CSS Neuse, 80
CSS Patrick, 67
CSS Planter, 10
CSS Raleigh, 253
CSS Roanoke, 67
CSS Seth Low, 72
CSS Teaser, 69
CSS Virginia (Merrimac), 66, 67, 69, 71, 73, 255
CSS Yorktown, 73
Cullipher, William, Private USA, 171
Curtin, Andrew Gregg, Governor of Pennsylvania, 156
Cushing, Alonzo, Lieutenant USA, 294
Cushing, Howard, USA, 294
Cushing, William B., Lieutenant USN, 129, 234, 237, 239, 241, **242**, 243, 244, 245, 248, 249, 251, 253, **254**, 257, 287, 288, 293, 294
Cushing, Mary Barker, 294
Dahlgren guns, 48, 123, 165, 234
Daily Richmond, 120, 207
Dare, Virginia, 29
Davenport, Henry K., Commander USN, 116, 165
Davenport, John, Lieutenant USA, 205
Davenport, Mary Cotton, 216
Davis, Jefferson, President of Confederacy, 3, **5**, 33, 50, 65, 73, 88, 103, 104, 139, 148, 149, 203, 234, 295
Day, David L., USA, 219
Dean, George A., USN, 116
Dearing, James, Colonel CSA, 106, 110, 111, 112, 116, 149, 209
Deming, Lorenzo, Landsman USN, 244
Dickey, Luther, Corporal USA, 41, 42, 91, 112, 120, 130, 163, 169, 180, 187, 194 208, 219, 261, 296
Dickinson, Samuel, 23
Dismal Swamp, 33, 62, 262, 281
Dixon, Chaplain USA, 102, 220
"Dog tags," 114
Donaghy, John, Captain USA, 48, 51, 109, 113, 114, 143, 147, 166, 194
Dotson, Jackie, 47
Double-ender, 78, 244, 245, 315
Douglass, Frederick, black abolitionist, 8
Drayton, Thomas, Brigadier General CSA, 7
Drayton, Percival, Captain USA, 7
Dred Scott decision, 8, 310
Drummer, George, Private USCT, 203

Duer, Rufus K., Lieutenant USN, 244
Dyer, W. R., CSA, 200
Eads, James B., 10
Edmondston, Catherine Devereaux, 80
Edward's Ferry Shipyard, 80
Elizabeth City, North Carolina, 42, 77, 78, 85, 131
Elizabeth River, 66, 67
Elliott, Gilbert II, Lieutenant CSA, 78, 79, 80, 85, **86**, 121, 122, 294
Elliott, Robert, author, 294
Ellis, John, Governor of North Carolina, 24, 25
Emancipation Proclamation, 56, 199
Enfield rifles, 47
English, Earl, Lieutenant Commander USN, 244
Ericsson, John, **71**, 72
Evans, Sergeant USA, 117
Ewer, Barnabas, Captain USA, 37, 43
Fagan, Levi, 221
Fairless, John, Lieutenant USA, 174
Faison, E. H., Colonel CSA, 117
Fancher, Amos, Private USA, 113
Fardella, E. H., Colonel USA, 95, 97, 163, 164, 170, 272
Fay, Lieutenant USA, 163, 190
Felice, Debra Miller, 101st Pennsylvania Volunteers' historian, 267, 313
Ferguson, Andrew, Corporal USA, musician, 49, 313
Fillmore. Millard, 174
Fisher, General, 122
Fiske, Joseph E., Captain USA, 192, 272
Florence, South Carolina, 184, 192, 278, 279
Flusser, Fanny, 105, 107, 129
Flusser, Guy, Lieutenant CSA, 3, 295
Flusser, Charles, Lieutenant Commander USN, 3, 29, 43, 78, 90, 92, 98, 101, 105, 107, 115, 116, 120, 123, 124, 127, 129, 130, 131, **133**, 147, 151, 164, 165, 166, 173, 220, 234, 253, 256, 257, 272, 273, 282, 295
Flusser, Mrs. Julianna, 3, 129, 130
Flusser, Ottaker, CSA, 3, 295
Flynn, John, USA, 116
Fogarty, Surgeon USA, 105
Foot, Lieutenant USA, Wessell's nephew, 143
Fort Barlow, 33
Fort Blanchard, 33
Fort Branch, 34
Fort Clark, 29
Fort Foster, 33
Fort Gray, 47, 77, 97, 106, 112, 114, 116, 117, 121, 122, 123, 154, 163, 165, 166, 192, 203, 271, 272, 273, 274, 277

Fort "Hal," 47
Fort Hatteras, 29, 85
Fort Huger, 33
Fort Jones, 47
Fort Monroe, Virginia, 29, 87, 88, 236, 260
Fort Parke, 33
Fort Pillow, Tennessee, 200, 206, 207
Fort Reno, 33
Fort Sumter, South Carolina, 9, 10, 25, 253
Fort Wessells, 47, 77, 97, 114, 117, 118, 119, 163, 164, 190, 277
Fort Williams, 44, **45**, 77, 114, 118, 119, 120, 136, 141, 142, 143, 144, 149, 150, 154, 166, 167, 201, 204, 215, 273, 274, 276, 281, 283
Foster, Henry H., Acting Master USN, 98, 116
Foster, J. G., Major General USA, 42, 259, 260, 275
Frank, John A., Acting Third Assistant Engineer USN, 116
Fredericksburg, Virginia, 1, 139
"Free persons of color" in Plymouth, 55
Freedmen's Colony, Roanoke Island, 63, 64, 226
Freeman, George, black Private USA, 200
Freeman, Miss Kate, Missionary, 63, 64
Freeman, Mrs. Sarah, Missionary, 63, 64
French, Charles A., Acting Lieutenant USN, 98, 116, 229, 272
French, George, Lieutenant USA, 171, 323
French, Sergeant USA, 204
Frick, Abraham P., Surgeon USA, 105, 169
Fulton, James, 192
Fulton, Ruth, 103rd Pennsylvania Volunteers' historian, 192
Fulton, William Allison, USA, 192, 267
Gardner, Laton, Private USA, 147
Garrett, Alfred D., 55, 59
Garrett, Dolphus, black Private USA, 200, 203
Gay, Thomas S., Acting Master's Mate USN, 244
Gayer, Henry, USCT, 56
Gemmill, John, Sergeant, USA, 189
Gettysburg, Pennsylvania, 1, 8, 101, 139, 294
Goe, Norval D., USA, 145, 195
Gosport Navy Yard, 33, 66, 67, 74
Grace Episcopal Church, 59, 95, 99, 215, 216, 217, **218**
Graham, John W., Major CSA, 106, 111, 208
Graham, Robert, Captain CSA, 106, 112, 145
Graham's Petersburg Virginia Horse Artillery, 110
Grant, Ulysses S., Lieutenant General USA, 3, 88, 89, 172, 181, 182, 183, 184, 289, 290, **292**
Granville, Samuel, black Private USA, 200
Gray, Benjamin H., black powder boy on *CSS Albemarle*, 10

Gray, Charles, Colonel USA, 47
Green, James G., Acting Master USA, 244
Grice, Charles, 85
Grice, Francis, 85
Grice Shipyard, 85
Guidon, 159
Gurion, Henry T., Colonel CSA, 110
Halifax, North Carolina, 80, 272, 285, 293
Halifax County, 221
Halifax Navy Yard, 79, 293
Hall, Provost Marshall, 183
Halleck, Henry W., Major USA, 11, 90, 147, 259
Hamilton, North Carolina, 34, 44, 81, 106, 121,173, 244, 278
Hamilton, Richard, coal heaver USN, 244
Hampton Roads, Virginia, 67, 71, 72, 73
Hand grenades, 118
Hanks, Benjamin, USA, 267
Hanks brothers, 179, 267
Hardee, William, General CSA, 50
"Hardee" hats, 50, 51, 176, **177**
Hardison, Seth, 211
"Hard Luck Regiment," 34, 267
Hardtack, 37, 114, 172, 190, 284
Hardy, Titus (Titus McRae), black Private USA, 200, 203
Harley, Bernard, Ordinary Seaman USN, 244
Harrisburg, Pennsylvania, 157, 267
Harrison's Landing, 91
Hart Island Prison, 296
Hartford Times, 159
Hassell, James, Private USA, 171
Hastings, George S., Lieutenant USA, 115, 135, 142, 166, 191, 194, **197**
Hawkins, Rush, USA, 172
Heckman, C. A., Brigadier General USA, 259
Hedrick, John A., 174
Herbert, Peter, USCT, 56
Higgins, Samuel, First Class Fireman, USN, 243, 244
Hilbert, John, USA, 195
Hill, James Charles, Acting Master's Mate USN, 243
Hilton Head, South Carolina, 259
Hintz, Captain USA, 42
Hoggard, Captain CSA, 97, 272
Hoke, Robert F., Brigadier General CSA, 81, 88, 89, 103, 104, 106, 109, 111, 112, 113, 117, 118, 119, 124, 135, 136, **139**, 142, 144, 145, 146, 148, 149, 166,171, 172 176, 207, 208, 209, 273, 274, 275, 283, 284, 285, 288, 295, 296

Holmes, Robert J., musician, USA, 184, 220, 263, **265**
Holmes, Scott, 16th Connecticut historian, 159
Holden, William Woods, editor, 101
Holt, Alonzo, black sailor, 59
Hopkins, Captain CSN, 287
Hopkins, James B., Acting Master's Mate USN, 116
Hoppin, Lieutenant USA, 122, 123, 163
Horton, Charles, black witness at Appomattox, 290
Houghton, Edward, Ordinary Seaman USN, 243, 244
Houghton, Reverend, 216
Howorth, William, Acting Master's Mate USN, 239, 249
Howitzer, 48, 165, 234, 235
Huddleson, Daniel, USA, 195
Hudson River, 235
Huger, Benjamin J, General CSA, 33, 73
Humphrey, Nee (Mrs. Charles), 213
Hurlbut, E. T., Corporal USA, 219
"Ironmonger Captain," 79
James, Alfred, black sailor, 59
James, Elizabeth, 63
James, Horace, Chaplain USA, 63, 115
Johnson, Alec, Private USA, 199
Johnson, Samuel, Sergeant USA, 204, 205, 207
Johnson, William, Connecticut black soldier not in USCT, 199
Johnson, Wyman, Sergeant USA, 185
Johnston, Joseph, General CSA, 3, 185, 295
Johnston, Stuart I., CSA, 216
Jones, Benjamin G., 149
Jones, J. G., Colonel CSA, 47
Jones, Mort, USA, 284
Jordan, Weymouth, researcher, 209, 210
Josselyn, Francis, Acting Master USN, 244
Judson, J. A., Captain, Assistant Adjutant General USA, 151
Keim, William H., General USA, 29, 91
Keister, W. H., Lieutenant USA, 195
Keith, Jeanette, 212
Keith, Joseph, 212
Keith, Mary Pettijohn (Mrs. James), 211, 212
Kellogg, Robert H., Major USA, 101, 169
Kepi, 51, 114, 176
"Keystone Regiment," 96
King, Robert H., Landsman USN, 244
Kinston, North Carolina, 47, 79, 86, 111, 149, 171, 172, 272
Kirk, J. B., USA, 62
Klingler, Peter, USA, 195

Krug, Daniel, Sergeant USA, 195
Lafler, John A., Lieutenant USA, 190, 191, 192, **193**
Lake Phelps, 23
Lamb, John C., Lieutenant Colonel CSA, 43, 44, 211
Lamphere, George, Private USA, 113
Langworthy, D. A., Captain USA, 194, 195, **197**
Latham, Charles, Sheriff, 7, 25, 59, 214, 215, 219, 225, 226
Latham House, **214**
Latham, Charles Louis, Major CSA, 25, **27**, 59
Latham's Farm, 47
Lee, Captain CSA, 251
Lee, George Washington, 289
Lee, Mary A., "free woman of color," 55
Lee, Maryann Parke Custis, 289
Lee, Richard H., Sergeant USA, 182
Lee, Robert Edward, General CSA, 3, 9, 89. 103, 104, 110, 139, 183, 289, 290, **291**
Lee, Samuel Phillips, Rear Admiral USN, 7, 164, 234, 254
Lee's Mill Road (Acre Road), 19, 77, 112, 113, 117
Lehmann, Theodore F., Colonel USA, 34, 97, 151, 170, 260, 262, 263, 272
Leonard, Margaret, 180
Leonard, Newton, Private USA, 180
Lewis, H. G., Captain CSA, 290
Libby Prison, Richmond, Virginia, 169, 170, 190, 275
Lincoln, Abraham, President of the United States, 3, **5**, 8, 10, 60, 91, 183, 199, 245, 286
Lincoln County, 295, 296
Lincoln Lithia Water Company, 296
Lincoln, Mary Todd, 7
Lockhart, Joseph G., Captain CSA, 136, 143
Luck, John, Pilot CSN, 81, 121
Luraghi, Raimondo, historian, 233
Lynchburg Artillery, 110
Mackey, James, Major USA, 101, 105, 143, 277
Macomb, William H., Commander USN, 244
Macon, Georgia, 179, 190, 194, 275, 279
Macon Prison (Camp Oglethorpe), 181, 318
Maffitt, John, Commander CSN, 81, 82, 239
Malaria, 63, 95, 175, 179
Mahoney, Frank, USA, 267
Mallory, Stephen Russell, Secretary of the Confederate Navy, 9, **65**, 66, 67, 73, 74, 86, 233, 247, 256
Malvern Hill, 91
Marsh, Alan, Andersonville Prison Museum, 187

Martin & Elliott Shipyard, 78
Martin, James, Brigadier General CSA, 85
Martin, William, Colonel CSA, 85, 86
Marvin, Hiram Leonard, Captain USA, 171, 322
Maxwell, William, USA, 113
Maxwell, Wilson C., Lieutenant Colonel USA, 41, 62, 166, 260
Mayflower Pilgrims, 176
McElroy, John, USA, author, 179
McHenry, Charles, 1st Lieutenant USA, 113
McLean, Wilmer, 289
Meade, George Gordon, General USA, 156
Mercer, Colonel CSA, 106, 110, 118, 119, 149, 150, 273
Merrill, Julian W., Sergeant USA, 41, 49, 63, 64, 154, 174, 175, 184, 219, 312, 313
Methodist Episcopal Church, 59, **218,** 219, 220, 221
Mexican War, 3, 91
Miller, Debra Felice, 101st PennsylvaniaVolunteers' historian, 267
Miller, Madison, Private USCT, 203
Miller, Nathaniel, Corporal USA, 147
Miller's North Carolina Artillery, 110
Mitchell, James, Sergeant USA, 147
Mizzell, Gilbert, Private USCT, 56
Moore, Jessie, poet, 7
Morgan, W. H., CSA, 111, 209
Morratock Primitive Baptist Church, 219
Morris Island Prison, 170, 275
Morris, Lieutenant USN, 67
Morrow, James, Captain USA, 114, 195
Mortimer, Benjamin, Corporal USA, 167
Moseby, Edgar Fearn, Major CSA, 110
Mosher, Charles, Private USA, diarist, 50, 52, **53,** 55, 90, 96, 113, 122, 144, 157, 163, 169, 171, 172, 174, 180, 183, 189, 195, 206
Mullin, David, Captain USA, 176
National Freedman's Relief Association (NFRA), 63
National Tribune Veterans' Newspaper, 7, 62, 123, 141, 157, 176, 206, 281
Neuse River, 47, 80, 103, 271, 272
New Bern, North Carolina, 77, 79, 87, 88, 89, 90, 97, 103, 104, 106, 109, 131, 139, 171, 201, 206, 229, 256, 263, 267, 271, 295
New York Daily Tribune, 115, 120, 206
Newberry, John, 61
Norcom, Willis, black sailor, 59
Norfolk, Va., 19, 33, 42, 66, 67, 73, 74, 93, 119, 129, 158, 189, 200, 256
Norfolk Navy Yard, 256
Norman, Annie, Latham slave, 59

North Atlantic Blockade Squadron, 164, 234, 248, 256
North Carolina Hall of History, 256
Norton, Major CSA, 111
Nott, W. H., 123, 157
O'Brien, Frank, artillerist CSA, 81, 157, 158, 159, 208, 209
Ould, Robert, 182, 205
Pacien, Crowder, black Private USA, 201, **202**, 267, **269**, 325
Palmer, Surgeon USA, 105
Palmer, General USA, 151
Pamlico Sound, 101, 145
Parrott guns, 48, 106, 112, 116, 118, 122, 165
Pascall, Samuel, USN, 116
Pasquotank River, 33, 85, 127, 256
Pate, Joseph and Susan, 215
Pea Ridge Plantation, 61
Peake, S. S., 2nd Lieutenant USA, 118
Peck, John J., Major General USA, 41, 87, 88, 89, 90, 151, 276
Pegram's Virginia Battery, 110, 117
Peterson, John, seaman USN, 116
Pettiford, Rev. Alford, 60
Pettiford, Nancy, 223
Pettiford, Reuben, 60, 223
Pettigrew, Ebeneezer, 41, 61
Pettijohn, John, C. 211
Petzinger, Conrad, USA, 154, 155
Phelps, Amanda, 43
Phelps, Lucretia, 43, 101
Philadelphia Inquirer, 206
Philadelphia Navy Yard, 48
Picket Boat Number One, 237, **238**, 239, 243, 244, 245
Picket Boat Number Two, 236
Pickett, George E., General CSA, 77, 88, 90, 103, **104,** 139, 142, 171, 172, 271, 294
Picot, Dr. Julian, 223
Picot, Louis, 99, 225
Picot, Peter P., 223
Pierson, Lieutenant USA, 195
Pinkney, Robert F., Captain CSN, 293
Pitt, George, Lieutenant USA, 195
Plasmodium falciparum, 95
"Plymouth Pilgrims," 1, 176, 179, 180, 181, 182, 190, 284
Plymouth, North Carolina, 1, 3, 7, 15, 19, 20, **21,** 23, **24,** 25, 29, 34, 37, 41, 42, 43, 44, 47, 48, 49, 51, 52, 55, 56, 59, 60, 61, 62, 63, 64, 77, 78, 81, 87, 88, 89,90, 92, 93, 95, 96, 97, 99, 100, 101, 103, 104, 105, 106, 107, 109, 110, 111, 112, 113, 114, 115, 116, 117, 119, 120, 121, 123, 124,

127, 129, 130, 131, 135, **137,** 139, 141, 142, 144, 145, 146, 147, 148, 149, 150, 151, 153, 154, 157, 158, 159, 161, 163, 165, 169, 170, 171, 173, 174, 176, 177, 179, 180, 182, 185, 189, 190, 192, 194, 199, 200, 201, 202, 203, 204, 206, 207, 208, 209, 210, 211, 212, 213, 214, 215, 216, 219, 221, 222, 224, 225, 226, 229, 233, 234, 243, 244, 245, 246, 248, 251, 256, 260, 261, 267, 271, 275, 277, 281, 284
Pollard, Edward, CSA, author, 144
Popple, Barber, USA, 171
Porter, D. D., Rear Admiral USN, 248
Porter, John Luke, 74
Port-O-Plymouth Museum, 159, **161**
Price, Selby O., 225
Pugh, Henry, black Private USA, 199, 203
Rainbow Bluff (Banks), 34, 77, 201, 272
Raleigh, North Carolina, 24, 37, 171, 174, 204, 256, 296
Raleigh Daily Confederate, 207
Raleigh News and Observer, 44
Raleigh, Sir Walter, 29
Ramsey, Hermine Ausbon, 213
Ransom's Brigade, CSA, 106, 109; command, 110; 112, 118, 119, 120, 135; 136; troops, 141; 146, 149; troops, 156; 163, 199, 215, 273
Ransom, Matthew, General CSA, 106, 109, 110, 111, 117, 118, 136; 141, 146, 149, 167, 283, 284
Reardon, Robert, USA, 195
Rebel "yell," 113, 117, 118, 149, 154, 166, 318
Reconstruction, 10
Redoubt Latham, 47, 136
Reed's Battalion, 110
Reed (Reid, Reade), Colonel CSA, 106; recorded as major; 111, 116; recorded as major, 117
Reed, Private. USA, 167
Rhodes, Arthur, map, 19, **21,** 211
Richmond, Virginia, 33, 34, 79, 87, **88,** 110, 148, 149, 169, 170, 190, 192, 204, 207, 275, 293
Richmond Fayetteville Artillery, 110
Rice, Abraham, USA, 179, 267
Rice, Isaac, USA, 179
Ripley's "Believe-it-or-Not," **217**
Roanoke Island, North Carolina, 29, **32,** 33, 47, 48, 60, 61, 63, 64, 97, 99, 100, 105, 109, 114, 115, 131, 147, 151, 189, 201, 202, 216, 226, 260, 261, 273, 281, 325
Roanoke River, 1, 19, 20, 29, 34, 37, 47, 48, 77, 78, 80, 81, 87, 90, 103, 104, 105, 107, 109, 116, 121, 122, 123, 124, 127, 130, 135, 142, 212, 225, 229, 233, **242,** 244, 245, 246, 248, 281, 285
Roberts, Surgeon USA, 105

Robinson, J. B., 113
Roche, Charles H., Captain USA, 97, 272
Roe, Francis A., Lieutenant Commander USN, 231
Rolack, John, black Private USA, 199, 203
Rose, William, USN, 116
Rowan, Stephen C., Commander USN, 11, 37
Rowlings, John, Chaplain USA, 220
Roy, G. G., Doctor CSA, 175, 184
Rupert, John F., Corporal USA, 195, 219
Russell, Lieutenant USA, 113, 271, 318
Sahara Plantation, 61
Samford, George W., Doctor, 263
Sampson, Ira B., Captain USA, 97, 119, 143, 272, 273
Sanderson, Aaron, black sailor, 59
Sanderson's Farm, 47, 117
Savannah, Georgia, 179, 181, 190, 275, 279
Scott, Winfield, General USA, 9
Scuppernong River, 23
Scuppernong Swamp, 23
Seneca Falls, New York, 52
Seymour, T., Brigadier General USA, 259
Shaffer, George, 195
Shaler, Alexander, Brigadier General USA, 259
"Shebangs," 179
Sheppard, Nelson, black Private USA, 199, 200, 201
Sherman, William Tecumseh, General USA, 7, 181
Sherwood, J. R., Acting Third Assistant Engineer USN, 116
Sickle-cell anemia, 95
Smalls, Robert, black pilot on *CSS Planter*, 10
Smellers, Henry, black sailor, 59
Smith, James, Private USA, 141
Smith, Melancton, Captain USN, 229, 251
Smith, Peter Evans, 78, 80
Smith, Seymour, 171
Smith, William Ruffin, 78
Smith, William, Ordinary Seaman USN, 244
Smithfield Herald, 288
Soldiers and Sailors Memorial Hall, 155
Soley, J. R., professor, 237
Somerset Place, Creswell, N.C., 59
Sparrow, Washington, black sailor, 59
Speller, Amanda, 59
Spotslvania, 1
Spruill, Hezikiah, 225
Spruill, Joseph, 221

Spruill, S. B., Mayor, 130
Stanley, Edward, Military Governor 37, 42
Stanton, Edwin, Union Secretary of War, 11, 182
Staplefoote-Whitley, Gladys Pettiford, 223
Stars and Bars, 153
Stars and Stripes, 144, 153, 154, 159, 285
Steever, Charles, Acting Third Assistant Engineer USN, 244
Stevens, Edwin Augustus, 66
Stevens, John, 66
Stevens, Robert Livingston, 66
Stockholm, Andrew, Acting Ensign USN, 236
Stoddard, S. A., Corporal USA, 189; 1st Sergeant, 219
Stokes, Thomas B., Acting Ensign USN, 98, 165
Stotesbury, William, Acting Third Assistant Engineer USN, 244
Stoney, Theodore, shipbuilder, 236
Stringham, Silas H., Flag Officer USN, 29
Stuart, J. E. B., General CSA, 7
Stubbs, Adolph, 225
Stubbs, W. H., 225
Stubbs House, 225
Sub-District of the Albemarle, 260
Sugar Creek Township, Pennsylvania, 154
Sutherland, William, First Class Fireman USN, 230
Swan, Francis, Acting Master's Mate USN, 244
Swift, Frank, USCT, 56
Tabor Island, 47
Tar River, 80, 86, 90, 174, 229, 271, 278
Tarboro Bridge, 174
Tarboro (Tarborough), North Carolina, 77, 80. 87. 89. 106, 111, 139, 146, 149, 170, 174, 176, 201, 275, 278, 284
Tarheel State, 79, 109
Taylor, A. W., Colonel USA, 96, 97, 99, 103, 219, 272
Terry, William R., Colonel CSA, 106, 110, 117, 149
Terwilliger, Lieutenant USA, 195
The Wilderness, 1
Thomas, Gerald, researcher, 173, 209, 210
Thompson, Harry, curator, 173, 221
Toodle, Edy, "free woman of color," 226, 227
Toodle, Harriet, "free woman of color," 225, 226, **227**
Toodle, William, "free man of color," 226
Torpedoes, 81, 121, 229, 235, 236, 282
Townes, Lieutenant Colonel CSA, 130
Townsend, E. D., 260
Tredegar Mills, Richmond, Virginia, 79
Truxton, William T., Lieutenant Commander USN, 89, 244, 271

Twist drill invention, 80
Tyrrell Territory, North Carolina, 20, 203, 221
Underground Railroad, 192, 223
Unionist, 3, 25, 37, 44, 159, 170, 174, 215, 261
United Census of 1820, 226
United States Census of 1850, 55, 226
United States Census of 1870, 59, 226
United States Colored Troops (USCT), 93, 119, 171, 199
USS Commodore Barney, 254
USS Bazley, tugboat, 244, 245
USS Belle, tugboat, 245
USS Bombshell, 98, 117, 123, 165, 229, 233, 273, 277, 285, 327, 330
USS Ceres, 48, 98, 116, 123, 147, 165, 229, 256, 272, 273, 295
USS Chicopee, 244
USS Commodore Hull, 244, 245, 249
USS Commodore Perry, 43, 88, 127, 129, 253
USS Congress, 67
USS Cumberland, 67
USS Dewitt Clinton, 98
USS Dolly, tugboat, 77, 98, 117
USS Fawn, 158
USS Fulton, 260
USS Guerierre, 127
USS Ida May, 229
USS Massasoit, 63, 97, 98, 100, 115, 273
USS Mattabesett, 229, 233
USS Maumee, 293
USS Merrimac, 66
USS Merrimack, 10, 66, 67
USS Miami, 15, 17, **48,** 90, 98, 115, 116, 123, 124, 125, 130, 148, 164, 165, 229, 272, 273, 277, 282, 285
USS Minnesota, 73
USS Monitor, 71, **72,** 73, 255
USS Monticello, 244, 249, 254, 287, 288
USS Ostego, 244
USS Robert Collyer, 34, 98
USS Sassacus, 229, 230, 234
USS Shamrock, 244, 245, 248, 249
USS Shokoken, 254
USS Southfield, 43, 48, 98, 116, 123, 124, **125,** 164, 165, 237, 239, 244, 248, 249, 272, 273, 277, 282, 285
USS St. Lawrence, 73
USS Tacony, 89, 90, 244, 245, 271
USS Valley City, 243, 244, 249

USS Whitehead, 48, 98, 244, 245, 272, 282
USS Wyalusing, 229, 244
Upjohn, Richard, 215
Vance, Zebulon, Governor of North Carolina, 37, 79, 171, 203, 296
Veterans, 52, 96; Alabama, 159; 189; Penna., 207; 267; 282
Vicksburg, Mississippi, 1, 101, 129, 319
Waddell, Alfred M., Lieutenant Colonel CSA, 124
Walker, Caleb, 225
Ward, John, Private USCT, 203
Ward, Warren M., Doctor, 225
Wardrop, D. W., Colonel USA, 151
Warley, Alexander, Lieutenant CSN, 237, 239, 245, 247
Warren's Neck, North Carolina, 47, 77, 117, 122
Warrenton, North Carolina, 25. 223
Washington College, 290
Washington County, North Carolina, 20, 37, 55, 59, 214, 215, 219, 296
Washington, D.C., 7, 62, 130, 147, 182, 187, 189, 203, 251, 259, 285, 296
Washington, George, Private USA, 59, 60, 199, 201
Washington, North Carolina (Little Washington), 77, 88, 89, 90,146, 147, 150, 151, 209, 271, 282
Washington Road, Plymouth, 19, 20, 47, 77, 111, 112, 113, 117, 163, 271, 273
Washington Street, Plymouth, 212
Welch's Creek, 20, 117, 272
Weldon, North Carolina, 34, 78, 170, 201, 204, 275
Welles, Gideon, U.S. Secretary of Navy, 11, 13, 15, 72, 131, 253
Wessells, Henry Walton, Brigadier General USA, 29, 34, 47, 48, 49, 61, 77, 87, 88, 89, 91, 92, **93**, 96, 97, 102, 113, 114, 115, 117, 118, 119, 135, 142, 143, 144, 145, 146, 148, 150, 151, 163, 165, 167, 169 170, 172, 180, 190, 208, 216, 220, 259, 260, 271, 276, 277, 281, 283, 285, 296, 297
West Pittston, Pennsylvania, 267
West, Richard, black Private USA, 200, 201, 207
Whitfield, John N., Colonel CSA, 251
Whitehurst, N. J., Captain CSA, **27**, 216
Wicomico Bay, Virginia, 236
Wilcox, George, Corporal USA, 113
Williams, Thomas, Brigadier General USA, 44
Wilmington, North Carolina, 34, 86, 146, 176, 179, 190, 278, 279, 284, 295
Wilmington Journal, 206
Wilmington Light Artillery, 110
Williamson, William P., Chief Naval Engineer CSN, 74
Williamston, North Carolina, 37, 106, 165, 278
Wilkes, Henry, Landsman USN, 244
Wilson, Charles, Lieutenant USN, 119
Wilson, Dr. Dean, 156
Wilson Street, 20, 47, 227

Winchell, Alfred, 226
Windley-Ausbon House, 211
Windley, Edmon, 211
Windsor, North Carolina, 60, 221
Wirz, Henry, Captain CSA, 185, **186,** 187, 190
Wise, Henry Alexander, Brigadier General CSA, 33
Wise, O. Jennings, CSA, 33
Woodman, John, Acting Master's Mate USN, 239, 244, 249
Woodruff, John G., Captain CSA, 200
Woods-lay torpedo, 235
Worden, John L., Lieutenant USN, 71, 72, 255
Yarrett, York, black sailor, 59

WORDS FROM THE "PLYMOUTH PILGRIMS" HISTORIANS

"To those of us with a deep interest in the battle of Plymouth, it has always been a puzzle why it has not been more publicized. When researching my ancestor who was captured at Plymouth, I had to look in three Civil War books to find mention of it. It had all the components of the more 'popular' battles and yet few people have heard about it. I am anxiously anticipating your book and the information your research has uncovered. I am sure it will assist in spreading the word about this interesting, relatively unknown piece of history."

John Ball, descendant of John Lafler and the historian of the 85th New York Volunteers.

"The actions at Plymouth, N.C. during the American Civil War have fascinated me since I first became aware of what happened there. I found precious little in the history books about the conflict and am pleased that a book has been written that will pull together the amazing facts about this significant military engagement involving infantry, cavalry, artillery, and navy on both sides of the conflict. An 'irresistible force' of the Confederate Army, overwhelming in number, surprise-attacked the 'immovable object' of a much smaller but entrenched and fortified Federal garrison.

For three days and nights the fierce conflict ensued. In the early morning hours of April 19, 1964 the naval battle took place on the Roanoke River and the ironclad ram prevailed, thus creating a critical problem for the Federals: their defenses were now vulnerable from the river. The Confederates moved quickly to seize this opportunity and took full advantage of it. On the morning of the third day, the superior numbers of the 'irresistible force' overcame the Federal defenses.

At the same time General U. S. Grant had declared that there would be no more prisoner exchanges, so as the majority of Federal soldiers captured at Plymouth made their way to Andersonville, they could not have fathomed the horrors that awaited them. Theintroduction of these 'Plymouth Pilgrims' to the piisoner population at Andersonville was so significant that it impacted the 'economy' within the prison and many of the 13, 000 graves at Andersonville are filled with the remains of 'Plymouth Pilgrims,' brave and patriotic men. The story of the 'Plymouth Pilgrims' must be told and I'm so pleased that a book has finally been written about this."

Scott Holmes, descendent of Robert Holmes and historian of the 16th Connecticut Volunteers

"This book is an excellent resource for the Battle of Plymouth, both for the causal reader and the in-depth researcher. Moss has left no stone unturned in her research of the battle, endeavoring to tell the story from the Northern and Southern perspectives. A nice addition to the book is the inclusion of a history of the town and its inhabitants. Never before have all of these sources been brought together in the same work."

> Edward Boots, President
> Civil War Plymouth Pilgrims Descendants Society

★★★★

"The 24th New York Independent Battery had its origins primarily in the Western New York Counties of Livingston and Wyoming. The men who served the battery came from all walks of life, but they were mainly from the farms of these rural counties. They put down their plows and took up artillery to serve their country and protect the Union. They did not participate in any of the large battles or campaigns of the Civil War, but that was not because they did not want to, it was caused by where the government's need sent them.

The Battery was well trained by Captain Jay E. Lee and following his discharge for illness by Captain A. Lester Cady. The men wrote home often stating that they disliked garrison duty at Plymouth because they felt the war was passing them by. This unfortunately did not happen as from April 17 to 20, 1864 Plymouth was besieged and despite valiant efforts by the small command they were overwhelmed by the Confederate General Hoke's army. Of the 110 men who entered the gates of Andersonville, sixty-nine died either in prison at Andersonville or at other prisons such as Savannah, Charleston, and Florence or shortly after their release before they could get back to their homes.

We cannot comprehend the conditions the men endured. We know that they left their wives and families to help their government uphold our way of life that we are so fortunate to have today. We can only remember their service and that of all the other countless veterans of our military service who have unselfishly put aside their pursuit of happiness so that we may have ours."

> C. Conrad Bush, historian of the 24th New York Independent Battery

"To date most books on the Civil War have been on the great battles. The second part of the plan to defeat the CSA has not—the economic blockade. This book describes the final battle of the Plymouth Pilgrims. Their mission was to destroy the CSA stores, capture or disperse the 17 NC and other armed guerillas, account for paroled CSA men and provide an administration for the civilians. A mission also against disease, boredom, no promotions, and no glory. The loss of records by CSA and Union and few accounts by the men makes this book important."

> Ruth Fulton, descendant of William Allison Fulton and a historian of the 103rd Pennsylvania Volunteers.

★ ★ ★ ★

"The town of Plymouth and its importance during the war has been often overlooked. Volumes have been written on Gettysburg and other such battles. The individuals who fought and died in Plymouth and those who ultimately went to prison, suffered and perished there, should be remembered for all time. This book will do just that—give 'Honor to whom honor is due.'"

> Debra Miller Felice, descendant of Abraham Rice and a historian of the 101st Pennsylvania Volunteers.

★ ★ ★ ★

"I can't thank you enough. As to me, I find real value in such a book. On a global scale, most Americans would be unable to identify the last Confederate vistory of the Civil War and probably would be surprised to find that the Battle of Plymouth in 1864 was that last victory. Imagine, those men continued fighting for a full year before finally surrendering. On a personal level, a book about the Battle of Plymouth will help record the last days that many of our men had freedom. Those last days either concluded in death on the battlefield, or as was the case with my ancestor, those last days of freedom were followed by nearly a year in prison captivity with death occurring just as the war was concluded."

> Evan Slaughenhoupt, descendant of Silas Haggerty, and a historian of the 103rd Pennsylvania Volunteers.

"As the Curator and Administrator of the Port-O-Plymouth Civil War Museum, which is the home of the 'Battle of Plymouth, April 17-April 20, 1864'--we are most pleased to announce and recommend this work on the 'Battle of Plymouth' by Juanita Moss as one of the most informative, well written, and best researched that has been done to date.

Mrs. Moss has shown previously in her first book involving her ancestor, to be very knowledgeable on the occupation of Plymouth by Union Forces from 1862-1864, and the resulting battle. She has created one of the most concise, accurate, and documented versions to date. You will enjoy it!"

Harry Thompson, Curator

ABOUT THE AUTHOR

Juanita Patience Moss is a former New Jersey high school biology teacher who since retiring has developed an interest in genealogy. After publishing her first book, the historical novel *Created To Be Free*, she has now written a detailed nonfiction version of the Battle of Plymouth, an important event in 1864 during the Civil War. Her interest in the subject developed because her great grandfather, Crowder Patience, a runaway slave from Chowan County, North Carolina, joined the 103rd Pennsylvania Volunteers on January 1, 1864 when it was garrisoned at Plymouth, North Carolina.

CREATED TO BE FREE
by
Juanita Patience Moss

ISBN: 1-58549-704-5

This historical novel is based on the life of an 18 year-old runaway slave boy who joined the 103rd Pennsylvania Regiment when it was garrisoned in Plymouth, North Carolina. The reason for writing the book was because several historians had told the author there had been no black men serving in white regiments during the Civil War. Juanita Patience Moss knew differently because her great grandfather had been one.

Her research to discover other such men led her to write about her ancestor's 83 year life journey from the sweet potato fields of North Carolina to the anthracite coal fields of northeastern Pennsylvania. Escaping from Chowan County, the slave boy, Toby, became the free man, Crowder Pacien (Patience).

Through the letters of a fictitious "Plymouth Pilgrim," the story of the Battle of Plymouth is told. A particularly poignant passage deals with what happened to two captured "Buffaloes" who were brothers.

Readers interested in the coal mining industry will want to read about the plight of seven and eight year-olds who were "breaker boys" working ten hour days, six days a week. The coal mining industry had created another kind of slave.

This book is about one American family, in some ways different from all others, but in many ways mirroring many because it is a story of tenacity and survival. There is something in this book for everyone, regardless of ethnicity.

SYNOPSIS

Are you familiar with the Battle of Plymouth?" Plymouth, Massachussetts? No, Plymouth, North Carolina. If you have never heard of it, you are in the company of many others, even those who consider themselves avid Civil War buffs. The Battle of Plymouth took place on April 17-20, 1864.

Even though the last shots were fired 138 years ago, the sounds of that terrible conflict are with us still. Interest in the Civil War does not wane and new facts continue to be uncovered.

In this book you will read about the second largest battle in North Carolina. It was fought at Plymouth where the Confederates tasted their last victory. Intense drama took place during four days filled with surprise, fate, intrigue, bravery, ingenuity, hope, daring, dedication, gallantry, victory, disappointment, and defeat.

Are you familiar with the names of Cooke, Cushing, Flusser, Hoke, and Wessells? Have you heard of the *CSS Albemarle,* a ship not built in a shipyard as expected, but in a cornfield? Are you aware of who is credited with having achieved the most daring venture in all of the Civil War, and that it happened at Plymouth, North Carolina? Even if you do know the answers to all of these questions, you will want to read still more about them in this informative, enlightening, and interesting book.

ABOUT THE AUTHOR

JUANITA PATIENCE MOSS, born in northeastern Pennsylvania, graduated from the West Pittston public school system; attended Bennett College in Greensboro, North Carolina; received a B.S. degree from Wilkes College, Wilkes Barre, Pennsylvania; and a M.A. from Farleigh Dickinson University, Rutherford, New Jersey. A retired New Jersey high school biology teacher, she recently has developed an interest in genealogy that led to her researching Union black soldiers whose service in white regiments has not been documented. Her great grandfather, Crowder Patience, who served in the 103rd Pennsylvania Volunteers, was one on them.

.